AMERICAN CONSERVATISM
AND THE
AMERICAN FOUNDING

HARRY V. JAFFA

The Claremont Institute
Claremont, California

Originally Published by Carolina Academic Press, 1984
Copyright © 2002 By The Claremont Institute
ISBN 0-930783-31-X

Printed in the United States of America

The Claremont Institute
250 West First Street, Suite 330
Claremont, California 91711
909/621-6825
info@claremont.org

This volume represents the fourth in a series. In 1999, in commemoration of Professor Harry V. Jaffa's 80th birthday and the 20th anniversary of the Claremont Institute, the Institute began to re-issue Jaffa's six out-of-print books. The present volume, originally published by Carolina Academic Press in 1984, joins *Equality and Liberty* (Oxford University Press, 1965), *The Conditions of Freedom* (Johns Hopkins University Press, 1975), and *How to Think About the American Revolution* (Carolina Academic Press, 1978).

The republication of this book was made possible by a generous gift from Mr. George Ball, Jr.

To the Memory of Calvin Coolidge

July 4, 1872 — January 5, 1933

President of the United States on the 150th Anniversary of Independence

Poet and Philosopher of the American Political Tradition

Great men are the ambassadors of Providence sent to reveal to their fellow men their unknown selves.

When the reverence of this nation for its great men dies, the glory of the nation will die with it.

It is only when men begin to worship that they begin to grow. A wholesome regard for the memory of the great men of long ago is the best assurance to a people of a continuation of great men to come, who shall still be able to instruct, to lead, and to inspire.

It was not because it was proposed to establish a new nation, but because it was proposed to establish a nation on new principles, that July 4, 1776, has come to be regarded as one of the greatest days in history.

ACKNOWLEDGMENTS

Thanks is given to the following for permission to reprint copyrighted material: *National Review, Modern Age, St. John's Review, The Tocqueville Forum* (Wake Forest University), the *Claremont Review of Books,* and *Current (The Public Affairs Magazine of Claremont McKenna College).*

TABLE OF CONTENTS

Foreword

WILLIAM F. BUCKLEY, JR.

I f you think Harry Jaffa is hard to argue with, try agreeing with him. It is nearly impossible. He studies the fine print in any agreement as if it were a trap, or a treaty with the Soviet Union.

Not that he *prefers* to disagree. On the contrary. It is his mission to purify and restore what he understands to be the original American consensus, the doctrine of the Founders and of Abraham Lincoln, whom he has constantly honored in terms that might astonish Lincoln's warmest eulogists. He doubts that we can recover our national well-being until we have recovered that doctrine.

But Jaffa also knows the dangers of a false and facile agreement. He understands that the American political tradition has been compromised, time and again, by an adulterated consensus about such problematic terms as *freedom, equality, democracy,* and *consensus* itself.

It would be only a slight exaggeration to say that Harry Jaffa is uninterested in debating those who disagree with him. His most fascinating debates engage those who seem to be, philosophically, his next-door neighbors: such eminent conservatives as Willmoore Kendall, Irving Kristol, Walter Berns, George Will, and Martin Diamond. These men, like himself, are patriots, lovers of freedom, principled enemies of tyranny, unmaskers of intellectual fraud. So why attack one's friends and allies?

Well, as Aristotle (another Jaffa hero) remarked, Plato is dear, but truth is dearer. And beyond that, the errors of excellent men are at once more instructive and more seductive than those of fools. So the relentless Jaffa logic pries at apparently trifling differences until they open like chasms. What is more, he is able to convey the full gravity of these differences. He can be difficult, contentious, abrasive. But petty, never. It simply is not in him. He magnifies all intellectual distinctions to the scale of first principles.

Most American conservatives naturally revere the American political tradition, since it is, after all, their tradition, and they are, after all, reverent men. Harry Jaffa has a somewhat different reason for cherishing it: he believes it to be true, as one might believe the theorems of Euclid to be true. He has devoted his career to vindicating its truth on rational grounds. One feels he would have done exactly the same for the Lithuanian political tradition, if he had found truth there.

To be sure, he has found truth in many places. His heroes include Aquinas, Shakespeare, Churchill, and his own great teacher, Leo Strauss. But the truth of politics is, for him, peculiarly embodied in the American tradition, starting with the Declaration of Independence. The Declaration sets down universal truths about man and government as a basis for political action.

Those truths have been (and are, and perhaps always will be) constantly menaced not only by direct denial, but also, more insidiously, by loose and unthinking assent. Most people are willing to agree, in some inexact and partial way, with this or that part of the creed of the Founders. They may like the idea that we are all equal; or they may feel that liberty is a good thing and ought to be maximized. They are, in short, heretics (literally, "choosers") who are willing to take the part, as it suits them, without regard to the whole.

Jaffa has made it his mission to remind us of the wholeness of the whole. Against all partial agreement, he has insisted on the integrity of the true American tradition, though it means opposing such great figures (indeed, to many conservatives, heroes) as Burke, Tocqueville, Calhoun. Consensus on first principles, yes. Syncretism, no.

In particular he has labored to refute the widespread opinion, Left and Right, that there is a cleavage between the democratic Declaration and the aristocratic (or oligarchic) Constitution. Both, he affirms, are rooted in identical principles of natural law and natural right, personal freedom and self-government. The Founders saw no opposition between liberty and equality: properly understood, these were, for them, what Acquinas would call "convertible terms." Following Locke, they held that men are by nature free *and* equal; that is, no man is rightfully another's subject. We are free because we are equals, equal in that we are all free. *Pace* Tocqueville and socialist egalitarians, there is no trade-off between equality and freedom.

In Jaffa's own words: "There is no difference between man and man, as there is between man and beast or between man and God, that makes one by nature the ruler of another." But the "crisis" of the American regime occurred because of the anomaly, in a free society, of black slavery. It was Lincoln's genius to see, and in fact to make obvious to posterity, what was not at all obvious to men as brilliant as Calhoun and Douglas: that it was nonsense to speak of "self-government" without universal personal liberty. Many (not just abolitionists) agreed that slavery was evil. Lincoln insisted that it corrupted the very principle of the Union.

On reflection it is astonishing that a man should come forth to uphold the American orthodoxy, as Lincoln did, in the swirl of violent times. But then, as Chesterton reminds us, orthodoxy is never static, but of necessity "wild and wheeling." It must be maintained by furious activity, by tacking and yawing through winds of doctrine and hurricanes of fashion. The heretic always wants to simplify a complex truth. It is the lot of the orthodox man to speak in what most people find incomprehensible paradoxes. We shall not remember why Lincoln was loved until we come to understand why he was hated. Jaffa reminds us that he was "a great teacher" of the American tradition, one whose teaching, when it is really grasped, is as controversial in the age of Andropov as it was in the age of George Fitzhugh, the determinist champion of an earlier form of slavery.

Jaffa the man is as generous as Jaffa the theoretician is severe, and this collection reveals more of him than any of his previous books. His best-known utterance gained national (and perhaps everlasting) attention when it fell from the lips of Barry Goldwater in 1964: "Extremism in the defense of liberty is no vice." Ever the aphorist, we find him explaining to a college audience: "Extremism in defense of liberty is not extremism in defense of extremism." He adds: "Rather, it is extremism in defense of moderation—that moderate regime in which people are not subject to the kind of censoriousness we associate with, say, the city of Geneva at the height of the regime of John Calvin."

It is especially gratifying to have his comments on the current political scene. He places the events of 1980 against the background of both theory and tradition, and declares: "Conservative Republicanism *is* the middle of the road." In a couple of pages he manages to compress a novel but compelling vision of our recent history:

> *Although the original New Deal counted the big city political machines as among its pillars, the later New Deal, and the still later welfare state, systematically destroyed these vital political structures. The death of Mayor Daley of Chicago probably marks the final passing of the old boss. For the essence of the policy inaugurated by FDR under the aegis of Harry Hopkins ("spend, spend, tax, tax, elect, elect") was to centralize political patronage in the federal bureaucracy, making the local political organization mere dependents upon the largess of the Great Machine of the Imperial Presidency. The rhetoric of ideological liberalism has glossed and painted over the brute fact of political power snatched and torn from its local roots and centralized in Washington.*

Since Lyndon Johnson especially, the number of "the officially designated 'poor'" has actually begun to *increase*. We now have "a permanent 'underclass' who are the permanent objects of concern of a permanent bureaucracy," this bureacracy in turn constituting "the principal beneficiaries of the contemporary Democratic Party." Such has been the real effect, and increasingly the actual intention, of the War on Poverty. "Anti-poverty programs," Jaffa observes, "have long ceased being nets *under* the poor. They are more nearly lids *over* the poor, preventing that upward mobility that has been the genius of the American regime from its origins." There is Jaffa in action, incisively defining large realities. He theorizes with his eyes open.

He even finds something fresh and profound to say about the Moral Majority, something which, at the time he said it, was drowned out by the frantic noises of frightened civil libertarians. As always Jaffa's observations have their roots in his Socratic understanding that virtue is necessary to citizenship. He disputes the very idea that there are "victimless crimes." Again the aphorist speaks memorably:

> *In a republic, the sobriety of the citizens replaces the force of authority as the principal source of order.*

> *Tolerance, as itself a moral virtue, cannot be indifferent to moral distinctions.*

> *In the last analysis, all our rights depend upon our willingness, not merely to tolerate each other, but to defend each other.*

> *Those who see each other as utterly alien cannot be fellow-citizens.*

> *For the forming of the laws ... is nothing less than the forming of the character of the citizens.*

Pointing back to our early documents, he reminds us: "The whole notion that morality is not a concern of government is denied by the very language of the American founding."

In one conversation reprinted here, Jaffa impishly turns a compliment aside by pointing out "what a dangerous man I am to praise." It is too true; but the risk must occasionally be taken. He is a very great teacher, one who does his master, Leo Strauss, proud. He is just the teacher America needs right now, to assist our recovery not only from misguided practice but from misleading theories. And a book in which the mind of such a teacher is brought to bear on so many subjects, lofty and topical, is a gift to the nation.

Introduction

The Special Meaning of the Declaration of Independence*

CHARLES R. KESLER

I n what was surely the most compelling speech of the past decade, Alexander Solzhenitsyn declared at the 1978 Harvard Commencement that the United States "has lost its civic courage." Another way of saying this would be that America has lost the courage of its convictions. But it is impossible to lose what we do not possess—and the real crisis of our times is the loss of confidence in what America's convictions or principles are. It should hardly come as a surprise that we find it difficult to decide what the U.S. ought to do in the world, since we cannot know what we want or need until we know what we are.

American conservatism is in the same boat. Conservatism presupposes that there is something worth conserving—but we can hardly know what to conserve without knowing what America is and what it stands for. To be sure, no one can justly accuse conservatism of having lived an unexamined life over the past forty years. But a political movement cannot form itself around a Socratic declaration of ignorance, however ironic (though in 1980 the Democrats almost succeeded). A political movement cannot philosophize, but a decent one has need of philosophy. In his great book on the Ancien Régime, Tocqueville observes that it is altogether understandable for a badly governed nation to desire to govern itself instead. "But a desire for independence of this kind, stemming as it does from a specific, removable cause ... is bound to be short-lived," he writes. "Once the circumstances giving rise to it have passed away, it languishes and what at first sight seemed a genuine love of liberty proves to have been merely hatred of a tyrant."

American conservatism sometimes resembles that false love of liberty, its self-examinations concluding in nothing more lasting or noble than ad hoc reactions to the New Deal, the Great Society, the New Frontier. But this sort of poking around in the detritus of liberal social programs, in the manner of Heinrich Schliemann uncovering Troy, proves nothing except that manifest follies should be avoided, and Greeks—or Georgians—bearing gifts, suspected. Historical sentimentalism in the face of the great changes wrought in

*This essay is a revised version of an article, sponsored by the Project in Public Philosophy of the Sabre Foundation, that originally appeared in *National Review* (July 6, 1979) and is used with permission.

American society since the New Deal will not provide conservatism with the meaning it is seeking. Nor will root-and-branch libertarianism, which in its own way is also a reaction to the New Deal.

What conservatism needs is an understanding of our political tradition that will free it from reaction and open it to action—action for the sake of the *genuine* love of liberty as expressed in the principles of that tradition. What this understanding would mean is that conservatives would choose those principles *again* if they had the chance. In other words, conservatism's commitment to the past makes political sense only to the extent that it implies a commitment to the future: conservatism, rightly understood, is less a commitment to the past than a commitment to certain *truths* applicable to past, present, and future.

Many conservatives have lately been mining the American political tradition in search of conservatism's golden meaning. But the scholar who, more than any other, has shown that the principles of that tradition, far from being "mere rubbish—old wadding left to rot on the battlefield after the victory is won" are in fact the living truths of just government and wise conservatism, is Harry V. Jaffa. A man of profound learning and sharp intellect, educated in the history of political philosophy by the incomparable Leo Strauss, Jaffa has dedicated the greater part of his career—he is now the Henry Salvatori Research Professor of Political Philosophy at Claremont McKenna College and Claremont Graduate School—to the recovery and elucidation of the American political tradition. He first set forth his interpretation of that tradition in 1959 in *Crisis of the House Divided,* a brilliant study of the Lincoln-Douglas debates and a refutation of the revisionist explaining-away of the Civil War. He has elaborated that interpretation in a series of books—*Equality and Liberty* (1965), *The Conditions of Freedom* (1975), culminating in *How to Think About the American Revolution* (1978) and now *American Conservatism and the American Founding,* volumes that provide a thorough, and thorough-going, defense of his lifework.

A defense is necessary because Jaffa has attracted many critics, not the least because he has been unstinting in his criticism of *them.* His preceding book, *How to Think About the American Revolution,* than which no more polemical work of scholarship has appeared in many years, is essentially a long series of replies to critics old and new, express and indirect—to Willmoore Kendall, M. E. Bradford, Martin Diamond, and Irving Kristol. These controversies over the nature of our political tradition, and hence over the meaning of conservatism, Jaffa wages in what he calls a "deliberately polemical" style. He adopts this "distinctly unacademic" manner, he writes, only because "academic disputation today has been aptly characterized by a prominent scholar who remarked that the proper way to refute someone is to ignore him." It was Santayana who coined the remark—saying that we no longer refute our adversaries, we quietly bid them goodbye—but it was Louis Hartz who adopted it in his book *The Liberal Tradition in America.* What was Santayana's lament became Hartz's guiding maxim, and therein lies the story of contemporary social science. For refuting someone by ignoring him is a mode ot (to speak loosely) argument appropriate only for those who believe that reason is powerless before the clash of irrational value judgments, and that science or philosophy cannot conclude anything concerning the fundamental human questions.

Strange to say, but Thomas Aquinas is in a way more liberal than our doctrinaire social scientists—more liberal even than *The Liberal Tradition in America*—since in the *Summa Theologica* he presents both sides of the argument, or at least versions of both sides, on every question. Contemporary social science has no need of the *disputatio*, however, because it denies that reason is able "to guide judgment, and therefore to guide human life ... concerning the true and the false ... the good and the bad ... the just and the unjust." That reason can guide life, and that political philosophy can guide political life, is a first principle shared in different ways by Thomas Aquinas and Thomas Jefferson. It is a principle, Jaffa declares, that neither shares in any way with "let us say, the last ten presidents of the American Political Science Association."

Leo Strauss, who is well-known for his rejection of the historicism and value relativism of modern social science in the name of natural right, was never president of the American Political Science Association; but some of his students and disciples may be enhancing their qualifications for the job, at least insofar as they seem to have lost a vivid or living appreciation of the task of political philosophy. In *American Conservatism and the American Founding*, Jaffa disputes with Walter Berns and Robert Goldwin, both students of Strauss's, over the thesis put forward by their fellow student, the late Martin Diamond. This argument starts from the question of the relation of the Amerian regime to the tradition of natural right—whether America truly is dedicated to a moral principle that renders citizenship meaningful and statesmanship necessary and desirable. But the argument ascends to the very possibility of political philosophy in the modern world—which is, Jaffa insists, the same question as the possibility of political philosophy simply, for if the activity of philosophizing cannot escape from or is not free of its historical situation, then political philosophy in the original sense of the term is and always has been an impossibility. At the same time, as the reader will discover, it is precisely the transhistorical ability of reason to take its bearings from nature, that makes it possible for political philosophy to be a guide to political practice here and now. Otherwise, reason would be the slave of history, and philosophy a set of *post facto* rationalizations or puzzles. From beginning to end, the debate over Strauss's legacy—which is also Socrates' legacy—is therefore a meditation on the proper relation between statesmanship and political philosophy, which meditation centers on the Declaration of Independence as the pre-eminent modern statement of that relation. For the Declaration is not only the *apologia* of the Founding Fathers, but also the touchstone of that only greater American statesman, Abraham Lincoln.

Jaffa writes polemically, then, in the interest of reason and truth, particularly in the interest of the reasonable truths of the American political tradition. It is, accordingly, almost as impossible to ignore him as it is to refute him, although his opponents have generally preferred trying the former to risking the latter. But America was not "raised to eminence by men who refused confrontation, either in the forum, or on the battlefield," he declares. "Nor can we long preserve this eminence, except by the means that raised us to it." Before we can defend American principles, however, we must know what they are. An act of recovery and reformation is needed. "I was interested in the political truth partly for its own sake," he writes in the Introduction to *Crisis of the House Divided,* "but also because I wished myself to know, and to teach others, the principles of just government."

II

In the period of the Bicentennial, the effort to understand the American political tradition necessarily concentrated on the Declaration of Independence, and on the Revolution that it proclaimed and justified. But in the opinion of some recent scholars, all of them conservatives of one stripe or another, it is difficult to say just what the Declaration has to do with our political traditions, or what the Revolution has to do with present-day conservatism. This is Irving Kristol's difficulty in his elegant essay "The American Revolution as a Successful Revolution," a contribution to *America's Continuing Revolution,* the Bicentennial *Festschrift* assembled by the American Enterprise Institute. Kristol, one of the finest political essayists writing today, is the celebrated leader — "the godfather," James Q. Wilson calls him — of the movement called neo-conservatism; and that movement's dedication to prudence, order, and a sense of limits shines through Kristol's praise of the Declaration as a "calm, legalistic" document. The victims of the French, Russian, and Chinese Revolutions would have been grateful for a little calmness and legalism in those upheavals. Which is precisely his point. The American Revolution is the only *successful* revolution of the modern age — the only one that "did not devour its children," that did not spawn a myth of "the revolution betrayed," that did not veer heavenward in quest of some "meta-political" transformation of the human condition. Yet such a revolution is, by the debauched standards of the modern world, not much of a revolution at all.

Harry Jaffa certainly agrees that the American Revolution is in a class by itself, but in *How to Think About the American Revolution* he questions, acidulously, the grounds of Kristol's praise of the Founding. The gravamen of his charge is that Kristol is not being true to the phenomena of the Revolution, which was neither as calm and legalistic as he thinks, nor as successful as he imagines. To begin with, it is hard to conceive that Americans would rise up to throw off British rule for reasons that could be embodied in a calm and legalistic document. Would *you* suffer Valley Forge for the sake of, say, the *Federal Register*? The Declaration that Kristol deradicalizes, Jefferson hailed as "the signal of arousing men to burst the chains, under which monkish ignorance and superstition had persuaded them to bind themselves, and to assume the blessings and security of self-government."

Now, Abraham Lincoln extolled the Declaration as "that immortal emblem of humanity," and praised Jefferson, its author, for introducing, into a "merely revolutionary document, an abstract truth, applicable to all men and all times." Of that abstract truth, "that all men are created equal," Kristol says nothing. Even more remarkable, in a discussion of "The American Revolution as a Successful Revolution" he says nothing of "the right of the people to alter or to abolish" their form of government. An encomium on the Revolution that does not mention the right of revolution is faint praise indeed, and it suggests that Kristol's admiration extends, in Jaffa's words, only "to something that might be called the [Founding] Fathers' 'practice' as distinct from their 'theory.'"

It is almost as if Kristol wished to do for our Revolution what Burke did for the English—namely, deny that it *is* a revolution. In fact, however, he wants to save the good name of "revolution" by restricting it to calm and legalistic ones like America's, condemning the others (following Hannah Arendt) as mere "rebellions." But he never meditates on the oxymoron that underlies his praise: a revolution may appear legalistic, but it can *not* be legal. Never being comfortable with "the abstract truth, applicable to all men and all times," that impelled the colonists to break Britain's laws, he never takes the full measure of the Revolution, never appreciates fully what made it so revolutionary.

The success of the Revolution, Kristol concludes, "turned the attention of thinking men away from politics, . . . so that political theory lost its vigor. This intellectual sloth . . . rendered us incompetent to explain this successful revolution to the world, and even to ourselves. . . ." Yet one wonders a) how his own essay escapes this indictment, and b) just when the attention of thinking men turned away from politics. Certainly his own attention has turned away from the most passionate and bloody political conflict in American history—the Civil War—which was preceded by decades of radical questioning of that "successful" Revolution's fundamental principles.

III

The Declaration and the Constitution each embody, in some sense, the principles of the Revolution, but the relation between them is unclear: which is the higher expression of those principles, and hence of the government and way of life that the Revolution established? To which should conservatives give precedence as a guide to what should be conserved? These questions divided Jaffa and Martin Diamond for a number of years. Diamond, who died in 1977, was the foremost expositor of the Constitution and *The Federalist* in our time, through his lucid, finely crafted essays on the Framers' view of democracy, liberty and federalism. Almost single-handedly he revived the study of *The Federalist* as a serious work of political philosophy.

In *America's Continuing Revolution,* the same work to which Kristol contributed, Diamond celebrates what he calls "The Revolution of Sober Expectations." Diamond points above all to the sober relation between the Declaration and the Constitution: the "silence" of the Declaration on certain constitutional questions is "the splendid distinction" of our Revolution. For, "noble document that the Declaration is, indispensable source of the feelings and sentiments of Americans and of the spirit of liberty in which their institutions were conceived, the Declaration is devoid of guidance as to what those institutions should be." The Declaration asserts merely that a people has the right to throw off despotic government and "to institute new government, laying its foundation on such principles, and organizing its powers in such form, as to them shall seem most likely to effect their safety and happiness." A people thus has the right to establish *any* form of government—monarchy, aristocracy, democracy—so long, Diamond argues, as it a) "secures equal freedom" and b) "is instituted by popular consent."

Not the Declaration, then, but the Constitution was responsible for our form of government. America was not a democracy (a democratic republic) until the Constitution made it so, by such provisions as the broadly democratic franchise in the federal election, the absence of property qualifications for federal offices, and the prohibition of titles of nobility. In short, we got liberty from the Declaration, democracy from the Constitution. This is exactly the reverse of what used to be the understanding of the American political tradition, which traced democracy to the "radical" Declaration, and liberty to the conservative, indeed counter-revolutionary, Constitution.

As opposed to both these interpretations, Jaffa argues that America's commitment to democracy *and* its commitment to liberty are present in the Declaration. Accepting Diamond's conclusion that the Constitution is a democratic document, he sets out to vindicate the Declaration's democratic character by driving a wedge into Diamond's analysis. Is it reasonable, he asks, for the Declaration "uncompromisingly [to] enjoin upon *all* governments the duty to secure the unalienable rights of *all* people, while supplying 'no guidance' toward that end?" What Diamond calls "equal freedom," the securing of every man's unalienable rights, is not equally the end of any and every form of government. "At least since Plato and Aristotle," writes Jaffa, "equal freedom" has been understood "as peculiarly a democratic end," even as wealth has been understood as the end of oligarchies, "honor of monarchies, and virtue (however understood) of aristocracies." All non-despotic forms of government may preserve "equal freedom" in some degree, but "surely they do not do so in the same degree."

If "equal freedom" points toward democracy, what of the other standard that Diamond extracts from the Declaration—that just government must be instituted by consent? Well, "something called 'consent,'" Jaffa explains, "may range all the way from the acquiescence of a slave whose life has been spared by his master on the battlefield, to that of a free man deliberating with his equals, as to what they deem best for their common good." As the Shah of Iran learned to his regret, all stable governments depend in some sense upon the "consent" of the governed. Even Hitler invoked the phrase, his plebiscites attesting to the fact that there is *nothing* to which some people will not consent. But when Jefferson wrote that the "just powers" of government derive "from the consent of the governed," he obviously meant something different from the "consent" that will acquiesce in anything. He meant what Jaffa calls "just or enlightened consent," which is to say that "men who understand their natural equality ... do not ... consent to governments which do not secure their rights." Only consent "enlightened by full consciousness of natural rights, and by the aptness of governments to secure those rights, is consent in the full or proper meaning of the term." The Declaration could hardly be (in Diamond's phrase) "neutral" as to forms of government unless it were "neutral," unrespecting, and disrespectful of human rights.

But why must "enlightened consent" result in democracy? Diamond had argued that "the people need not *establish* a government which *operates* by means of their consent." To which Jaffa retorts: "it is unfortunate for Professor Diamond's argument ... that he did not take note of the fact that 'consent' occurs not once, but three times in the Declaration." Its first mention indeed refers primarily to the *institution* of government; but its later occurrences refer "unmistakably and unequivocally" to the *operation* of government. King George III, the Declaration accuses, has "kept among us, in times of peace, standing armies without the consent of the legislature," and has—above all—imposed taxes "without our consent."

No taxation without representation! It is passing strange that one of the great rallying cries of the Revolution—probably the *only* one Jude Wanniski knows—has virtually escaped Diamond's attention. The right to consent to taxes is merely the other side of the right of property (or of the pursuit of happiness), and implies a right to approve or disapprove all operations of government that depend on taxes, which is to say nearly all operations of government. "For the preservation of property being the end of government," Locke explains in the *Second Treatise*, "and that for which men enter into society, it necessarily supposes and requires, that the people should *have property*, without which they must be supposed to lose that by entering into society, which was the end for which they entered into it, too gross an absurdity for any man to own."

No man will own this absurdity because all men own property, which the government cannot take from them without their consent. "For I truly have no property in that, which another can by right take from me, when he pleases against my consent." At least since Locke it has been understood that "this is not much to be fear'd" in governments where the people from time to time elect their own representatives. "A pure implementation of the principles of the Declaration of Independence," concludes Jaffa, "one unmitigated by any prudential accommodation to circumstances, would then result in a purely republican—or democratic—form of government." The Declaration is every bit as democratic as the ordinary American thinks it is.

Yet it does not lack a teaching about the "prudential accommodation to circumstances." That democracy is everywhere desirable does not mean that it is everywhere possible. In the language of the Declaration, "all experience hath shown, that mankind are more disposed to suffer, while evils are sufferable, than to right themselves by abolishing the forms to which they are accustomed." Accordingly, "prudence indeed will dictate that governments long established should not be changed for light and transient causes...." Prudence modifies the *application* of the Declaration's teaching about rights, since many nations must make do with governments less enlightened than they might wish, or than they ought to wish. It is for this reason that the long, detailed indictment of George III appears: the American revolutionaries must pay "a decent respect to the opinions of mankind" by showing that the evils they formerly suffered have now become *insufferable.*

The democracy that the Declaration shows to be everywhere desirable nowhere appears except in constitutional form. Democracy "rightly understood" *is* a constitutional process, according to Jaffa, who points to the Declaration's distinction between consent in the institution of government and consent in its operation. This distinction is the *sine qua non* of constitutionalism, since it underlies the distinction between constitutional law and statute law.

Jaffa's way with the text of the Declaration, like his earlier exegesis of the Lincoln-Douglas debates, is a wonder to behold. Beneath the most trodden and dusty ground he uncovers fresh streams of meaning, their headwaters in the distant mountains of ancient political philosophy, their flow, swift and powerful, cutting channels through the present, finally mixing and spilling into the future, that great ocean beyond our horizon. His interpretation of the Declaration in *How to Think About the American Revolution* is a "universal confrontation of the text" that his old foe Willmoore Kendall would have acclaimed, and reconfirms Jaffa's title as the foremost contemporary interpreter of the American political tradition.

IV

Lincoln's reflection on the relation of the Declaration to the Constitution (and the Union) took the form of a meditation on Proverbs 25:11, "A word fitly spoken is like apples of gold in pictures of silver." To Lincoln, the word fitly spoken was the assertion of principle in the Declaration; the pictures of silver were the Union and Constitution subsequently framed around it. "The picture was made, not to conceal, or destroy the apple; but to adorn, and preserve it." Lincoln's task, of course, was to preside over the dissolution and reconstitution of the Union, and in so doing to affirm that a nation "conceived in liberty, and dedicated to the proposition that all men are created equal . . . can long endure." Though the dispute over the extension of slavery into the Western territories was the proximate cause of the Union's dissolution, the more fundamental cause was the existence of negro slavery in a nation "so conceived and so dedicated."

For this reason, writes Jaffa, "however admirable the character of the American Constitution, it was not . . . the most admirable expression of the regime. The Constitution is the highest American thing only if one tries to understand the high in the light of the low. It is high because men are not angels, and because we do not have angels to govern us. . . . But the Constitution, in deference to man's nonangelic nature, made certain compromises with slavery. And partly because of those compromises, it dissolved in the presence of a great crisis. The man—or the character of the man—who bore the nation through that crisis, seem[s] to me . . . the highest thing in the American regime." Above the Constitution, even above the Declaration, as an expression of American principles, is the magnanimous figure of Lincoln, who preserved the Union and Constitution by restoring them to their true foundation, the Declaration; and who ennobled the Union and Constitution by leading them to "a new birth of freedom," based upon a nobler understanding of the Declaration's principles.

That, in brief compass, is the thesis of *Crisis of the House Divided,* Jaffa's magisterial interpretation of the Lincoln-Douglas debates. Lincoln led America through "a new birth of freedom"—through a spiritual rebirth—because the first birth, the Founding, had been defective. Not merely because of the Constitution's compromises with slavery, but because of what those compromises represented. To Lincoln, slavery was the pre-eminent expression of human selfishness, of the evil to which men's passions could lead them; constitutional compromises with slavery, however necessary, meant that American government had not been established on an entirely proper understanding of the relation between passion and reason. Which is not to say that the Founders' handiwork was erroneous, only that it was insufficient or incomplete. In the Founding, the passion of the few for distinction and honor, and of the many for revenge and hatred, had assisted the struggle for free government, according to Lincoln. But once the struggle had been won, these former allies became threatening foes. The people had been taught—Jefferson had taught them, Jaffa explains—"to assert their rights. But they had not yet learned to respect what they had asserted."

Distinguishing between rights and passions has always been the *pons asinorum* of democracy. To claim respect for their rights the people themselves must first respect them: in Jaffa's words, they must "demand only those things in the name of their own supreme authority that are reasonable, i.e., consistent with the implications of their own equal rights." But Americans had *not* been reasonable in their demands. In escaping the "absolute despotism" of George III, they had retained a tyranny of their own over hundreds of thousands of Negro slaves: equality in the sense of "the consent of the governed" parted company with equality in the more fundamental sense of each individual's natural rights. The possessors of equal rights warred upon the philosophy of equal rights.

The statesman's task—Lincoln's task—is to bring these two aspects of equality together. The tension between the two is, in one sense, *the* tension in American politics, the moral spring that puts our politics in motion—the continual test of the capability of a free people to govern itself. For the policy of ambition checking ambition—Madison's language for "politics-as-usual"—works for all of the people some of the time, and some of the people all of the time, but never for all of the people all of the time. Occasionally a policy that transcends the play of ambitions is needed, and that is the occasion for great statesmanship. Jaffa's view of the character of our politics unfolds easily into an interpretation of the whole of U.S. history: which becomes the moral drama of conflict between self-government as *what the people will* and self-government as *what the people ought to will.* This is history on the grand scale, similar to Charles A. Beard's or Louis Hartz's comprehensive interpretations, but truer to the moral character—one should say, truer to the facts—of American political life.

Lincoln's effort to form public opinion on true republican principles, his reconciliation of men's rights and passions, can be summed up in one of his famous epigrams. "As I would not be a *slave,* so I would not be a *master.* This expresses my idea of democracy. Whatever differs from this, to the extent of the difference, is no democracy." To be free requires that men know, and respect, what it is that makes them free. The point of Lincoln's analysis is that *respect* demands more than mere acknowledgment of human rights—it demands a duty to strive for their achievement. In this sense, Lincoln can be said to have transformed the doctrine of natural rights in the Declaration from "a norm which prescribes what civil society ought *not* to be, into a transcendental affirmation of what it *ought* to be." Properly speaking, this is not a rejection of the Declaration's minimalist doctrine, but a transcendence of it; the direction of this transcendence is from passion to reason: from men's indefeasible passions to reason, in the form of distributive justice—giving to each man his due—as the proper ground of human rights.

With the foundation of human rights laid in reason, in the "discernment of what is due to a man," rights never appear without corresponding duties. Every man is charged to strive for justice, to see that all his relations with men are governed by the rights belonging by nature to all men. It follows that loyalty to the Constitution must ultimately be based upon a nobler motive than the selfish connection between one's interest and the rights of one's place, otherwise expressed in the famous "policy of supplying, by opposite and rival interests, the defect of better motives." Sometimes there is no substitute for better motives.

Jaffa never tires of repeating Woodrow Wilson's remark that the phenomenon of Lincoln has made it possible to believe in democracy. By that, Jaffa means that Lincoln was America's political savior, the man who led the nation back from apostasy to its ancient faith, but who transcended that faith through "a new birth of freedom." The "ancient faith" Lincoln defended was found above all in the Declaration of Independence, the "apple" for which the "pictures of silver" were made. The assertion of principle in the Declaration was the "word fitly spoken"—America's word, in a special sense. American conservatives who want to know what it is they should be engaged in conserving should look first to this great and wonderful truth, that "all men are created equal." It is this truth, said Lincoln, that gave liberty "not alone to the people of this country, but hope to the world for all future time. It was that which gave promise that in due time the weights would be lifted from the shoulders of all men, and that *all* should have an equal chance."

V

Forthrightly, Jaffa titles one of his essays in *How to Think About the American Revolution*, "Equality as a Conservative Principle." Imagine that: "Equality" being defended by conservatives—by unequal conservatives—unequally! But "equality" as Jaffa means it is not equality of condition, of virtue, knowledge, strength, good looks, or anything else so unnatural, but rather *equality of natural rights*—of the rights to life, liberty, and the pursuit of happiness. In this sense, equality is the same thing as liberty (a word to which conservatives are more accustomed), inasmuch as men have a right to liberty only because they are born equal, i.e., born without natural superiors: "No man," said Lincoln, "is good enough to govern another man, without that other's consent." To borrow one of Jaffa's striking images, liberty and equality are as inseparable as the concavity and convexity of a curved surface.

Who defends liberty must therefore defend equality. But there is also a prudential reason why conservatives should want to defend equality: it is generally a more potent political term than liberty, as Tocqueville understood, so that he who controls the political meaning of "equality" controls the discussion just so much. Conservatives should make it clear that it is we who hold the genuine title deeds to equality, and that other claimants are squanderers of a precious legacy who, in the name of a spurious equality, would abolish true equality, and with it all hope for liberty, justice, and happiness.

Not every conservative will or has embraced equality as a conservative principle, although no American conservative that I have ever heard of has renounced the Revolution made in the name of that equality. Instead, some conservatives have tried to read equality out of the Revolution by denying that the equality clause means what Lincoln, Jaffa, and most ordinary Americans say it means.

Now, one of the pleasures of reading Harry Jaffa is the art, at once sublime and merciless, with which he exposes the intellectual pedigrees of his opponents' arguments. He demonstrates (what is quite in keeping with a certain type of conservatism) that Diamond's argument—that the Declaration provides "no guidance" concerning forms of government—is derived from another conservative's argument, Willmoore Kendall's in *The Basic Symbols of the American Political Tradition* (completed, after Kendall's death, by his friend and collaborator George W. Carey). Kendall, who taught at Yale and the University of Dallas and was for many years a senior editor of *National Review*, asserts that the equality clause in the Declaration has no theoretical significance for the American political tradition. That equality came to be regarded as a fundamental American principle, he attributes to a radical "derailing" of the tradition by Abraham Lincoln, whose Gettysburg Address was the climax of a grand scheme to pull the wool over Americans' eyes. "The Declaration itself," Kendall writes, "gives no guidance on how or in what ways" America's government should be structured; it anticipates merely that the people will shortly "engage in some sort of deliberative process to establish that form of government...." America, in short, may have been conceived in liberty, but it was not dedicated to any proposition, much less the proposition "that all men are created equal."

By enshrining that clause, Lincoln paved the way for a series of future derailments under "an apostolic succession of great leaders...Abraham Lincoln, Roosevelts I and II...John Kennedy, each of whom sees more deeply than the preceding leader into the specifically American problem...posed by the 'all men are created equal' clause." Jaffa's interpretation of Lincoln and our political tradition would "launch...the nation upon a political future the very thought of which is hair-raising," Kendall warns—"an endless series of Abraham Lincolns, each persuaded he is superior in wisdom and virtue to the Fathers, each prepared to insist that those who oppose this or that new application of the equality standard are denying the possibility of self-government, each ultimately willing to plunge America into Civil War rather than concede his point."

In effect, Kendall argues that equality of natural rights is an *ignis fatuus* that leads inevitably to farther-reaching kinds of equality, each more pernicious than the last, each more difficult to attain than the last, and each requiring a harsher shake-down of society by an increasingly domineering government. Such a commitment to equality culminates in "the cooperative commonwealth of men who will be so equal that no one will be able to tell them apart." But then why is the equality clause in the Declaration at all? It is there, Kendall concludes, because the Founders wished to declare the American people's independence from the British people: "the Americans are equal to the British and are, therefore, as free as the British" to establish their own form of government.

This argument has been taken up recently by M. E. Bradford, a professor at the University of Dallas, who maintains that what Jefferson and his "sensible friends" meant in the equality clause was that men "together—as a group—" are equal. The "we" who hold certain truths to be self-evident are the "one people" spoken of in the Declaration's first sentence. This initial "we" governs the rest of the Declaration, which is not "a piece of reasoning or systematic truth" but above all a rhetorical document. Like Kendall, Bradford sympathizes with the Confederacy, makes great sport of the freedom-loving-slave-holding Founding Fathers, and is scornfully critical of Lincoln, whom he anathematizes as a "gnostic" force.

On the issue of Lincoln, by the way, there is no middle ground. Either he is a "self-made Caesar," an "enemy of the 'founding,'" as Bradford would have it, or he is a wise and magnanimous leader, the savior of the Republic, as Jaffa maintains. Bradford and Kendall imagine that Lincoln's "opposition to slavery leads to slavery," that when the last trumpet shall sound Lincoln will be standing rather closer to Hitler than to, say, Churchill. For Hitler, like Lincoln—cracks Bradford, in what is surely the most outrageous footnote in modern scholarship —was "a firm higher-law man, and no legalist or historicist," a man who was convinced he was "'fighting for the Lord's work.'"

But, really, this is an old question. "Professor Bradford and I," writes Jaffa, "are carrying on a debate which reached a climax in the 1850s." In this exchange, as elsewhere, Jaffa's method is to reveal "the contemporary academic debate concerning the meaning of the American political tradition as itself a form of political debate within that tradition. In short, I argue that the 'academic' debate is not strictly speaking academic at all." The same argument advanced by Kendall—taken up in part by Diamond and Kristol, in whole by Bradford—was made by Chief Justice Roger Taney in the *Dred Scott* decision of 1857 and by John C. Calhoun before him in 1848. In a speech to the Senate, Calhoun, who defended slavery on the grounds that it was a "positive good" for blacks and whites, denied that the Declaration had "any weight in constructing the governments which were substituted in place of the colonial," and attacked the proposition that "all men are born free and equal" as "the most false and dangerous of all political errors." Taney, in the Supreme Court's most ignominious decision, argued that the equality clause was meant only to distinguish the equal rights of the American nation from those of the British. The Founders could not have meant that all men are created equal because they did not abolish slavery. The Negro, according to Taney, was regarded by the Founders as "an ordinary article of merchandise and traffic," who might "justly and lawfully be reduced to slavery" inasmuch as he was "so far inferior that [he] had no rights which the white man was bound to respect."

The enormity of this calumny against the Founders is matched only by its fragility; a single glance at the Declaration is enough to dispel it. The Declaration states plainly that "all men are created equal"—not all white men; not all British citizens; all men. The Founders were claiming their rights as men, not their rights as British citizens; accordingly, they appealed not to the laws of Britain but to the "laws of Nature and of Nature's God." It is possible to reconcile the Taney-Kendall-Bradford interpretation of the Declaration with the language of the Declaration only, as Jaffa says, "by means of the proposition that all true men are by nature British"—a proposition that "might find its place in some undiscovered operetta by Gilbert and Sullivan," but could hardly be located in the thought of the Founders.

Nor is the argument that equality of natural rights yields inevitably to equality of condition a sound one. Bradford asserts that the distinction between the two types of equality is "nothing less than sophistry" because "only those who are equal can take equal advantage of a given circumstance." Retorts Jaffa, "I confess myself unable to assign any intelligible meaning to this assertion." For if Bradford means that "a fair start in a race is advantageous only to someone who is fast enough to win it" he is clearly talking nonsense: "The purpose of the race is to find out who is the fastest, and this can be done only if the start of the race is fair." The protection of the "different and unequal faculties of acquiring property," which Madison hails in *Federalist* Number Ten as the "first object of government," derives from the natural right of every man to his own body, and hence to the labor of his body. It is slavery, not the principle of equal natural rights, that is the philosophical enemy of private property, through its denial of that most elementary right.

While Kendall denies that equality is part of the American political tradition, he never doubts that there is a tradition, which he identifies as the virtuous people (or their representatives) deliberating under God. The emphasis upon virtue and deliberation in unobjectionable, but his formula is insufficient on two counts. It cannot explain how the "people" came to be a people; and it provides no guidance concerning what the people may reasonably consent to. Discrete individuals come to be a sovereign people through the exercise of consent—but consent is not, as Kendall seems to believe, an ultimate principle. On the contrary, it is derived from the fact that every individual is born free and equal, without a natural ruler in the sense that God is the natural ruler of man, or man the natural ruler of dogs. It is only through consent that the people become a people with the authority to choose a form of government. But that choice is not unbounded or unprincipled, since the source of the people's right to give their consent—the equality of men—"limits and directs what it is to which they may rightfully consent," as Jaffa puts it. The virtuous people deliberating under God may decide to de-liberate—to enslave—their fellow men, unless they understand the ground of their own rights, and know "what kind of a people a free people ought to be."

VI

"In 1776," Jaffa declares, "the United States was so to speak nothing; but it promised to become everything. In 1976, the United States, having in a sense become everything, promises to become nothing." The U.S. will become nothing if it suffers a great military defeat in the next war; but, more profoundly, the U.S. will become nothing if it becomes persuaded that it stands for nothing. When the central ideas of our political tradition become blurred and obscured, when Americans no longer understand what it is that makes them a people, then they will cease to be a people, and that noble and reasonable tradition will decay into ideology. A people's spiritedness, if in the service of something higher than the people's passions, can be a great ally to virtue. But when spiritedness, the prideful assertion of dignity and independence, is severed from its connection to reason, it collapses upon itself and, like one of those invisible black holes said to populate (or depopulate) space, pulls in everything around it. All virtue disappears into appetite, and even the light of the Founders' words and deeds is overwhelmed by darkness.

Conservatives who look to Jaffa's teaching, and to Lincoln's example, will see a kind of conservatism that lies between, and above, the extremes of libertarianism and traditionalism. What is extreme about libertarianism is the insistence that freedom, in one way or another, is the solution to all the problems of human life. Like abolitionists of slavery, many libertarians are abolitionists of government—indeed of all authority superior to the individual —who are willing to pay any price for freedom, regardless of the consequences to a decent human life, or to the basis of their own rights. Other libertarians are less radical and do not hope for the immediate uprooting of government; they trust in the working of impersonal economic "laws" which, if only the government would get out of the way, would take care of things, leaving government to run only a watchman state.

Now, Stephen Douglas, Lincoln's opponent in the famous debate, could say he didn't care whether slavery was voted up or down because he counted upon America's economic growth and westward expansion to defuse the whole slavery question. Like Douglas, these libertarians believe that the laws of economics will inevitably produce peace and freedom if only they are allowed to work. Economics will supplant politics. But we may well question the price of this exchange: when men choose to rely on economics instead of politics, they choose to deny human choice—particularly choice in matters of right and wrong, which is what politics is all about. Lincoln's criticism of Douglas' program was that slavery was inconsistent with the principles of republican government, and that a people could not be indifferent to the one without being indifferent to the other. Freedom is a matter of choice, and a people must choose well in order to establish and preserve it. But no people can choose well who do not respect their ability to choose, who barter that ability away for the spurious guarantees of economics.

At the other extreme of conservatism today is traditionalism, which may be defined as a reverence for the past that gets in the way of understanding the past—and present, and future. The danger in traditionalism's reverence for the past is that it is unreasonable, unprincipled—and fundamentally no different from liberalism's unprincipled commitment to the future. It does not acknowledge any objective standards by which we may distinguish just from unjust, good from bad, true from false, and so provides us no guidance in choosing what elements of the past should be conserved as a matter of expedience, and what elements must be conserved as a matter of justice. Nor, needless to say, can it provide us with what the past does not furnish —living statesmanship and virtue.

Jaffa's interpretation of the American political tradition points toward a politics that prizes virtue more highly than does libertarianism, and reason more highly than does traditionalism. Virtue and reason are essential parts of liberty if liberty is grounded in the equality of man properly understood. That equality, the equality of natural rights, is the central idea of our political tradition—the principle from which all others radiate. And as liberty is not complete without virtue and reason, so equality of rights is not perfected without duty. Education in the rights of man means in the last analysis a noble dedication to the justice that stands behind—and above—those rights.

"That all men are created equal" is the foundation on which all else is built; it is the seed of a virtuous and reasonable liberty, the first principle of civil and moral education. Success, sobriety, the virtuous people, deliberation, limited government—all are important conservative principles, but all are given form and direction by the "abstract truth" of human equality. At the same time, no appreciation of the American political tradition is possible without an appreciation of American statesmanship, so that a prudent conservatism must be ever alive to the virtues of statesmanship and to the presence of statesmen. We must beware of rigid formulas and of a foolish reliance on impersonal forces or laws, lest we be left, in Solzhenitsyn's words, "completely helpless before the trials of our time." It must above all be our hope, kindled by the numinous inquiries of Harry V. Jaffa, that conservatives who know what is worth conserving in our political tradition will be able to inspirit America, so that we may regain our convictions *and* our courage.

One

Another Look at the Declaration

A merican conservatives have, as conservatives, regarded themselves as guardians of tradition. The tradition they guard is of course the American political tradition. (They cannot guard "tradition in general" because that is an abstraction and, as conservatives, they are enemies of abstractions.) The most famous document of the American political tradition is the Declaration of Independence. The most famous words of the Declaration are those that affirm as a self-evident truth "that all men are created equal." It is this proposition —enshrined as well in the Gettysburg Address—that Lincoln called "an abstract truth, applicable to all men and all times." Yet it is this proposition that is anathema to American conservatives. It is hardly too much to say that they regard it with an aversion equal to that with which they regard "all history is the history of class struggle." Not a few of them think of it as belonging properly, not to the American Declaration, but to the Communist Manifesto. One puts the matter in its mildest form in saying that American conservatism has been stultified by the presence of a self-contradiction within its being.

An example of this is supplied by Mr. William T. Couch, writing in the September 14, 1979 *National Review* ("Muddled Meanings"). Mr. Couch takes exception to Charles Kesler's "The Special Meaning of the Declaration of Independence," in the July 6, 1979 *National Review*. Mr. Couch thinks that Mr. Kesler—and I, and Abraham Lincoln—have found meaning in the Declaration where none in fact exists. As evidence whereof he cites the celebrated letter of May 8, 1825 from Jefferson to Henry Lee. According to Couch, in that letter Jefferson referred his correspondent to a series of sources where he might discover the presumable enigmatic construction of "equal" in the Declaration. Jefferson, writes Couch,

> suggested [to Lee] *as sources "the elementary books of public right...Aristotle, Cicero, Locke," that Lee should read if he wanted to discover Jefferson's meaning of the word "equal" in the Declaration.*

However, adds Couch,

> *one will not find in Aristotle or Cicero any explicit support for the famous phrase "all men are created equal." Aristotle clearly regarded slavery as existing by nature. Cicero never denies this. Locke asserts inequality in his second* Treatise *of Civil Government. VI, 54. He also asserts equality in the "the state of nature." II, 4.*

Mr. Couch concludes this line of argument by citing Leo Strauss to the effect that Rousseau destroyed the credibility of the Lockean state of nature (in which alone men are said by Locke to be equal) by proving that, had it ever existed, it would have been a subhuman state in which it would be "absurd . . . to find a norm for man."

Mr. Couch has misunderstood and misrepresented—however unintentionally—Jefferson's letter to Lee. The brief quotation is bowdlerized and out of context. Yet this letter is also one of the great documents of the American political tradition. It shows Jefferson, in his 83rd year—14 months before his death—possessed of that same "masterly pen" with its "peculiar felicity of expression" that had earned him the place of draftsman for the Congress and for the American people nearly a half-century before. It provides us, not only some of our profoundest insights into the meaning of the Declaration itself, but into that historical moment that produced the Declaration. It too is a priceless heirloom that conservatives should treasure.

The context of the letter to Lee is supplied by a correspondence between Timothy Pickering and John Adams, on the one hand, and between Madison, Jefferson, and Lee, on the other. Most of the relevant texts are collected in *A Casebook on the Declaration of Independence*, edited by Robert Ginsburg (Crowell, 1967). Pickering, in a widely circulated "Fourth of July Observations on the Declaration of Independence," had given notoriety to a remark he had made to John Adams, and which Adams had echoed back to him. In a letter to Pickering August 6, 1822, Adams wrote,

> *As you justly observe, there is not an idea in it but what had been hackneyed in Congress two years before.*

The letter to Lee is in the main Jefferson's response to this use of the word "hackneyed." In it, he turns a term of disparagement into a badge of honor. He does not deny the charge, nor does he accuse his old friend—and sometime enemy—of malice. Rather, he agrees with him, while translating the offending word into synonyms fitting the requirements of the task that he had faced as the draftsman of the Congress.

In the letter to Lee, Jefferson says that, when independence was decided upon, there was "but one opinion on this side of the water" concerning American rights and British transgressions. "All American whigs thought alike on these subjects." He continued:

> *When forced therefore to resort to arms for redress, an appeal to the tribunal of the world was deemed proper for our justification. This was the object of the Declaration of Independence.*

It was not the purpose of the Declaration, Jefferson went on,

> *to find out new principles, or new arguments, never before thought of, not merely to say things which had never been said before; but to place before mankind the common sense of the subject; in terms so plain and firm as to command their assent, and to justify ourselves in the independent stand we were compelled to take.*

Jefferson, to repeat, was the draftsman of the Congress, which in turn was the body which represented the American people. It was his high honor to be selected to put their thoughts and convictions into words fitting for the occasion. Of course, they were his own thoughts and convictions, since he was one of the American people. But nothing merely idiosyncratic to Jefferson would have been proper in such a place. Hence the letter to Lee continues thus:

> *Neither aiming at originality of principle or sentiment, nor yet copied from any particular and previous writing, it was intended to be an expression of the American mind, and to give to that expression the proper tone and spirit called for by the occasion. All its authority rests then on the harmonizing sentiments of the day, whether expressed in conversations, letters, printed essays or in the elementary books of public right, as Aristotle, Cicero, Locke, Sidney, etc.*

Recalling the brief quotation by Mr. Couch, we see that Jefferson was not sending Lee to "sources" for the meaning of "equal." "That all men are created equal" was of course one of the leading "hackneyed" ideas. It was certainly one concerning which there was "but one opinion on this side of the water," as it was one concerning which "All American whigs thought alike." It was so far from needing explanation that, in "the American mind," it merely expressed "the common sense" of the matter. Lee did not dream of asking Jefferson what he meant by "equal." I know of no single instance (I do not say that none exists) in which any one of the Revolutionary leaders, or any one of the Founding Fathers, either themselves asked, or were asked by others, what "equal" in the Declaration meant. For them its meaning was indeed "self-evident."

Mr. Couch, in commenting on Jefferson's list of "the elementary books of public right," says that Aristotle "clearly regarded slavery as existing by nature." But Aristotle distinguished between *natural* slavery, and slavery that rested merely on convention and force. Natural slaves are those whose bodies are apt for useful work, but whose minds are not apt to direct them in that work, and require someone else's brain for that purpose. Today, we would call most of such persons mentally retarded. Their enslavement is just, Aristotle says. But those who are slaves merely because they, or their fathers, had been captured by physical force, are not slaves by nature, and they are slaves unjustly. We might add that such was the case of all, or nearly all, those who were slaves in the antebellum United States.

That Aristotle had some influence upon the teaching of the Declaration is suggested in part by the presence in it of the idea of human nature. Such an idea did not originate with Aristotle, but he certainly gave it its most powerful development within the Western world. This evolved in later writers—Cicero among them—into the idea of "laws of nature and of nature's God." But the Declaration, in one of its most notable passages, speaks of the dictates of "prudence." And it is the sixth book of the *Nicomachean Ethics* that is the *locus classicus* for the development of the meaning of prudence. Although the concept of prudence descended into the eighteenth century through a thousand sources besides Aristotle, his texts were its headwaters. The same may be said of "happiness," as in "the pursuit of happiness" and in "their safety and happiness." Although the substantive meaning of happiness had been modified in the writings of many seventeenth and eighteenth century writers, its classical meaning was still powerful. Jefferson may have rejected Aristotelian metaphysics. But it is doubtful that he or his contemporaries had reservations in regard to it as the *summum bonum* both for individual human beings and for civil society.

Mr. Couch says that Locke "clearly asserts inequality" in the sixth chapter of the *Second Treatise*, while he "also asserts equality in a 'state of nature'" in the second chapter of that same work. This is not very helpful for understanding either Locke or the Declaration. Here is an ample quotation from the second chapter.

> *To understand political power aright . . . we must consider what state all men are naturally in, and that is a state of perfect freedom to order their actions . . . within the bonds of the law of nature, without asking leave, or depending upon the will of any other man.*

It is in this respect that men are also in a state of equality, Locke continues,

> *there being nothing more evident* [this is the Lockean antecedent of "We hold these truths to be self evident . . ."] *than that creatures of the same species . . . should be equal one amongst another without subordination or subjection . . .*

In Chapter Six, Locke makes it clear that this equality is fully consistent with the recognition of all the important qualitative distinctions and differences among men.

> *Though I have said above that all men by nature are equal, I cannot be supposed to understand all sorts of equality. Age or virtue may give man a just precedency. Excellency of parts and merit may place others above the common level . . . And yet all this consists with the equality which all men are in, in respect of jurisdiction or dominion, one over another.*

I have often, in my writings, rendered the foregoing doctrine thus: There is no difference between man and man, as there is between man and beast or between man and God, that makes one by nature the ruler of another. This does not mean that there are not wide differences among men, or that it is not often to the advantage of some to be ruled by others. For the rule of the wise over the less wise to be advantageous, however, it must come about by a process of consent. And the requirement of consent can be understood only in the light of, and by recognition of, natural equality. Let us illustrate this by analogy with other arts, in which we seek the advantages of the wisdom of others.

I permit myself to be ruled by my doctor, not only because I think him wiser than I concerning health. I do so because I believe that he will actually devote himself to my health. This I am satisfied he will do because I am confident that he wants to collect my fee, and because he wants to have the reputation of having benefited me, so that he can collect fees from others as well. In addition, there is the fact that if he practices medicine negligently he can be sued for doing so; and if he were to join in a conspiracy to injure me in any way, he can be prosecuted under the criminal law. These things testify to the fact that medical knowledge — like all the arts — is in itself morally neutral. It can be used either to help or to harm. It is the Hippocratic oath, not his medical knowledge, which commits the physician to healing. Similar considerations govern the employment of lawyers, architects, engineers, economists, and generals.

The problem of civil society is twofold: how to identify and select wise rulers, and how to assure that their wisdom will be used for the benefit of the ruled — or of the common good as distinct from their private good. Governments, like physicians, must simultaneously be the masters and the servants of those whom they govern. The case of governments is, however, infinitely more complicated than that of physicians. By the teaching of the Declaration, we repeat, it is the recognition of natural equality which is the ground, the necessary condition, for assuring that governments serve those they rule. For once again, it is natural equality which requires that authority be grounded in consent. It is natural equality which leads logically to the requirement that no superiority, whether in intelligence, strength, or virtue, justifies government in preferring the advantage of the few to that of the many. The process of consent, arising from the recognition of natural equality, becomes the "Hippocratic oath" of free government.

Seen from this perspective, the "state of nature" is not something belonging to the past. It is an analytical distinction within an eternal present. I know that Mr. Carter, who happens now to be President of the United States, remains my equal in nature, even as he is, temporarily, my superior in law. But it is because I know that we are equal in nature that I know that the law that makes him my superior also makes him my servant. He is there for my benefit, and for the benefit of all of our fellow-citizens, and not for any private benefits of his own. And he, like the physician, is given private compensation for performing public services. His tenure of office — indeed all tenures of office in a free government — is for a limited time only. Even offices whose tenure is indefinite — as is the case of federal judges — are so only "during good behavior." A free people always has the right to dismiss its rulers — whom it regards as its servants — at any time. This it may do either by constitutional or by revolutionary means, as Lincoln carefully observed in his first inaugural address.

Here I should like to correct a widespread misconception, arising largely from a misreading of the tenth and 51st *Federalist,* of the meaning of constitutional morality. In a celebrated paragraph, Madison writes that the great security against a tyrannical concentration of power

> *consists in giving to those who administer each department the necessary constitutional means and personal motives to resist encroachments of the others. The provision for defense must in this, as in all other cases, be made commensurate to the danger of attack. The interest of the man must be connected with the constitutional rights of the place.*

It is sometimes assumed from this that "personal motives" and the "interest of the man," neither of which are directed toward the common good nor toward the public well-being, constitute the sufficient ground for constitutional morality. It is thought that, in a well constructed constitution, some kind of "invisible hand" presides over the good of the whole, without any conscious direction toward that end. But if one reads to the end of this same paragraph one finds Madison saying,

> *A dependence on the people is, no doubt, the primary control on the government; but experience has taught mankind the necessity of auxiliary precautions.*

Connecting the interests of the officeholders to the rights of their offices are then "auxiliary precautions." In the very next paragraph Madison calls them "inventions of prudence." Now prudence, according to the philosophic tradition going back to Aristotle, relates entirely to means, and not to ends. Prudence, Aristotle says, presupposes moral virtue. It is moral virtue which directs men toward their proper ends, and prudence which finds out the means to those ends. Absent moral virtue, there is absent any possibility of prudence. The prudential utilization of self-interest for the sake of ends which are good because they are in accordance with "the laws of nature and of nature's God" is what the *Federalist* may properly be said to argue.

Mr. Couch, finally, has attempted to bring in Leo Strauss, as a witness against Mr. Kesler and myself. He quotes from pp. 273 and 274 of *Natural Right and History,* to the effect that Rousseau, by thinking through the "modern natural right teaching," had reduced it to absurdity. And Mr. Couch assumes that the Declaration of Independence is thereby reduced to absurdity.

In the sentence following the last one quoted by Couch, Strauss continues, saying, "Hobbes had denied that man has a natural end." And Couch rightly interprets Strauss as holding that, in this decisive respect, Locke had been a secret follower of Hobbes.

If the Declaration of Independence was merely and simply a Lockean document, Mr. Couch's argument would be decisive. Yet every schoolboy knows — or at least once knew — that Jefferson departed from Locke in declaring that among man's unalienable rights were life, liberty, and the pursuit of happiness — happiness, mind you, and not "property" or "estate." If man, in the state of nature, or by nature, pursues happiness, then by nature he pursues a *summum bonum* and does not merely flee a *summum malum*. This theoretical defect in Hobbes' and Locke's teaching is then not a necessary defect of the Declaration. The limited relevance of Rousseau's critique of Hobbes and Locke has never been better expressed than by M. J. Sobran, in his review of *How to Think About the American Revolution (National Review,* December 22, 1978, p. 1602).

> *Never mind Leo Strauss's contention that Locke was an intellectual hypocrite who gave his tongue to Hooker and his heart to Hobbes: the Fathers weren't Straussians, and they interpreted Locke in an innocent and traditional way.*

To this I would add that Leo Strauss himself appears to have interpreted the Declaration of Independence in much the same way that Mr. Sobran says that the Fathers did. One does not understand *Natural Right and History*, or Strauss's work as a whole, without understanding that he was in the highest sense a political writer. The controlling purpose of *Natural Right and History* is supplied by the Introduction, which begins with a solemn invocation of the Declaration of Independence, one that reminds us as well of the Gettysburg Address. After repeating the Declaration's most famous sentence, Strauss continued,

> *The nation dedicated to this proposition has now become, no doubt partly as a consequence of this dedication, the most powerful and prosperous of the nations of the earth. Does this nation in its maturity still cherish the faith in which it was conceived and raised? Does it still hold those "truths to be self-evident?"*

The answers to those questions have unhappily become more negative every year since Strauss asked them, more than a quarter-century ago. Yet it is certain that Strauss believed those questions ought to have been answered in the affirmative. Until they could be so answered, he did not believe this nation, or the West, could recover its moral health or political vigor. Nor would it in the end preserve its freedom or material well-being. For Leo Strauss, no less than for Abraham Lincoln, the United States was the "last best hope on earth." And this was so because in the Declaration of Independence there was preserved that vital spark of natural right from which could always be rekindled another "new birth of freedom."

July 1980

Two

The 1980 Presidential Election
A Watershed in the Making?

R onald Reagan's election as fortieth President of the United States is a beginning and not an end. The liberal commentators may say all that they want to say about Reagan abandoning his "extreme conservatism" during the campaign, and his movement to the "middle" in which all presidential elections are won and lost. But anyone who watched the Democratic Convention, and heard the acceptance speeches of both Mr. Mondale and Mr. Carter, will recall that the Democrats were unrelenting in reminding the electorate of Mr. Reagan's conservative opinions, expressed consistently over the years. The results of the election suggest that the voters reacted in a manner exactly the opposite to what the Democrats (and liberal commentators) expected and wished. They *liked* what they heard of Mr. Reagan's opinions, past as well as present. Certainly Mr. Reagan expressed himself somewhat differently when he was speaking to country-club Republicans, than when he spoke more recently to national television audiences. But the main thrust and purport of his speeches has not changed. We will have a conservative Republican administration. Perhaps even more important will be the public realization that conservative Republicanism is *not* right wing extremism. Conservative Republicanism *is* the "middle of the road."

The election of 1980 may be a "watershed." By that we mean one of those elections — 1800, 1828, 1860, and 1932 — in which one political party replaces another political party, as the nucleus of a governing majority, a governing majority that becomes the political core of the country for several generations. In the election of 1860, the Republicans were not yet a majority party, but were becoming one. They remained the majority party, from after the Civil War until 1932. In 1932, Franklin D. Roosevelt began a process of transforming the party of Woodrow Wilson into a majority that has controlled the basic instruments of government until the present day. Dwight D. Eisenhower enjoyed a Republican Congress for only two years of his eight. The eight years of Nixon and Ford did not see a single term in which the Republicans controlled either branch of the Congress. In the forty-eight years since F. D. R.'s first election, there has been Republican rule, in the proper sense, for only two years. Mr. Reagan's election, bringing with it Republican control only of the Senate, does not yet constitute a thorough realignment of American politics. Neither did Mr. Roosevelt's election in 1932. It was Mr. Roosevelt's transformation of the old Democratic Party into the New Deal coalition—of which the old Party was but one element—which in retrospect made 1932 into a watershed election.

Notwithstanding the foregoing, the transformation of the Democratic Party into the New Deal coalition may be said to have begun in 1896, with the nomination of William Jennings Bryan. The heart of Bryan's populism—which thrust aside the old Democracy of Grover Cleveland—was his campaign for the free coinage of silver. This ancient slogan should not conceal from us the now familiar commitment to "soft money" and inflation, so familiar as a feature of the New Deal and its successors. Bryan's party came to power somewhat moderated and "high-toned" in the person of Woodrow Wilson. Wilson actually received fewer popular votes in 1912 than Bryan had received in 1908, but the Bull Moose Party, dividing the Republicans, enabled him to capture a majority in the Electoral College. Franklin D. Roosevelt became in time the political heir of his cousin, Theodore Roosevelt, no less than of Bryan and Wilson (whom he served for seven years as Assistant Secretary of the Navy, the post that TR held under McKinley).

Looking at the Republican Party today, we can see that Mr. Reagan is the political successor of Barry Goldwater, in much the same way that FDR was of Bryan and Wilson. Strange to say, Mr. Reagan is also the political heir of the Democratic Party whose symbolic hero was—once upon a time—Al Smith. It was that party, as much as the party of Herbert Hoover, that was driven into the political wilderness by the New Deal. Smith was a reformer, but he was also a product of the old big city machine, the machine that was the primary political instrumentality for the assimilation and upward mobility of the post-Civil War immigrant groups. Although the original New Deal counted the big city political machines as among its pillars, the later New Deal, and the still later welfare state, systematically destroyed these vital political structures. The death of Mayor Daley of Chicago probably marks the final passing of the old boss. For the essence of the policy inaugurated by FDR under the aegis of Harry Hopkins ("spend, spend, tax, tax, elect, elect") was to centralize political patronage in the federal bureaucracy, making the local political organizations mere dependents upon the largess of the Great Machine of the Imperial Presidency. The rhetoric of ideological liberalism has glossed and painted over the brute fact of political power snatched and torn from its local roots and centralized in Washington.

The nomination of Barry Goldwater in 1964 was not—contrary to everything that has been written—a victory of the "Right" over either the Left or Middle of the Republican Party. Rather was it a defining of the ground upon which the Party's mainstream would fight the political battles of the next generation. Right, Left, and Center are always relative terms. The victories of the New Deal transferred the wild-eyed radicalism of the thirties into the mainstream—and center—of American politics. Viewed from that center,

Senator Goldwater's older liberalism was called a newer conservatism. I took part in the Goldwater campaign of 1964, and debated Democrats on campuses up and down the east coast. Whenever I was asked about Senator Goldwater's alleged plans to tear down the institutional structure of the New Deal—to abolish Social Security, sell TVA, etc, etc. —I truthfully, if vainly, denied that he had any such intentions.

The heart of the Goldwater campaign, as it related to domestic policy, was as follows. The G.N.P. of the United States, in 1964, was expanding at an annual rate of about 4%. This was due in no small measure to the success of the "Kennedy" tax cuts, which were in fact bipartisan. Kennedy's greatest success as President was a tax policy which flowed from Republican rather than Democratic imperatives. But we Goldwaterites knew—and said as loudly as we could—that under the Democrats, the prosperity of the economy would become an excuse for vast *new* government spending programs. For along with the rising G.N.P., and because of it, federal tax revenues were increasing by a factor of four or five. When G.N.P. went up by 4%, federal revenues, largely from the personal and corporate income tax, went up as much as 20%. We in the Goldwater campaign knew—and predicted—that Lyndon Johnson's next administration would be characterized by programs like the "war on poverty." We knew that such a "war" would be nothing but a vast federal program, designed to soak up the federal revenues that a prospering free market economy was producing. But we also knew that that free market economy would not continue prospering, if its marginal revenues were absorbed by the federal budget, and did not get into the capital markets, to seed and re-seed on-going prosperity. During the recent Carter-Reagan debate, President Carter charged that Mr. Reagan's tax-cut proposals would be inflationary, by putting too much purchasing power into the hands of consumers. But Mr. Reagan retorted by demanding to know why purchasing power in the hands of private citizens —who might at least save some of it—was inflationary, while purchasing power in the hands of bureaucrats—who never save any of it—was not.

The significance of the Goldwater campaign was lost to the public at the time, in part because of the assassination of President Kennedy. Had Kennedy lived, he would almost certainly have been re-elected. The election would have been decided by the flush of prosperity which followed the tax cuts, which had not yet been soaked up by the war on poverty or the war in Vietnam. But the election would have been much closer. As it was, Kennedy could not be attacked, because he was a dead martyr, and Johnson could not be attacked, because he had too recently assumed the reins of power under tragic circumstances.

But the stagnation, inflation ridden economy of today is the direct result of policies put in place by the Democratic Party headed by Lyndon Johnson. The fallacy of the "war on poverty" is shown by the fact that the ranks of the officially designated "poor" had been undergoing steady attrition for a genera-tion *before* the "war," a trend which has been reversed *by* the "war." Instead we have a permanent "under-class" who are the permanent objects of concern of a permanent bureaucracy. It is this bureaucracy—a highly paid clique of privileged ideologues—not altogether unlike their opposite numbers in the planned economies elsewhere in the world, who are the principal beneficiaries of the contemporary Democratic Party. Relatively little of the public money goes to the poor. All those crocodile tears that Senator Edward Kennedy shed at the Democratic Convention in New York last summer were for the deserving Democrats who would be *ministering* to the poor. The last thing in the world that Senator Kennedy would want is to have too few poor for his crocodile tears. Anti-poverty programs have long ceased being nets *under* the poor. They are more nearly lids *over* the poor, preventing that upward mobility that has been the genius of the American regime from its origins.

There is a striking parallel between 1964 and 1980. Once again, federal revenues are soaring. But now it is inflation, not economic growth, that is putting taxpayers into higher brackets. As nominal incomes go up, taxes are paid at higher rates, and real income goes down. Mr. Reagan repeated almost the precise arguments of the Goldwater campaign, but whereas Mr. Goldwater's arguments, being prophetic, were unheeded, Mr. Reagan's, describing a present and very painful condition, were. The continual transfer of the country's marginal income from producers to consumers, and from savers to spenders, cannot continue without causing a crisis. All segments of the economy and of the population are now aware of this. The continual growth of non-productive government functions, and the continual process of income transfer, is perfectly well understood by everyone in terms of the ancient fable of killing the goose that laid the golden eggs.

The foreign and defense issues of the 1980 presidential campaign can be summed up by reference to President Carter's Notre Dame speech, in the first year of his term, in which he warned us to beware of "an inordinate fear of Communism." Less than three years later, after the Soviet invasion of Afghanistan, he confessed that he had been completely misled concerning Soviet intentions. In short, the premise upon which his foreign policy and his defense policy had rested, when he cancelled the B-1 Bomber, vetoed the new nuclear carrier, delayed the building of the Trident missile and submarine, delayed the M-X missile, *and* signed the Salt II Treaty, had been in error. Yet even after Afghanistan, and after a year of impotent flailing over the hostages, Mr. Carter had made no moves to restore the military credibility of the United States in the world. His most widely publicized move was his 3% real increase in the 1981 defense budget. Yet, as the *Wall Street Journal* showed, this increase was accomplished *not* by *adding* to the FY 1981 defense budget, but by *reducing* the FY 1980 defense budget. This invisible budget increase, along with the equally apocryphal revelation of an invisible bomber, showed a cynicism towards the most vital interests of the nation that enraged its patriotic instincts. What it proved was, that although Mr. Carter could "whup" Senator Kennedy's "a--"

in the party primaries, it was the latter who controlled party policy when the chips were down. For Senator Kennedy's wing of the party, national defense rests not on guns, but on "character," the latter being defined with reference to "social reform," and not with reference to a willingness—or ability—to fight.

The Democratic National Convention in New York proved beyond a reasonable doubt that the controlling wing of the Democratic Party was indeed Senator Kennedy's, along with his cohorts, such as Senators McGovern, Bayh, Church, Magnuson. For them, the motto of the Democratic Party might well be, "Extremism is no vice, if it is in defense of an ever-larger federal bureaucracy, affirmative action, busing, homosexual rights, federally funded abortions, and aid to Third World countries that burn the American flag." To this might be added, that "Moderation is no virtue, when attacking the F.B.I., the C.I.A., nuclear power, and United States corporations that build the weapons of our defense." With such slogans, and the Party dominated by them, the American people are sick unto death. The silent majority—whom the pollsters certainly missed in 1980—has finally emerged. Let us hope that the Republican Party, reconstituted to become their spokesman for the next generation, will comprehend and fulfill its responsibilities, "as in the olden times."

November 1980

Three

For Good Government and the Happiness of Mankind

The Moral Majority and the American Founding

I mmediately after the election of Ronald Reagan, I wrote that "the silent majority, whom the pollsters missed in 1980, has finally emerged." I expressed the opinion that this election might prove to be a watershed election, and that the Republican Party, duly reconstituted, might become the spokesman for a new majority, for the next generation. Certainly there is a possibility that Mr. Reagan's election—accompanied by decisive gains in the Senate, and large gains in the House—foreshadows a reconstitution of American politics on the order of magnitude of that presided over by Franklin D. Roosevelt. This of course depends in the first instance upon his success in facing the immediate crises in the economy and of American security in the world. Mr. Reagan must have his own "hundred days," whatever its actual length may turn out to be. If he can restore the nation's confidence in its future, then the political movement he leads may turn out to be one of "many years of sunshine days."

Whether the "silent majority" turns into a "new majority" may in the end depend very much upon what it does, or is able to do, about the "Moral Majority." This self-proclaimed majority has been anything but silent. It has claimed much credit as part of Mr. Reagan's constituency, and has been more than plausible in its asserted responsibility for the defeat of many of the great and conspicuous old guard liberals of the Senate establishment: notably, Senators Bayh, McGovern, Church, Magnuson, Culver. The aforesaid Senators have made the claims of the Moral Majoritarians more plausible than they might have been, by blaming them—that is, giving them credit—for their defeats. On the whole the pundits of the press—joined rather loudly of late by the President of Yale University—have not been kind to the Moral Majority. The discussion of the Moral Majority's role in the campaign has has been dominated by the silly charge that they have transgressed the margins separating church and state by injecting religious demands into political campaigns. I say "silly" in part because of the historic role of the churches and of churchmen—and churchwomen—in such nineteenth century political movements as the crusade against slavery, the crusade for temperance (that is, against strong drink), and the crusade for women's suffrage. Moreover many of the most prominent critics of the Moral Majority were themselves enlisted almost yesterday—as it were—in the ranks of the Southern Christian Leadership Conference, led by the Reverend Doctor Martin Luther King, Jr. I do not think that Dr. King himself doubted for a moment that the movement he led was advancing the cause of true Christianity, as much as the cause of true political freedom. Certainly the Christianity he preached, in advancing civil rights, was non-sectarian, and nothing about it was invidious in its bearing upon Judaism, Islam, Buddhism, or any other religion. Yet the dynamism of his movement drew, first and foremost, upon the enthusiasm of a fundamentalist Christianity, in exactly the same way that the Reverend Jerry Falwell does, in his appeals for the restoration of a traditional morality. I can see no more tension between the claims of church and state, in the one case, than in the other. The only difference lies in whether one sees religion reinforcing political demands coming from the Left, or from the Right.

Early in the 1980 campaign Mr. Reagan himself was treated with scorn by the ideologists of the Left when he ventured the opinion, almost in passing, that "creationist" doctrine should have place, along with the "evolutionist," in school instruction dealing with the question of the origin of the universe. From the reaction of the press, one would have thought that Mr. Reagan was reopening the Scopes trial and replaying the role of William Jennings Bryan in his celebrated clash with Clarence Darrow. Yet one wonders how in the world one is to explain to a child "that all men are created equal" and that they are "endowed by their Creator with certain unalienable rights," without resorting to "creationist doctrine."

The other remark for which Mr. Reagan was much taken to task was the one in which he said that the Vietnam war, or America's part in it, was a "noble cause." I suspect that both of these "gaffes" or "blunders" (as they were called at the time) reached deeply within the soul of the people, and found an answering response that contributed profoundly to his victory. Vietnam was the first unambiguous repulse or failure of American military power in American history. It was the first time that American forces had withdrawn from a contested field, leaving the enemy in sole possession. Yet our forces were never defeated in that field. Their withdrawal was not accomplished by the arms of the enemy, but by internal political pressures generated within the United States. The United States military was driven from the field by the domestic opponents of the war, demonstrating in the streets—and in particular on the campuses—of the United States. These demonstrations were then repeated and replayed by the media—notably television—in such a way as to greatly intensify their effects. I remember an NBC television crew arriving on a Claremont campus in the mid-sixties, to tape a debate on the war. They arrived complete with made-up anti-war signs and paraphernalia, which they handed out to the students as a backdrop for the cameras. In this particular instance, the students indignantly refused to participate in NBC's fraud. But there must have been thousands upon thousands of such episodes, in which the media and the anti-war forces conspired to magnify the political opposition to the war. In the end, they defeated the United States.

The great Tet offensive by the Viet Cong was catastrophic for the Viet Cong. Yet the military defeat of the Viet Cong became a political victory, by its misrepresentation by the press and television media. American opinion became wavering and uncertain, and support for our forces in the field, in the Congress, faltered and eventually broke. Those whose sons fought bravely in that war, many of them never to return, have had accounts to settle with those who nullified their sacrifices. There is a deep inner attachment of traditional America to the honor and dignity of the fighting services—as indeed there must be within any regime that is to survive. Many of the Senators who went down to defeat so resoundingly in 1980, apparently on the "social" or "moral" issues, were also pre-eminent among the architects of our defeat in Vietnam. The taking of the hostages by the Iranian militants, and the year-long stream of abuse and insolence to which this nation was subjected, has accentuated the resentment against what happened in Vietnam. The sneering superciliousness of the claque that tried to "make a monkey" out of Mr. Reagan for his remarks on evolution and Vietnam turned against his political opponents.

As Governor of California, Mr. Reagan made clear his understanding of the connection between the life-styles and the political causes espoused by the protestors and demonstrators. (One might say that "causes" were the only thing that they did "espouse.") Because of this he became the favorite politician of those who, on varying grounds, and with differing degrees of emphasis, have been against the drug and pornography culture, against abortion-on-demand, against the so-called Equal Rights Amendment, against mandatory busing, against race quotas or "affirmative action" in employment and education, against equal rights for homosexuals, or at least for those flaunting their homosexual life styles, against transvestitism and transsexualism, against easy and frequent divorces (not to mention their horror at the rising disregard of marriage in the formation and dissolution of families), and in favor of some mild and modest form of non-sectarian school prayer. At the root of the social protest against the recent assaults upon traditional moral conventions and traditional proprieties is the conviction that, whatever adaptations to changing times and circumstances may prove to be necessary, the traditional family, in some recognizable form, can and must be preserved. There is a moral fundamentalism in this country, which is by no means identical with religious fundamentalism, however much it may be supported by religious fundamentalists. The enemies of moral fundamentalism, for obvious interested motives, have tried to reduce this moral fundamentalism to the religious convictions of the religious fundamentalists. To listen to these critics, one would think that the argument for chastity, for example, rested squarely upon the acceptance of the literal interpretation of the story of Jonah and the whale (with a nod in the direction of George Gershwin's *Porgy and Bess*). The publicists and pundits who have dominated the media and the academies have thus equated moral conservatism with religious fundamentalism, and both with intolerance. They would have us believe that "all lifestyles are created equal," and equally entitled to the protection, not only of enlightened opinion, but of law. They think that morality, like religion, has no place in political life. They speak of conscience — or moral inhibitions — as "Hang-ups," much the way that Puritans once spoke of Original Sin. That this is an inconsistency, is something of which they seem wholly unaware. But they are wrong about the relationship of morality to political life. A free, self-governing society, more than any other kind, depends upon the qualities — the virtues — of its citizens. Even the *Federalist*, the most "realistic" example of political reasoning, declares in number fifty-five, that, "As there is a degree of depravity in mankind which requires a certain degree of circumspection and distrust, so there are other qualities in human nature which justify a certain portion of esteem and confidence. Republican government presupposes the existence of these qualities in a higher degree than any other form."

In a republic, the sobriety of the citizens replaces the force of authority as the principal source of order. Anarchy and tyranny are the eternal antinomies of political life, and each breeds the other. Aristotle, in the second book of the *Politics*, says that the power of the law lies essentially in the power of habit, which is "second nature." That is why the formation of good habits is the primary task of the law. The moral virtues are good habits. The habit of law-abidingness is called by Aristotle legal justice, which he also describes as justice in its most comprehensive sense, since it commands us to do all the acts of all the virtues. When men have good habits they are in no need of external restraints. Gentlemen, properly so called, do not even have a sense of shame, according to Aristotle. Shameful behavior is not even possible, for a true gentleman. To have a sense of shame is to be restrained by fear of the opinion of others, and even to be subject to such a fear is, according to Aristotle, a sign of inferiority. A gentleman is restrained only by his own inbred or innate sense of what is fitting.

In a democratic republic, those who make the laws live under the laws they make. The relationship between law and opinion, in our form of government, was stated by Abraham Lincoln when he declared that "In this and like communities, public sentiment is everything... Consequently he who molds public sentiment goes deeper than he who enacts statutes or pronounces decisions. He makes statutes and decisions possible or impossible to be executed." Hence the character of such a society, more than any other kind, consists in the character of its citizens. A free society is undoubtedly "pluralistic." But pluralism implies diversity *within* unity. It cannot be an unbounded diversity. *E pluribus unum* is the motto of the United States. On the surface, it refers to the legal unity — or the sovereign Union — compounded of many sovereign states. But it also refers, less obviously, but more profoundly, to the moral unity that underlies the moral diversity comprehended by the same

Union. By virtue of this moral unity, the American people are "one nation, under God." It is the antecedent moral unity that makes the political unity possible. Tolerance, for example, is certainly one of the virtues of a free, republican people. But tolerance, as itself a moral virtue, cannot be indifferent to moral distinctions. George Washington, on a famous occasion, speaking of religious freedom, declared that "It is now no more that toleration is spoken of, as if it was by the indulgence of one class of people, that another enjoyed the exercise of their inherent natural rights." A condescending tolerance can, in certain circumstances, be a reprehensible tolerance. Nor can tolerance of diversity extend to such diversity as will destroy the possibility of genuine tolerance. Tolerating slavery, for example, may be a necessity in certain circumstances: in the formation of the Union, for example. But tolerating slavery as a necessary evil is different from regarding it either as a positive good, or as a matter of moral indifference. Freedom of speech cannot be understood to extend to such speech as is destructive of the equal rights of others, or of the right of the community to preserve itself. There is no inherent right to civil liberties by totalitarians, either on the Right or the Left, who would destroy all civil liberties. "Must I shoot the simple-minded soldier boy who deserts," asked Abraham Lincoln, in the midst of a great civil war, "while I must not touch a hair of the wily agitator who induces him to desert? I think that, in such a case, to silence the agitator and save the boy is not only constitutional, but withal a great mercy." If libel and slander laws, as well as laws against obscenity, place limits upon speech, so must the possibility of a "diversity of life-styles" be understood to have limits. The first platform of the Republican Party, in 1856, spoke of the "twin relics of barbarism ... polygamy and slavery." Neither polygamy nor polyandry (any more than slavery) are compatible with that equality of the sexes and equality of families which is fundamental to a republican form of government. It may sound or seem merely prudish to object to "families" which arise without legal marriage. But there is much more at stake than whether or not sex needs a license. The wreckage caused to lives by divorce, a wreckage that almost invariably extends to children, and children's children, is certain to be much worse, where the "marriages" which are dissolved were never formed in the first place.

In the last analysis, all our rights depend upon our willingness, not merely to tolerate each other, but to defend each other. In acting to defend the nation—or union—we cannot be supposed to be defending "life-styles" we regard as abominable or disgusting. The life-style of the Manson clan (note that it *was* an extended polygamous family of the counterculture) had enough to discommend it even before it proved to have murder as an element of its ritual. The Mansons were only a dramatic example of the commonplaces of the counterculture of the 1960's, but they help to place in perspective the fallacy, common then and now, that there are "victimless crimes." The idea that there are no rules that ought to govern the behavior of "consenting adults" leaves out of account the fact that such adults are supposed to be fellow-citizens. It is a mere redundancy—but a most instructive one—to say that those who see each other as utterly alien cannot be fellow-citizens.

* * *

For some generations now, there has been a steadily growing alienation of the American political order from its historic roots in the tradition of reason and of revelation. This alienation has proceeded from that radical modernity expressed in positivism and historicism, culminating in nihilism. Even the fashionable depreciation of Marxism-Leninism in our academies is a sign, not of the healthy rejection of an unhealthy doctrine, but of the morbid depreciation of *any* principles that claim a ground in objective reality, whether that of a living God, or of reason, nature, or history. When American intellectuals—so called —say, as they often do, that Marxism-Leninism has few genuine adherents behind the Iron Curtain, they are more likely to be projecting upon others their own incredulity, than telling us something they know to be true. If they think that others do not believe in the doctrines of the *Communist Manifesto* (or of *State and Revolution*), it is because they themselves do not believe in the doctrines of the Declaration of Independence. I recall a public debate, in which my opponent brushed aside my citations of statements by Soviet leaders, repeating and reaffirming their goal of world revolution. "Those," he said, "are merely ceremonial. They mean no more to them than Fourth of July orations mean to us."

Positivism and historicism have so dominated the academies of the western world that there have been few university professors in this century who have given—or would give—a moment's consideration to the question of whether they should, whether as men or citizens, be guided in their lives by such principles as Thomas Jefferson once called "the common sense of the subject." This alienation from the principles of the Founding has of course made its way downward and outward through the ranks of all the professions— in literature, the arts, politics, and the media—until it can be said that a condition not unlike schizophrenia exists within the soul of the polity. Our institutions, beneficent and prosperous as they may be, subsist only on the inertia of old loyalties and narrow self-interest, unsupported by anything resembling a rational faith, either in divine guidance or philosophic wisdom. Machiavelli warned of the fate of any nation that depended for its safety upon mercenaries. We have become mercenaries to ourselves, because we recognize no higher purpose being served by our institutions or our way of life than that served by mercenaries—or fanatics. Those who live without any purpose derived from any wisdom, whether human or divine, are equally open to the contemptible and the fanatical. That is something all of us learned—or should have learned—who lived through the violent oscillations between mindless radicalism and the soulless materialism, on the campuses, in the last generation.

The Moral Majority is one symptom, however, that the legacy of the Founding Fathers will not be abandoned altogether without a fight. The fashionable criticism of the Moral Majority, is that their horizon, moral and intellectual, is a narrow one. If it is narrow then, of course, it should be broadened. But one suspects that true ground of hostility to the Moral Majority—such as that of the President of Yale University—stems less from the alleged narrowness of the Majority, than from the genuineness of their convictions with respect to the authority of traditional morality. And the truth is that the Moral Majority represents but a mild form of the old code. Even Thomas Jefferson —surely no Puritan—in his "Bill for Proportioning Crimes and Punishments" (1779), proposed castration as the fitting punishment of rape or sodomy. But the details of an evolving criminal code are not what is at issue here. What is important is the question of public recognition of the utility and necessity of moral principles, in the formation of the character of those who are to be citizens of a democratic republic. No one expressed the proper political concern for morality better than George Washington, in his Farewell Address. "Of all the dispositions and habits which lead to political prosperity," he declared,

> *religion and morality are indispensable supports. In vain would that man claim the tribute of patriotism who should labor to subvert these great pillars of human happiness—these firmest props of the duties of men and citizens. The mere politician, equally with the pious man, ought to respect and cherish them...Let it be simply asked, Where is the security for property, for reputation, for life, if the sense of religious obligation desert the oaths which are the instruments of investigation in courts of justice? And let us with caution indulge the supposition that morality can be maintained without religion. Whatever may be conceded to the influence of refined education on minds of a peculiar structure, reason and experience forbid us to expect that national morality can prevail in exclusion of religious principle.*

Lest the foregoing advice of the Father of his country be thought merely an old man's piety, we recall the flaming words of the author of the Declaration of Independence, still a young man, as set down during the Revolution in his *Notes on Virginia.*

> *And can the liberties of a nation be thought secure, when we have removed their only firm basis, a conviction in the minds of the people that these liberties are of the gift of God? That they are not to be violated but with his wrath?*

Here we have another perspective on religion and morality, as the "firmest props of the duties of men and citizens." It may be true that "minds of a peculiar structure" can recognize what they owe to others in what they ask for themselves. But the generality of mankind think much more of what others owe to them, than of what they owe to others. They need to be reminded that an offense against the other is an offense against the God who equally endowed all with unalienable rights.

*   *   *

The Northwest Ordinance of 1787, according to the United States Code, is one of the four "organic" laws of the United States. These are, in order, the Declaration of Independence, the Articles of Confederation, the Ordinance, and the Constitution (and amendments thereto). It is the Ordinance which provides the basic legal pattern that has been followed in the expansion of the original thirteen states to the present fifty. The Constitution says that Congress may admit new states to the union, but does not describe or prescribe how this is to be done. The Ordinance was adopted in July of 1787. While the proceedings of the Convention were secret, those of the Congress were not. The Convention probably knew what Congress was doing, and may have assumed that the Ordinance would supply the procedures which are not given by the Constitution. This at any rate is what the first Congress under the Constitution effected in 1789, by adopting an act for the enforcement of the Ordinance, thus making it for all practical purposes part of the Constitution. The Ordinance detailed steps by which territorial governments were to be instituted in unorganized territories, and by which territorial governments might become states. And it provided that the new states, when admitted into the union, would be equal in all legal and political respects to the older states, and that their citizens would be the equal, in all legal and political respects, to the citizens of the older states. This, as much as the division of the powers of government between the United States and the several states (and their people) constitutes the uniqueness of American federalism. For the preservation of equal rights throughout the whole, as the whole became a larger whole, has made the United States the first empire in the world that is an empire of freedom.

The foregoing remarks are necessary to remind ourselves of the greatness of the Northwest Ordinance as a constitutional document, and hence of its authority as a source of the doctrines of the American Founding. As the Ordinance provided that the new states were to be equal with the old, some care was needed to describe in what that equality was to consist. It was to consist in more than equal representation in the Senate of the new states as states, or of the equal representation of the people of the new states with the people of the older states, in the House of Representatives. The Constitution provides that the United States shall guarantee to each state in the union a republican form of government." But the Constitution does not say what a republican form of government is. The *Federalist* defines "republic" in distinction from "democracy," as that form of popular government in which the people conduct their business by elected representatives rather than "in person." This is very far from being a sufficient definition of a republican form of government. It is the central maxim of popular government—republican or democratic —that the majority shall rule. Again, majority rule is one of the necessary conditions, but it is not a sufficient condition, for genuine republicanism. No one ever stated this more eloquently or succinctly than Jefferson, in his first inaugural address, when he said,

> *All, too, will bear in mind this sacred principle that though the will of the majority is in all cases to prevail, that will to be rightful must be reasonable; that the minority possess their equal rights, which equal law must protect, and to violate would be oppression.*

Jefferson, during the Revolution, and immediately thereafter, tried to spell out many of those conditions that constituted both necessary and sufficient conditions for republicanism. Among the "equal laws" which were necessary, and for which Jefferson himself fought during this period, were the abolition of primogeniture and entail, and the abolition of religious establishment, the securing of religious freedom. The emancipation of the slaves was another element of republican freedom, for which Jefferson declared in the *Notes on Virginia*. The "way [I] hope is preparing," he wrote, "under the auspices of heaven, for a total emancipation...." Jefferson attempted, and failed to secure a clause abolishing slavery in the Report of Government for the Western Territories of 1784. But Jefferson's attempt succeeded—although it was others who carried the attempt to success—in the Ordinance of 1787. Lincoln, in his Cooper Union speech of 1860, relied mainly upon the anti-slavery clause of the Northwest Ordinance to support his contention that it was the Founding Fathers' intention to treat slavery as a necessary evil, and not as either a positive good, or as a matter of moral indifference. Lincoln analyzed in some detail the actions of those members of the Constitutional Convention, who sat in the Congress of 1789, when the Northwest Ordinance come to a vote. By this analysis he argued forcefully that it was the intention of the Framers of the Constitution to put slavery "in the course of ultimate extinction." Slavery, according to Lincoln, was the very negation of the principle "that all men are created equal," the principle that was the very "sheet anchor of American republicanism."

These remarks help to put into perspective the most famous of the precepts embodied in the Northwest Ordinance, and the one most to our present purpose. That is that

> *Religion, morality, and knowledge, being necessary to good government and the happiness of mankind, schools and the means of education shall forever be encouraged.*

This exhortation is perhaps unsurpassed, as a text upon which to preach the purpose of the American Revolution and the American Founding. Jefferson, we recall, caused three things to be inscribed upon his tombstone, as the "testimonials" by which he wished "most to be remembered." These are, that he was "author of the Declaration of American Independence," and "of the Statute of Virginia for Religious Freedom," and that he was "Father of the University of Virginia." The relationship between religion, morality, and knowledge is involved both in the Declaration of Independence and in the Statute of Religious Freedom, although in different ways. But the purposes of these two great documents can be made intelligible only as they are the causes and consequences of a certain kind of education, without which republican freedom and human happiness would not themselves be possible.

The Declaration of Independence, we recall, speaks of "self-evident truths," and implies thereby a ratiocinative process, in the minds of those endowed with unalienable rights, by which they recognize those rights in themselves and in others of their kind. Let us place all possible emphasis upon "others of their kind." The Declaration in its assertion of human equality implies that men will see the humanity common to men as men, a humanity that man does not share with all creation. The distinction of creation into man and non-man is grounded in the same judgment of the mind as the one that teaches the unity of the human race. It is such a judgment of the mind that gives rise to that consent from which the "just powers of government" are derived. That consent is not an act of the will alone. It is an act of the will informed by intelligence, it is *enlightened consent.* Unless consent is enlightened by intelligence, the resulting powers of government are lacking in justice, and the laws are lacking in morality.

The characteristic understanding of the relationship of political man—and the republican form of government—to the order of creation, was expressed with the eloquence characteristic of the American Revolution, in the instructions of the town meeting of Malden, Massachusetts, in favor of American independence, May 27, 1776. According to Commager "On May 9 the Massachusetts House of Representatives ... appointed a committee to bring in a resolve that the Towns of the colony instruct their representatives with respect to independence" (*Documents*, I, 96). In the course of their instructions, the town fathers declared

> ... *we are confirmed in our opinion, that the present age would be deficient in their duty to God, their posterity and themselves, if they do not establish an American republic. This is the only form of government which we wish to see established; for we can never be willingly subject to any other King than he who, being possessed of infinite wisdom, goodness, and rectitude, is alone fit to possess unlimited power.*

The natural superiority of man to the sub-human creation entitled man to lordship over it, as the Bible teaches. But that same distinction between the human and the sub-human instructs man that the proper rule of equals in nature is by law. Law means a system of ruling and being ruled in turn, and it means that those who make the laws also live under the laws that they make. For if man is to be distinguished from the beasts beneath him, so also is he to be distinguished from the God above him. This distinction arises in the mind from the operation of unassisted human reason, which from its observation of the human and the sub-human, frames the equation, as man is to beast, so God is to man; or, conversely, as man is to God, so beast is to man. It follows from this, that when man attempts to govern man, as man governs beast, the rule is not divine but bestial. For it is as self-evident as any proposition that is not merely analytical, that human wisdom, goodness, and rectitude is limited, and that autocratic rule could be justified only by myths about rulers that reason could never justify. Regimes that do not recognize how man's nature is circumscribed within the order of creation do not rise above its limits, but rather fall below them. This is implied also in that famous passage of the fifty-first *Federalist*, in which Publius declares that men are not angels, and do not have angels to govern them. (Jefferson, in his inaugural address, asked "... have we found angels in the form of kings to govern [(us)]? Let history answer this question.") The problem of human government is to enable the government to control the governed, while also compelling it to control itself. Publius' solution to this problem is, first of all, by law: that is, by governing and being governed in turn. Second, it is enlarging the sphere of government by the principle of representation. Third, it is by separation of powers. Fourth, it is by federalism, the division of the separated powers between a central government and states. It is by combining representation with federalism, that the republic becomes an *extended* republic, in which the multiplicity of factions assists in preventing the tyranny of the majority.

In the discussion of separation of powers, Publius explains that the separation is accomplished in such a manner as to give each of the separated powers a partial agency in the exercise of each other's functions. By this, each of the separated powers is given an interest in compelling the others to do their duty, or to act justly. Publius tries throughout the *Federalist* to design the regime so that, as much as possible, interest will be in the side of duty, and the rewards for acting justly will be greater than the rewards for acting unjustly. But it is nonetheless true that "Justice is the end of government. It is the end of civil society." What "the rules of justice and the rights of the minor party" are, however, is not itself a matter of mere opinion. These are in accordance with "the laws of nature and of nature's God." The practical teachings of an enlightened political science—such as those of the *Federalist*—arise from the contemplation of a structured and ordered—that is, purposeful—universe.

Without education in these laws of nature, without education, that is, in the ends of government, the means become unintelligible.

In the foregoing, we see at least some of the ground upon which Jefferson believed that the will of the majority must rest, if it is to be reasonable. The most famous of the limitations upon the will of the majority—or, more generally, upon the legitimate powers of government—concerns the rights of conscience. In the *Notes on Virginia* Jefferson declared that

> ... *our rulers can have no authority over* [our] *natural rights, only as we have submitted to them. The rights of conscience we never submitted, we could not submit. We are answerable for them to our God. The legitimate powers of government extend to such acts only as are injurious to others. But it does me no injury for my neighbor to say there are twenty gods, or no God. It neither picks my pocket nor breaks my leg.*

The remark about pocket-picking and leg-breaking has often been taken as a sign of indifference to religion, and its role in political society. But this is to mistake Jefferson. We have already cited the passage in the *Notes* in which he calls the conviction that our liberties are the gift of God, "their only firm basis." In the same query as the one in which he speaks of twenty gods or no God, he also declares, as he will do again in the Virginia Statute, that it is error alone that needs the support of government. "Truth can stand by itself." Coercion, he argues here and in the Statute, can make men either knaves or hypocrites, but it can never make them truer men. "Had not the Roman government permitted free inquiry, Christianity could never have been introduced. Had not free inquiry been indulged at the era of the reformation, the corruptions of Christianity could not have been purged away." It is Jefferson's larger argument then that the separation of church and state, the making of our civil rights absolutely independent of our religious opinions, is above all necessary to the purity of religion itself.

The supreme axiomatic proposition of the Statute of Religious Freedom, is that

> *Almighty God hath created the mind free. . . .*

Because of this

> *all attempts to influence it by temporal punishments or burthens, or by civil incapacitations, tend only to beget habits of hypocrisy and meaness . . .*

Such attempts, moreover,

> *are a departure from the plan of the Holy author of our religion, who being Lord*

both of body and mind, yet chose not to propagate it by coercions on either, as was in his Almighty power to do. . . .

From this Jefferson concludes

that our civil rights have no dependence on our religious opinions, any more than our opinions in physics or geometry. . . .

But the corollary of this is that Jefferson is not indifferent to religious truth. He was most certainly not indifferent to truth in physics or geometry. Perhaps the most famous words Jefferson ever wrote, equal if not surpassing the great annunciation of human equality in the Declaration of Independence, are those in which he says

that truth is great and will prevail if left to herself, that she is the proper and sufficient antagonist to error, and has nothing to fear from the conflict, unless by human interposition disarmed of her natural weapons, free argument and debate, errors ceasing to be dangerous when it is permitted freely to contradict them.

This great statement would, however, be meaningless, if nothing final were ever known, or if all propositions were equally open to contradiction, or if the seeking of truth was a process which had no end or ends in view. No one would, by Jefferson's principles, be forbidden to question whether the earth was round, or whether it revolved around the sun. But anyone who seriously pursued such questions would certainly be subject to some doubts as to his sanity. What would Jefferson think of someone who questioned the truth of the proposition that the mind was, in its own nature, free? What would he think of someone who believed that the truth of religion, or of science, could be propagated by coercion? Merely to ask these questions is to instruct ourselves that both religious and civil liberty rest upon assumptions concerning God, man, and the universe. These assumptions may, as a matter of theory, be questioned, by virtue of the very principles embodied in the assumptions. Yet they cannot as a practical matter be discarded, without discarding the premises upon which the argument in favor of free institutions rests.

Let us, for example, reflect upon the proposition that the mind of man is created—or by nature—free. ("Created" and "by nature" are used inter-changeably in the American Founding.) The proposition is at once moral and metaphysical. To say that the mind is free is to say something about both the world and the mind, about the whole and a part. It is to say that the mind is capable of deciding what is true and false, what is right and wrong, upon the basis of reason and experience, or by reasoning about experience. It means that the process of ratiocination is, in the decisive sense, what it seems to be:

that is, that the mind, before it decides what is true or false, right or wrong, is actually undecided, that it is not predetermined to its conclusion. In short, the mind is not a puppet, whose master (whether God, chance, or necessity) "knows" in advance what it will do. This does not mean that the mind cannot be deceived. The mind does not by nature know. As Aristotle says, the mind by nature desires to know. But this desire, for Jefferson as for Aristotle, cannot be vain. The possibility of knowledge must be genuine. The mind needs facts about the world, before it can reason about those facts. Some of these facts are accessible only with instruments: e.g. only by the use of a microscope or a telescope can that part of the visible world inaccessible to the unassisted eye become accessible to observation, and hence to unassisted reasoning. The accumulation of records of a wide variety of experiences, extending sometimes over many generations, is a pre-condition for the development of those methods of reasoning about those experiences by which the natural powers of the mind are converted into the intellectual virtues of knowing. The obstacles to the moral virtues are no less formidable than are the obstacles to the intellectual virtues, although the former lies mainly in the power of the passions, rather than in the difficulties of reasoning. But knowledge is useless—or even pernicious—to those who cannot use it well. A human mind that knows, but is disabled by the violence of its passions from using that knowledge properly, is one in which truth cannot prevail. For truth prevails only when the passions are in harmony with the truth concerning human well-being. The knowledge that enables men to become powerful, but to become powerful for evil and not for good, is a defective form of knowledge. Morality, knowledge, and religion are then interdependent, as the Northwest Ordinance implies. Human happiness depends upon all three together.

Consider for a moment the negative of the proposition that the mind is free. No one ever characterized it more precisely than Abraham Lincoln. In his circular letter to the voters of the Seventh Congressional District of Illinois, in 1846, in which he repelled charges that he had been "an open scoffer at Christianity," he remarked that it was true that in early life he "was inclined to believe in what I understand is called the 'Doctrine of Necessity'—that is, that the human mind is impelled to action, or held in rest by some power, over which the human mind itself has no control." This doctrine, in and of itself, is a declaration that the human mind is enslaved. For there can be no more perfect definition of slavery, than that of a condition, in which one being is moved, or prevented from moving, by a power outside itself, over which it has no control. This is to say that one being is perfectly in the power of another being. If this doctrine were taken to express the metaphysical truth about the human mind, then all human beings would be perfect slaves by nature. Political slavery, or slavery by human law, could add nothing to their pre-existing slavery by nature.

The doctrine of necessity—or determinism—is the natural correlate of despotism. The argument for despotism becomes conclusive, if men are by nature slaves, and if every attempt at emancipation results only in a worse form of slavery. If, as in the case of Marxism-Leninism, human beings are taught to think of the perfect human condition as one of perfect freedom, then they must be taught as well that the perfection of their slavery is the perfection of their freedom. Orwell's *1984* dramatized this. Everything there is called by a name proper to its opposite: not only is slavery called freedom, but peace is called war, and so on. George Fitzhugh, the most articulate spokesman for slavery in the ante-bellum South, expressed this thought long before Orwell, but without Orwell's cynicism. In his argument, he seems merely to have carried forward the logic of Rousseau's *Social Contract*, in which men are "forced to be free." Rousseau had written that men are born free, yet are everywhere in chains. One thinks himself the master of others, he said, yet is a greater slave than they. In this spirit, Fitzhugh argued that the only condition possible for man was one of slavery. (He differed, or seemed to differ, with Rousseau only in denying that men are born free.) The best human condition was one in which the best kind of slavery prevailed. The master (the greater slave, he) must be enslaved to the slave by benevolent bonds, so as better to enslave the slave by beneficent bonds. The only difference between this, and the Marxist-Leninist argument for the dictatorship of the proletariat (that is, for the dictatorship of the Central Committee of the Communist Party), is the different and opposite names they apply to the same things.

* * *

If the truth about the human mind is the truth of determinism, then truth as well as freedom must be an illusion. The quintessential philosopher would be the Cretan who said that all Cretans are liars. The absurdity of this statement, far from being an objection to it, would be its highest recommendation. Not mystery, but absurdity, lies at the heart of reality. The theater of the absurd, *par excellence*, is the universe. Any attempt to live a consistent life, whether upon the principles of reason or of revelation, would be regarded as impossible. Moral wisdom would be that wisdom which recognized the impossibility of such consistency.

The American Founding, as symbolized by the Northwest Ordinance's assertion concerning the relationship of morality, religion, and knowledge, assumed the possibility of philosophy in the traditional sense. The quest for knowledge was believed to be what Socrates believed it to be. It was an enterprise in which the purpose of human life was realized in the progress of knowledge. This progress might ironically be described as a progress in the knowledge of ignorance, but one had somehow to know what one did not know, to know that one did not know it! But the long tradition which had flowed, during two millenia, from the Socratic quest for knowledge through the awareness of ignorance, had formed the canons of civilized community, and these canons had become the tradition known as the natural law. There was substantial agreement between the traditions of reason and of revelation, as to what morality was, and *that* the moral rules were binding, however much there might have been disagreement as to *why* these rules were binding. There is an important difference in saying that a moral rule is binding, because God has commanded it; and in saying that it is binding because reason has found out that it is necessary for the good life. But surely, men can live together, not only peaceably, but as friends and fellow-citizens, if they share this common code of morals, even if they differ as to what its highest ground or cause is. But they cannot so live together, if they do not share any such code, or if they think that any attempt even to discover what that code is, violates the freedom enshrined in the principle of absurdity.

Science is the great authority for modern man. But science, when it takes up the question of man's humanity, is the source of the greatest superstitions that have afflicted the human mind. Science declares that facts and values are absolutely discrete, and that nothing can be known as to which are more choice-worthy, and hence that nothing can be known about what is the right way of life. Since what is declared concerning the right way of life in Plato's *Apology of Socrates* and Aristotle's *Nicomachean Ethics* is regarded thereby as a mere matter of faith, the distinction between the way of knowing the right way of life, in these books, and in the Bible, becomes irrelevant. In short, education becomes irrelevant.

The American Founding presupposed a harmony between the quest for knowledge, and the moral rules that men observed in civilized society. The Founders separated church and state because, but only because, they were confident that no particular revealed dogmas regarding God and the universe, were necessary to uphold their common moral code. Thomas Jefferson, in his inaugural address, counting our blessings as a nation, gave high place to the fact that we were "enlightened by a benign religion, professed indeed, and practiced in various forms, yet all of them inculcating honesty, truth, temperance, gratitude, and the love of man." The Virginia Bill of Rights, adopted three weeks before the Declaration of Independence, declared "That no free government, or the blessings of liberty, can be preserved to any people, but by a firm adherence to justice, moderation, temperance, frugality and virtue, and by frequent recurrence to fundamental principles." The fundamental principles are those we are most familiar with from the words of the great Declaration, beginning, "We hold these truths to be self-evident . . ." But the Virginia Declaration insists that the moral qualities are a necessary prerequisite. Here is but a distant echo of Aristotle's dictum, that knowledge is unprofitable for those who merely follow their passions, that is, who lack the moral virtues.

The Massachusetts Bill of Rights of 1780, is even more emphatic. It says that "a constant adherence to . . . piety, justice, moderation, temperance, industry, and frugality, are absolutely necessary to preserve the advantages of liberty and to maintain a free government." The reference to piety merely assumes what Jefferson later asserted, that Americans were "enlightened by *a* benign religion," however "various" the "forms" in which it was "professed." But Massachusetts then continues, that "The people ought, consequently, to have a particular attention to all those principles, in the choice of their officers and representatives: and they have a right to require of their lawgivers and magistrates an exact and constant observance of them, in the formation and execution of the laws necessary for the good administration of the common-wealth." As far as I understand the purpose of the Moral Majority—certainly as far as I approve of the purpose of the Moral Majority—it is in reminding the people of the particular attention that they ought to give those moral principles, "in the choice of their officers and representatives," and in the manner in which they judge the performance of these same officers and representatives, in forming and executing the laws of the commonwealth. For the forming of the laws—taking into account example along with precept—is nothing less than the forming of the character of the citizens. And, to end where we began, the character of the citizens is nothing less than the character of the city—of the political community. Bad characters do not make good citizens, and bad citizens do not make good laws. The Moral Majority, at the very least, retains that link with the Founding, that declares that the just powers of government rest upon the consent of the governed, and that the governed ought not to consent to laws which are indifferent to the moral distinctions which "are absolutely necessary to preserve the advantages of liberty and to maintain a free government."

December 1980

Four

A Conversation with Harry V. Jaffa at Rosary College

The following conversation took place at Rosary College, River Forest, Illinois, December 4, 1980. Professor George Anastaplo is Lecturer in the Liberal Arts at the University of Chicago, Professor of Political Science and of Philosophy, Rosary College, and Visiting Professor of Law, Loyola University of Chicago. Among his publications are The Constitutionalist: Notes on the First Amendment, Human Being and Citizen: Essays on Virtue, Freedom and the Common Good, *and the forthcoming* The Artist as Thinker: From Shakespeare to Joyce. *Among the participants, in addition to Mssrs. Jaffa and Anastaplo, the following are members of the faculty of Rosary College: Dr. Christopher A. Colmo (Political Science), Dr. Robert Rusnak (History), and Mr. Gregory Smith (Political Science). Mrs. Kewalek and Mrs. McGrail are students at Rosary College. Special thanks are due to Mr. Robert L. Stone of the University of Chicago, for recording and transcribing the conversation, and in particular to Sister Candida Lund, President of Rosary College, for making the conversation possible.*

Anastaplo: It is my privilege to introduce on this occasion a friend of a quarter century and a distinguished political scientist, Harry V. Jaffa, of Claremont McKenna College and Claremont Graduate School. Professor Jaffa, whose appearance at Rosary College has been made possible by the support of him by the Intercollegiate Studies Institute, is available for an extended conversation with us about matters ancient and modern.

Mr. Jaffa is, to my mind, the most instructive political scientist writing in this country today. The things he writes about range from Socrates and Aristotle to Thomas Aquinas and William Shakespeare, from the Founding Fathers to Abraham Lincoln, from Tom Sawyer and Winston Churchill to contemporary politics and the joys of cycling.

I am reminded, when I encounter Mr. Jaffa, of another provocatively influential American, a great woman who died only this past weekend, Dorothy Day of the *Catholic Worker* movement (whom I was privileged to see close-up only once). It was true of Miss Day, as it is true of Mr. Jaffa, that it was virtually impossible for her not to be interesting about whatever she wrote. Intelligence, hard work and a gift for language no doubt contribute to this capacity to invest every discourse with significance. But fundamental to such influence is a certain integrity, even a single-minded moral fervor. Thus, it could be said of Miss Day in her obituary in the *New York Times* on Monday of this week that she had sought "to work so as to bring about the kind of society where it is easier for people to be good." Much the same can be said about Mr. Jaffa. Indeed, Miss Day, in the way she lived her life, in an unrelenting effort to better the lives of the downtrodden, could be said to have put into practice the much-quoted proposition by Mr. Jaffa which was used by Senator Goldwater in his Acceptance Speech upon being nominated for the Presidency by the Republican Party in 1964, "I would remind you that extremism in the defense of liberty is no vice. And let me remind you also that moderation in the pursuit of justice is no virtue."

A little more should be said by me about Mr. Jaffa now, if only to suggest matters that we might want to talk about on this occasion. A few differences between us, of which I was reminded when I heard him speak yesterday at Loyola University, could usefully be indicated.

Mr. Jaffa not only makes far more of exercising than I do—I limit myself to walking whenever possible and to the avoidance of elevators for ascents or descents of less than five floors—but he also is a much more vigorous moralist than I am, both in regulating his own conduct and in judging the conduct of others. I believe that I allow more than he does for good-intentioned errors, for inefficiency on the part of people, and for circumstances which account for, sometimes even justify, what seem from the outside to be moral aberrations. Compassion can be almost as important as moral indignation in these matters, particularly with respect to domestic relations, whether the subjects be abortion, divorce or homosexuality. Perhaps also I make more than he does of the importance—if only out of respect for the sensibilities of others and for the moral tone of the community—of discretion, if not even of good-natured hypocrisy.

We differ as well with respect to the conduct of foreign relations. We do share an abhorrence of tyranny, whether of the Right or of the Left. But we sometimes part company on assessments of how constitutional government and American republicanism can best be defended abroad. Thus, he was much more hopeful than I could ever be that our involvement in the Vietnam War (however noble in intention that involvement might have been, and *that* it was, in some respects)—he was much more hopeful than I was that our Vietnam involvement could do the American *or* the Indo-Chinese people some good.

Today we differ as to precisely what kind of a threat the Russians pose to us. I see them as much more vulnerable (both politically and militarily) than does he; and I consider all too many calculations about nuclear war "scenarios" to depend too much on game theories and not enough on political judgment. I believe, for example, that the Russian leaders are much more constrained by domestic public opinion (by a pacific, even though patriotic, public opinion) and by other factors than many of us recognize. They have suffered, at home and abroad, a considerable setback in Afghanistan; we can only hope that they, and we, do not suffer an even greater setback by a Russian invasion of Poland. But whatever happens in Poland, it is now evident that the cause of freedom is bound to be in better shape in Eastern Europe than it has been since the Second World War—in part because of what Polish workers have done in showing the world how things really stand there. The only question may be what price the Polish people will have to pay, and this may depend, in part, on their prudence and on ours.

Perhaps at the heart of the differences between Mr. Jaffa and me—whether the differences be as to the status of exercise or as to assessments of the Russians—is with respect to how much one should be concerned with the preservation of one's life. An immoderate cherishing of what happens to be one's own can lead, it seems to me, to psychic paralysis or to undue combativeness: either can undermine that relaxed competence which makes healthy statesmanship more likely. Certainly Mr. Jaffa responds much more than I do to the apocalyptic as against the comic, and somewhat less than I do to "liberty" as against "equality." Obviously, we touch here on questions about the nature of human existence, of virtue, and of happiness.

On the other hand, at the heart of our deep affinities—besides the fact that we were both fortunate enough to share a great teacher in Leo Strauss—is our minority belief that fundamental to sensible political science and to a decent life as a community is a general respect for natural right and what is known as natural law. This means, among other things, that discrimination based on arbitrary racial categories cannot be defended, especially by a people dedicated to the self-evident truth that "all men are created equal." It also means that the family as an institution should be supported.

I mention in passing that we do differ with respect to the Equal Rights Amendment—but here I believe that Mr. Jaffa, even though he puts what he says in terms of nature in his opposition to that amendment, has allowed himself to be unduly influenced by the antics and "principles" of a minority of the proponents of that largely symbolic grace note for our Constitution.

Be all this as it may, an informed study of nature in human things is perhaps the most pressing demand in education today—and for this Mr. Jaffa, with his profound grasp of the classical writers, of Shakespeare's thought, and of the career of Abraham Lincoln, is an invaluable guide.

Permit me to close these introductory remarks by returning to something else that has been said about Dorothy Day, something which (with appropriate adjustments) can be applied to the tireless dedication Mr. Jaffa devotes to his "conservative" creed and to his graduate students. We are reminded by Dorothy Day's *New York Times* obituary that Church officials in New York were "often sorely tempted to rebuke Miss Day—her ardent support of Catholic cemetery strikers a number of years ago especially irked Cardinal Spellman —but they never could catch her in any breach of Church regulations." Besides, the editor of *Commonweal* has observed, one of the bishops she fought with, James Francis McIntyre (who later became a cardinal himself), "was afraid he just might be dealing with a saint." "He was alluding to what has been called Miss Day's 'indiscriminate and uncompromising love of the Mystical Body' as well as to her courage and her care for the poor in hospices she established in New York and elsewhere."

But enough of this canonization of Harry Jaffa, who does remind me in certain ways of St. Augustine. Any effort at canonization, you recall, requires that the devil's advocate have his say also. As you can see, I have had to take on more than one role in introducing to you a gifted colleague whom we are privileged to have with us today.

Some of you must have questions — but first, Mr. Jaffa may have something to say in response to the remarks I have made in an effort to guide the conversation I look forward to in the hours and years ahead.

Jaffa: Well, thank you very much, Professor Anastaplo. I must say that that is the most remarkable introduction I have ever had or that I am ever likely to have.

Anastaplo: This means you must come here more often.

Jaffa: I shall make an effort to do so. I shall not, however, climb up on that pedestal you have prepared for me. I trust that in the next hour it will have disappeared as I speak. I am not quite certain what aspect of that ambiguous canonization I should respond to. My instincts have always been to spring right at the throat of objections, to show what a dangerous man I am to praise. However, if I did that I might not be gratifying the genuine curiosity among you. I don't know if you have read any of my "justly decried" writings and have any questions about them you would like to ask. I would like to take questions or challenges from the floor. If I turned it into a discussion of foreign policy, that might miss what you really want to talk about. I spoke at Loyola yesterday about the Moral Majority, and of the fact that the political principles of the Goldwater campaign have become respectable because of the election of Ronald Reagan. And I would remind Mr. Reagan of something he seems not to recall, namely that his political career began with a very fine speech in defense of Goldwater's candidacy in 1964. The principles of his political career were embodied in that speech, and he has built a more successful career than Senator Goldwater was able to do, on those principles. But now that those principles have at least for the moment become respectable, the question is what *terra incognita* of shocking extremism I can now find to defend, to reestablish my position on the right. It is as if everyone has moved over so that I am now in the middle. Yes?

Colmo: Did they really move to the right, or did they just move away from Carter?

Jaffa: It's quite obvious that the expressions "left, right, and center" are, to use a cliche, relative terms. What is "right" depends on where you put the center. The principles of Progessivism at the turn of the century represented radicalism. By 1936 they represented the middle of the road, and have been more or less ever since. American politics is characterized by a certain series of (to use bad Latin) "consensuses." There is no such thing as a political consensus, that is to say an agreement, or set of agreements, among people who differ on various things, unless it is made up of some core to which or around which their concessions to each other turn. For example, the election of Lincoln in 1860: the heart of that election was the decision to limit the expansion of slavery, and a new political constellation formed around that core. You could say that the Republican party in 1860 represented, to a large extent, programmatic Federalism: the policies of Hamilton, which were the core of the old Whig Party, itself an attempt to revive Hamilton's, and to some extent Adams's Federalism. Those were defeated repeatedly by the Jeffersonians and Jacksonians. Federalism was the radical right, if you will, of American politics at the turn of the nineteenth century. And yet by, say, 1864, or certainly by 1868 or 1872, the Republican Party's policies — internal improvement, tariffs, and the central banking system — revived as the heart of a new consensus, which was now the "middle of the road," Then again, the "middle" moved to the "right" with what you might call "old-guard" Republicanism, in the person of William McKinley. McKinley served for four years in the Union Army; he left college and volunteered and served throughout the war, and, of course, Lincoln was his hero. But for him protectionism was the heart of Republicanism, once the slavery issue was ended. And the slavery issue itself would never have been the basis for a major party, unless it had been joined by that complex of economic issues which were represented by protectionism (along with internal improvements of rivers and harbors, and things like that). Yes?

Colmo: Are you suggesting that Messrs. Goldwater and Reagan are now the middle of the road?

Jaffa: Yes. Let me put it this way: what Mr. Reagan represents *will* be the middle of the road if he is successful, if the victory lays down the kind of program that can endure for the next generation. What was the New Deal? Certainly the New Deal represented a thorough realignment of American political life. The coming of the New Deal meant nothing less than the end of the era that was begun by Abraham Lincoln. Symbolic of this fact is that most black voters were Republican, from the Civil War until the age of Roosevelt. After that they became overwhelmingly Democrat. The same thing is true of Jews. What Roosevelt meant to Jews because of Hitler, Abraham Lincoln meant to blacks because of slavery. I am reminded, by the way, of a discussion with Willmoore Kendall years ago. He said, "Harry, what have you got against slavery? You wouldn't be one of the slaves," I said "Willmoore, did you ever hear of Moses?" [laughter] I said, "We Jews tried it once, and now we settle for constitutional government."

Anastaplo: You were immunized.

Jaffa: That's right. And there was that time in Chicago when George Nash was describing, from Willmoore's letters, how he felt when he went back to Oklahoma,

and to Dallas, after having been at Yale and selling his professorship, and he said
he was returning to the land of his youth like a Moses returning to his people.
And I got up and said, "Yes, the greatest anti-slavery leader before Lincoln."
Rusnak: Is it possible to summarize what you said about the Moral Majority,
what it means in terms of (a) a real power base, and (b) its effects on the
Reagan administration in terms of policy?
Jaffa: I will give you a couple of paragraphs, or a couple of pages, from the
beginning of my prepared text at Loyola yesterday. I began this way:

> *Immediately after the election of Mr. Reagan I wrote that, "The silent majority,*
> *which the polls had certainly missed in 1980, has finally emerged." I expressed the*
> *opinion that this election might prove to be a watershed election, and the*
> *Republican Party, duly reconstituted, might become the spokesman for a new*
> *majority for the next generation. Certainly there is a possibility that Mr. Reagan's*
> *election, accompanied by decisive gains in the Senate and large gains in the*
> *House, could show us a reconstitution of American politics on the order of*
> *magnitude of that presided over by Franklin D. Roosevelt. This of course,*
> *depends, in the first instance on the immediate crisis of the economy and of*
> *American security in the world. Mr. Reagan must have his own hundred days. If*
> *he can in this period, whatever length it may turn out to be, restore the nation's*
> *confidence in its future, then the political movement he leads may indeed be one of*
> *many years of sunshine days (Richard II). Whether or not the "silent majority"*
> *turns into a "new Majority" may in the end depend on what the Republican Party*
> *does about the "Moral Majority." This self-proclaimed majority has been anything*
> *but silent. It has claimed much credit, as part of Mr. Reagan's constituency, and*
> *has been more than plausible in its asserted responsibility for the defeat of such*
> *great and distinguished Old-Guard Senate liberals as Senators Bayh, McGovern,*
> *Church, Magnuson, Culver, and a number of others. The aforesaid senators*
> *have made the claims of the "Moral Majoritarians" even more plausible by*
> *blaming them—i.e. giving them credit—for their own defeat. On the whole, the*
> *pundits of the press and the media have not been kind to the Moral Majority, and*
> *discussions of their role in the election have been dominated by the rather silly*
> *charge that they have transgressed the margin separating church and state by*
> *injecting religious demands into political campaigns.*

I spoke at some length about that, and I said that this notion, that they were
injecting religious demands into political campaigns, rests upon the assumption
that morality is essentially a religious matter. And I pointed out that many of the
pundits of the liberal press talk about "hangups" the way Puritans talked about
original sin. Sometimes they seem to wrestle with the Ten Commandments
(particularly the seventh) the way their ancestors wrestled with the Devil. I
said this was an inconsistency of which they are seldom aware. But, I argued, a
concern for morality, a morality supported by a non-sectarian natural theology
(as in the Declaration of Independence), was an essential element of the
Founding. I supported this with a number of quotations from documents, of

Washington, Jefferson, and others. Here is just one, from the 15th article of the Virginia Declaration of Rights: "No free government, or the blessings of liberty, can be preserved to any people but by a firm adherence to justice, moderation, temperance, frugality, and virtue—and by frequent recurrence to fundamental principles." This article is part of an enumeration in the prologue to the Virginia Constitution, adopted during the Revolution. This is called the "basis and foundation of government." In other words, the moral virtues are seen as the foundation of republican freedom, in the sense which was articulated by political philosophers from Aristotle to Montesquieu. Republics, more than monarchies, need virtue, because the laws come from the people, and ruling and being ruled in turn depends upon morality as the foundation of legislation. In fact the most important legislation, in the classical sense, is that which provides for the virtues. So I think the whole notion that morality is not a concern of government is denied by the very language of the American founding, which embodies a very old and wise tradition. Separation of church and state was not understood, and I think cannot be understood, to mean a separation of religion and politics. Separation of church and state only means that the churches best perform their political function without any patronage of sectarian religion by the government or any discrimination among them. But the assumption is—and I think Tocqueville says this with very great clarity—that it is the support, and to some extent even the creation, of a moral consensus by the churches outside of the formal realm of political authority which makes possible majority rule and minority rights. Confidence that the majority will rule according to principles accepted by the minority depends upon a moral consensus, without which the possibility of self-government and majority rule would not be practical. Tocqueville argues, I think, that the separation of church and state makes it possible for the churches to agree on morality without having to agree on church dogma. Sectarian religion contributes to the moral consensus by enlisting, you might say, the enthusiasm of its church members for a moral consensus, which would be ruptured if people had to fight with each other over which set of revealed dogmas is to be official. The churches could not support morality together, were they to quarrel politically over dogma. But by putting the dogma outside the realm of politics, they enable the churches to cooperate in a role which makes a democratic politics possible.

And I argue in my paper that, at the period of the founding, the assumption was that education, the increase of knowledge, would increase the rational religious commitment of the citizens, that it would supply more enlightened foundations for morality, and that virtue and morality would thereby contribute to good government and the happiness of mankind. But we have seen in the last several generations, perhaps from a period going back to not long after the founding, the gradual attrition of that constructive relationship between education, religion, and morality. I remind you of the resounding proposition in the Northwest Ordinance: that "Religion, morality, and knowledge, being necessary to good government and the happiness of mankind, schools and the means of education shall forever be encouraged." There is nothing in the Declaration of Independence itself which speaks more deeply to the soul of America than this belief that education will promote morality and reasonable religion and good government. But we now find in the schools philosophic doctrines (or, more properly, anti-philosophic doctrines) which have been patronized in the universities for more than a hundred years with a kind of cumulating force, that have culminated in doctrines of moral relativism. The notion is that the more enlightened one is the more one sees that there is no objective foundation for morality or religion, and that they are mere illusions. Morality, we are now taught in school, like beauty, lies in the eye of the beholder, and "choice of lifestyle" is something the human soul is free to make without any guidance from either God or nature. So education has become the enemy of the regime. And I think that the Moral Majority is in part a visceral reaction to the attack on morality by the skeptics, by the "supercilious sophisticates," as I call them, the people who think that the case against morality was decided long ago by science, in general, and by evolution in particular.

And I mentioned in my paper the reaction to Mr. Reagan for having said in the campaign that the schools should teach creationist doctrines along with evolutionist doctrines. You would have thought from the reaction of the commentators on television and in the newspaper, that he had suddenly emerged as a new William Jennings Bryan doing battle with Clarence Darrow. But intelligent men and women have known for a very long time that the conflict between the Bible and evolution is spurious, and that the assumption that you cannot believe in one without rejecting the other has been disproved. The physicists have been patronizing the Big Bang theory for a long time now, and everybody knows that not all the seven days of Creation in Genesis can be "days" in the same sense, since the sun was not created until the Fourth Day. In fact, the Bible even says that the sun was created "for seasons and for days and years," meaning that it is using "day" in two distinct senses, one of which must be symbolic. Hence neither naked evolutionism nor naked fundamentalism is sufficient ground for instructing the young. And there is no reason for thinking that they are mutually exclusive explanations of the origin of the universe. In fact they *agree* on what is the most important single question about that universe: that it had a beginning in time. It is the Aristotelian view, that the universe is eternal, that stands in opposition to both.

Rusnak: Concerning the people who are broadly identified as being members of the more fundamentalist churches, I agree with what you said about the importance of separating morality and the political, but I think it is the pursuit of *righteousness* that may be upsetting to some people, the sense that we are not only going to remoralize the country, but you are going to be moral whether you like it or not, in the political sense.

Jaffa: If you remember the history of the Reformation, what people are afraid of is a Puritan Savonarola or of a Cromwell smashing the idols in the temple in the name of sanctity and moral purity. You could say that that is a kind of fanatical moralism which can be destructive of human freedom. That's very possible, but you can say also that this type of fanaticism can be brought on by a regime of moral laxity which outrages the moral sentiments of decent and moderate people. Those are two extremes which one ought, as a good Aristotelian, to avoid. Extremism in defense of liberty is not extremism in defense of extremism. Rather, it is extremism in defense of moderation—that moderate regime in which people are not subject to the kind of censoriousness we associate with, say, the city of Geneva at the height of the regime of John Calvin. On the other hand, we don't want to live in Sodom and Gomorrah either. And I think that the experience particularly of the sixties and the seventies indicated a kind of Sodom and Gomorrah, or the spirit of Sodom and Gomorrah being loose in the land. Charles Manson's family was one of perhaps several thousand like it scattered throughout California; this one happened to go off on a kick of murder. There is something very much in common, and worth mentioning, between Charles Manson's murders and the Jonestown "suicides." They were both, in a way, expressions of a kind of perverted religious sentiment. But the atmosphere was one of disintegration of traditional morality and an attempt to reconstitute a sense of community, through an act of will unguided by any rational principles. My thesis is that the Moral Majority may become a legitimate majority if it conforms to what I would consider a natural law teaching. This provides a secular foundation for morality in agreement with the religious teaching. But it also would provide a moderating influence and a rational guide to the religious sentiment which is engendered in support of religion. Tocqueville saw the natural law teaching (for example, that of the Declaration of Independence) enlisting the enthusiasm of the churches while placing rational boundaries on it. And that is exactly what I am suggesting needs to be done. Now, I would also, as a political man, like to see the Moral Majority identify itself with the Republican Party and not remain a kind of independent single-issue group outside of the party structure, which would be out to elect or defeat individual candidates solely on their "morality" without reference to the range of policies these people represent. I'd like to see them go out and mop up as many Democrats as possible and, as far as I am concerned, the Republican liberals in the primaries. But I would not want to see them opposing Republicans in the general election, even if they don't agree with them, because I would like to see them accept the idea of a responsible party system. Among the great defects of American politics today is the continuing decline of the party system as a ground of government. And I'm not sure that is a reversible phenomenon; a lot of it is due to television. Out in California people run for election as Republicans, yet you rarely see party identification in their political advertising. Yes?

Rusnak: Let me put it a different way. The German people thought they could simply use the Nazis and then cast them aside. Is this not what the Republican Party is trying to do with the Moral Majority? They want to use this as the "hit-group" versus the immoral minority of Democrats, who will find themselves moving a little bit toward *enforced* morality? Is not morality a matter of personal choice?

Jaffa: Well, yes and no. At bottom the answer is "No," People should be well brought up. Children should be instructed in sound moral principles long before they have the power of choice as mature rational beings. This is the dilemma that Aristotle poses at the end of the *Nicomachean Ethics:* it's not easy to have a good upbringing if one lives in a corrupt regime, and that is why he goes from ethics to politics—how we can make good laws so that people will be well brought up. And that problem has never changed; it is very difficult to make intelligent decisions as an adult if you have not been well brought up as a child.

Rusnak: But who makes the judgment of what is private morality in this case?

Jaffa: The parents have to make it for the children.

Rusnak: Then, who is making it for the parents?

Jaffa: That's right. Who is making it for the parents? Well, we are not using the term in its literal but in its general significance—we are not barbarians. It is a matter of great good fortune that we have an inheritance as civilized beings from a tradition that is more than three thousand years old. Our possibility as human beings is decisively created for us by the civilization we have inherited, which civilization does provide us with more than one principle of moral choice, but it is not an arbitrary or infinite spectrum of choices. Aristotle says at the beginning of the Seventh Book of the *Politics* that the man who was a perfect coward, who was frightened by anything, and a man who would sacrifice his best friend, who was so intemperate that in order to get food or sex he would sacrifice anyone or anything for his immediate appetite, would be a miserable human being. I think we do have rational knowledge of the highest degree of certitude as to the value of the basic moral virtues for a good life. I don't think anyone should be at liberty to choose between virtue and vice, as principles of choice. How those principles should be *exercised* in particular cases, this certainly provides a wide latitude for human freedom. But I think that we have inherited a body of—I won't say merely knowledge—but of structured behavior that is more than a mere way of knowing. We don't have to start out as children to rediscover what Newton and Einstein discovered in order to find out what the universe is like. We may study their reasoning, and part of our education is just this. But we do not count it part of our "Freedom" to pretend that they never lived. We inherit a great deal of information about the physical universe which enables us to become intelligent beings oriented in a universe of matter and form, of light and sound, of touch and taste, and smells and so on. Similarly, we are beings who are born into a world that has placed a great deal of reason and experience about morality at our disposal and which we would be mad to disregard merely in order to exercise some hypothetical freedom. The human mind has come to terms with the problem of moral choice in a variety of circumstances over some millennia, and that information has been reduced into various books, to a form which is accessible to us. And I think it would be insane to identify human freedom with the ability to disregard the experience —the reason and experience—of all these millenia.

Rusnak: I agree with your distinctions, but, nonetheless, certain groups tend to be absolutely *arbitrary* on their position on the Bible, for example, or what some dogma should be. They do *not* partake of either experience or reason.

Jaffa: I agree with that. One of the things I am anxious to do is to share it with them. [laughter]

Rusnak: Oh, so you intend to teach Aristotle to the Moral Majority?

Jaffa: That's it. But let me say one thing further. I think that in all human circumstances the most important thing is to have a grasp on sound principles. But those principles of themselves do not provide simple answers or directions on how to act in every case that arises. Courage, Aristotle teaches, is a mean between fearfulness and overconfidence. Yet there may be a situation in which a man may run away from danger out of bravery, and another in which he may run into it out of folly. Yet this does not mean that the distinction between courage and cowardice is arbitrary. Aristotle also points out that courage is closer to overconfidence than it is to fearfulness. What most people need most of the time, in facing danger, is not to moderate their boldness, but to bolster their confidence. For some generations now we have been seeing a "brute relativism" arising in the schools (and also in many of the churches), which declares that since there is no rule that governs every situation, principles are merely illusions, that there is no objective ground for morality whatever, and, perhaps most important of all, that there is no objective ground for what is called human nature. So they think that all old fashioned notions of morality are myths, and that human beings should take their pleasures where they find them. I told the story yesterday of a senior honors seminar I had in 1966 at Claremont Men's College, when it was not co-ed, and when there were no young ladies present. I think there were sixteen or seventeen young men. We were going to read the *Protagoras*. As part of an introductory discussion—to prove that we were going to read something that was still "relevant"—I mentioned that there was a moral crisis in modernity, and suggested that Plato—or Socrates— might assist our thought about it. The class wanted to know, what did I mean by moral crisis? I had much more than sexual morality in mind, of course, but I responded by saying, "Well, Once upon a Time, [laughter] young people were instructed that they should be chaste because of the terrible penalties that are connected with unchastity, the so-called 'natural' sanctions: pregnancy, disease, etc." And I said, "Of course, without these sanctions, the status of chastity as a desirable thing is more doubtful. With birth-control and penicillin the 'natural' sanctions would seem to be abolished." So the class responded, I must say as a single man, "Well, what is the crisis?" [laughter] I gave them an argument, which, at least, did not have any rebuttal at the end. I won't go through that argument now, except to say that I raised for their consideration the question, not only "What is right and wrong?" but "What is happiness?" I suggested that the conception of human "well-being" has something to tell us about human "ill-being." There is, I said, no action, or series of actions, which does not form you into a character of a certain kind. In overcoming moral inhibitions to gratify yourself now, you make it easier to do the same thing again in the future. But you also make it difficult, if not impossible, to gratify yourself in different ways in the future. There are surprisingly few reversible consequences of moral decisions, and the price that may be paid to reverse them, if that is possible, may be greater than fools and children can easily imagine. It is easy to admire the tyrant's pleasures—to wish to put on the ring of Gyges—but who admires the tyrant? Who would want to live without friends, surrounded by loud sycophantism and silent hatred? Read Strauss's *On Tyranny*. Most people lack the thoughtfulness to take into account long range consequences of moral decisions—that was one theme of the *Protagoras*—and so moralists through the ages have pointed to hell-fire, disease, death, and shame, to persuade those who cannot be persuaded by the truth, which is that virtue and happiness are intrinsically compatible, and the good life is also the most pleasant. The evil done by "situation ethics" is precisely to make philosophically respectable the intellectual limitations of children and morons.

Smith: Something that I noticed in this election, besides the emergence of the Moral Majority, was the renovation of *laissez-faire* capitalism, which was fairly important to Mr. Reagan. And while coalitions sometimes have strange bedfellows, Jerry Falwell and Milton Friedman sort of struck me as strange.

Jaffa: Yes, I think Jerry Falwell is exactly what Milton Friedman needed. [laughter] Because Milton Friedman's free market economics is in itself absolutely amoral. I won't call myself a free market economist because I'm not an economist at all. I am however a devotee of the free market as a most desirable ground for constitutional government. But I don't regard it as a great gift in the cause of human freedom if unrestricted choice becomes an end in itself. I don't believe that at all. I think that "freedom to choose" guided by moral considerations and by proper education becomes a great vehicle of human well-being. But only then. Yes?

Kewalek: I was just wondering if I understand Mr. Strauss's writings on natural right correctly: the biggest problem for the ancients was the matter of individualism. Can you explain that a little bit?

Jaffa: That was the heart of my presentation yesterday. I argue that, first of all, properly speaking, there is no such thing as individualism—for the very simple reason that there is no such thing as an individual. It's part of our vocabulary; I can't speak at any length without speaking of "individuals" myself. But the word "individual" is an adjective. And an adjective ain't nothin' 'till there's a noun to which it is attached. It's an attribute without a substance. There are individual dogs, individual cats, individual trees, and individual human beings. And, as a matter of fact, when you look at individual human beings, what do you see? You see individual women, or girls, and individual boys, or men. There are no human individuals that are neither the one nor the other. There are some monstrosities, but there are always monstrosities. Nature has accidents too. But, any individual human being not a monstrosity is (or grows up to be) either an individual man or an individual woman. Now, in Hobbes's teaching the first law of nature is certainly self-preservation, and all rights are derived from the right of self-preservation. But Hobbes's argument is radically defective, in that he sees the state of nature as one in which each "individual" is in a foxhole. He doesn't have a wife, and he (or she) doesn't have a child. You never are told if it's a man or a woman in that foxhole. Yet is is right and proper to speak of self-preservation as Hobbes and Locke do, but also as James Madison does in *Federalist* No. 43, where he speaks of the great law of nature and of nature's God. (That is one of the few places in the *Federalist* where you hear the echoes of the Declaration.) But the truth is that a cock robin will attack a cat if the cat comes too close to the nest where the hen is brooding. I know from the personal observation that self-preservation in nature is primarily the preservation of the species and not of the individual. By nature, individuals act to preserve their families first. According to the old view, which I think is in Augustine's *City of God,* if two human beings are adrift on a raft that can support only one, it is not unjust—it is not just, but it is not unjust—for one to shove the other off. However, we know that as a matter of nature, if the two people clinging to the raft are father and son, that the father will usually prefer the life of his son to his own life. There are very few parents who would not, I think, sacrifice their lives for their children, in the same spirit as the cock robin who attacks the cat. Radical individualism has no foundation in nature and is *against* natural law. The other example I give is the old rule, which is also a law of nature, that when a ship is sinking, "women and children first." Among ancient cities, you would suffer great losses in battle among the men, but the city could come back if the women and children survived. One man might have to have several wives in the aftermath of a battle. Or, bachelors might be required to marry. That frequently happened in ancient times. That was why Socrates married. He obeyed the law which commanded him to marry after a battle in which Athenian men died in large numbers.

Smith: Sort of the same question: you mention the Moral Majority in a commercial society. Now we don't have a lot of magnanimous men running around these days—

Jaffa: There never were a lot.

Smith: —but rather bourgeois types. And supposedly the argument is that if we accept a lot of economic freedom, then in the interstices there will be a lot of political freedom. What happens if you pursue this more conditional understanding of moral virtue?

Jaffa: Let me come back to the argument I made against radical individualism. I think that, merely from the point of self-preservation, the fundamental unit is not the "individual" but the family, and morality comes to sight as those things which enable the family to survive, and of course to develop, which in turn enables the members of the family eventually to take their roles as citizens. The "individual" is incomplete without the family: there are clear grounds in nature for the union of male and female to provide the fundamental form of human association without which there is no self-preservation. But the prohibitions against, murder, theft, adultery, and incest are all fundamental prohibitions relating to the preservation of the family and its property. Just as the family needs property to survive, so ultimately the family must, I think, become part of the city or the political community for the family to perfect itself. And, you see, in the first instance the family needs the city, partly for self-preservation but also for the enhancement of that morality which is ultimately needed but which the family really cannot provide for itself, because there must be laws, and they must be good laws. That argument, which is from the first book of Aristotle's *Politics,* stands today as ever a model of what nature is and of the role of morality in relationship to nature. But, again, what we need to be reminded of now, in this modern civilization of ours, is not to be told over and over again how complex it is. We know that. We need to be reminded about the simple elements out of which this complexity arose. We need to be reminded of what we are according to nature, to see what guidelines we can find amidst the enormously wider range of choices available to us. And one of the things I mentioned yesterday was, of course, that the family has to change; and that the law of the family has to change. Certainly the family in nature, in its primitive character, is one in which the division of labor between husband and wife is spelled out by necessity. The husband must provide food, and the wife must be in the house guarding the children and providing for them. And no other division of labor is conceivable. And, of course, the growth of the economy and of technology have changed all that, and for the most part changed it in ways that are very desirable, because our ability to survive mere nature is much greater, the life span is much longer, the lives of women are not bound down to those immediate functions which are connected with child-bearing and the consequences of child-bearing. The nature men and women share in common comes more to the fore, and the nature which distinguishes them falls more into the background. But that doesn't mean that either the one or the other ceases to operate. To show how rapidly things have changed, and how necessary it is that we not lose our perspective on the fact of change, I said I am sure that if Mrs. Jerry Falwell were to be confronted with the situation of one of Trollope's heroines—less than a hundred years ago—where many of the novels turn around the fact that a woman, when she married, passed from being a ward of her father to becoming a ward of her husband, I'm sure Mrs. Falwell wouldn't tolerate the consequences of that for five minutes. And I hope that nobody would want her to. Surely, desirable changes have happened in the past, and will happen in the future, modifying the internal life of the family, because of external changes in the environment. Trollope's novels derived from an earlier, agricultural society. The legal limitations of women in agricultural societies were not perceived as such, because they did not hinder any freedom that women actually wanted. In fact most of them were looked upon as protections for women, rather than limitations. Women were too busy performing their functions, as the queen-bee within the hive, to notice that there was any liberty that was being taken away from them. So circumstances do change, and morals, and the laws regarding morals, will, in certain contingent respects, change with them. But the notion that because some things changed everything changes, and there is *no* ground for morality, or that there is nothing durable in the structure of the family, because some elements of the traditional family have shown themselves to be changeable, that is the danger we are faced with now. And the reaction of the Moral Majority, however undirected in some respects, nevertheless supplies an energy which should force us to reconsider. And I think that this reconsideration should be assimilated within a framework of a civilized understanding of the changing relationship of the sexes and of the need to preserve the family within the context of those changes. Because certainly this attitude —that the traditional family must be abandoned —was common in the Sixties (a great record of this is in the "Doonesbury" cartoons): the communes and the new experiments and all sorts of things —some of them were bizarre and some were obscene, but you know what they were. Yes?

McGrail: Could I ask a different question about political elections in general? It seems that after different candidates are nominated they get up and give a rousing speech calling for virtue and morality. But then when they get running against their opposition they get more into pragmatic things, and then all they do is appeal to people's self-interest, and they sort of forget that they were idealists. They are schizophrenic about it. Do we want to uphold virtue and morality? Or do we want to solve inflation? It's like an article I saw recently in the newspaper about Army recruiters. They say, "We no longer appeal to their sense of patriotism. We say, 'Come join the Army and learn a skill.'" It is as if we were afraid to appeal to man's better instincts, to the democratic ideals.

Jaffa: Well, Abraham Lincoln once said that the element of will in man is a compound of moral sense and self-interest. Convince a man that something is right *and* in his interest, then you get action.

McGrail: I wouldn't mind if they said that what is in his interest is also moral.

Jaffa: I think that if you examine political rhetoric you will find that every politician in some measure appeals to both. Now, it's true that he might not do it at the time. Certainly Mr. Reagan made all sorts of accommodations. For example—and I can't think of anything more absurd from the point of view of his principles and everything he stood for—he endorsed federal aid to New York City. It reminds me of the story of F.D.R. on the drafting of his speech to be given in Boston in September, 1940. (This story is told in Sherwood's *Roosevelt and Hopkins.*) It concerns the speech in which he said, "I promise you Mothers of America, a-gain and a-gain and a-gain, that your sons will not be sent to fight in any foreign wars." And Sherwood himself, who was a red-hot interventionist, nevertheless, in his anxiety to get F.D.R. elected, said "Don't say anything about *foreign* wars." And F.D.R. exploded, "You mean to say we won't fight if we are *attacked?*" So the joker was "foreign wars." Here was F.D.R. doing everything he could to get us into war and making that promise. The voters are sophisticated enough to know that when Ronald Reagan defended both the federal aid to New York and the federal bail-out of Chrysler Corporation, he was simply bending to the pressures of the campaign, and it didn't mean he would do such things later. It's just that in politics you get subjected to pressures you don't anticipate, and sometimes the heat is too strong. Remember that Abraham Lincoln's presidency was characterized by two policies: (1) the promise in the first inaugural that he would never interfere with slavery in the States and (2) the Emancipation Proclamation, which required the Thirteenth Amendment. Remember the great peroration, at the end of his message to Congress in December, 1862. "The dogmas of the quiet past, are inadequate to the stormy present. The occasion is piled high with difficulty, and we must rise — with the occasion. As our case is new, so we must think anew, and act anew. We must disenthrall ourselves and then we shall save our country." Never was an excuse for repudiating a campaign promise — and one repeated in his inaugural address — made in such beautiful language. That is politics, high and low. Because there can be noble reasons for abandoning old promises and old policies, does not mean that it is always noble to do so, anymore than the fact that such repudiations may be base does not mean that it is never noble to do so. I think that you will find, though, that it is simply against the laws of our democratic political nature for any politician to campaign without appealing to what he claims to be noble and right, and trying to connect that with base self-interest, certainly self-interest understood at a very low level.

Rusnak: Could you please tell us about something mentioned earlier, some of the details about you Extremism Statement in '64: how that emerged, how it got into Goldwater's speech, and what you think of it now?

Jaffa: I would say *"imprudent."* I wrote the whole paragraph in which it was encapsulated or incorporated as a memorandum when I was attending the hearings before the Platform Committee in the week before the Republican National Convention. I was with a group of people who were being shepherded around under the auspices of John Rhodes. (We were therefore known as "Rhodes Scholars," and that's the only way I could ever become a Rhodes Scholar.) I wrote that statement, in part, as a repudiation of the critique of extremism that was made by Rockefeller and Scranton witnesses before the committee. Sometimes these things get out of hand. They are like letters you did not intend to send. But they blow out the window and somebody picks them up and they are delivered. And this one was delivered to the Senator, who fell in love with it and ordered that it be incorporated in his Acceptance Speech, which in turn led to my becoming the principal drafter of the speech. And, there it was. It was not my political judgment that the thing be used in the speech at all, although I must say that I was flattered at the time and didn't think too much of what the consequences would be. I couldn't make a political judgement myself because I was isolated from the Convention and had no contact with the political currents on the floor. The Senator liked it because he had been goaded by mean-spirited attacks through the long months of the primaries. Nothing in the political history of the country surpasses in fundamental indecency the kind of attacks that were made on Goldwater by Nelson Rockefeller and his followers. These attacks were followed up by William Scranton at the end, and also to some extent by Henry Cabot Lodge and some of the other "gurus" of the Eastern Republican Establishment—who, by the way, I think, were not merely ideologically hostile to Goldwater. If you look at the electoral process over the last twenty years, you have to bear in mind that the seemingly ideological changes in principle in the Republican platform, which I think will change and are changing the axis of the whole two-party system, are in part due to great demographic shifts going on in the country. The country is moving southwest, and it is no accident that from 1960 on all of the Republican candidates, with the exception of Gerald Ford, who wouldn't have been the candidate except for Watergate and his appointment as Vice President followed by the resignation of Richard M. Nixon, have been from the Southwest. But I was responsible for another statement of the Senator's, the press release he issued on the eve of the Convention when Scranton had made a particularly brutal criticism of him. I offered him some excerpts from Lincoln's response to Horace Greeley, "The Prayer of Twenty Millions," when Greeley severely and unfairly criticized Lincoln for not issuing an emancipation proclamation. Lincoln responded with magnanimity when he said, "If there be in it [Greeley's statement] an impatient and dictatorial tone, I pass over it in deference to an old friend whose heart I have always believed to be right...." Then he goes on, "I would save the Union ... the shortest way under the Constitution." So I was also responsible for that soothing and accomodating statement of Goldwater's.

But I was not asked for the extremism statement; I had written it as an in-house memorandum, and it was appropriated. I'm not making an excuse for myself in saying I wasn't responsible for it. I was certainly enthusiastically in favor of it at the time. As I said, I had not been present on the floor of the Convention, nor had I any contact with the delegates as a political observer, and so had no sense of the temper of the Convention. But the Senator *did*, and he knew what he was doing. I don't blame him for his feelings, because he had been subjected to character-assassination from within the party, which was very unfair. I have one sort of sidelight on the aftermath of the whole episode. I don't know if any of you saw the review of *Equality and Liberty* that George Kateb published in *Commentary* magazine in the spring of 1965. He praised *Crisis of the House Divided* and then said, in effect, "But I cannot understand how anyone who could have written *Crisis of the House Divided* could have supported Senator Goldwater." He read *Equality and Liberty* with the sole intention of trying to find some explanation of the strange "change." And he read through it and couldn't find any explanation, which was good as far as it went, except that he never got around to writing a review of the book. But I met him at Amherst in late April (1980) when I was there. In the meantime Kateb had been one of the most strident campus voices against the Vietnam war. So I greeted him, and said, "George, I have an apology to make. You were right about my politics in 1964. I should never have supported a man who promised to keep us out of a land war in Asia." [laughter]

Anastaplo: This raises questions about the role of academic people in political activity—in a campaign or in an administration. Should they be in there? Is it likely that they will be misused and misunderstood?

Jaffa: I don't think there is any formula for that. The model for thinking about this, at least for me, was the passage in Strauss's essay "On Classical Political Philosophy" when he said that the political philosopher comes to sight as the good citizen, who attempts to moderate political conflict and move it to its resolution. But he had to really *seem* to be a citizen, and to some extent really be a citizen, in order to play that role. Now there is a difference of course between the political philosopher who comes to sight as a good citizen and the political philosopher who is the teacher of legislators. I think ultimately they are the same person, or they *can* be. There is a continuity between these roles, even if they are different. I think whether or not one should be a visible and conspicuous part of the political process is a prudential decision which can only be made in the circumstances at a certain time. I think there is such a thing as "normal" times, when the "normal" party conflict engenders the kind of consensus which is necessary. At such time, I would say on the whole that political activity is not called for, *may* not be called for, on the part of the scholar who understand the role of political philosophy in political life. But, on the other hand, my feeling is that today we are somewhere near a terminal process in the history of Western civilization—not just in the history of this republic—in which a dark night of the soul could very well be the fate of the world if certain cataclysms with which we are threatened come to pass. In that circumstance, I don't think that there can be any conflict between one's civic duty and one's scholarly and professional duty. I think that both thermonuclear war in all of its horrors and the tyranny of the universal homogeneous state are evils which it behooves every man—so far as in him lies—to avert. *My* understanding of Marxist Communism is that—whatever its own understanding of itself—its necessary result is the extinction of the memory of the past. There will always be a fictitious memory of sorts, which will call itself a memory. But the idea of the leap into freedom—which is essential for the self-justification of Marxism

—implies the radical superiority of the future over the past in all fundamental human respects. Any memory of that past, any genuine memory of the past, destroys the illusion of that superiority and hence would have to be extinguished. Remember: our identities, whether as individuals, nations, or cultures, depend on memory. The way the history of the Communist Party of the Soviet Union is rewritten every time there is a change within the regime is, I think, a model of what would happen to the memory of everything we call civilization. History, properly so called, is nothing but civilization's memory. In that case we would really be deprived of our heritage, as we would be deprived of our identities, without which I think there is nothing in our lives which would be essentially valuable; we would be reduced to mere subhuman animals in our relationship to nature and to each other. And even if we were animals in control of sophisticated machinery, we would have no human characteristics, no recognizable characteristics. You would have to do over again all the work which has been done since man emerged, whether by divine creation or by evolution from the nothingness of protozoic slime. I myself find the question of origins relatively uninteresting. I am not interested in what man was before he became man, nor in the efficient causes, as much as I am in the achievement itself. And as a matter of fact, I like to point out, whenever the occasion arises, that the mystery of *Genesis* is not an archaeological question, because if we ask how anyone begins to think at any moment in time now, we have to face the problem of *Genesis*. And the problem of *Genesis* at some remote point in archaeological time is no different from the point of how we begin to think *now*. So, there is always a new beginning for human life in each one of us every time we think, which is a mystery which cannot be explained. Any time it were possible to explain how men began to think, they would no longer be able to think, because that is where human freedom resides, in the mystery of the origin of the motion of the soul, in which the mind apprehends an external reality and transforms it into the symbolic forms of language and of art, which are all different forms of the expression of the grasp of an abstract reality which is separate from the thinking soul itself. Man commands the matter (or energy) in nature because there is something within him which is free from determination by that which he apprehends. All totalitarian regimes rest upon deterministic theories of the soul, upon denial of any metaphysical freedom. All theories of the soul which dominate the academy today are deterministic. The most powerful intellectual forces in the free world today are accordingly forces for despotism. And this is the problem we have to face and encounter. But I see no fundamental conflict in our duties as scholars in fighting the false theories of determinism which underlie all our relativism, and our civic duty to oppose the totalitarian political consequences of that determinism and relativism. I think that our responsibilities as scholars and as citizens are ultimately one and the same. Yes, please.

Colmo: Is there any tension between your recurrence to education and history and tradition, on the one hand, and your recurrence to nature on the other hand?

Jaffa: Nature is the great foundation for *being*. I think we exist within a framework. As Leo Strauss used to say, speaking of genius, he would mention Plato sometimes, Aristotle sometimes, sometimes Shakespeare, as an example of the peak of human genius, you might say the crown of human nature as revealed in such genius. Yet he would always insist that there was one thing greater than Shakespeare, and that is the nature that made Shakespeare possible. So we must always look beyond that "individual" to the species, and when we speak of species we are speaking of course of an order within a whole. It is impossible to speak of man without speaking of human nature, but once we say "human nature," we are making a subdivision within a larger whole, "nature," one part of which is human nature, but not the whole. That whole, of which human nature is a part, is a greater whole and the ultimate object of speculation which we may never apprehend except in part. Even though we cannot understand the whole we can understand that there *is* a whole, because if there were no whole there couldn't be a part.

Colmo: But the "nature" that makes Shakespeare possible was very much a nature transformed by man.

Jaffa: No. Shakespeare was indeed born into a culture, it was a *human* culture, meaning a culture that arose because human nature lay at its foundation. I mean, London existed because human beings do create civilization, in which *nomos* is supposed to replace *phusis*. But law does not replace nature. To use Burke's phrase, "Art and nature may be opposites, but yet there is a sense in which art is man's nature." Nature made it possible for man to have artifacts. Bees and beavers build artifacts which are not artifacts in the same sense in which human artifacts are artifacts, because the bees can only build a beehive one way, and the dams are built only in the way nature intended beavers to build dams. But nature does not tell man how to build cities; it only requires that they make decisions about the just and the unjust, as Aristotle says at the end of the first book of the *Politics*. It is true that, had Shakespeare been born into some barbarian tribe, then he wouldn't have become the William Shakespeare we know, because London and the English renaissance provided opportunities for actualizing his genius. But he had to leave Stratford for London, much as Moses had to leave the desert and return to Egypt. His genius would also have remained unfulfilled without that positive action on his part. Still, there were also circumstances that he did not create that were necessary to his art. Clearly the actuality of the natural potentiality that was William Shakespeare required circumstances — cultural circumstances — extrinsic to his genius. But bear in mind that these circumstances were also actualizations of natural potentialities. The nature that we wonder at, the nature more wonderful than either William Shakespeare or the English Renaissance, was the nature whose actuality became both Shakespeare and the Renaissance. Both were manifestations of a freedom that human beings exercised, but which they did not create. Piety might lead us to call it a gift of God, but it is surely not impious to call it a gift of nature.

Smith: It sounds as if the entire history after Shakespeare was somehow a natural necessity, because that history was contingent on one being civilized. And that is something of an act *against* nature as well as an outgrowth of nature itself.

Jaffa: What if I were to try to understand the essential difference between, say, a fifth-century B.C. Athenian, Sophocles or Aeschylus or Euripides, and Shakespeare? I think in particular of Sophocles. I promised, in my essay on *King Lear,* which I wrote almost thirty years ago, that I would somehow, sometime write a comparative analysis of *Oedipus* and *Lear* as the two peaks of pre-Socratic and Socratic tragedy. I never got around to doing that, although in some ways I set a foundation for doing such a thing (maybe somebody else will do it) in my essay on "The Shakespearean Universe."* In some ways *Oedipus* could be looked upon as a precursor of Christianity, because, remember, Oedipus becomes the scapegoat of the gods. He becomes a kind of guilt-bearer who purchases (now I'm using Christian eschatological terms) a freedom from guilt for his people, just as he saved them earlier by answering the riddle of the sphinx. But, still, that is a pre-Socratic tragedy. Now, when I call Shakespeare a Socratic tragedian, I also mean that in some sense he is a Christian writer of tragedies, and the decisive difference between Shakespearean tragedy and Sophoclean tragedy has something to do with the intervention of Christianity. The idea of human civilization is decisively transformed in the Shakespearean universe by reason of this intervention. And Shakespeare himself comments on that. He wrote an absolutely perfect pagan tragedy in *Coriolanus,* where man and god were part of a continuous process, and there is no radical difference between man and god. But the radical difference between man and god, and man's natural guiltiness and his need for redemption, complicates and even, if you will, confuses his role as a citizen. Now, I leave it to you to decide whether the intervention of Christianity is a matter of history, necessity, or divine intervention.

Smith: [pause] I hope you're not waiting for a decision.

Jaffa: No, I'm leaving it to you, whether or not my interpretation is really Hegelian.

Student: [inaudible] I noticed you spent much time trying to separate Thomism and Aristotelianism. It seems to me that what you said was more at home with the Thomist point of view.

Jaffa: Then I was very successful in my rhetoric. [laughter]

Student: Was that just rhetoric or isn't that in your book, to separate the two?

Jaffa: Yes, and ever since then I have been putting them back together again. I think it's good sometimes to look at things in separation and sometimes to look at them in combination. I would certainly think that, looking at the political crisis of our time, which is not really of yesterday, today, or tomorrow, and which is destined to last (if we survive) many generations—that there is a tradition which we are all defending, or all should be defending, a tradition constituted by the principles of reason *and* revelation. And I share in Leo Strauss's analysis of the relationship between reason and revelation. Classical rationalism is always accompanied by skepticism as by its shadow, and that shadow of skepticism provides a foundation for doctrines drawing on divine revelation. I think neither side can refute each other. Both represent human possibilities, the exploration of which, and the dynamic tension between which, has been the glory of Western civilization. Both reason and revelation are threatened now. Modern philosophy at its roots was an attempt to free reason from skepticism—an intellectual task which I have compared to trying to jump over one's shadow. That's what Cartesianism is. The famous dualism, between *res extensa* and *res cogitans,* is repeated over and over again in every characteristically modern doctrine. In Marxism it repeats itself in the fact that Marxism is the dialectic of history which reveals that all human thought —except Marxism—is ideology. It exempts itself from its own analysis of human thought, but that is what every philosopher from Descartes to Hume to Kant to Hegel has been doing. And ultimately the attempt to free rationalism from scepticism was also an attempt to free reason from the challenge of revelation by assimilating the argument for revelation into the framework of reason. Because if reason can be freed from skepticism then there would be no rational doubt to provide a ground of revealed religion. Marxism is the clearest example of this. In the attack on all revealed religion as the opiate of the people, Marxism asserts that revealed religion is an attempt to substitute false pleasures after death for real pleasures now, and thus to cheat people out of their humanity. And by this attempt to solve the problem of reason and revelation by abolishing skepticism as an attribute of reason, they attempted to abolish the tension between reason and revelation, and ultimately to abolish the claims *both* of reason and revelation as these were understood before. However, the modern principles ultimately destroy themselves. While I have great respect for modern science and for scientific rationalism in a limited sphere of human existence, I think that the idea is impossible that modern scientific rationalism, founded upon determinism, can say *anything* (not something, but anything) about the problem of human choice. Once you accept the deterministic metaphysics and try to found a method on that, I think you are bound ultimately to end with nihilism in philosophy and with totalitarianism in politics. So, as far as Thomas and Aristotle are concerned, they may be, at a certain level, theoretical antagonists. But one of the things I admire most about Aquinas is that in trying to make Aristotle acceptable to the church authorities, he tried to make Aristotle someone who, instead of being banned, would be read. Now I think Thomas himself understood very well this tension between reason and revelation. Certainly his whole work was designed to overcome this tension. Whether his intention was to abolish it or only to *seem* to abolish it, so as to make possible the fruitful study of theology and philosophy without fear of punishment and persecution, I cannot say. Aquinas, as far as I know, wrote the first tract designed to produce tolerance toward Jews in the history of the West in his "Letter to the Duchess of Brabant on the Treatment of Jews." Of course it's not a call for the kind of freedom you would find in Locke's *A Letter Concerning Toleration,* or in Jefferson's Statute of Religious Freedom, but it laid the foundation for them, and probably went as far as he thought he could go in that direction. Thomas should be judged more by the direction in which he pointed than by the ground he covered. He moderated theological passion and showed that civilized men could differ, without being indifferent to truth.

Student: In some sense, then, you are changing where the money is. You're almost seeming to say that Thomas would be more important than Aristotle (but you can't understand Thomas without Aristotle; I understand that).

Jaffa: No, I thought that in Thomas I had an enlightened teacher, an unsurpassed teacher, someone who led me, paragraph by paragraph, and sentence by sentence, through the text of *Ethics,* even though I didn't ultimately agree that the most important way to understand Aristotle was always in the way that Thomas *seemed* to understand him. He pointed out alternatives. As in the *Summa Theologica,* he would give you the objections to his position, as well as the replies to those objections. In the last analysis, he left it up to you. And you could see in the design of his interpretation the magnificent effort to show the place of every sentence in that great book in relationship to every other sentence, in a kind of architectural structure with a cathedral-like outline of the whole.

Student: But Thomas and Aristotle must differ on the relationship between reason and revelation because there really was no revelation available to Aristotle.

Jaffa: As a matter of fact there was. I would say that Aristotle teaches revelation as much as any Christian theologian—in his own way. If you read the treatise *On the Soul* everything comes down in the end to the problem of the agent intellect, which absolutely cannot be explained. You want me to give you a brief rundown?

Student: Okay.

Jaffa: How does Aristotle explain sense perception? Let's take sight, which is the most interesting and the most noble of the senses. In order for seeing to take place, there must be a visible object and an eye capable of seeing things. But in order for the eye which is capable of seeing to actually see, there must be a third thing, light. Now, for thinking to take place, there must be an object capable of being understood, an intelligible, and there must be a mind capable of thinking it. But there has to be a third thing. If I say "light," I'm using a metaphor. Often when we are trying to understand something, there will be a certain moment ("now I see it") when we do understand it. Sometimes we say that we have seen the light. What we mean, however, is that the object of our understanding has been there all the time, but somehow became "uncovered" (that is what apocalypse, or revelation, means). But who uncovered it, or who turned on the light? How were we transformed from potential seers into actual seers. I do not want to refer to the many stories of revelation within the sacred tradition as mere stories for children; only to point out that the mystery underlying reason is a genuine mystery. Within that mystery lies the mystery of human freedom. Now from Aristotle's point of view, I think there is no necessary conflict between reason and revelation—if you get down to the real question, which is how thinking takes place. There is the tradition of reason and the tradition of revelation, but I think the problem with revelation is as much in reason itself—it has its own problem within its own structured framework. That's the problem of the active intellect. Where does it happen? Why does it happen? How can I *will* to know? Here I am; I want to know something; but I still don't know it. And then, all of a sudden, "Yes, now I see it." Why?

Student: So, what you are saying is that in the Greek world that continuum you were talking about between gods and man is *almost* as discontinuous as in Christianity, because, after all, that is the distinction you were making before.

Jaffa: Yes, one of the explanations of this is in the *Metaphysics.* There is a discussion of inductive reasoning. For example, I say that I understand that this is a chair. When I say that this is a chair, that means two different things. First is the positive or affirmative statement that this particular object is a chair. But implicit in this is the proposition that if this was the only chair in the world I wouldn't be able to make such a statement. This is a particular object constructed in such a way so as to support the body in a semi-recumbent posture. But there are an infinite number of possible ways in which that can be done. That object over there is also a chair; it doesn't look like this one at all. But I perceive something in common between them. Now how is it that my mind makes the jump from the particular to the universal? It's because, on the basis of a series of comparisons, I see with the eye of my mind an *eidos* or *species,* a form which is common to all possible chairs, and in virtue of which they are chairs. And yet this form lacks all the characteristics in virtue of which any particular chair is not merely possible, but actual, and hence a "this." For the form of the chair is at once something that is *like* every possible chair, and yet *different* from any actual chair. This experience of likeness and of difference underlies what I call the miracle of the common noun, which is truly the most miraculous of all possible human experiences. For it is the essential experience which makes language—and hence man—possible. This, incidentally, is the meaning of that bad argument that Socrates uses in the first book of the

Republic, in which he defeats Thrasymachus by getting him to agree that a thing *is* what it is *like.* Aristotle, in the *Metaphysics,* speaks about sense perception in relationship to understanding in this way. He compares it to an army which is fleeing in confusion. It has been defeated, running away, and the soldiers run pell-mell, helter-skelter away from the enemy. Everything is in disorder; everything is chaotic. And that is what sense perception is, you might say, in its purest form. Now, Aristotle says that the soldiers are fleeing, and all of a sudden one of them stops, stops running, and turns and faces the enemy. And then another forms behind him. And another. And another. And pretty soon ranks form. Chaos is replaced by cosmos. This is the genesis of which I spoke earlier. This is what happens when the mind, understanding, imposes order on sense perception. In this Aristotle anticipates Kant's "synthetic *a priori.*" Unless the mind has certain *a priori* capacities for imposing itself, for synthesizing experience, experience doesn't happen.

Smith: Isn't that phrase "impose itself" somewhat unfortunate for your position? [laughter]

Jaffa: No.

Smith: We know only what we make?

Jaffa: There is a certain natural making which takes place. Remember Jacob Klein's lecture, "On the Nature of Nature"? Klein says that in every tree there is a little carpenter making new trees. Every acorn has a little carpenter in it, ready to make a new tree. In other words, art imitates nature, and nature imitates art. There is that affinity between art and nature. This would lead to brute positivism only if one said that the "artisan" in nature was not there, only in the eye of the beholder.

Smith: You might call it "brute realism."

Jaffa: No, it is not a brute projection of reality upon a screen from something that has no intrinsic cause: or four causes, or five causes, whatever, however you count them. Concede that skepticism, which follows reason as its shadow, opens the door not only for faith but also for scientific positivism. But I think that the very attempt to eliminate skepticism by scientific positivism is an ultimately self-defeating enterprise. Yes?

Smith: You mentioned that modern science is deterministic. Do you really think that is still true?

Jaffa: It may not be true from the perspective of those who are facing the mysteries of reality on the frontiers of modern physics. The genuine sophisticates seem to be much more modest in their pretensions than the routine members of the profession. But the word doesn't seem to have gotten down to the "philosophers" and social scientists at all.

Student: Perhaps when it does it will be worse.

Jaffa: The latter-day followers of Copernicus will probably react very much as the former-day followers of Ptolemy did. I think it should be open, the whole question of what we mean by the human soul: is it a by-product of atoms and the void, or what? Every attempt at reductionism, which finds an underlying common cause which is said to explain all higher things, is self-defeating. If again I may quote Leo Strauss, "I think we must understand the low in the light of the high, and not the high in the light of the low." Modern science attempts to understand the high in the light of the low. And that is ultimately self-defeating because the very attempt at explanation becomes low, and hence becomes self-contradictory. For example, if you say, "I, the scientific knower of all things, know that morality is an illusion because all human freedom is an illusion," then you have to ask, "Are you a Cretan who says that all Cretans are liars?" They're all calling themselves liars, and at the same time proclaiming their authority as knowers of the truth. I love that Cretan who says that all Cretans are liars. He was the first modern philosopher.

Anastaplo: Is there a final question someone would like to pursue? [pause]

Colmo: Yes, actually. [laughter] That skeptical shadow that has been following reason around all the time. You said that it provided a sort of opening for revelation. But why can't you say, instead, that the difference between Aristotle and a believer is that Aristotle insists on naming problems but that a believer, when confronted by some mystery like the ability to think and understand, explains it away by saying, "God made it possible." I mean, that seems to be a much more straightforward presentation of it.

Jaffa: But the Bible commands us to love God with all our heart and with all our soul and with all our mind, and our neighbor as ourself, and tells us the attempt to know the universe as the ground for our behavior is impossible because God himself is mysterious. But God, out of his mysterious nature, nevertheless, vouchsafes his love for us by letting us know those things that are sufficient for us to lead the right kinds of lives. And, that there are mysteries at the heart of the universe is as much a conclusion of philosophy as it is of divine revelation. Socrates would say, I think, that this mystery should preoccupy us. Although I think that the conclusions he drew with respect to human conduct are neither altogether the same, nor altogether different, from those that stem from the Biblical tradition. The Socratics, I think, go on speculating on mysteries; the children of faith worship God rather than trying to speculate on his mysteries. Those are differences. I have no fault to find with those who worship, and I'm not saying that there is any contradiction between speculating sometimes and worshipping sometimes. Those are valid human alternatives. I think that a regime like the Soviet Union—towards which I think we are tending very much, impelled by the dominant teaching of our academies—is one in which those who show awe before the mysteries of the universe are ridiculed and treated as if they are somehow the reactionary slaves of an alienated consciousness and of a false ideology.

Colmo: And you think that when that ridicule becomes directed against religion, it will also become directed against those who show that same awe in terms of philosophy?

Jaffa: Absolutely. I recommend to everyone to look at that book called *Fundamentals of Marxism-Leninism,* which is published by Progress Publishers, Moscow, and which I think is a very sophisticated handbook of Marxism-Leninism, done by a committee of academicians on the basis of the Seventy-Fourth Party Congress, which was in 1974. There the alternative to Marxism is simply "idealism." And philosophy and revealed religion are simply two species of "idealism."

Smith: But are not some forms of religion dubious?

Jaffa: Let us say that there are a variety of spurious enthusiasms which pass themselves off as religion.

Smith: Would you care to name any?

Jaffa: Jim Jones. As Strauss says in *Natural Right and History,* it's only those who think in terms of a value-free social science who cannot distinguish between high religions and vulgar enthusiasms. In some cases high religions in the persons of certain congregations and certain people degenerate. Although I admire many things about fundamentalist Protestantism, I think that what the Puritans did to the churches in the sixteenth century is indefensible. They went through with hammers smashing statues and altar pieces, everything that they thought violated the commandment against graven images—just as Moses did with the Golden Calf. I think they were wrong in interpreting their instructions from God in that way. But, still, there is no good thing in this life which cannot be perverted to bad ends by either the stupid or the evil. Plenty of people were burned at the stake for holding heretical opinions in the course of the wars of religion. And it was done by both Protestants and by Catholics. And I think that if you drew your picture of either the Catholic or the Protestant churches on the basis of the excesses of the Reformation, you would have to condemn Christianity across the board. And I think that would be wrong. The fact that Savonarola was a fanatic doesn't mean that Thomas Aquinas was. I must say that I like Christianity best when it has a large infusion of Aristotelian moderation. But I think that it would be a great mistake for us not to utilize the enthusiasm of those who want to preserve what can be preserved of the traditional *family.* Here the Moral Majority has a constructive role to play. The problem of recent generations has been the attrition of the family, the destruction of the family partly because of the notion that morality is a mere matter of choice, a mere matter of *opinion* I should say. Human happiness for most people most of the time depends perhaps more than anything else on having a good family life. That is something which those young men in my class who thought there was no moral crisis because it was *over* did not understand. I tried to convince them, and I think I may have convinced some of them that the argument for chastity is in some ways an argument for happiness and for the family—which doesn't mean you have to put a big letter "A" on everybody that you catch doing naughty things. There it is.

Anastaplo: Well, what it is that *is* has been a very interesting discussion for us. I hope we can do it again on another occasion.

Jaffa: Thank you. And thank you for your introduction, which certainly inspired me, or gave me a sense of responsibility for something that I had to live up to. [laughter]

Anastaplo: Very good.

*Published in *Shakespeare as Political Thinker,* edited by John Alvis and Thomas G. West, Carolina Academic Press, Durham, 1981.

Five

Inventing the Past

Garry Wills's Inventing America *and the Pathology of Ideological Scholarship*

And this too is denied even to God, to make that which has been not to have been.

THOMAS AQUINAS

G arry Wills's *Inventing America: Jefferson's Declaration of Independence* is a book that should never have been published, certainly not in its present form. Its errors are so egregious that any intelligent graduate student—or undergraduate student—checking many of its assertions against their alleged sources, would have demanded, at the least, considerable revision.

It has been widely hailed as a great contribution to our understanding of the American political tradition. There have been "rave" reviews in the *New York Times Book Review*, the *New York Review of Books*, the *Saturday Review*, the *New Republic*, the *American Spectator*, and *National Review*, to mention but a few of many. It has been praised by such glittering eminences of the academy, and of the historical profession, as David Brion Davis, Edmund Morgan, and Arthur Schlesinger, Jr. These are men who can, if they wish, split a hair at fifty paces. In this instance, their critical faculties seem to have gone into a narcotic trance, proving the truth of the aphorism that ideology is the opiate of the intellectuals. Among the reviewers hitherto, only Professor Kenneth Lynn, writing in *Commentary*, October, 1978, has seen Wills's book for what it is. "*Inventing America*," he writes, "does not help us to understand Thomas Jefferson, but its totally unearned acclaim tells us a good deal about modern intellectuals and their terrible need for radical myths." The myth promoted by *Inventing America* "is that the Declaration is not grounded in Lockean individualism, as we have been accustomed to think, but is a communitarian manifesto derived from the common-sense philosophers of the Scottish Enlightenment..." By this myth, says Lynn, Wills would have "transmogrified" a "new nation, conceived in liberty ... into a new nation, conceived in communality," and thus have supplied "the history of the Republic with as pink a dawn as possible."

I think that Professor Lynn is correct as far as he goes. But he does not go far enough. *Inventing America* was received with virtually the same enthusiasm on the Right as on the Left. The reviews in *National Review* and the *American Spectator* were both written by current editors of *National Review*, surely the most authoritative of conservative journals.* (Ronald Reagan's message to the Twentieth Anniversary banquet declared he had read every issue from cover to cover.) But the current editors, we must note, are apostolic successors to Wills himself, who wrote for the journal for a number of years. His account of his days as an *NR* staffer may be found in *Confessions of a Conservative*, published shortly after *Inventing America*. The title of the book is not meant in irony. Wills thinks of himself as a Conservative still, and somehow traces all his serious ideas to St. Augustine. At the deepest level of Wills's being, there is indeed a kind of Lutheran hatred (and Luther was an Augustinian Monk) of classical rationalism. Lynn calls Wills "the leftist (formerly rightist) writer." Yet there is more inner consistency between the two "Willses" than Lynn perceives. That is because there is more inner consistency between the Right and the Left than is commonly supposed.

* * *

To understand where *Inventing America* "comes from," to employ a popular neologism, one must read an essay Wills published in 1964, entitled "The Convenient State." It was originally published in a volume edited by the late Frank Meyer (an *NR* editor, and Wills's close friend), called *What is Conservatism?* Later, it achieved neo-canonical status, by its inclusion in an anthology of *American Conservative Thought in the Twentieth Century*, edited by *NR*'s Editor of Editors, William F. Buckley, Jr. (It is only fair to add that an essay of mine, "On the Nature of Civil and Religious Liberty," was included in the same volume. My essay, however, represented Conservative heresy; Wills's Conservative orthodoxy.) Frank Meyer and I exchanged dialectical blows in the page of *NR* in 1965, after Meyer published an article attacking Abraham Lincoln as the enemy of American Constitutionalism and American freedom. (Meyer's own best known book is called *In Defense of Freedom*.) Meyer in 1965 and Wills in 1964 follow exactly the same line: Calhoun is their hero and their authority, Lincoln the villain of American history. As we shall see, both of them, in the decisive sense, follow a pattern of thought which seems to have been worked out for them by Willmoore Kendall. Kendall was a professor of political science at Yale when Wills was a graduate student in classics there. For Wills, as for Meyer and Kendall, there is no contradiction, nor even any paradox, in identifying the cause of constitutionalism and freedom with the defense of chattel slavery. For all three, the defense of freedom turns, in the decisive case, into the defense of the freedom of slaveowners.

The main thesis of Wills's 1964 essay was that something called

*See Postscript.

"rationalism" is the root of all political evil. This attack on "reason" has been the stock-in-trade of Conservatism since Rousseau's attack on the Enlightenment was fortified by Burke's polemics against the French Revolution. Most present-day Conservatives would be horrified to learn that they are disciples of Rousseau, yet such is surely the case. For it was Rousseau who, in going all the way back to the "state of nature" discovered that man by nature was free, but not rational. The celebration of freedom, divorced from reason, has a theoretical foundation in Rousseau which is nowhere else to be found. The Rousseauian denigration of reason, and the elevation of sentiment to take its place, is the core of nineteenth century romanticism, both in its Left phases (e.g. anarchism, syndicalism, socialism, communism), and in its Right phases (e.g. monarchism, clericalism, feudalism, slavery). Romantic nationalism has been equally a phenomenon of the Right and of the Left. "Rationalism," Wills declared as a man of the Right, "leads to a sterile paradox, to an ideal freedom that is a denial of freedom." What such a remark means can be inferred only from the use to which it is put. Here it clearly refers to the question of slavery, and to the Civil War. Concerning slavery, he remarks, somewhat vaguely, "One cannot simply ask whether a thing is just." Certainly, to ask whether slavery was just was never sufficient, but it was always necessary. One cannot distinguish a greater from a lesser evil, unless one can distinguish evil from good. Wills concedes that "the abolition of slavery [may have] been just," but insists nevertheless that the only politically relevant question was "whether it [was] constitutional." For "what is meant by constitutional government" Wills turns to that statesman of the Old South, the spiritual Father of the Confederacy, John C. Calhoun. According to Calhoun, we are told, constitutional government means "the government in which all the free forms of society—or as many as possible—retain their life and 'concur' in a political area of peaceful cooperation and compromise." We can now better understand Wills's polemic against "rationalism," since among the "free forms" which, by the foregoing statement, ought to be retained, was the institution of chattel slavery.

It was not the slaves whose concurrence Calhoun's constitutional doctrine required, but only those who had an interest in preserving, protecting, and defending slavery. Calhoun provided the slaveholders a constitutional mechanism, in the supposed rights of nullification and secession, to veto any national (or federal) legislation that they regarded as hostile to the interests of slavery. Calhoun's constitutionalism, based upon supposed rights of the states, was originally forged in the fires of the nullification controversy, between 1828 and 1839. Later it was elaborated in two books, the *Disquisition on Government*, and the *Discourse on the Constitution*. Calhoun's main dialectical adversary in 1830 was no one less than the Father of the Constitution, James Madison, although his principal political adversary was President Andrew Jackson, backed in the Senate by Daniel Webster. It was as the heir of Madison, Jackson, Webster (and others) that Lincoln compounded his constitutional doctrine. Lincoln's genius proved itself less by its originality than by the ability to reduce a complex matter to its essentials, and to express those essentials in profound and memorable prose. The essence of a constitutional regime, according to Lincoln, was that it was based upon the consent of the governed. And the consent of the governed was required, because "all men are created equal." In 1964, Wills rejected Lincolnian constitutionalism because (like the Declaration) it was rational. In 1978, he rejects it because it is based upon an allegedly mistaken understanding of the Declaration. In *Inventing America*, he will undercut what Lincoln has made of the Declaration, by unleashing a barrage of fanciful scholarship designed to transform the Declaration's lucid doctrine of self-evident truths into esoteric eighteenth century mysteries.

Wills's 1964 essay follows the conventional path of Confederate apologists since the Civil War (and Wills is a native of Atlanta). He tries to make it appear that, on the one hand, Lincoln's war was an abolitionist crusade and, on the other, that the South was defending, not slavery, but constitutionalism. Nothing could be further from the truth. As we shall presently see, however, *Inventing America* is less a book about Thomas Jefferson and the Declaration of Independence, than it is a book against Abraham Lincoln and the Gettysburg Address.

* * *

Let us here make the record straight, as against the 1964 Garry Wills and his preceptors of the Right, as to what purposes were in conflict, that led to the Civil War, or the War for the Union. (It was not a War between the States.) First of all, there was no disagreement between Abraham Lincoln and the followers of John C. Calhoun that slavery was a lawful institution in some fifteen of the States. Moreover, it was agreed that where slavery was lawful, it was under the exclusive control of the States, and that the federal government had no jurisdiction over it. In his inaugural address, Lincoln quoted from a statement he had made many times before, in which he said that he had "no purpose, directly or indirectly, to interfere with the institution of slavery in the States where it exists." He said that he believed that he had "no lawful right to do so," and added that he "had no inclination to do so." Lincoln's anti-slavery policy was comprehended completely by his avowed purpose to have excluded slavery, by federal law, from the national territories, where it had not already established itself. It is true that Lincoln believed, as, indeed, his pro-slavery antagonists believed, that slavery as an institution in the United States was highly volatile, and that if its expansion were prevented, its contraction would set in. And, it was further believed—on both sides—that if contraction once set in, slavery would be, in Lincoln's words, "in course of ultimate extinction."

Lincoln believed that, in the understanding of the Founding Fathers, slavery was an evil. It was an evil condemned by the principles of the Declaration, which Lincoln called "the father of all moral principle among us." It was an evil to which certain constitutional guarantees were given, in the political arrangements of the Founding, because at the time there did not appear to be any alternative arrangements which would not have been disruptive of the Union. Yet the Fathers showed their opposition to its perpetuation in various ways: by the limit placed upon the foreign slave trade, and by the prohibition upon slavery in the Northwest Territory, among others. They had left the institution of slavery where, to repeat, "the public mind might rest in the belief that it was in course of ultimate extinction." Such a belief, Lincoln held, was absolutely necessary, if the slavery question were not to agitate the public mind, and threaten the perpetuity of the Union. Yet the expectations of the Fathers had been upset: by the invention of the cotton gin, by the progress of the factory system, by the enormous expansion of the cotton economy, and with the latter, the expansion of the demand for slave labor. These changes culminated, in time, in the most sinister change of all: that change in at least a part of the public mind which, from regarding slavery as at best a necessary evil, now began to look upon it as a positive good. With this, slavery sought expansion into new lands: into the lands acquired from France in 1803 (the Louisiana Purchase), and into the lands acquired from Mexico as a result of the war that ended in 1848. To prevent this *expansion* of slavery, the Republican Party was formed in 1854, and, in 1860, elected Abraham Lincoln to be sixteenth President of the United States.

The great ante-bellum political question, the one that dwarfed and absorbed all others, was the question of whether slavery should be permitted in the territories of the United States, *while* they were territories, and *before* they became states. The dialectics of this dispute became as complicated as any thirteenth century theological controversy. Yet in the end the legal and political questions resolved themselves into moral questions, and the moral questions into a question of both the meaning and the authority of the Declaration of Independence. The Constitution itself was ambiguous—if not actually self-contradictory—as to whether Negro slaves were human persons or chattels. In fact, the Constitution refers to slaves (which are never explicitly mentioned before the Thirteenth Amendment) only as persons, even in the fugitive slave clause. But by implication, it also refers to them as chattels, since they were so regarded by the laws of the states that the fugitive slave clause recognized. But the logic of the idea of a chattel excludes that of personality, while that of a person excludes that of chatteldom. The Fifth Amendment of the Constitution forbade the United States to deprive any person of life, liberty, or property, except by due process of law. Did this forbid the United States to deprive any citizen of a slave state of his Negro chattel, when he entered the territory of Kansas? Or did it forbid the United States to deprive any Negro person of his liberty, when he entered that same territory? Since the language of the Constitution was equally consistent with two mutually exclusive interpretations, there was no way to restore the meaning of the Constitution, from the language of the Constitution alone. For Lincoln the question was resolved by the Declaration of Independence, by the proposition that all men are created equal. The right of persons to own property under the Constitution as under "the laws of nature and of nature's God," was derivative from their right, as human beings, to life and to liberty. Such an understanding of the Declaration alone gave life and meaning to the Constitution. Wills, in "The Convenient State," repudiates the Declaration. In *Inventing America*, he denies that it has any such meaning as Lincoln found in it. In the course of denying that meaning, he denies some of the most undeniable facts of American history.

* * *

It was not possible, in the free states of the ante-bellum United States, for public opinion to acquiesce in the proposition that slavery was in itself neither good nor evil, and that it was best to leave to the people of a territory the decision whether they should permit slavery as one of their domestic institutions. This was the famous doctrine of "popular sovereignty," advanced by Lincoln's redoubtable opponent, Stephen A. Douglas. Douglas's doctrine was both appealing and plausible, since it seemed to rest upon and embody the very kernel of the idea of popular self-government, that "the people shall be judge." Here is how Lincoln dealt with it. The following is from Lincoln's Peoria speech, of October 1854:

> *The doctrine of self-government is right—absolutely and eternally right—but it has no just application as here attempted. Or perhaps I should rather say that whether it has such application depends upon whether a negro is not or is a man. If he is not a man, why in that case, he who is a man may, as a matter of self-government, do just as he pleases with him. But if the negro is a man, is it not to that extent a total destruction of self-government, to say that he too shall not govern himself? When the white man governs himself that is self-government; but when he governs himself, and also governs another man, that is more than self-government—that is despotism. If the negro is a man, why then my ancient faith teaches me that "all men are created equal;" and that there can be no moral right in connection with one man's making a slave of another.* [All emphasis is Lincoln's.]

I have quoted so much of classic Lincolniana here, to bring before the reader an example of that reasoning that Garry Wills dismisses and ridicules. For Lincoln, of course, the article of his "ancient faith" was such, not because it was inherited, but because it was true. *Inventing America* was written for no other reason than to obfuscate and deny what Lincoln here affirmed. The Declaration, Wills writes, "is written in the lost language of the Enlightenment." "It is dark with unexamined lights." It embodies "the dry intellectual formulae of the eighteenth century" which according to Wills "were traced in fine acids of doubt, leaving them difficult to decipher across the intervals of time and fashion." Wills does not think that Lincoln—like Calhoun—was a political thinker of any substance. Rather was he "the great artist of America's romantic period." By his "democratic-oracular tone" he invested the Declaration with a meaning that the Gettysburg Address canonized, but which has nothing in common with the document drafted by Thomas Jefferson in 1776!

The Civil War was not, however, fought because of any merely abstract moral judgment concerning the ethics of treating human beings as chattels. It was fought because eleven states of the Union "seceded," meaning that they repudiated and took arms against the Constitution and the laws of the United States. They did so because they refused to accept the lawful election of a President who believed that slavery ought to be excluded by law from United States territories. (The President, by himself, had no authority to accomplish that exclusion. Nor was there a majority in Congress to pass such a law, before the representatives of the "seceding" states left Washington.) Slavery was, in fact, abolished as a result of the Civil War. This abolition was accomplished, in part, by the Emancipation Proclamation. It was consummated by the Thirteenth Amendment. The former was a war measure, aimed at the property of the enemies of the United States, in arms against the United States. But we cannot forget that the destruction of property by the Proclamation had a double effect, due to the peculiarity of the "peculiar institution" at which it was directed. By the laws governing this institution, certain human beings were legally defined as chattels. Interestingly, the root meaning of both "peculiar" and of "chattel" refers to "cattle." But some eighty-six thousand of these human beings who had hitherto been regarded by law as no more than cattle enlisted and fought in the Union armies, many of them sealing with their blood their right to that freedom that the Declaration of Independence had proclaimed to be the universal birthright of mankind. Nevertheless, the Civil War was not, we repeat, an abolitionist crusade. It was a war to preserve the Union, to prove that there could not be a successful appeal, as Lincoln said, from ballots to bullets. Emancipation and abolition became, in the course of the war, and because of the war, indispensable constitutional means to a constitutional end. Let us never forget this just but tragic consummation of our history: that men who had been called cattle proved their manhood in arms, and provided indispensable help to save a Union which thereby became theirs. They also vindicated the Declaration of Independence, by proving that human laws which rest upon a denial of the laws of nature cannot long endure. The Union endured, but only by repudiating that denial and becoming a different Union. The original Union—or nation—embodied the Original Sin of human slavery. Without "a new birth of freedom" it must needs have perished from the earth. It is this understanding of the Declaration of Independence, in the light of what "fourscore and seven years" had revealed as to its meaning, that is immortalized by the Gettysburg Address, but that *Inventing America* maliciously attacks.

* * *

When Wills wrote in 1964 that in a constitutional regime "the free forms of society ... 'concur' in ... peaceful cooperation and compromise," he was using Calhounian Confederate code language, implying the rightfulness and constitutionality of "secession." Conversely, he was implying the wrongfulness and unconstitutionality of Lincoln's executive action to preserve the Constitution and the Union. But what was this vaunted "right of secession"? Lincoln called it an "ingenious sophism" according to which "any State of the Union may, *consistently* with the national Constitution, and therefore *lawfully* and *peacefully*, withdraw from the Union without the consent of the Union or of any other State." [Lincoln's emphasis.] But, Lincoln asked, if one can reject the constitutional decision of a constitutional majority, whenever one dislikes that decision, how can there be any free government at all? Unanimity is impossible. Government that is both constitutional and popular also becomes impossible, if the principle of "secession" is once granted. With what right, Lincoln asked, can the seceders deny the right of secession against themselves, if a discontented minority should arise amongst them?

In 1848 Henry David Thoreau published his essay, "Civil Disobedience." At the same time, Thoreau called for the secession of Massachusetts from the Union. He adopted the pattern of abolitionists generally, who declared that there should be "No Union with slaveholders." Thus Thoreau invoked an alleged right of secession *against* slavery, as Calhoun's followers would invoke it for *the sake of* slavery. But Thoreau brushed aside any such notion as that of the "concurrent majority" in Calhoun's sense. Thoreau saw quite clearly that the argument of a minority veto upon majority action, in any matter of interest that could be called one of conscience, did not admit of any stopping point, short of the minority of one. Thoreau declared frankly that, although he preferred "that government ... which governs least," he would not be satisfied except with that government "which governs not at all." Thoreau believed in the withering away of the state quite as much as Karl Marx, and saw the best regime as an anarchist regime, also quite as much as Marx. But Lincoln, in 1861, showed by unrefutable logic that Calhoun's premises led to Thoreau's conclusions. In short, despotism leads to anarchy, as surely as anarchy leads to despotism. The Garry Wills of 1964 defended despotism. In the later sixties and early seventies, Garry Wills joined those who were protesting and demonstrating in behalf of their Thoreauian consciences, in behalf of those causes which, in the name of conscience, would arrest the process of constitutional government.

But the earlier Wills and the later Wills are like two segments of the same circle. Each leads into the other: like anarchy and despotism.

* * *

If the earlier Wills differs from the later one, as John C. Calhoun differs from Henry David Thoreau, so also do the two "Willses" differ as George Fitzhugh and Karl Marx. Fitzhugh (1806-1881), after the death of Calhoun in 1850, became the leading publicist and intellectual protagonist of the thesis that slavery was a positive good. Of all the pro-slavery writers, none roused the anger of Abraham Lincoln more than he did. Yet Lincoln viewed Fitzhugh's argument with a certain grim satisfaction, since it arrived at the conclusion that Lincoln always insisted followed from the pro-slavery premises: namely, that if slavery was a positive good for black men, then it must also be good for white men. Calhoun had already argued that, in the burgeoning conflict in the industrial North between capital and labor, the South, with its stability rooted in chattel slavery, would be the force making for equilibrium between the two great factions. Fitzhugh went a step farther: only by the enslavement of the white work force, could the North achieve that equilibrium. By way of contrast, Lincoln declared, in March, 1860, "I am glad to know there is a system of labor where the laborer can strike if he wants to! I would to God that such a system prevailed all over the world."

It is a matter of the highest moment for students of the political scene today, to understand that what is now called Conservatism, and what is now called Liberalism (although neither is properly so called), have their common ground in the rejection of the principles of the American Founding, above all in the rejection of the principles of the Declaration of Independence. On both sides, there is a peculiar hatred of Abraham Lincoln, because of the renewed vitality he gave to the authority of the Declaration, in and through the Gettysburg Address. The Liberalism of today—or, more properly the Radical Liberalism of today—stems largely from the Abolitionism of the ante-bellum North (not to mention its successor in the Reconstruction era). And the abolitionist critique of Northern free society, and the critique by Fitzhugh and his pro-slavery coadjutors of that same free society, were not only virtually identical, but were hardly distinguishable from the Marxist critique of capitalism.

Anyone today reading the pro-slavery literature of the ante-bellum South, must be struck by the constant reference to Northern workers as "wage slaves." Indeed, if someone reading these tracts did not know where they came from, and when, he might reasonably suppose that they were written by Marxists of a later period, or even by Bolsheviks. The general argument against Northern capitalism—which as we noted was shared with the Abolitionists—ran as follows. The "free workers" depended upon the owners for their livelihood. But the owners employed them only when they could make a profit from their labor. There was no provision for the workers during the slack periods of business; but neither was there provision for them when they were too young, too old, too sick, too feeble, or too handicapped to be profitably employed. In these respects, Fitzhugh (and all the other defenders of slavery) argued, slavery, with its traditions of paternalism and patriarchalism, with its ethics of responsibility for masters no less than of obedience for slaves, was morally as well as economically superior. Thus Fitzhugh, at the end of *Cannibals All!* (1857) addresses the Abolitionists as follows. (In today's parlance, a Conservative addressing a Radical Liberal, or Garry Wills, vintage 1964, addressing Garry Wills, vintage 1978):

> *As we are a Brother Socialist, we have a right to prescribe for the patient; and our Consulting Brethren, Messrs. Garrison, Greeley, and others, should duly consider the value of our opinion. Extremes meet—and we and the leading abolitionists differ but a hairbreadth. We...prescribe more of government; they insist on No-Government. Yet their social institutions would make excellently conducted Southern sugar and cotton farms, with a head to govern them. Add a Virginia overseer to Mr. Greeley's Phalansteries, and Mr. Greeley and we would have little to quarrel about.*

Extremes do indeed meet. "Phalansteries" were the Fourierist anticipation of the later and better known "communes" and "soviets." Nearly a century before Hayek's *Road to Serfdom*, Fitzhugh saw with perfect clarity the inner identity of the slave system and a socialist system.

*   *   *

Today it seems as if Conservatism is wedded to the free market economy. But that is true only on the surface. Garry Wills deserted Conservatism rather than embrace the free market. Others embraced the free market, rather than submit themselves to the authoritarianism of the Left. But Conservatives who embrace the free market, not as Abraham Lincoln did, because it implements the moral principles of the Declaration of Independence, but because it is "value free," are building their politics on that same "House Divided" as the ante-bellum Union. For a free market economy committed to nothing but "consumer sovereignty" does not differ essentially from a "popular sovereignty" that is free to choose slavery. Those who look backward to slavery, and those who look forward to the dictatorship of the proletariat, will always have the better of an argument founded upon "ethical neutrality." Critics of Marxism in our time, notably the patrons of the free market economy, constantly marvel at the survival of Marxism as an intellectual force (notably in the minds of college professors of the liberal arts). They marvel at the apparent immunity of Marxism to the disastrous fate of every single one of Marx's predictions, based upon his analysis of the dynamics of capitalism. And this, moreover, despite his claim of "scientific" status for his analysis, and his staking of his claim to that status upon the verification of these same predictions. But the magnetic core of Marxism, the source of the power of its attraction, consists not in its economic analysis, or its economic claims, but in its moral analysis, and in its moral claims. What follows is a representative passage from the *Manifesto*:

> *The bourgeoisie, wherever it has got the upper hand, has put an end to all feudal, patriarchal, idyllic relations. It has pitilessly torn asunder the motley feudal ties that bound man to his "natural superiors."*

We noted earlier the denigration of reason, and the elevation of sentiment, that characterized the radical thought—equally of the Left and the Right—of the nineteenth century. Capitalism, Marx declared, reduces all human relations to "the naked cash nexus." It is this "nakedness," this reduction of man to a "commodity," which "alienates" him and leaves him feeling alone in a world without meaning. It is Marxism's promise to restore "community" (where all men will be "comrades"), that is the source of that magnetism to which we have adverted. No promise of wealth to mere "individuals" by a market economy can possibly compete for long with this secularization of Christian eschatology. But Marx's communist moral vision is itself adapted from the moral vision of the *ancien regime* that we find in Edmund Burke. From the standpoint of historical dialectics, it is true that the bourgeois regime is "progressive" compared with its predecessor. That is because, in stripping away "illusions," it prepared the way for the revolution of the proletariat. Intrinsically, however, the *ancien regime* is more humanly desirable, even to Marx, because these self-same illusions made man at home in his world. Men are not as "alienated" under feudalism as they are under capitalism. For in the *ancien regime* there is the illusion that, in being governed by his "natural superiors" the superiors and inferiors are joined together in "community," an organic relationship in which the whole gives independent meaning to each of its human parts. In the meaning that the proletarian whole gives to the lives of each of the comrades, it resembles the feudal order. This is why R. H. Tawney —himself a socialist—could remark, with profound insight, that "the last of the Schoolmen was Karl Marx." Both feudalism and communism see themselves as bonded into a community, which is denied to man in "the lonely crowd" of the de-humanized bourgeois-capitalistic order.

* * *

Here is how Burke's romantic imagination dignified the morality of inequality of the *ancien regime*. Here, in truth, is the inspiration of Marx's moral imagination. What follows are excerpts from the *Reflections on the Revolution in France*:

It is now sixteen or seventeen years, since I saw the Queen of France, then the Dauphiness ... and surely never lighted on this orb, which she hardly seemed to touch, a more delightful vision....

Little did I dream that I should have lived to see such disasters fallen upon her in a nation of gallant men. ... I thought ten thousand swords must have leaped from their scabbards to avenge even a look that threatened her with insult. But the age of chivalry is gone. That of sophisters, economists, and caluclators has succeeded; and the glory of Europe is extinguished forever. ...

All the pleasing illusions ... are to be dissolved by this conquering empire of light and reason. All the decent drapery of life is to be rudely torn off. All the superadded ideas, furnished from the wardrobe of a moral imagination, which the heart owns and the understanding ratifies, as necessary to cover the defects of our naked, shivering nature ... are to be exploded. ...

On this scheme of things, a king is but a man, a queen is but a woman....

In another famous line, Burke also spoke of that "dignified obedience, that subordination of the heart, which kept alive, even in servitude itself, the spirit of an exalted freedom." Here was the very spiritual charter or gospel of the Confederacy, in building a polity upon chattel slavery. For make no mistake, it was this spiritual justification of the *ancien regime* that became the ideology of the Holy Alliance, and that served the cause of American slavery, when it came across the seas. For the "exalted freedom" of the slaves was compared, to its disadvantage, with the debased freedom of the "wage slaves" of the bourgeois order. How these "superadded ideas" appeared to the leaders of the American Revolution, may be inferred from what Washington wrote in 1783:

The foundation of our empire was not laid in the gloomy ages of ignorance and superstition; but at an epoch when the rights of mankind were better understood and more clearly defined, than at any other period.

Everyone knows that Karl Marx called revealed religion "the opiate of the people." But Marx's critique of Christianity, the very foundation of his system, also had its luminous antecedent in Burke. Here is what Burke wrote, in the *Reflections*, before Marx was born:

The body of the people ... must respect that property of which they cannot partake. They must labor to obtain what by labor can be obtained; and when they find, as they commonly do, the success disproportioned to the endeavor, they must be taught their consolation in the final proportions of eternal justice. Of this consolation, whoever deprives them, deadens their industry, and strikes at the root of all acquisition as of all conservation.

To convert Burkean Conservatism into Revolutionary Communism, all that was necessary was to declare that the disproportion between labor's endeavor and labor's success was the "surplus value" appropriated by the owning classes. To make the proletariat revolutionary, it was necessary to deprive them of that meretricious consolation in the "final proportions of eternal justice." Marx did not state more clearly than Burke the utility of revealed religion for maintaining a regime of unmerited privilege.

* * *

It is desirable here to compare the proto-Marxism of Burke, and the Marxism of Marx, with Abraham Lincoln. Here is how Lincoln teaches respect for private property:

> *Let not him who is houseless pull down the house of another, but let him work diligently and build one for himself, thus by example assuring that his own shall be safe from violence when built.*

Concerning the priority of labor to capital, Lincoln was as emphatic as Marx:

> *Labor is prior to and independent of capital. Capital is only the fruit of labor; and could not exist if labor had not first existed. Labor is the superior of capital and deserves much the higher consideration.* [Nevertheless] *Capital has its rights, which are as worthy of protection as any other rights. . . .*

What the rights of Capital are, is seen in the following:

> *That men who are industrious and sober and honest in the pursuit of their own interests should after a while accumulate capital, and after that should be allowed to enjoy it in peace, and ... to use it to save themselves actual labor, and hire other people to labor for them is right.*

The common ground of Burke and Marx is the idea that morality—whether illusory or real—is ineluctably grounded in stratified and invincible class distinctions. For Burke, this stratification follows the arbitrary lines of the feudal regime. It requires, in the name of the myths of such a regime, an unequal distribution of the rewards of life, along the lines of class and caste. Yet the proletarian society of the future—the classless society of Marx—is nothing but a mirror image of that very same feudalism. For it is as arbitrary in its commitment to an equal distribution of the rewards of life, as the other is to an unequal distribution. For arbitrary equality—that is to say, giving equal rewards to unequal persons—is as unjust as unequal rewards to equal persons. Both are equally unjust, *for the same reasons.* The regime of the American Founding, however imperfect the implementation of its principles, is in its principles the perfectly just middle way between these two extremes. As a regime of equal *rights*, it recognizes the justice of unequal *rewards*. There is, said James Madison, "a diversity in the faculties of men from which the rights of property originate." "The protection of these faculties," he added, "is the first object of government." Because of this equal protection of unequal faculties, wealth accumulates and social classes become distinguishable. But neither accumulations of wealth, nor social classes, are fixed in any immutable pattern. As Lincoln declared, on one of many similar occasions,

> There is no permanent class of hired laborers among us. Twenty-five years ago I was a hired laborer. The hired laborer of yesterday labors on his own account today, and will hire others to labor for him tomorrow.

And again:

> The progress by which the poor, honest, industrious and resolute man raises himself ... is that progress that human nature is entitled to [and] is that improvement in condition that is intended to be secured by those institutions under which we live....

It is this *moral* vindication of the "bourgeois" regime, as the regime which is truly in accord with human nature, that makes Abraham Lincoln, and his interpretation of the Declaration of Independence, that "hard nut" that the tyrannies of both Right and Left must crack, to establish their sway and domination. It explains the extraordinary efforts in *Inventing America*, of that symbol of the union of Left and Right: Garry Wills.

* * *

Inventing America begins in this way:

> Americans like, at intervals, to play this dirty trick upon themselves: Pollsters are sent out to canvass men and women on certain doctrines and to shame them when these are declared—as usually happens—unacceptable. Shortly after, the results are published: Americans have, once again, failed to subscribe to some phrase or other from the Declaration of Independence. The late political scientist Willmoore Kendall called this game "discovering America." He meant to remind us that running men out of town on a rail is at least as much an American tradition as declaring unalienable rights.

But Wills is not accurate even in this reference to Kendall. The game Wills calls "discovering America" is called by Kendall "Sam Stouffer discovers America," and may be found described in pages 80 and 81 of *The Conservative Affirmation*. It is Kendall's commentary on a book by Stouffer published in the early fifties under the title of *Civil Liberties, Communism, and Conformity.* It is one of the "classic" liberal attacks on the reactionary public opinion of the so-called McCarthy era; and one should bear in mind that Kendall was one of McCarthy's staunchest defenders. Hence Kendall's testimony is unusual, in this context, for a *guru* of the Left to take as his authority! Here is how Kendall actually described Stouffer's book:

> *Mr. Stouffer and his team of researchers asked a representative sample of Americans a number of questions calculated to find out whether they would permit (a) a Communist, or (b) an atheist, to (1) speak in their local community, or (2) teach in their local high school, or (3) be represented, by means of a book he had written, in their local public library. And consider: some two-thirds of the sample answered "Nothing doing" right straight down the line ... nor was there any evidence that they would have been much disturbed to learn that the Supreme Court says that the Fourteenth Amendment says they can't do anything legally to (e.g.) prevent the Communist from speaking.*

In the poll conducted by Stouffer there is, we see, literally nothing about the Declaration of Independence. What Kendall observes the American people saying "Nothing doing" to—at the period in question—is what the Warren Court (not the Declaration) was saying in interpreting the First and Fourteenth Amendments. And on this point I think the American people (thus polled) were right, and the Court wrong. In 1964 I myself published an essay "On the Nature of Civil and Religious Liberty" in which I argued that precisely on the ground of the principles of the Declaration, Communists and Nazis had no just claim to the constitutional privileges of the First Amendment. Moreover, I know of no such polls or studies, that Wills asserts exist, in which Americans have "failed to subscribe to some phrase or other from the Declaration of Independence."

In any event, it is not phrases that count, but ideas or principles. These must be stated in terms intelligible to the respondent. Perhaps the best known slogan of the American Revolution was "Taxation without Representation is Tyranny." In accordance with it, the Declaration denounced the King "For imposing taxes on us without our Consent." The premise underlying these judgments is that the power to tax is the power to destroy. Does Wills think that Americans today do *not* agree with these judgments or their underlying premise? The Declaration says that the just powers of government are derived from the consent of the governed. Suppose a pollster, asking whether the respondent thinks that any government that governed him, might do so justly without his consent. Does Wills believe that Americans today would answer differently from those in 1776? Does he think that they think that any government might justly levy taxes upon them—*or on anyone else*—without the consent, given by their elected representatives, of the ones taxed?

But perhaps Wills thinks that the arch mystery of the Declaration is the great proposition, upon which Lincoln so concentrated attention in the Gettysburg Address, that all men are created equal. Certainly many are today puzzled by this doctrine. This is not, I think, because of its intrinsic difficulty, but because publicists like Wills have for so long told them that it is a mere vague abstraction. But let us re-phrase the proposition, in some of its applications. Suppose, in conducting a poll, one asked whether the respondents thought it reasonable to divide all human beings (men and women) into the superior and the inferior, the latter to be ruled by the former, and without their consent? Or, to put the same question slightly differently, suppose one asked whether those who made the laws should live under them, or whether the government might reasonably and justly exempt itself from the laws it made for others. (One example might be whether the lawmakers might exempt themselves from the payment of taxes; another might be whether the punishments for either civil damage or criminal offenses might be different for those in office, as compared with those out of office.) How many today would reject Lincoln's simple maxim—interpreting the proposition that all men are created equal—that no man is good enough to govern another man without that other's consent?

All the foregoing questions are based upon that simplified Lockeanism that Jefferson thought was to be found in the American mind, no less than in the common sense of the subject. One need not have ever heard of the names of Hume or Hutcheson or Reid or Stewart—indeed one need not have heard of John Locke—to know that the power to tax is the power to destroy, and to draw all the long series of inferences that follow from it. Wills wants to turn the Declaration into an esoteric mystery, by convincing us that we do not know things that we know perfectly well. He would have us think that eighteenth century beliefs are necessarily different from twentieth century beliefs, and that the veil between them can be pierced only by the magic of the cultural (or professorial) elite. This is the priestcraft of our contemporary Dark Age.

To end this discussion, I would like to make one further comment on Kendall's assertion, endorsed by Wills, that

> *the true American tradition is less that of our Fourth of July orations and our constitutional law textbooks, with their cluck-clucking over the so-called preferred freedoms, than, quite simply, that of riding someone out of town on a rail.*

Note that even here Kendall says something different from what Wills represents him as saying. Kendall does not mention unalienable rights. The closest he comes to it is when he mentions Fourth of July orations. "Preferred freedoms" refers almost certainly to the constitutional doctrines of Mr. Justice Black, not to those of Thomas Jefferson, or of any other of the Founding Fathers. Yet Kendall here is in fact being squeamish, something certainly unusual for Kendall. Riding someone out of town on a rail is a quasi-euphemism for lynching. Someone—perhaps a specialist in Burlamaqui or Hutcheson —might not know that riding on a rail was usually preceded by tarring and feathering. And tarring frequently resulted in second (and sometimes third) degree burns. Since the tar covered the whole body, the minimum result was usually pneumonia. Not many more survived a tarring and feathering than survived a hanging. But it was a more protracted process, and accompanied by terrible suffering. In the thirty-third chapter of *Huckleberry Finn* we bid our farewell to the Duke and the King. These bunco artists have by now forfeited all of our — and Huck's — sympathy, by betraying Jim back into slavery. In their last appearance Huck sees them being whooped along by the townsmen they had cheated. Huck says he knew it was the Duke and the King,

> *though they was all over tar and feathers, and didn't look like nothing in the world that was human....*

Although he had loathed them before, and hates them now, he says that

> *It was a dreadful thing to see. Human beings can be awful cruel to one another.*

When Kendall or Wills tell us that lynching is as much an American tradition as declaring that there are unalienable, or natural human rights, they are telling us no more than that evil is as deeply engrained in the American tradition as good. This is a difficult proposition to contest. All that I would contend is that the principles of the Declaration, which embody the principles of the rule of law, stand in direct opposition to lynching, which is the denial or repudiation of lawfulness. And by a disposition of Providence, as poetical as it is historical, Abraham Lincoln's first great speech — his Lyceum Address of 1838 — was a denunciation of the growing and dangerous habit of lawlessness, which he observed to be abroad in the land then. In that speech, Lincoln warned that lynch law and free government were enemies of each other; and that one could not long survive in the presence of the other. Lynch law, we repeat, was but one expression of the repudiation of the Declaration of Independence. Slavery was another. Slavery and lynch law went together. Kendall's (and Wills's) tacit patronage of lynch law is but another aspect of their tacit patronage of slavery.

According to Wills, Abraham Lincoln was "a great artist of America's romantic period." This, however, is not intended as a compliment. Rather is it intended as an *a priori* explanation of how Lincoln was able to substitute a fallacious myth of our origins as a nation for the truth about those origins. Lincoln's artistry, he says, fits the antiscientific, biblical mood of mid-century, so that the "biblically shrouded" figure of "Four score and seven years..." presumably evoked acceptance, as "eighty-seven" might not. And Wills is not tender with Lincoln's character, in regard to this alleged deception about the date of the founding of the nation. "Useful falsehoods," he writes, "are dangerous things, often costing us down the road." The Gettysburg Address, beginning with its magisterial invocation of the year 1776 as the point of our origin as a nation, is a "falsehood," and even a "dangerous" one. Wills has summoned up a strict standard of truthfulness, by which he, no less than Abraham Lincoln, must then be judged.

Wills's entire work, as we shall see, actually stands or falls by this claim that 1776 is not, and cannot be regarded as, the birth date of the nation. Lincoln, he says, "obviously gave some thought" to his "Four score and seven." Indeed he did.

* * *

In *Crisis of the House Divided* I pointed out, more than a score of years ago, that the beginning of the Gettysburg Address marked as well the end of the long debate with Stephen A. Douglas. For Douglas had declared that we existed as a nation only by virtue of the Constitution. Notwithstanding the fact that, in other respects, Douglas was a Jacksonian Unionist, in this he echoes Southern—and Calhounian—doctrine. It was axiomatic for Jefferson Davis—and for all who voted for secession in the winter and spring of 1860-1861—that the United States could be regarded as a single nation, solely by virtue of the Constitution. Each state, it was held, became part of the Union or nation by virtue of the process of ratification. The ordinances of secession were regarded as—and in some cases were actually called—acts of de-ratification. And there can be no doubt that, were the Union or nation created solely by the process by which the Constitution of 1787 was ratified, then it could lawfully have been uncreated by the same process. Willmoore Kendall, whom Wills is obviously following, repeats this Confederate dogma, saying that there was a "baker's dozen" of new nations resulting from the Declaration of Independence. By this interpretation, in the Declaration of Independence the thirteen colonies were not only declaring their independence of Great Britain, they were declaring their independence *of each other*.

Wills thinks that Lincoln would have had some ground for treating 1777 as the year of birth of the nation, since in that year the Articles of Confederation were adopted. But best of all, as a proposed birth date, he thinks, is 1789, the year in which the Constitution came into operation. For this date, he says, Lincoln should have written "Four score minus six years ago. ..." With this ill-placed facetiousness Wills shows himself completely oblivious of the great ante-bellum debate. He seems unconscious of the existence of the masterful brief—legal, historical, and philosophical—that Lincoln presented, notably in his inaugural address, and still more copiously, after Sumter, in his message to Congress, in special session, July 4, 1861. Lincoln's argument, as to the nature and origin of the Union, is presented with Euclidean precision and classic beauty. It is surpassed by nothing in Demosthenes, Cicero, or Burke.

Wills writes as if Lincoln had suddenly invented the notion that the nation had been born in 1776 as he composed the Gettysburg Address, and that he relied upon the mesmerizing influence of his vowels and consonants (e.g. "by mere ripple and interplay of liquids") to secure his deception. But Lincoln's audience in 1863 and thereafter, unlike Wills, knew very well that the Gettysburg Address was but a moment in a dialectical process that had been going on for more than a generation. Neither Lincoln nor the nation ever imagined that he was appealing to their sentiment, apart from an argument, laid in fact and reason. It would have been perfectly honorable for Wills to have taken up the weapons of the controversy against Lincoln's side, as statesmen and scholars have done since the days of Calhoun, Jefferson Davis, and Alexander Stephens. But mere malicious sneering has no place in such a debate.

Wills tells us, with easy assurance, that "there are some fairly self-evident objections to that mode of calculating," viz., the mode expressed by "Four score and seven years ago. . . ." What are these objections?

> *All thirteen colonies* [writes Wills] *subscribed to the Declaration with instructions to their delegates that this was not to imply formation of a single nation. If anything, July 4, 1776, produced twelve new nations (with a thirteenth coming in on July 15) — conceived in liberty perhaps, but more dedicated to the proposition that the colonies they severed from the mother country were equal to each other than that their* inhabitants *were equal.* [Wills's emphasis.]

We note that Wills does not say that the delegates were not instructed to form a single nation. He says that they *were* instructed *not* to form (or imply formation of) a single nation. If Wills had said that the instructions for independence were in some cases ambiguous, as to whether the thirteen colonies were to form a single union, state, or nation, he would have asserted what would certainly have been plausible. But in positively asserting an unambiguous intention not to form a single nation, he is asserting something for which there is not a shred of evidence.

Not many readers will take the trouble to look up the colonial instructions to the delegates to the Continental Congress, in the spring of 1776. Like most reviewers, they will assume that someone with a prestigious professorship at a major university, with a doctorate from Yale (all things advertised on the dust jacket), will of course have read documents carefully, and reported them faithfully. Errors like Wills's, launched with such authority, spread like plague germs in an epidemic. And although it takes few words to put such errors in circulation, it takes painstaking effort, and detailed analysis, effectively to contradict them.

Turning now to the instructions, we note that they do not contain the word "nation" at all. The word "union" is its nearest equivalent. (We note also that in Lincoln's political vocabulary, the words "union" and "nation" were virtually synonymous.) In the instructions, the word "confederation" is also used in a sense, at least quasi-synonymous with "union."

The important question we must ask, in examining the language of the instructions for independence, is whether the colonies were, in making a single and common declaration of independence, implying or assuming or declaring that they did so as members of a common government. And further, we would want to know whether they implied or stated that they expected their association in and through the Congress to become a permanent one. An affirmative answer to these two questions is all that would be needed to sustain Lincoln's thesis with respect to the "Four score and seven years." Wills, we repeat, by asserting that in July of 1776 thirteen nations or states came into existence by virtue of the Declaration, asserts that the thirteen were not merely declaring their independence of Great Britain, but their independence *of each other*.

Rhode Island, by its General Assembly, on May 4, 1776, instructed its delegates

> *to join with the delegates of the other United Colonies in Congress ... to consult and advise ... upon the most proper measures for promoting and confirming the strictest union and confederation....*

Virginia's instructions — May 15th — called simply for such measures as might be thought proper and necessary

> *for forming foreign alliances, and a confederation of the colonies.*

Here "confederation" is synonymous with "union and confederation" in the Rhode Island instructions.

*   *   *

We should be aware, in reading these documents, that we are witnessing a transformation in the use and application of certain key terms. The word "confederation," like the words "federal" or "confederal," was an old bottle into which new wine was being poured. The American Revolution, and the American Founding, produced a form of government unprecedented in the history of the world. In later years, James Madison called the government of the United States a "nondescript," because there was still no word that properly expressed what it actually was. In 1787, in the *Federalist*, Madison called the government of the new Constitution, "partly national, partly federal," although by the traditional understanding of "federal" and "national" such an expression would have been a self-contradiction. As the late Martin Diamond has pointed out, the expression "federal government" would have been a solecism, prior to the emergence of the American form of government. What had hitherto been regarded as federal, could not properly be regarded as a government, and what had hitherto been regarded as government, could not properly admit any distinct or separate sovereignty in any of its parts. In these instructions we see an early application of "confederation" in a sense consistent with what was later understood clearly in the expression "federal government." It would be a mistake to assume that the later meaning was clearly present to the minds of the men of 1776. Yet it would be an equally great mistake to fail to perceive, in 1776, the genesis of the later meaning. Lincoln, one should remember, said that the nation had been born in 1776, he did not say it had already matured.

Connecticut, on June 14, 1776, instructed its delegates in Congress to

> *move and promote, as fast as may be convenient, a regular and permanent plan of union and confederation of the Colonies....*

New Jersey, on June 21st, called for

> *entering into a confederation for union and common defense....*

Maryland, on June 28th, in authorizing independence, also authorized

> *such further compact and confederation ... as shall be judged necessary for securing the liberties of America....*

Most extraordinary of all is the instruction of the House of Representatives of New Hampshire. For in this case, the instruction for independence and the instruction for union, given separately in the other cases, were here combined into one. New Hampshire instructed its (single) delegate

> *to join with the other colonies in declaring the thirteen United Colonies a free and independent state....*

Concerning what might justly be called the burgeoning national consciousness, consider the language with which the Georgia Colonial Congress addressed its delegates in the Continental Congress, in April of 1776. They exhorted their representatives that they

> *always keep in view the general utility, remembering that the great and righteous cause in which we are engaged is not provincial, but continental. We therefore, gentlemen, shall rely upon your patriotism, abilities, firmness, and integrity, to propose, join, and concur in all such measures as you shall think calculated for the common good, and to oppose all such as appear destructive.*

We see the coordination of "patriotism" with the "common good," and that this good is said to be "continental" and not "provincial." Can anyone, reading these words, think that in 1776 Georgia (any more than New Hampshire) was engaged in declaring its independence from its sister colonies?

* * *

Let us ask what could lie behind Wills's assertion about these colonial instructions. It is certainly true that the full implications of single statehood, or union, or nationhood, were not visible in 1776. And it is true that all of the colonies, while endorsing union in varying terms, nonetheless did so with reservation. For example, while calling for the formation of the "strictest union," Rhode Island required that the greatest care be taken

> *to secure to this colony ... its present established form, and all powers of government, so far as it related to its internal police and conduct of our own affairs, civil and religious.*

Virginia, in like manner, asked that

> *the power of forming government for, and the regulating of the internal concerns of, each colony, be left to the respective Colonial Legislatures.*

Pennsylvania required that there be reserved

> *to the people of this colony the sole and exclusive right of regulating the internal government and police of the same.*

And New Hampshire, the same New Hampshire which thought that the United Colonies should declare themselves a single "free and independent state," nonetheless required that

> *the regulation of our internal police be under the direction of our own Assembly.*

Could there be any clearer demonstration, than these words by which New Hampshire reserved its right of internal or local government, that such reservations did *not* constitute obstacles, in the minds of those making the reservations, to national unity?

These reservations of local or state autonomy represent, in generic form, the great principle of American federalism. They reappeared, the year following the Declaration, in the Articles of Confederation, in Article II, which reads as follows:

> *Each state retains its sovereignty, freedom, and independence, and every power, jurisdiction, and right, which is not expressly delegated to the United States, in Congress assembled.*

The Tenth Amendment to the Constitution contains a similar reservation of the "internal concerns" to the jurisdiction of the governments of the states—and to the people of the states—as is found in those colonial instructions of the spring of 1776. It reads:

> *The powers not delegated to the United States by the Constitution, nor prohibited by it to the States, are reserved to the States respectively, or to the people.*

The notable difference between these two articles is the presence of the words "sovereignty" and "expressly" in the former. But John Quincy Adams, among others, thought that the spirit of the Declaration (and of the instructions authorizing the Declaration) was stronger in the Constitution than in the Articles. The Tenth Amendment, by not referring to the powers delegated as being "expressly" delegated, opened the door to the great contest, begun by Hamilton and Jefferson, between liberal—or broad—construction, and strict—or narrow—construction, a contest which continues until this very day. But the ambiguity in the Constitution which permits two schools of constitutional interpretation is not different from the ambiguity in the original instructions for forming a union. If that ambiguity is regarded as militating against the formation of a national union, then we are no more a nation today than we were on July 4, 1776.

Wills, we have noted, denies any credibility to Lincoln's character-ization, in the Gettysburg Address, of July 4, 1776, as the birth date of the nation. We have seen that his alleged grounds for this denial, the colonial instructions to the delegates to the Continental Congress in the spring of 1776, do not bear out what he says about them. But Edmund Morgan, writing in *The New York Review of Books*, August 17, 1978, in a generally favorable notice of *Inventing America*, has pointed to a very good test of single statehood in the Declaration itself. For the Declaration reads, near the end, as follows:

> *That these United Colonies are, and of right ought to be Free and Independent States ... and that as Free and Independent States, they have full power to levy War, conclude Peace, contract Alliances, establish Commerce, and do all other Acts and Things which Independent States may of right do.*

"Which of these free and independent states," asks Morgan, "undertook to do the acts and things Jefferson specified as characteristic of a state?"

> *It was Congress* [Morgan continues] *that levied war through the Continental Army; it was Congress that concluded peace through its appointed commissioners; and it was Congress that contracted the alliance with France. Congress may not have established commerce, but in the Association it had disestablished it, and in a resolution of the preceding April 6, it had opened American ports to all the world except England.*

In denying that there was "one nation" or anything like it, resulting from the Declaration of Independence, Wills makes the extraordinary assertion that the Declaration is not a legal document of any kind. He calls it and the Gettysburg Address mere "war propaganda with no legal force."

Now the Gettysburg Address was an occasional address of the President of the United States. Its force, as such, was moral rather than legal. Its chief feature, however, was to reaffirm the principles of the Declaration, and to reaffirm them in conjunction with another Presidential act, namely, the Emancipation Proclamation. The latter of course *was* a legal act, although its permanent force depended upon the adoption of the Thirteenth Amendment. The purpose of the Gettysburg Address was to help to generate the political forces which would lead the nation from the Emancipation Proclamation —whose legal effect was limited to what could be inferred from the war powers of the Commander-in-Chief— to that permanent abolition of chattel slavery that could only be accomplished by an amendment to the Constitution. It is that fulfillment of the promise of equal human rights by the Declaration, in the Thirteenth Amendment, that constitutes the "new birth of freedom" wished for by the Address. If Wills regards this as mere "war propaganda" then he can have little regard for the abolition of slavery as an event in American history.

To assert, as Wills does, that the Declaration of Independence is not a legal document, is simply amazing. It is among the more stupendous reasons why we think that *Inventing America* should have been shipped back to its author in manuscript. Evidently Wills—and the readers of his manuscript—have never held in their hands the Statutes at Large of the United States, the Revised Statutes of the United States, or the United States Code. The 1970 edition of the United States Code, which is before me as I write, classifies the Declaration among the "Organic Laws of the United States." Of these, the Declaration of Independence is the first. Second is the Articles of Confederation. Third is the Ordinance of 1787: The Northwest Territorial Government. Fourth is the Constitution of the United States and Amendments.

Let us recall that Wills preferred both the Articles and the Constitution to the Declaration, as marking the beginning of American statehood or nationhood. But the Articles declares, in its preamble, that it was done "in the second year of the Independence of America." Moreover, the Constitution, in the form in which it left the Convention, over the signature of George Washington, dates itself

> in the Year of our Lord one thousand seven hundred and Eighty seven and of the Independence of the United States of America the Twelfth.

Both these notable documents—which Wills thinks Lincoln should have preferred to the Declaration—themselves refer to the Declaration as the originating document of the United States.

This dating of the union, at the end of Article VII of the Constitution, has moreover a particular legal application. Article VI reads, in its first paragraph, that

> *All debts contracted and engagements entered into, before the adoption of this Constitution, shall be as valid against the United States under this Constitution, as under the Confederation.*

From the foregoing, it is clear that there was a "United States under the Confederation" before there was a "United States under this Constitution." The fact that the United States in its subsequent form (that of "a more perfect Union") acknowledges the debts of the earlier United States, shows that it remains the same moral person. But Article XII of the Articles of Confederation accepts responsibility for the debts contracted by the Congress before the adoption of the Articles, just as the Constitution accepts the debts of the government of the Confederation. In short, the United States is continuously the United States, is continuously the same collective identity, the same moral agent, from the moment that it became independent, viz., since July 4, 1776.

In what sense then is the Declaration of Independence a law of the United States; or, rather, in what sense is it the first of the organic laws of the United States? The United States Code does not say. In 1825, however, Thomas Jefferson and James Madison, both members of the Board of Visitors of the University of Virginia, together prepared a list of books and documents to serve as authorities for the instruction to be offered by the faculty of law. On "the distinctive principles of government of our State, and of that of the United States," they wrote, the first of the "best guides" to this end was

> *The Declaration of Independence, as the fundamental act of union of these States.*

We see then that the Declaration was not regarded by Jefferson and Madison, as it is by Wills (and Kendall), as an act whose sole effect was to *separate* thirteen colonies from Great Britain. It was an act whereby the *separation* from Great Britain was simultaneously accompanied by *union* with each other. It was the accomplishment of *union* that makes it the primitive organic law of the United States. This is why all acts of the United States are dated from the Declaration.

But the Declaration is more even than an organic law. Its statement of principles remains that statement of the principles of natural right and of natural law which is the ground for asserting that the government of the United States (and of each of the States) represents law and right, and not mere force without law or right.

In 1844, for example, in a great speech in the House of Representatives,

John Quincy Adams declared that the assertion of principles in the Declaration of Independence, beginning with the proposition that "we hold these truths to be self-evident ..." constituted the "moral foundation of the North American Revolution." It was, he said, "the only foundation upon which the North American Revolution could be justified from the charge of treason and rebellion."

But Wills hates the very idea that the United States was born out of a dedication to liberty and justice. For him, the belief that our political arrangements are in some particular sense in accordance with universal principles of natural right, breeds only a sense of self-righteousness, and makes us a danger to ourselves and to others. As an example of the latter, he cites John F. Kennedy's alleged willingness "to throw Communist devils out of Russia, China, Cuba, or Vietnam." As an example of the former, he cites "the House Un-American Activities Committee"!

In 1823, Jefferson, writing to Madison on August 30th, referred to a meeting that had taken place the previous month as an anniversary assemblage of the nation on its birthday. When Jefferson thus referred to July 4th as the nation's birthday, Abraham Lincoln was fourteen years old. By this time, such references to the Glorious Fourth were traditional and customary. No one seemed to doubt then that the principles that accompanied our beginnings were as luminous as they were true. It was some years later that men began to discover the "positive good" of slavery, and to mutter that the so-called self-evident truths might after all be self-evident lies. Then was the foundation laid for Garry Wills's discovery that the Declaration was, after all, written in "the lost language of the Enlightenment."

* * *

Wills contends that the major influence upon Jefferson, and upon the writing of the Declaration, was not John Locke, but Francis Hutcheson. Hutcheson was a Scottish philosopher who wrote a generation or so after Locke. The dates of his books, as given by Wills, are from 1725 to 1755. Locke died in 1704. Indeed, the principal explicit thesis of *Inventing America* is that the Declaration is an Hutchesonian and not a Lockean document. Wills's principal antagonist, within these lists of controversy, is Carl Becker. Becker's *The Declaration of Independence*, published in 1922, has long been regarded as a classic. And in certain respects, its authority—as Wills notes—has gone unchallenged. We would note that Becker was himself an historicist and a relativist, and as such took no more seriously than Wills the Declaration's assertion (in Lincoln's words) "of an abstract truth, applicable to all men and all times." However, Wills cites one noted scholar after another, who has cited Becker, assimilated Becker, built on Becker. "The secret of this universal acclaim," writes Wills, *lies in the inability of any later student to challenge Becker's basic thesis — that Jefferson found in* John Locke *"the ideas which he put into the Declaration."* [Wills's italics.]

According to Wills, the thesis of a "Lockean orthodoxy . . . coloring all men's thought in the middle of the eighteenth century" is one which has not been challenged by "any later student." That is to say, it has not been challenged by a single student prior to Wills.

Wills's bold challenge to Beckerian — and all later — orthodoxy, concerning the Lockean orthodoxy of the American Founding, comes to a climax in Chapter 18. This chapter is prefaced by a paragraph from an influential pamphlet essay by James Wilson, first published in 1774. This passage from Wilson, says Wills, was used by Becker "to establish the orthodox Lockean nature of Jefferson's Declaration." Here it is, as it appears in *Inventing America.*

> *All men are, by nature, equal and free: no one has a right to any authority over another without his consent: all lawful government is founded on the consent of those who are subject to it: such consent was given with a view to ensure and to increase the happiness of the governed, above what they could enjoy in an independent and unconnected state of nature. The consequence is, that the happiness of the society is the* first *law of every government.* [*Wilson's emphasis.*]

Next, we will repeat what Wills says about this passage from Wilson's essay, and what he says about Becker's use of it. We give this paragraph from page 250 of *Inventing America* exactly as it appears there. If the reader finds the paragraph confusing, he must ask the apology of Wills. For Wills has the muddling and confusing habit of using no footnotes, but incorporating all his reference notes in parentheses within his text. As we shall presently see, however, Wills does not only not *use* footnotes, he does not know how to *read* them. Becker, says Wills,

> *calls the Wilson quote "a summary of Locke"* (Declaration, *108), part of America's common heritage of ideas. But if the idea was so common, why did Wilson give a* particular *source for it, and only* one? *Here is his own footnote to the passage (in his* Considerations on the Nature and Extent of the Legislative Authority of the British Parliament *of 1774): "The right to sovereignty is that of commanding finally — but in order to procure real felicity; for if this is not obtained, sovereignty ceases to be a legitimate authority, 2 Burl., 32, 33." He is quoting in summary Burlamaqui's* Principes du droit politique, *1, v, 1; 6 (* =Principes du droit naturel, *1, x, 2). Now Burlamaqui was a disciple of Hutcheson's philosophy of moral sense (*Naturel, *2, iii, 1) and therefore he differed from Locke on concepts of right (ibid., 1, v, 10) and property (1, iv, 8), of the social contract (1, iv, 9) and the state of nature (2, iv, 11). If Wilson*

meant to voice a Lockean view of government, as Becker assumed, he
clumsily chose the wrong source.

The unsuspecting reader, confronted by this witches' brew of scholarship, is apt to think that Carl Becker must certainly have been clumsy, and not James Wilson. And it would certainly seem as if a whole generation—or more—of scholars had followed Becker, "like sheep, through the gates of error." It takes two or three readings of this paragraph before one can accustom one's eyes to the forest of parentheses, and then slowly begin to distinguish the sentences within. This, however, is what can be seen at last. Wilson has quoted something in a footnote. At the end of the quotation, and within the quotation marks, he has given a source for that quotation. Wills calls the quotation "a summary" of a certain chapter in a book of Burlamaqui, which parallels another chapter in another book of Burlamaqui. Having read with some care both chapters in both books, I would call the quotation a paraphrase rather than a summary. But that is not important.

What is important is that Wilson does not present the paraphrase or summary of Burlamaqui as a source for what he himself has written. Wills's assertion that the passage from Burlamaqui is the "*particular* source" and the "only" source for Wilson's alleged "summary of Locke" is simply untrue. It is easier to see this if one has Wilson's essay before one, and if one sees the footnote separated from the text at the bottom of the page. Let us suppose, for example, that after saying that "all lawful government is founded on the consent of those who are subject to it" Wilson had appended this footnote: "'Our authority is his consent', Sh., 2 Hen. 6, 4, 1, 316." Would this have meant that Wilson had declared that the source of the idea expressed in the text was the second part of Shakespeare's *Henry VI*? Would it have meant more than that Wilson had found a felicitous expression of his thought in Shakespeare, and that such an expression lent a certain cogency or weight to what Wilson had said?

Wills's assertion that this note gives the "only" source of Wilson's thought, is all the more absurd because Wilson's essay has forty-eight separate footnotes. Some cite Blackstone, some cite Bolingbroke, but the majority refer to decisions of British courts, and opinions of British judges. As Becker rightly observes, the main point of Wilson's entire essay, is to show the close approximation of the principles of British constitutionalism to the principles of natural law. All of Wilson's footnotes are designed to confirm his judgments, not to give sources for his ideas. To repeat: the quotation in the footnote is a paraphrase of Burlamaqui. The reference to Burlamaqui is simply to give the source in Burlamaqui of the passages thus paraphrased. The reference then is to *the source of the footnote*, not to *the source of the text*. All that buckshot spray of alleged differences between Burlamaqui and Hutcheson, on the one hand, and Locke on the other, is simply pretentious nonsense. Wilson has throughout spoken in his own name, not in that of either Locke or Burlamaqui. That he has, in the main followed Locke, as Becker says, is not to be doubted on the basis of any evidence supplied by Wills.

* * *

In his anxiety to re-write the intellectual history of the American Founding, Wills goes to lengths of hyperbole and exaggeration which are inconsistent with serious scholarship. He says, for example, that there is "no demonstrable verbal echo of the *Treatise* [Locke's *Second Treatise of Government*] in all of Jefferson's vast body of writings." Against the many writers who have said that the Declaration repeats not only arguments, but even the phraseology of the *Second Treatise*, Wills airily asserts that "no precise verbal parallels have been adduced."

Wills, however, thinks that verbal parallels to the Declaration abound in Hutcheson. Here, for example, is a passage from Hutcheson, adduced by Wills as an example of the proximity of Hutcheson to the Jefferson of the Declaration:

> *Nor is it justifiable in a people to have recourse for any lighter causes to violence and civil wars against their rulers, while the public interests are tolerably secured and consulted. But when it is evident that the public liberty and safety is not tolerably secured, and that more mischiefs, and these of a more lasting kind, are like to arise from the continuance of any plan of civil power than are to be feared from the violent efforts for an alteration of it, then it becomes lawful, nay honorable, to make such efforts and change the plan of government.*

Here is the passage in the Declaration it is compared with:

> *Prudence indeed will dictate that governments long established should not be changed for light and transient causes; and accordingly all experience hath shown that mankind are more disposed to suffer while evils are sufferable than to right themselves by abolishing the forms to which they are accustomed.*

But here is what Locke, in the *Second Treatise* (para. 230) had written:

> *For till the mischief be grown general, and the ill designs of the Rulers become visible, or their attempts sensible to the greater part, the People, who are more disposed to suffer, than right themselves by Resistance, are not apt to stir.*

Who cannot see that the words of Locke are much closer to the words of Jefferson than those of Hutcheson? The phrases "disposed to suffer" and "right themselves" may or may not be echoes, but they are key phrases, and they are identical in Locke and Jefferson.

Here is another example of Hutcheson, provided by Wills:

> *A good subject ought to bear patiently many injuries done only to himself, rather than take arms against a prince in the main good and useful to the state, provided the danger extends only to himself. But when the common rights of humanity are trampled upon, and what at first attempted against one is made precedent against all the rest, then as the governor is plainly perfidious to his trust, he has forfeited all the power committed to him.*

Here is the parallel passage in the Declaration. This is from the Declaration in the draft originally reported, as distinguished from that finally adopted:

> *But when a long train of abuses and usurpations, begun at a distinguished period and pursuing invariably the same object, evinces a design to reduce them under absolute despotism it is their right, it is their duty, to throw off such government. . . .*

And here is Locke, in the parallel passage in the *Second Treatise.*

> *But if a long train of abuses, Prevarications, and Artifices, all tending the same way, make the design visible to the people, and they cannot but feel, what they lie under, and see, whither they are going; 'tis not to be wonder'd, that they should then rouze themselves, and endeavor to put the rule into such hands, which may secure to them the ends for which Government was first erected. . . .*

Once again, we have, not echoes, but identical phrases in Jefferson and Locke. The "long train of abuses" has been the phrase most cited by generations of scholars—although Wills stubbornly denies that they have ever "adduced" such parallels. Even more to the point, is the key word "design," which occurs in both Locke and Jefferson, and which is peculiarly vital to the Declaration's argument.

Edmund Morgan, in the review to which we have already referred, says flatly that the resemblances of Jefferson's language to Locke are closer than anything Wills has found in any Scottish philosopher. But even more to the point—and we will let Morgan make this point for us—is that in the parallels between Hutcheson and Jefferson cited by Wills, "the distance from Locke's political principles is not noticeable, indeed it is non-existent." Yet so insistent is Wills upon this very distance of Jefferson from Locke, that he asserts that: "There is no indication Jefferson read the *Second Treatise* carefully or with profit. Indeed, there is no direct proof he ever read it at all (though I assume he did at some point)." Wills is aware that Jefferson recommended the book to others but thinks that, like many a professor puffing himself to students, "There would be nothing dishonest about his general recommendation of the *Treatise*, made to others while he lacked any close acquaintance with the text. . . ." Yet in 1790, writing to an intimate friend, Jefferson pronounced "Locke's little book on government" to be "perfect as far as it goes."

Forty-five years later, near the end of his life, Jefferson collaborated with Madison—as we have already noted—in drawing up a list of books and documents for the faculty of law at the University of Virginia. Again—and for the last time—he turned to Locke, as he sought by university education to preserve the principles of the Revolution. In a resolution, prepared for, and adopted by the Board of Visitors, if was affirmed to be

> the opinion of this Board that as to the general principles of liberty and the rights of man, in nature and in society, the doctrines of Locke, in his "Essay concerning the true original extent and end of civil government," [the full title of the Second Treatise] and of Sidney in his "Discourses on government," may be considered as those generally approved by our fellow citizens of this, and the United States. . . .

From this recommendation of Locke and Sidney for "general principles" Jefferson went on, as we have already seen, to recommend the Declaration for the "distinctive principles" of American government. The pairing of Locke and Sidney was, as Wills notes, a traditional Whig custom. I do not see how this detracts from the importance of Locke. Wills says that the famous letter to Henry Lee is the only place in which Jefferson ever links Locke and the Declaration. In this resolution however, Locke and the Declaration are again linked, and linked in the most authoritative manner. Coming at the end of Jefferson's life, this resolution has a peculiar and final authority.

Among the many absurdities of Wills's work is that Adam Smith, as a "moral sense" philosopher, becomes a "communitarian." Thus the spiritual father of capitalism—or the system of natural freedom, as he called it—becomes part of the anti-individualism which prepared the way for Marx and today's Left. Had Wills read that notable book linking the *Theory of Moral Sentiments* with *The Wealth of Nations*, Joseph Cropsey's *Polity and Economy: An Interpretation of the Principles of Adam Smith*, he would not have committed such an egregious error. For he would have learned from Cropsey that the Scottish school were emenders of Locke, rather than negators or opponents. All their thought moves within a circle previously defined by Locke, and before Locke, by Hobbes. Indeed, the quotation from Burlamaqui, relating the purposes of civil society to sovereignty, points back from Locke towards Hobbes, rather than forward toward the Scottish school.

An important book may still be written about Hutcheson and the school he represents, and their influence upon the American Founding Fathers. No responsible scholar has ever claimed that the Declaration of Independence is purely (or merely) a Lockean document. The substitution of "pursuit of happiness" for "property" in the famous enumeration of rights is a sufficient obstacle to such a simplistic view. So is the appeal to the "dictates of prudence." The ultimate authority for the meaning of the intellectual virtue of prudence is Aristotle. For it was Aristotle who separated philosophic wisdom from practical wisdom, *sophia* from *phronesis, sapientia* from *prudentia.*

* * *

There is accordingly a great deal in the Declaration that points backwards from Locke, towards the ancients. In that famous letter to Henry Lee in 1825, Jefferson wrote of the Declaration:

> *All its authority rests then on the harmonizing sentiments of the day, whether expressed in conversation, in letters, printed essays, or in the elementary books of public right, as Aristotle, Cicero, Locke, Sidney, etc.*

Wills attempts to brush this aside and ridicules the reference to Aristotle, because elsewhere Jefferson depreciates him. But Jefferson makes clear in the Lee letter that in drafting the Declaration he was the agent of the Congress, and of the American people. What he wrote was not intended as a personal statement, but "as an expression of the American mind." That Jefferson listed two ancients—Aristotle and Cicero—before two moderns—Locke and Sidney—was not casual or accidental. Patrick Henry's famous apostrophe began by noting that "Caesar had his Brutus." The Senate, the Capitol, and many other symbols from the Founding period remind us of the power of the example of ancient Rome, and of ancient freedom. Perhaps Rome was more looked to than Greece. But Cicero himself looked to Athens to discover the principles of Rome's greatness. Cicero was an "academic skeptic," who, although he wrote both a *Republic* and a *Laws,* came closer in many respects to Aristotle than to Plato.

Wills ends his Prologue, his apology for writing his book, with an appeal to the authority of Douglass Adair. He cites an essay by Adair published in 1964, in which Adair said, among other things, that

> *An exact knowledge of Jefferson's ideas . . . is still lacking . . . We know relatively little about his ideas in the context of the total civilization of which he was a part. . . .*

This, Wills thinks, authorizes his flat rejection of the Lockeanism of orthodox scholarship. Certainly, Adair was himself something of a rebel against orthodox scholarship. He was also the author of what has often been referred to as the most influential unpublished dissertation of our time. Adair was restrained more by modesty and perfectionism, than by fear of the orthodox. Adair—who died in 1968—was my colleague and my friend, and a copy of his 1943 dissertation is before me. It is entitled *The Intellectual Origins of Jeffersonian Democracy*. Its exceedingly bold hypothesis is: that the most important source of Jeffersonian ideas on the connection between virtue, freedom, agrarianism, and republicanism, was to be found in the Sixth Book of Aristotle's *Politics*. Adair's argument, although brilliantly set forth, is not altogether persuasive. But it adds plausibility to the notion of an Aristotelian influence on the Declaration —particularly since Jefferson mentions that influence himself. When the Declaration speaks of the people, instituting new government, such as "to them shall seem most likely to effect their Safety and Happiness," he is appealing to a tradition of more than two thousand years. For safety and happiness are the alpha and omega of political life, according to a tradition originating with Aristotle. Political life, Aristotle had written, originates in the desire for life, that is, for self-preservation. But it moves on a scale of dignity, from mere life, to the good life. And the name for the good life is happiness.

In his straining to credit everything Jeffersonian to Hutcheson, Wills makes much of the fact that Hutcheson coined the phrase, "the greatest happiness of the greatest number." He is sure that this is what caused Jefferson to write "pursuit of happiness" instead of "property" or "estate", in the famous enumeration. He tells us confidently that from the teachings of the Scottish school "public happiness" is "measurable" and "is, indeed, the test and justification of any government." That public happiness is the test and justification of any government is also the teaching of both the *Nicomachean Ethics* and of the *Politics*. Such public happiness would not, however, be measurable in any mathematical sense. Happiness, according to Aristotle, is the *summum bonum*. As such it cannot be counted *among* good things, since it represents the presence of *all* good things, in the proportions that make them beneficial to their possessor. For example, you cannot be made happier by becoming richer, if you already have all the wealth that you can use well. But where does Jefferson ever speak of measuring happiness, in the mathematical or geometrical manner that Wills imputes to Hutcheson? It bears repeating, that in sketching the literary sources of the Declaration—or, rather, of the American mind that the Declaration expressed—Jefferson names Aristotle first of all. Then, after naming Cicero, he mentions Locke. But the name of Francis Hutcheson, in connection with the Declaration of Independence, is never mentioned at all.

Postscript

The two reviewers in question were M. J. Sobran, for *National Review*, and Richard Brookhiser for the *American Spectator*, In a later article in *NR*, "Saving the Declaration" (December 22, 1978) Mr. Sobran wrote as follows.

Six

On Political Education

Whatever the world thinks, he who hath not much meditated, upon God, the summum bonum, *and the human mind, though he may possibly make a thriving earthworm, shall indubitably make, a sorry patriot, and a sorry statesman.*

BISHOP BERKELEY (1685-1753)

C laremont Men's College is an academy of the liberal arts, specializing in public affairs. In the deepest sense, it is contradictory to speak of public affairs as a specialization. What is public is political, and what is political concerns the whole rather than the part. The liberal arts are the arts that liberate the minds of men, that fit them for the duties of freedom. They are the arts that turn the mind from the part to the whole, from the merely idiosyncratic to the universal, from the realm of necessity to that of free choice. Statesmanship requires above all understanding the fundamental choices open to a free people. It implies possession of the intellectual skills required for comprehending those choices, and for communicating what has been comprehended.

As a member of Congress, Abraham Lincoln devoted the greater part of his leisure time to the study of Euclid's *Geometry*. Later, he would refer to the "principles of Jefferson" as "the definitions and axioms of free society." At Gettysburg, of course, he said that the nation had, at its birth, been "dedicated to a proposition." In his debates with Douglas, he appealed repeatedly to the nature of proof in Euclid, to evaluate the arguments that he and his opponent had put forth. The precision of Lincoln's mature thought owed much to that perfectly non-political discipline: geometry. The elevation of that thought derived in equal measure, from the contemplative study of the Declaration of Independence, and of the Bible. His greatest utterances are a unique blend of doctrines derived from those two sources, expressed with the eloquence, and in the temper, of Shakespearian tragedy.

Abraham Lincoln was not a learned man, in the usual sense of that term, but he was probably the best educated of all American presidents. Claremont Men's College has many learned men on its faculty. It does not neglect the progress of learning in a world in which learning is highly specialized, and constantly changing. But it attempts to fit the need for this learning into a framework of education in the liberal arts, education in the permanent things, those things that not only enable a man and a nation to survive in a troubled and a hostile world, but so to live that life may be a blessing.

*The Declaration is a republican document, based squarely on Locke's theory....
Which brings me to a personally embarrassing point. In his recent book,*
Inventing America, *Garry Wills persuaded me (*NR, *July 7), that the Declaration can be understood without reference to Locke. He denied, in fact, that
there are any distinct echoes of Locke, either in the Declaration or in
Jefferson's writings generally. But a careful reading of the* Second Treatise
*makes overwhelmingly clear that Wills is wrong. In diction, terms, turns of
phrase, structure, and of course destination, the resemblance is so close that
it is hard to feel that the Declaration is anything but a sustained* allusion *to
Locke.* [Emphasis by Mr. Sobran.]

The reader will, of course, have perceived that in our opinion the Declaration is
in fact much more than an allusion to Locke. Without that allusion, however,
nothing of substance in the Declaration comes to sight. I am pleased to be able
to record that Mr. Brookhiser has authorized me to declare his association with
Mr. Sobran's revised judgment of *Inventing America*. This is a most hopeful
sign, that for better reasons than mere success, the Right may become the
Center of American politics.

Seven

Looking at Mr. Goodlyfe

T he Spring Semester, 1979, has brought forth yet another new official publication of Claremont Men's College, called *Current 79*. Being new, the current issue is Volume 1, No. 1. We expect the Spring issue, 1980, to be called *Current 80*, which would therefore also be Volume 1, No. 1. To be perpetually resurrected each Spring, to be forever Volume 1, No. 1., to be always current, seems clearly to be the aim of *Current*. It seems also to be the aim of a CMC education, as seen from the editorial chair of *Current*.

Current takes great pride—and properly so—in the selection of the College by the National Association of Business Economists for its first award for excellence in business economics. The recognition of excellence in any form is so unusual these days—being "affirmative" means recognizing anything but excellence—that we should rejoice in it. Never mind that Claremont Men's College calls itself a liberal arts college, and that business economics can hardly be called a liberal arts subject. Moreover, there is a certain inner consistency, both symbolic and nonsymbolic, between this award and the love of currency that runs through the new journal. For American business, notable in its advertising and merchandising, has ever turned upon the axis of the prototypical word and concept *New*. Alexis de Tocqueville noted this in the 1830's, and the attraction of the "new" has remained unchanged.

> *One touch of nature makes the whole world kin, That all with one consent praise new born gawds....*

This has ever been the thematic approach of American business to the marketplace. *To neon* is the word that is with God, and in God according to the Gospel of Wall Street and Madison Avenue. It now seems to be equally the *logos* of Claremont Men's College. "Let us have no innovation in our time," said George III. American business arose to the challenge not by the Declaration of Independence, but by its unshakable and unchanging grip upon the *new* within the *now*, within the *current*.

As in all good merchandising operations, the dominating feature of *Current 79* is not what is on the inside, but what is upon the outside of the package. There we find a cartoon of "Mr. Goodlyfe," who, we are told is "what we like to think of" as a CMC graduate. This pudgy and vacuous figure is surrounded by creatures of his imagination, who sing his praises like angels at the throne of Grace (or, in this case, of Success). I suspect that the artist was spoofing the editors, without their knowing it. He draws with something of the spirit—if not the skill— of a Hogarth or a Daumier. But *Current* thinks that Mr. Goodlyfe's "reveries of the 'good life'" capture "what we like to think of as a guiding principle at CMC." This "guiding principle" which serves to guide the education of "leaders for business, professions and government" is the recognition of "the importance of personal values." One is struck by the fact our editors think that what guides the education of leaders is recognition of personal values. But they say nothing at all of *what* personal values ought to guide these leaders. Certainly no one in our time had stronger commitments to their personal values than did Joseph Stalin and Adolph Hitler. Some fifty million people died, as witnesses—that is, martyrs—to the power of their personal values. Now I do not think that Mr. Goodlyfe represents the personal values of either Hitler or Stalin. In his consuming desire to be praised, he does in fact represent the principle of tyranny. One classic definition of tyranny is of a regime in which one man is the object of indiscriminate and universal (that is, uncontradicted) praise. But Mr. Goodlyfe is a weak fellow, with much more in common with such "boneless wonders" as Ramsay Macdonald, Stanley Baldwin, and Neville Chamberlain, than with Hitler or Stalin—or Churchill. As a representative of business enterprise, he does not care how he makes his money, so long as he makes it. He would as soon follow in the footsteps of Larry Flynt or Hugh Hefner, as of Andrew Carnegie. Let us bear in mind that the phrase "personal values" is itself "value free"; that is, it is itself neutral as between the different and conflicting values that men may hold. Yet it fits the CMC emphasis upon business economics, and the concept of "economic man." For the latter is indifferent to the difference between citizens and sybarites, between lovers of liberty and lovers of libertinism. One may go to the marketplace for photography, pornography, or geography. One does not go there as a patriot or a citizen, but as a buyer or as a seller, and the heterogeneity of the demand and of the supply schedules is homogenized by the pricing mechanism. All values, as values, are created equal.

Mr. Goodlyfe's "personal values," insofar as he can be said to have any, seem to consist—as we have noticed—in his being the object of unstinted praise. The cartoon does not imply that anyone actually admires Mr. Goodlyfe (except the staff of *Current*), only that he admires himself. To admire oneself, however, does not mean that one is admirable. Self-admiration is not the same as self-respect, although it is doubtful if Mr. Goodlyfe (or *Current*) understands the difference. In his idolatry of himself, and of the money which is the basis of that idolatry, Mr. Goodlyfe is the quintessence of what Rousseau called the *bourgeois* as distinct from the *citoyen*. His revery, or fantasy, places him in a solipsist universe, consisting of himself (*ipse*) alone (*solus*). Without the slightest consciousness of sharing things with others who are his friends and fellow citizens, he is utterly devoid of public spirit. He is, in fact, in the precise and original meaning of the word, an *idiot*, which is to say one who is completely *private*. Yet he represents what "we like to think of as a guiding principle at CMC," which calls itself a college of *public* affairs.

Mr. Goodlyfe appears in the cartoon as the snappy junior executive. He sits at a desk with his nameplate on it, wearing a three piece suit and striped tie, and he is clean shaven. No hairy sixties radical he! Behind him is a bookcase, with Plato's *Republic*, Adam Smith's *Wealth of Nations*, and the *Federalist Papers*. These books clearly are not *current*. There are also Rutledge's *A Monetarist's Model*, Thomson's *Laws*, and Samuelson's *Economics*. The important thing about the books, whether current or not, is that they are behind him. In front of him are his telephone, and a stock market ticker, from which sparks are shooting. His eyes are rolled upwards, away from his fat cheeks and puffy hands, and the air is filled with his dreams and visions. Of these, most notable are three bound bundles of bills, amounting in all to three million dollars. They are topped by a cascade of coins, from one of which protrudes the face of George Washington, declaring "A Great Guy, this one!" Of this we may be certain: Mr. Goodlyfe's contact with the heroic figures in the American past will henceforth come exclusively from *Currency*, from his contact with treasury and federal reserve notes, and with coins. Below the piles of bills is a chauffeur driven antique sports car, bearing the license plate RICH, the driver also declaring "Now there's a great guy!" On Mr. Goodlyfe's desk is the figure of an overblown female with a tennis racket on her shoulder (although one doubts that tennis is her racket), chorusing "Truly, a wonderful guy." Other impish figures exclaim "How does he do it?" and "One heck of a golfer, too!" One is as struck by the poverty of Mr. Goodlyfe's vocabulary, as of his imagination. A tiny figure of a Mr. Chips-type professor, with tasselled academic cap atop his grey head, and book beneath his arm, sits on Mr. Goodlyfe's shoulder. His eyes are rolled towards his patron with an expression of owlish skepticism. No balloon tells his thoughts, which he may be prudently keeping to himself, as he speculates on the chances of Mr. Goodlyfe helping to endow his chair.

The lead article of *Current 79* is entitled "Looking for the Good Life," by Professor Steven Smith. The editors tells us that it is from Smith that the students learn "how to understand their own values in their search for the good life." Smith's course in "Theories of the Good Life," which the article describes is, we are told, "a classic at CMC sought out by econ majors and English lit majors alike. It is as much a part of our public affairs emphasis as Economics 52 or Political Science 10." Let us then see how Professor Smith links Mr. Goodlyfe to the College's "public affairs emphasis."

The article seems to have two epigraphs, one general, the other particular. The first is "The unexamined life is not worth living," attributed to Socrates. The second is as follows.

The good life is money in the bank ... not needing to work ... eating steak and lobster three times a week ... Charlie's Angels ... gambling in Tahoe or Vegas without worrying about how much you lose ... close friends.

These definitions of the good life are unattributed. But Professor Smith explains that he begins his course on "Theories of the Good Life" by asking the students to complete the sentence "The good life is ..." This second epigraph must be taken from these completions. These definitions of the good life clearly have much in common with Mr. Goodlyfe. To give them the politest characterization, they are all sybaritic. Only the last definition of the good life, as having "close friends," seems to suggest any variation. But we are reminded that "close friends" are not necessarily "good friends." A close friend may be one who eats steak and lobster with you, or who goes with you to Tahoe or Vegas to gamble. Without attempting here to explain in any detail what Socrates meant by the examined life, we would observe that it was at the farthest remove from the foregoing definitions. Like Jesus, Socrates urged ambitious young men to abandon wealth and power, unless they were instrumental to virtue. In fact, Socrates did not say that the unexamined life was not *worth* living. Professor Smith has used a defective translation, for there is nothing in the Greek corresponding to the word "worth." There is nothing in the Greek that would justify thinking of the examined life as a "value." The Greek word means that the unexamined life is "not to be lived," implying that it is not a life at all, and that those who "live" it are dead souls.

I would summarize my impression of Mr. Smith's course by saying that I cannot discover a word in his article which suggests that students starting out with vulgar definitions of the good life would end up with anything less vulgar. The emphasis of his instructional method, according to Smith, is upon something called "values clarification." I can see that a student, clarifying his values, might come in time to realize that it is unlikely that he will keep money in the bank while patronizing Tahoe and Vegas. Or, alternatively, he may be made to realize that gambling and not worrying about losing, are incompatible with each other. Perhaps he will decide that eating steak and lobster three times a week is a modestly attainable goal, compared with the others. But I fail to see how "value clarification" can lead someone, for example, to disinterested devotion to justice or the common good, when such were not among the values to be clarified. If in time this student turns to TM, Yoga, or Zen, or some other ascetic ideal, it is not likely to be the result of leading an examined life, but rather a reaction of disgust to his own clarified values. After all, how many years of steak and lobster can you take, without getting a little restless? Smith himself is quite frank in declaring that he himself has no idea of what the good life is, and therefore has no advice to give his students. They are not, for example, exhorted to shun baseness and self-indulgence, while studying the alternatives presented by the story of the great lives and great doctrines that the heritage of civilization presents for their contemplation and improvement. Instead, they are invited to rate and rank all values, their own and others, the way they would a consumer market research survey of canned vegetables. And they will end up, we may be sure, rationalizing their passions for gluttony, venery, money, and gambling, while dreaming of what "great guys" they are—so many Mr. Goodlyfes!

In explaining the origin of his "Theories of the Good Life," Professor Smith tells us that for a number of years he had taught "a fairly conventional course in ethical theory." "Its primary aim," he says, "was to help students understand the thought of others." Among the "others" he mentions are Hobbes, Kant, and Mill. I assume however that along the way he—and his students—stumbled over such other "others" as Plato, Aristotle, Aquinas, Hegel, Marx, and Dewey. If so, Professor Smith and I have been teaching substantially the same subject matter, albeit in different departments. But I would never dream of describing these giants of the mind and spirit as "others," as if there were some equality between them and myself. Professor Smith says that he was troubled by criticism by the students—and in particular by the serious and thoughtful students—which went like this:

> these materials are interesting and stimulating, but they don't help me to get a bearing on life and how I ought to live it.

For some time, says Professor Smith, he did not see how to meet this criticism. Then, he tells us,

> events in my personal life intervened. I encountered a period of personal crisis, a deeply troubled time of despondency, self-doubt, and anxiety. Many of my former values no longer seemed to be worthy of my allegiance, and I began to cast about for a better foundation for my own life.

It was, he tells us,

> under the double impetus of student interest and my own personal concerns [that he] developed and began to teach a course called Theories of the Good Life—not because I knew what the good life is, but because I needed to know.

Let me now disavow any wish or desire to intrude upon Professor Smith's privacy. If I allude to his personal crisis, it is because he has made it part of his public explanation of his professional development. I have no knowledge of Professor Smith's personal circumstances, other than what is mentioned in *Current 79*. Let me say that, over the last generation—and I have been a college teacher for thirty-four years—it seems to have become almost obligatory, in some departments, to have had a "personal crisis." There are places—or so it sometimes seems—in which a young scholar would not even be considered for tenure unless he presented affidavits from three psychiatrists that he had had an "existential" or "identity" crisis.

Professor Smith tells us that, in the midst of his crisis, he remembered that

It was philosophy's concern with the deepest questions of human existence and value which, when I was a boy, had quickened my heart, sent my thoughts soaring, and had eventually drawn me to devote my career to the field.

But we must wonder what had happened to Professor Smith during all those years between his boyhood and his crisis to obscure this fact about the nature of philosophy? What did he think he was doing when teaching his "fairly conventional course in ethical theory" except to explore what some of the greatest minds had said and thought about these deepest questions of human existence? Most pertinent, why did he turn to a new approach, and why is that new approach more satisfactory than the old one?

In his new course, says Professor Smith, the students were "forced to think for themselves and to formulate their own views of the good life ..." Now, strictly speaking, it is as impossible to force anyone to think, as it is to force him to be free. I see no objection to asking students to formulate their own views of the good life, provided that they are then asked to defend those views in the light of what has been said on the same subject by Plato, Aristotle, Kant, Marx, and others. This implies subjecting them to authority—the authority of reasoned argument. But Professor Smith says that in his new course he "shifted [his] teaching role from that of authority figure and pundit to that of facilitator and discussion leader." But what does a "facilitator" facilitate? Towards what does the "leader" lead? Professor Smith does not say. He says however that he tried to create "a personalized learning environment" in which students "could pursue their deepest concerns, try out their thinking, and learn from one another." But what are the students' "deepest concerns"? Philosophy, Professor Smith said earlier, was concerned "with the deepest questions of human existence." Are not the students' deepest concerns of necessity the same as philosophy's, since they too are human? Will not the students, like Professor Smith as a boy, have their hearts quickened and their thoughts sent soaring, merely by discovering philosophy?

Professor Smith tells us he has changed the manner of his classroom, by attempting to create a "personalized learning environment." But what does this mean? "Personalized" along with "customized" are vogue words, neologisms (that is, words that pass as *current*) of modern advertising. Their fashion can be explained by the phenomenon of the "the lonely crowd," to borrow the title of David Reisman's book, itself the exploitation of a theme from Alexis de Tocqueville's *Democracy in America*. American democracy, as a modern mass society, although nominally devoted to the rights of the individual, undermines the sense of individuality by the very means by which the individual is supposedly served. Mass production, designed to emancipate the common man—and woman—from the burdens of poverty and inequality, tends to convert the consumer along with the worker into a depersonalized unit. More and more, society seems to resemble a giant factory on the one side, and a giant supermarket on the other. Not only do class distinctions tend to vanish. Everyone becomes more and more alike, as a consumer no less than a producer. But above all, they become more and more alike in their "life styles." But people rebel against becoming more and more alike. Although this rebellion is mainly a middle class, or upper middle class phenomenon, the rebels think of themselves as "everyone." However, in America the distinction between the middle class and everyone is not very great. And so everyone rebels against becoming more and more alike; and never are they more alike than in their rebellion against becoming more alike. From this one can trace at least one of the sources of the fashionable "identity crisis." One can also trace to this many elements of the "counterculture" of the sixties, and of the "counter-counter-culture" of the late seventies, of which Mr. Goodlyfe is a notable specimen. In the homogenized rebellion against homogenization, we can identify a central problem of modern merchandising, and the characteristic response to it. Advertisers try to make customers *feel* different when consuming standardized products, by persuading them to identify themselves with models and actors who (via the script-writers) represent to them life styles which become the customer's fantasies. Thus, in his imagination the consumer (everyone a "Goodlyfe") becomes one of these beautiful and extraordinary people (that is, beautiful and extraordinary *to him*) by virtue of drinking their beer and smoking their cigarettes. In some cases, the illusion of individuality is built into the product itself. By the use of computers, automobiles, for example, can be marketed in an extraordinary variety of combinations of colors and accessories. And even the governments can cash in on this, by marketing license plates that reflect individuality (like RICH). In short, mass production, and mass psychology—the two tend eventually to merge into one—are employed in the mass marketing of "individuality." This is what, at bottom, a "personalized environment" means, whether for "learning" or for any other kind of consuming. Professor Smith, it seems to me, has brought the Marlboro cowboy of personalized consumption into the quest for the good life. But I predict that the one will be as carcinogenic to the soul, as the other is to the body.

Turning again to Professor Smith's conception of "values clarification," I believe we may confirm our analysis of it, as a form of the reduction of moral philosophy to marketing. Professor Smith employs something called "The Rokeach Value Survey Scale." This is to help the student put his "values" in perspective, by ranking them. He is given a list of 18 "values" and asked to put a number opposite to each one—from 1 to 18—corresponding to how he ranks them in relationship to each other. Among these "values" are: Freedom,

Happiness, Inner Harmony, Pleasure, Salvation, Wisdom, True Friendship. Let us make the gratuitous assumption that the student has a sufficient understanding of what these things mean—how can they be ranked? How can one rate wisdom before self-respect, or self-respect before wisdom? Is it possible to imagine a wise man lacking in self-respect? Surely, a fool can rank pleasure before wisdom, but can one imagine a wise man who does not regard wisdom as among the pleasantest of things, if not the most pleasant? Can anyone who believes in the possibility of eternal salvation, think that any worldly wisdom can be preferred to it? Perhaps most illogical of all, is to ask anyone to rank happiness *among* the good things. Since Aristotle, happiness has been defined as the *summum bonum*, that highest good which comprehends all lesser goods, and renders them beneficial to their possessor. One cannot, for example, imagine a happy man, who was a fool, lacking in self-respect, a slave, and without friends. Happiness implies the presence of the other good things, in such manner and proportion, as to contribute to the well-being of their possessor.

"The Rokeach Value Survey Scale" does not in fact ask the student to compare and contrast such things as wisdom, freedom, or self-respect. What it asks him to compare and contrast are the *value* of wisdom, with the *value* of freedom, with the *value* of self-respect. Wisdom and happiness are objective states or conditions; but the *values* placed upon them are the preferences or attitudes of evaluating subjects. What are being ranked then are not the things regarded as good in themselves, but the values placed upon them. "Values," as such, are both discrete and homogeneous. But wisdom, and freedom, and self-respect, and happiness, are neither discrete nor homogeneous. Without understanding why they are neither discrete nor homogeneous, one can understand nothing whatever about them. Professor Smith's procedure does not clarify, it only obfuscates, the meaning either of "values" or of the ends valued.

From the point of view of a free market economist, the distinction between ends which are objective, and values which are subjective, is unnecessary. From his point of view, the Gross National Product, is the sum of the value of all the goods and services produced and consumed in a given year. In comparing last year's GNP with this year's, he is not expected to say whether there has been an increase or a decrease in the "goodness of life," only whether the aggregate of goods and services was greater or lesser. And such goods and services are rated simply by the market prices that they bore. For the economist, the goods and services properly labelled "art" are not distinguished from those properly labelled "trash." Even if they were, he would not change his estimate of the GNP by reason of the relative proportions of the two. Yet from the point of view of the art critic, the difference between art and trash is (or ought to be) vital. And for the statesman, for the one liberally educated to be a leader in public affairs, the question whether art or trash has been on the increase in the nation, is a vital one. In recent years, the size of that part of the GNP devoted to "education" has increased enormously. Yet according to all judges of what makes an educated people, we are becoming less educated year by year. When I came to CMC in 1964, the principal extra-curricular event of that year, and of several subsequent years, was the Seminar in the American Political Tradition. In the last decade at CMC, less has been heard of the American political tradition. Out of those seminars of the mid-sixties, came the James Madison Society. It was intended to promote and preserve the study of the Founding, as a continuing extra-curricular activity. In speaking to the current president of the James Madison Society, and several of its members, I could find no one who knew how or why the Society had been founded. One will search in vain for anything to do with either James Madison or the Founding among its current activities. The Bicentennial passed virtually unnoticed here.

What follows is the 15th paragraph of the Virginia Declaration of Rights, June 12, 1776. To it corresponds the 18th paragraph of the Massachusetts Declaration of 1780.

> *That no free government, or the blessings of liberty, can be preserved to any people, but by a firm adherence to justice, moderation, temperance, frugality and virtue, and by a frequent recurrence to fundamental principles.*

The idea of a "frequent recurrence to fundamental principles," as the ground for educating leaders in public affairs—indeed, as the most important element in such an education—was the guiding purpose of the James Madison Society. Today, I doubt that many—or any—of the members of the Society could explain what the Virginia or Massachusetts Declaration meant by such language, or what the principles of free government are. And I doubt that Professor Smith's "Theories of the Good Life" with its "personalized learning environment" will teach them a firm adherence, or any adherence, to justice, moderation, temperance, frugality, or virtue.

Does anyone think that the "value" of a CMC education has gone up, along with its price? Don't ask Mr. Goodlyfe, he is off in a world of his own. But I can assure everyone that, if we do not in our education in public affairs once again recur to fundamental principles a world more real than Mr. Goodlyfe's—without illusions, without reveries, and without mercy—will presently intrude with devastating harshness. Mr. Goodlyfe will have shown us all the way to a very bad death.

* * *

Someone may ask, why should a busy scholar waste such heavy ammunition upon something so trite and shallow as *Current 79*. Why take images—such as Mr. Goodlyfe—projected by a college PR department, as if they were theses nailed to the door of the Capitol? My answer is, first of all, that these images are an accurate reflection of how the governing bodies of the college —administration, faculty, and trustees—see the college and its educational mission. In their claim that they furnish leaders for public life they are correct: but if Mr. Goodlyfe represents the quality of those leaders, then clearly our public life is doomed. Moreover, the college's constituencies—students, alumni, donors—also take these things pretty much at face value. For anyone who thinks the light tone of the articles—and the cartoons—indicates that all this is not meant too seriously I would retort: this lack of seriousness about the most serious thing in the world is itself revealing.

I am also told, from time to time, that Claremont Men's College is too small and too insignificant to preoccupy someone, even if he is a member of its faculty, whose job it is to attend to the larger crises of civilization, national and international. I am constantly exhorted and admonished, by friends and well-wishers, to exhort and admonish the nation and the world, but not Claremont. But political philosophy, like charity, also has its domestic duties. Socrates went about the streets of Athens, admonishing and exhorting his fellow-Athenians, not because they were Athenians, but because they were his neighbors. Socrates did not exhort Athenians because Athens was the home of political philosophy. Athens became the home of political philosophy because Socrates exhorted Athenians. There are some who think that, because political philosophy originated in the Socratic critique of the opinions of Athenians, that political philosophy ought properly to remain a critique of the opinions of Athenians. To subject the opinions of Americans—and even of Claremonters— to the same kind of critique to which Socrates subjected the opinions of Athenians, seems to them to lower the dignity of the discipline. But I think I am right and even Socratic in my procedure, and I shall persevere. If I cannot equal Socrates in other respects, I hope I shall not equal him in this respect either: that my critique comes too late.

Eight

In Defense of Political Philosophy
Two Letters to Walter Berns

*Let us all be lovers of victory when it comes to virtue, but without
envy. The man of this sort—always competing himself but never
thwarting others with slander—makes cities great.*

PLATO, *Laws*, 731 a-b
[Pangle, trans.]

Introduction

In 1978 I published *How to Think About the American Revolution*, which I
characterized in the subtitle as "A Bicentennial Cerebration." It would be
presumptuous to say that there was no other cerebrating in the celebrations
commemorating the occasion of our two hundredth anniversary as a nation.
However, nothing I know of, published in connection with this anniversary,
compares in depth of thought or beauty of expression with the address delivered by President Calvin Coolidge, in Independence Hall, Philadelphia, 1926,
observing the one hundred and fiftieth birthday of the United States.

Coolidge's speech, entitled "The Inspiration of the Declaration of Independence," was an exploration of the historical and philosophical meaning of
that famous document. For Coolidge never had the slightest doubt that the
importance of American independence was to be found primarily and essentially
in the principles by which that independence was originally justified. The truths
expressed in the Declaration were, he said, very old. But never before had they
been adopted by a duly authorized and constituted representative body, a body
supported by general public opinion, and by armies in the field. It was this
uniting of philosophical thought with political action that made the Declaration of
Independence "the most important civil document in the world," and the Fourth
of July "one of the greatest days in history."

In the course of his oration, President Coolidge remarked that there was,
about the Declaration, "a finality that is exceedingly restful." The assertions of
man's equality, of his endowment with inalienable rights, of the derivation of the
just powers of government from the consent of the governed, are all, he said,
final. "No advance, no progress can be made beyond those propositions."
Anyone wishing to deny them, he continued, can only go backward. And those
who wish to proceed in such a direction "are reactionary."

Coolidge spoke in what was still the heyday of the so-called Progressive

Era. The idea that a final political truth might be pronounced at any time was wholly inconsistent with the evolutionary and historicist theories that dominated Coolidge's world—as they still dominate our own. Carl Becker's *The Declaration of Independence*, published four years before Coolidge's speech, was then—and still is—regarded as the last word in historical and philosophical criticism of its subject. And Becker had written that, "To ask whether the natural rights philosophy of the Declaration of Independence is true or false is essentially a meaningless question." In saying this, Becker was casting aside a philosophical tradition of more than two thousand years, a tradition that discovered the very purpose of human life in asking such questions as Becker had pronounced to be meaningless. There is a tragic irony in the sequel to what Becker thus wrote in 1922. In a new preface to his book, written in 1941, Becker confessed that the challenge of Hitler and his bestial doctrines had renewed interest in "the immemorial problem of human liberty." Men everywhere were being forced "to reappraise the validity of half-forgotten ideas," among them presumably those of the Declaration of Independence. Becker did indeed turn again to the ideas of the Declaration, like a frightened child in the night. He embraced them with the will of a convert and, as a matter of faith, willingly suspended his former disbelief. Yet his reason never overcame the relativism that he had been taught by historicism and scientific positivism, concerning "the laws of Nature and of Nature's God."

Today, thanks to the work of Leo Strauss, it is the relativism taught by positivism and historicism, that must rank among the most thoroughly exploded superstitions of the human mind. In the court of reason, the integrity of the Declaration of Independence stands where it stood in the mind of Calvin Coolidge, as it had before so stood in the mind of Coolidge's hero, Abraham Lincoln. But superstitions do not die merely because they have been shown to be baseless. In *How to Think About the American Revolution* I examined a number of opinions about the Declaration widely thought to be authoritative —particularly in circles called conservative—and subjected them to dialectical commentary. In each case I discovered—or perhaps I should say uncovered— a core of meaning that corresponded to, if it was not identical with, opinions that had been advanced earlier by John C. Calhoun, and that were associated with the historicist and positivist defense of slavery in the ante-bellum debate.

This was notably true of the two lectures which inaugurated the American Enterprise Institute's Distinguished Lecture Series on the Bicentennial of the United States. The late Professor Martin Diamond maintained that the "sobriety" of the American Revolution consisted primarily and essentially in the fact that it culminated in a Constitution that had received "no guidance" from the Declaration of Independence. Professor Irving Kristol has said substantially the same thing in the opening lecture of the series, in which he hailed the Revolution as "successful" mainly because in it the leaders of the Revolution ignored their own rhetoric. "To perceive the true purpose of the American

Revolution," Professor Kristol asserted, "it is wise to ignore some of the more grandiloquent declamations of the moment." Of course, the quintessentially "grandiloquent" declamation was that which began, "We hold these truths to be self-evident ..."

Martin Diamond had found his "no guidance" thesis in Willmoore Kendall's *Basic Symbols of the American Political Tradition*, published posthumously in 1970, a book which, however, capped more than a generation of Kendall's warfare against the Declaration, or, rather, against Abraham Lincoln for using the Declaration to "derail" the American political tradition. Kendall, however, was himself merely echoing what Calhoun had said in his speech on the Oregon Bill, June 27, 1848, when he said that the principles expressed in the Declaration "made no necessary part of our justification in separating from the parent country ... [and did not have] any weight in constructing the governments which were substituted in place of the colonial." The principles themselves, Calhoun declared, were "false" and "dangerous."

Needless to say, my work exposing the character and intellectual pedigree of these lectures was not universally well received. Now, however, the American Enterprise Institute has inaugurated its celebration of the forthcoming Bicentennial of the Constitution. As nearly as I can tell, this series seems destined to have as the "central idea" from which all its minor thoughts "radiate," the same negative view of the principles of the regime, as its predecessor. Hence my letter to Professor Berns of January 14, 1981, and his response, from which I have quoted in my reply to him of March 18, 1981.

January 14, 1981

Professor Walter Berns
American Enterprise Institute
1150 Seventeenth Street, N.W.
Washington, D.C. 20036

Dear Walter:

About a week ago I received a copy of *How Democratic Is the Constitution?* . . .

I have only had time to skim most of the essays, though I gave yours a rather careful first reading. I think you are mistaken in your understanding of what is meant in *Federalist* #63 by "the total exclusion of the people in their collective capacity" from any share in the government. But this is symptomatic of your deeper failure to understand the question of whether and how the Declaration of Independence is or is not a fundamentally democratic document. I also think you misunderstand Locke, as well as unwarrantably assuming that the Declaration is to be read merely and simply in the light of Locke. But enough of that for the moment.

The editors claim that the volume presents "spokesmen as authoritative, thoughtful, and instructive as could be found" upon the main questions. Among these spokesmen was Michael Parenti who, I take it, is there as a representative of Marxism. It seems to me that if Parenti is the best representative of Marxism who could be found, then Marxism is in worst shape than I had thought. But I concede that it was not out of place to include a Marxist. However, was it not out of place *not* to have included a representative of that contemporary of Karl Marx—for whom, incidentally, Marx himself expressed great admiration—Abraham Lincoln? In passing, let me note that there is no representative in the book of that "Marx of the Master Class," John C. Calhoun. Or are we to assume that Martin Diamond's "no guidance" thesis is there as an esoteric symbol of Calhoun's presence?

I assume that you have not yet forgotten that at Gettysburg Lincoln declared that this nation, at its birth, was dedicated to the proposition "that all men are created equal," and that in virtue of that dedication "government of the people, by the people, for the people," came forth upon the earth. Lincoln believed that the government of the United States was democratic. But he also believed that the principles of that government—and of the Constitution —were to be found in the Declaration of Independence. The principles were the "apples of gold" for which the Constitution and the Union were no more than "pictures of silver." For Lincoln it was sufficient, in discussing the principles of government, to discuss the principles of the Declaration. This you, like Diamond (and Calhoun) deny. Perhaps you are right, and Lincoln is wrong, and the Declaration is merely "neutral" as between forms of government. But surely you would not contend that Lincoln is of too little moment, and his opinions too slight, to be included in A.E.I.'s inaugural volume of the Constitution's bicentennial. Surely, his view of the Constitution deserves inclusion with a gutter Marxist, as "authoritative, thoughtful, and instructive."

I have it in mind to write a piece entitled, "How to Think About How Democratic is the Constitution." Would you be willing to debate this with me at a panel at the next APSA meeting? Or do you now believe, with Louis Hartz, that the proper way to refute someone is to ignore him?

As ever,
Harry

March 18, 1981

Dear Walter,

   Your letter to me of January 30, was an attempt to turn questions of scholarship and of political philosophy into personal differences. You seem to have lost all confidence in your ability to debate, or even to discuss, the points upon which our views appeared to be in conflict: concerning Locke, the *Federalist*, Abraham Lincoln, and the Declaration of Independence. Instead, you have mounted a savage attack upon my character. You say that the letter you have written to me is the one I deserve. May I assure you, my choleric old friend, that that is something of which you will *not* be the judge. On my part, let me say that the letter you are about to get, is one that you do *not* deserve. I do not mean to be gentle with you. In your present state of mind, nothing less than a metaphysical two-by-four across the frontal bone would capture your attention. And yet I will offer you an "apology," in the sense of the philosophic tradition. For your attack is only incidentally against me personally. It is, in essence, against anyone who stands by the conclusions of "free argument and debate." It is against the idea of political philosophy.

   The intention of your letter was clearly to break off all communication between us. But it was also meant to solicit the aid and comfort of all those others who you think nurse wounds from my "polemics," and who, like yourself, cannot meet me on the ground of the argument. How deeply in love you are with your grudge against me, I cannot tell. I have little optimism on that account. We are old men now, but once, when we were young, we shared in a springtime of the rediscovery of political philosophy, of the power of the *logos* to lead us, whither we should go. Together we sat at the feet of Leo Strauss. We were a happy few, a band of brothers then, ready to stand against the world, "whither the god had stationed us," in dialectical combat. The matter between us now, is very much one of where we stand, respectively, in relationship to what was once our "ancient faith."

   I must and shall repel what I conceive to be slanders. But I sorrow that anyone who has been to me as you have been, should endorse and circulate such slanders. I do not write to put a thorn in your—or any man's—bosom. But I cannot place your friendship—or any one's—before the truth that is in me. Aristotle, in the only reference to piety in the *Nicomachean Ethics*, says that virtue requires us to honor truth before our friends. That is because we would not otherwise be worth having as friends. If I can no longer have your friendship, I intend nonetheless to be worthy of it. Abraham Lincoln tells us to "Stand with anybody that stands RIGHT. Stand with him while he is right and PART with him when he goes wrong." That saying was beneath a framed silhouette of Lincoln in my room when I was a child. Its meaning did not become apparent to me until many years after I had ceased to be a child. Yet it is a comfort to me now to remember it with the glow of a distant past, in the truth that time has revealed.

* * *

The kind of attack you have made upon me is full of the malice of ideological sectarianism. It is like a chapter out of *Darkness at Noon*. This is the Alice-in-Wonderland, where guilt is assumed rather than proven, and where the imputation of base motives takes the place of reasoned argument. "Off with his head, the jury said, this villain must be tried." Your jury is comprised of all those who, you think, are resentful of the contents of one or another of the chapters of *How to Think About the American Revolution*, not one word of which you or they have challenged. But you would like them all to think, that if only they join together with you in saying what a bad man I am, that they can in good conscience go on—like you—in ignoring the force of my arguments.

The occasion of this assault of yours, is my letter to you of January 14, which, you declare, was "outrageous" and "insulting." When I called you on the phone to ask if we could schedule a debate at the APSA meeting next fall—since the deadline for the Preliminary Program was February 1st—you told me that the letter was "offensive." Now you write that I had "affected surprise" at that. I certainly am given to candor, but not to affectation. There was not a word in my letter to which someone writing on controversial matters could properly have taken offense. Since when is it a personal insult to tell someone that he has misread a text of John Locke? I had stated in a perfectly straightforward way the points in your essay "Does the Constitution 'Secure These Rights'?" which I thought were mistaken, and which might form the agenda of a debate. What was I supposed to do? Grovel and fawn and beg permission to disagree? It seems to me, that a man who has written and spoken as you have done, about Oliver Wendell Holmes, Jr., and Earl Warren ought not to be so delicate.

* * *

I can understand your irritation at my question, at the end of my letter, whether you had joined the ranks of those who think that the proper way to refute someone is to ignore him. Charles Kesler, in his article in the Independence Day issue of *NR* in 1979, took note of my use of that saying. It was Santayana, he said, who had observed that "we no longer refute our adversaries, we quietly bid them goodbye." "Santayana's lament," he continued, "became Louis Hartz's guiding maxim." He noted that I had said that that maxim was appropriate for those "who believe that the foundations of reason are laid in unreason, and that nothing can ever be concluded concerning the noble and the base, or concerning the just and the unjust." That is to say, it was appropriate for those who deny the possibility of political philosophy.

However irritating my question, it was necessary and just. You had indeed ignored my argument, in *How to Think About the American Revolution* concerning whether the Constitution of 1787 "secured these rights." In ignoring it, you ignored the question of whether the Constitution, and the American polity generally, had any foundation whatever in natural, as opposed to positive right. You were, whether you understood what you were doing or not, putting yourself squarely on the side of radical modernity. You had every right to be angry—but the anger should have been directed at yourself. I have no illusions about why you should prefer me as an object of your anger; but neither should you have any illusions as to the likelihood of your success in concealing the real issues between us. How could you—and Goldwin, as editor of *How Democratic Is the Constitution?*—simply ignore the position represented by Abraham Lincoln and the Gettysburg Address? How could you preen yourselves on patronizing a vulgar Marxist, while ignoring that position? Why would you want to? How is it that you are insulted only by me? You say that Goldwin wants nothing further to do with me. Well, I can understand that. To be saddled with an argument and a conscience that you cannot defend, is not pleasant. But if either of you think that you will find safety in flight, you are mistaken. As Joe Louis said about Billy Conn, "He can run, but he can't hide."

* * *

You say that I accused you and Martin Diamond "of denying what neither of us ever denied." But that accusation—as you called it—is something that I had *documented*. I had said that *according to Abraham Lincoln* (with whom I happened to agree) the principles of the Constitution and government of the United States were to be found in the Declaration of Independence. Diamond denied that the principles of the Constitution and the government it established were to be found in the Declaration, and he insisted that Abraham Lincoln agreed with him! Here are his exact words, in his Bicentennial Lecture.

> *He* [Lincoln] *carefully limits his indebtedness to the Declaration only to certain sentiments and feelings . . . Indeed, he could not have done otherwise for there is nothing in the Declaration which goes beyond that sentiment . . . the Declaration is devoid of guidance as to what those institutions* [i.e. Constitution and government] *should be.*

And you supported this position when you wrote in your essay, "Contrary to Carl Becker [Never mind Abraham Lincoln!] I think that the Declaration does not contain a presumption against kings in general, but only against tyrannical kings." Now you knew that I had quoted Lincoln in my book ridiculing just such an interpretation of the Declaration, when he said that "it gave no promise that having kicked off the King and Lords of Great Britain, we should not at once be saddled with a King and Lords of our own." How then can you say that I accused you and Diamond "of denying what neither of us ever denied"?

* * *

You say that because of my "vanity" and "overweening vanity" I have lost "any sense of proportion as to what is important and what is not," and add that I "engage in petty polemics with persons . . . [whom I] owe it to myself to ignore." Because of this, you also say, I cause my friends to become "embarrassed defenders of [my] earlier self and work." But these accusations are not accompanied by a single illustration of what you mean. You ask me whether—since twenty-two years have passed since *Crisis of the House Divided* appeared, and *A New Birth of Freedom* has not appeared—I am "pleased with what *[I]* have done instead?" But, in truth, I have never done anything "instead" of writing the sequel to *Crisis*. That still unfinished book has been the *telos* and the *entelecheia* of my life's work. It has therefore been the *cause* of everything I have written. This is perfectly compatible with the proposition that what is prior in order of *being*, may yet be posterior in order of *becoming*.

Are you suggesting that the work published in *Equality and Liberty, The Conditions of Freedom*, and *How to Think About the American Revolution* is in some fundamental way different from, and below the level, of my earlier work? How? *Crisis of the House Divided* is in the form of a Thomistic *Questio Disputata*, and the *Questio* is whether or not Abraham Lincoln was the bad man that he would have to be, if the dominant opinions in then contemporary historiography were true opinions. Certainly, my polemics against "revisionist" historians in general, and Richard Hofstadter in particular, were not less trenchant than anything I have written since. The critique of Hofstadter, in *Crisis*, to which I returned in *How to Think*, is one link between the two books.

But what about *Equality and Liberty*? No one encouraged me to publish it more than Robert A. Goldwin. Three of the essays are slashing critiques of historians: Donald A. Riddle (*Congressman Abraham Lincoln*), Avery Craven (*The Coming of the Civil War*), and Daniel Boorstin (*The Genius of American Politics*). One was a dialectical refutation of a philosophical positivist (Felix Oppenheim), and still another was a critique of David Easton's *The Political System*. Do you not, as an "embarrassed defender of my earlier self and work," owe it to me and to yourself, to point out the errors of my ways?

* * *

Who are they, among those I have noticed recently, that I "owed it to myself to ignore"? Willmoore Kendall? Martin Diamond? Irving Kristol? Garry

Wills? Walter Berns? Abraham Lincoln took note of what Stephen A. Douglas said and wrote because, he said,

> *Judge Douglas is a man of vast influence, so great that it is enough for many men to believe anything when they once find out that Judge Douglas professes to believe it.*

Now it is precisely upon this principle, which is also the principle of Socratic political philosophy, that I have noticed opinions that I have undertaken to refute. One reason I paid such attention to the Kristol and Diamond lectures was because of the conspicuous role that they played in the Bicentennial. The A.E.I. series was the most prominent political academic recognition of the two-hundredth anniversary of the United States of America. Since the A.E.I. is itself recognized as a center of "conservatism," this did indeed give the series a political cast. Since so-called modern "liberalism" looks upon the past as reactionary, the only positive recognition of the principles of the Revolution would of necessity be "conservative." The A.E.I. lectures were therefore directed towards the same "constituency," that is, the same body of opinion that I too hoped to influence as an interpreter of the American political tradition.

As I said, the critique of opinions that are popular, or influential, or both, has supplied the ground or matter of political philosophy, since Socrates first brought it down from the heavens and into the cities. When Socrates went about refuting the opinions of poets, politicians, and artisans (but not philosophers), he too appeared to be occupying himself with persons whom the Walter Berns's of his day thought it his duty to ignore. How else account for Callicles' reproach to him, for being "childish," and imploring him to leave off his endless "refuting"? I am reminded of a lecture Allan Bloom gave some years ago on the *Ion*. He had his audience laughing with him at Socrates' ridicule of the rhapsode. In the discussion, however, I pointed to a serious opinion, underlying Ion's opinion, which was not to be refuted so easily. I put this to Allan. He replied, to loud applause, that he only replied to unintelligent objections, not intelligent ones. I mention this, not to disagree with Allan, but to agree with him, at least up to a point. Political philosophy does come to sight as the ridicule of unintelligent opinions, although it certainly does not remain such. In saying that I should ignore opinions to which I give my attention, you think that I am "stooping to conquer." But what appears "stooping" to you, I regard as bringing philosophy down from Heaven, and into the City. Oddly enough, the one who first praised me for doing this, was Martin Diamond. It was he who, more than twenty-five years ago, noted that the "orthodox" Straussians held that political philosophy, which originated in the Socratic critique of the opinions of the Athenians, consisted thereafter in the Socratic critique of the opinions of the Athenians. It was Jaffa, he declared, who discovered that political philosophy might also consist in the Socratic critique of the opinions of the Americans. In his characteristically pungent manner, he added that it all depended upon which cave you were in!

* * *

I find that Peacock is publishing *The Founding of the Democratic Republic*, which will consist of Diamond's chapters 1, 3, 4, and 5, from *The Democratic Republic*. According to the publisher, the *raison d'etre* for doing so, is in the following excerpt from early in the text.

> *Few countries have a national political creed. Fewer have a formal constitution vitally related to that creed. It is not accident, therefore, that much American political debate and scholarship has focused on the relationship between the Declaration and the Constitution; or to state the issue more precisely, on the relationship between democracy and the restraining tendencies of the Constitution. This relationship is at the center of the American political existence. Everything depends upon its proper understanding.*

When he wrote these lines, Diamond was much closer to the mark than when he came to regard the Declaration (as you also now seem to do) as neutral towards forms of government (and hence unable to supply "guidance" with respect to the Constitution and government). That "everything" depends upon the proper understanding of the relationship between the Constitution and the Declaration is what I believed when those lines were written and what I believe today. Carrying on the debate and the scholarship that is focused on this relationship, to secure, as far as possible, that "proper understanding," is the core of my life and work.

The central thesis of Revisionist historiography, when I began work on the Lincoln-Douglas debates, was that the Civil War was an "unnecessary war." It was held to have been unnecessary for two reasons. First, because the slavery question, which agitated the country, was a moral question. And moral questions were held to be incapable of resolution by any rational means. Morality —so the historians, like the social scientists, believed—was a matter of subjective opinion, and there was no way that anyone could be proved "right" or "just," or, conversely, "wrong" or "unjust." Yet in those faraway days, moral relativism and democracy were held to go hand in hand. So it was thought that the proper way to have dealt with slavery was to abstain from inflaming passions by talking about it, either as an evil or a good thing, while somehow working out a compromise. But American politicians of the period, the Revisionists held, were notably irresponsible, and fanned the flames recklessly, to advance their political fortunes. The "responsible" politician, *par excellence*, was Stephen A. Douglas, because "popular sovereignty" was a way to stop talking about slavery at least on the national level. And of all those who continued to talk about slavery, none was more reckless than Abraham Lincoln. By insisting, at a moment of high tension, that a decision was at hand, whereby the country must become all free, or all slave, he insisted upon a policy that could only result in civil war.

Secondly, however, the Civil War was unnecessary, because at the moment that Lincoln made the House Divided speech, the territorial issue, the focal point of the slavery question, was virtually solved. And it was solved because of the policy embodied in Lincoln's rival, and the Revisionists' favorite, Stephen A. Douglas. Whether or not "climate" would have kept slavery out of Kansas is immaterial, because the battle for Kansas had been won by the superior numbers and greater force of the free-soil settlers. The sole remaining chance for slavery in Kansas by 1857 lay in the attempt of the Buchanan administration to force the acceptance of the Lecompton Constitution on Congress, which would have admitted Kansas as a state with a foothold for slavery remaining there. But the fight against Lecompton was led every inch of the way by Stephen A. Douglas. The winning of that fight vindicated popular sovereignty as an effective means to assure freedom in the territories. The virtue of popular sovereignty, as seen by Revisionism, was then two-fold: first, that it did not treat slavery as a moral question; and, secondly, that it assured the victory of freedom in the territories. Most Revisionists conceded that this was the proper outcome, not because slavery was wrong, but because such an outcome was in keeping with the trends of the nineteenth century. The South, they felt, would and could have accepted the loss of the territories because of the operation of popular sovereignty—although the demand in 1860 for a federal slave code for the territories seems to contradict this—just because it did not involve any moral condemnation of the peculiar institution.

The defeat of the Lecompton Constitution, with the Republicans in Congress marshalled under the leadership of Douglas, occurred before Lincoln made his House Divided speech. By the early spring of 1858, Horace Greeley, and other eastern leaders of the Republican Party, felt that Douglas should be supported, not opposed, for re-election to the Senate, by the Illinois Republicans. The principal thrust of the House Divided speech was directed against just this political sentiment. Douglas had once been anathema to free-soilers, because of his role in repealing the Missouri Compromise restriction of slavery. It is worth recalling, that the original blast against this repeal, which led to the formation, first of the anti-Nebraska coalition, and then to the Republican Party, was called the "Appeal of the Independent Democrats in Congress." It denounced that repeal as "an atrocious plot . . . to convert [a vast unoccupied region] into a dreary region of despotism." But it was no longer possible to believe that Douglas was the arch-conspirator in such a plot, when he had fought tooth and nail against the President of his own party, to assure that the victory won by the free-soilers on the plains of Kansas was not taken from them in Washington. Any suspicion that "popular sovereignty" was a secret formula for extending slavery—as Lincoln, like the Independent Democrats, had charged—seemed now to have been dissipated. That is why Lincoln, in the House Divided speech, went to such extraordinary lengths to revive the conspiracy charges, in the account of the four "workmen," Stephen, Franklin, Roger, and James. But there was no question but that Douglas had burned his bridges Southward, and had done so long before the Freeport Question. The Southerners had believed the charge of the Independent Democrats in 1854, and had believed Douglas was their man. Henceforth they would regard him as renegade and traitor.

In the minds of the eastern Republicans, the success of the fight against Lecompton pointed towards an alliance between Douglas Democrats and Republicans. After all, it was not long since most of those Republicans had *been* Democrats, as the Appeal reminds us. Had Lincoln not repelled this possibility by his candidacy for the Senate in 1858, that alliance might well have come to full fruition in 1860, with Douglas supported for the presidency by Republicans. Would the Southern Democrats have walked out of the Charleston Convention in such a case? Probably. But when we think of the Douglas Democrats at Charleston, we think of a Northern Democratic Party badly splintered by the presence in the field of a hostile Republican Party. By the spring of 1860, the Republicans were rapidly absorbing the remnants of the Know-Nothings, and most of the remaining Whigs, outside of the border slave states. And they were absorbing droves of free-soil Democrats, who could see that a majority coalition in the free states was forming around the Republicans, and not around the Douglas Democracy. In this movement, the tariff probably played as large a role as free soil. We are then faced with the might-have-been that, had Douglas been supported for the Senate by Lincoln and his followers in 1858, that he would have been supported by Republicans nationally (or sectionally!) for President in 1860. Douglas, under such circumstances, would have been elected President by a much larger majority than Lincoln's 39% of the popular vote, and perhaps by an even larger majority of the electoral vote. The South would have faced a North much more politically united than the one it faced in the case of Lincoln's election. Would secession and Civil War have followed nonetheless? No one can tell, but the probabilities are infinitely less that it would have done so. Even if the bolt at Charleston had occurred, the obstacles to secession that followed Lincoln's election would have been far greater. For the South to secede in the face of the election of a Democratic President, however personally unpopular there, would have been much, much more difficult. Besides, that President would have commanded an effective lever in the patronage. All he would have had to do was offer offices to a handful of the firebrands, whose defection would have broken the back of the secessionist movement.

It is worth repeating, and repeating often, that however Douglas may have been looked upon as a traitor to the South, his doctrine of popular sovereignty did *not* involve any moral judgment upon the peculiar institution. It is impossible to read the debates of the period, without feeling that this moral judgment, more than anything else, drove the slave South into rebellion. Yet it was just this moral condemnation that Lincoln insisted upon, in the House Divided speech, throughout the joint debates, in the Ohio speeches of 1859, and in the Cooper Union speech. He made it a kind of doctrinal means test, to drive Douglas away from the Republican Party, and of course to keep open the place of leadership that he himself filled. In 1858 Lincoln did not, I think, aim at the Presidency for himself. Yet he certainly knew that he was destroying a possible coalition of Republicans and Douglas Democrats in 1860. Douglas's charges throughout the 1858 campaign, that the House Divided speech embodied a policy that could only lead to civil war was a valid one, and did not require any prophetic insight on Douglas's part. How candid was Lincoln's denial that his policy had any such import?

Lincoln's policy is indefensible, if there was not a profound reason for preferring the moral condemnation of slavery, as the basis for restricting its extension into the territories, to popular sovereignty. The ground for this preference was its embodiment in the Declaration of Independence. For Lincoln, the principle that condemned slavery was the same principle that justified American independence. John Quincy Adams had declared that the only thing that kept the "North American Revolution" from being mere "treason and rebellion," was the principles contained in the first two paragraphs of the Declaration of Independence. Lincoln inherited this view. And the principle that justified American independence required the "republican form of government," also required by Article 4 of the Constitution. Americans could not, Lincoln held, accept slavery as a matter of moral indifference, without coming to accept their own freedom as a matter of moral indifference. What they owed to Negroes, they owed to themselves and what they owed to themselves, they owed to Negroes *because* they owed it to themselves. "As I would not be a slave, so I would not be a master."

The "national political creed," of which Diamond once wrote, is to be found in the Declaration. It is not to be found in the Constitution. The compromises with slavery, in the Constitution of 1787, called into question *all* the compromises of the Constitution, raising the doubt whether any of them were in accordance with principles, or were merely concessions to necessity, that is, reflections of the bargaining power of the contending factions. Without recourse to the Declaration, there is no way of distinguishing principled from unprincipled compromises. Diamond's latter-day "no-guidance" thesis simply severs that relationship between Declaration and Constitution which he himself had called the vital principle of the regime.

Here is how Lincoln regarded the logic of the principle of equality. Here is how he thought that "all men are created equal" implied, not only a condemnation of slavery, but a condemnation of slavery *because* it was inconsistent with the idea of republican government. And republican government, to him, meant a government of equal political rights—or, as we would say, democracy—*and* the rule of law. The following is from the Peoria speech of 1854.

> *Judge Douglas frequently, with bitter irony and sarcasm, paraphrases our argument by saying: "The white people of Nebraska are good enough to govern themselves, but they are not good enough to govern a few miserable negroes!!"*

> *Well, I doubt not that the good people of Nebraska are, and will continue to be as good as the average of people elsewhere. I do not say the contrary. What I do say is, that no man is good enough to govern another man, without that other's consent. I say this is the leading principle—the sheet anchor of American republicanism.*

Lincoln then quotes the first two sentences of the second paragraph of the Declaration of Independence, and continues.

> *I have quoted so much at this time to show that according to our ancient faith, the just powers of government are derived from the consent of the governed. Now the relation of masters and slaves is PRO TANTO, a total violation of this principle. That master not only governs the slave without his consent; but he governs him by a set of rules altogether different from those which he prescribes for himself. Allow ALL the governed an equal voice in the government, and that, and that only, is self-government.*

According to Lincoln, the principles of the Declaration are the principles of self-government, and they are the principles of American republicanism. They require that those who make the law *live under the law*—which means *constitutionalism*. But they also require that those who live under the law *make the law*—which means *democracy*. Democracy, I should add, is the same as American republicanism.

That self-government, properly and strictly understood, requires allowing "All the governed an equal voice in the government," is an unequivocal assertion. But this clearly refers to political justice in its fullest sense, the sense implying the best regime. The cast of Lincoln's thought, is in this respect classical, not modern. Political justice—democracy understood as the best regime—is a *terminus ad quem*, not a *terminus a quo*. (Hobbes, remember, substituted the turning away from evil, for the turning toward the good, as the ground in nature of moral and political choice. This replacement of a natural end, with a natural beginning, coincided with the abolition of prudence, as the political and moral virtue *par excellence*.) The actual requirements of political justice—that is, justice as an act of prudence—for Lincoln as for Aristotle—always required taking into account circumstances. He had ample authority for this in the Declaration of Independence, which is a sufficient reason why the American

Founding cannot be understood entirely or solely in the light of modern political philosophy. But there can be no prudence, except in the light of a goal or end of political life. One cannot measure and give due weight to the obstacles to the goal if the goal itself is lost to view. This goal, or the symbol of this goal, is found within the American political tradition, in the Declaration of Independence, if it is to be found anywhere. All my efforts to restore the classical element in Lincoln's statesmanship have thus been linked to the restoration of the teaching of the Declaration of Independence to its proper role.

* * *

I have written repeatedly that the Civil War is "the most characteristic phenomenon in American politics . . . because it represents the innermost character of that politics." I have, I think, sufficiently proved that the academic debate about the American political tradition is for the most part little more than a concealed (or unconscious) form of the political debate. Conducting my argument by political, rather than academic speech, is part of my attempt to restore to this debate both its seriousness and its vitality. Surely, this is necessary when someone of Irving Kristol's place and eminence, solemnly declares, in the inaugural of A.E.I.'s Bicentennial Distinguished Lecture Series, that the American political tradition is "an inarticulate tradition." Would it not be fair to say that Irving Kristol became inarticulate, when confronted with the articulateness of the American political tradition?

You have reproached me for not becoming, as you think I might have become, "the great historian and poet of the American regime." Now history is concerned with particulars, and poetry with universals, and these might seem to be antithetical enterprises. (Aristotle calls poetry "truer" than history, because universals are objects of knowledge, but particulars, at best, yield true opinion.) Yet history and poetry form part of a single discipline in political philosophy. (Shakespearian history, which is neither tragedy nor comedy, and yet both, represents this unity. See my "The Unity of Tragedy, Comedy, and History: An Interpretation of the Shakespearian Universe."*) Writing as I do, about the Civil War, and the American Revolution, both as events in the past, and as elements of an "eternal present," is of the essence of my project. *Crisis of the House Divided* was not meant to be a book about American history, except incidentally. It is in the form of a scholastic disputed question, which is itself a form of the Socratic dialogue. It was born in my mind when I discovered—at a time when I was studying the *Republic* with Leo Strauss—that the issue between Lincoln and Douglas was in substance, and very nearly in form, identical with the issue between Socrates and Thrasymachus. The beauty of Lincoln's argument was that he made the case for popular government depend upon the acceptance of a standard of right and wrong, independent of mere opinion, and one which was not and could not be justified by the counting of heads. Hence the Lincolnian case for popular government was inherently proof against "permissive egalitarianism." The American tradition of popular government in the person of Lincoln, was thus seen to depend upon the statesman as prophet. And prophecy, as I learned from Strauss, who had it from Maimonides —and ultimately from Plato's Athenian Stranger—was the political name for political science. The relationship of history and poetry, in the American political tradition, may be indicated by saying that if Lincoln had not existed, we would have had to invent him! Existing as he did, however, involves showing his life as itself a work of art, and not of chance events. Lincoln's best known noble lie is "the world will little note, nor long remember, what we say here." Perhaps more significant is "I claim not to have controlled events, but confess plainly, that events have controlled me." The art of the dialogue, as Strauss interpreted it, was to produce a surface that appeared to be governed by chance. (Socrates did not intend to go down to Piraeus: and, being down, intended to return immediately. It was necessary to the dialogue on justice, a dialogue governed by the strictest necessities of Plato's art, that it seemed to have been the result of chance, and to have been forced upon Socrates against his will. Lincoln took great pains to characterize the Emancipation Proclamation as "an act of justice . . . upon military necessity.") Plato himself found many of the materials of his art in "history," the central historical event being the life and death of Socrates (seen, however, in the context of both the Persian and the Peloponnesian Wars). Without these materials of history there would have been nothing to form into his art. (There really were a Cephalus, a Polemarchus, and a Thrasymachus, whose names chanced to represent the roles assigned to them by art.)

Do I not bring philosophy down from the heavens and into the city —making it practical and political—when I demonstrate by my critiques of Kendall, Bradford, and Wills, that their doctrines are merely varieties of Confederate doctrine, and that the vital center of their beliefs is derived from John C. Calhoun? Do I not do that even more profoundly, when I show that the "Marx of the Master Class" is not, in the crucial respect, so very different from Marx himself, since the proslavery attack on free society, and the Marxist critique of capitalism, closely coincide? In showing that the struggle today over the interpretation of American tradition is "the Civil War continued by other means," do I not thereby illuminate my thesis that the Civil War is "the most characteristic phenomenon in American politics"? Is it not vital and necessary to this project, to show that Kristol and Diamond represent (like mirrors reflecting each other) two images of the position held by Stephen A. Douglas in 1858? The one called the principles of the Revolution "rhetoric," and the other called them "noble," but without correlative practical implications. The severing of the Founding from natural right and natural law, leaves it with nothing to guide it but positive right. At that point, Kristol and Diamond, like Douglas, under the withering and relentless analysis of Lincoln, become followers willy-nilly of John C. Calhoun. (In Diamond's case, I traced his precise words, from Calhoun via Kendall.) Is not my challenge to interpret the American political tradition identical in its terms to Lincoln's challenge to the eastern leaders of the Republican Party in 1858, as to the propriety of Douglas leading the free-soil movement? And is not this also a demonstration of the "eternal presence" of the question of whether justice is the interest of the stronger, or whether it must not be based upon natural right?

Leo Strauss's life and work had a motive that was not less political than philosophic. The political motive was to arrest and reverse "the decline of the West." That decline consisted in the West's loss of its sense of purpose. It no longer believed in its purpose, because it no longer understood that it had a purpose. Its purpose had become unbelievable to it, because certain objections to belief had arisen which had sapped, if they had not destroyed, the foundations of belief: belief had become unbelievable. At first, it appeared that "man made himself," that the human, and not the divine, was the "measure of all things." But the human, detached from the divine, did not long remain human: it quickly turned into the bestial. Man himself presently appeared as the mere epiphenomenon of his own blind and destructive urges. The destruction of philosophy appeared completed, in contemporary social science, when Reason appeared finally as nothing more than the mask worn by Unreason. Today, terrorism is a symbol of the fact that to *avant-garde* modernity not even self-preservation can be called a rational goal.

The West, Strauss taught, was constituted at its highest by Reason and Revelation. These two different and contradictory principles, neither of which could refute the other, had come to subsist, in the minds of the West's greatest souls — for example, in Moses Maimonides, William Shakespeare, and Thomas Aquinas — in an uneasy but fruitful tension. The greatness of the West lay in the quiet but firm refusal of the human soul, nurtured by both, to acquiesce in the destruction of either, by closing the eyes of the soul to the possibility of either. Yet Reason and Revelation came to be threatened, or more than threatened, by Modernity. The theoretical tension between Reason and Revelation came to be replaced by a practical alliance — an alliance forged in Strauss's life's work — in the face of this threat of destruction to the West. For Modernity culminates in the claims of Science, to have replaced God, and of History, to have replaced Philosophy. Strauss's career, his peculiar genius, and his particular achievement, was to have proved — as no one in four hundred years had done — that neither Science nor History had vindicated its claims, and that the power and dignity both of Reason and Revelation, as guides to human life, were inherently untouched by Modernity. In this he vindicated the claims both of Athens *and* Jerusalem.

Strauss proved that the *problem* of natural right remained what it had always been since its first discovery: the problem whose solution was the solution to the human problem. Nor was it any accident that he found the most lucid examples of the necessity of natural right in two passages of the Old Testament, which provided the epigraph of *Natural Right and History*. But the contemplation of a problem, while it may be a sufficient guide to action for philosophers, is not a sufficient guide to political men. Socrates' refutation of Thrasymachus was not sufficient, from Socrates' point of view, nor was it sufficient from that of Glaucon and Adeimantus, Plato's brothers (and surrogates). But it *was* sufficient for Thrasymachus, who became Socrates' disciple, when he perceived that Socrates was the stronger of them. At that point Socratic natural right became political right for Thrasymachus. One might say that for Horace Greeley and the free-soil movement, natural right became political right, when Lincoln defeated Douglas in the political dialectic of the joint debates, and their sequel, ending in the Cooper Union speech. At that point, Lincoln had succeeded in turning the free-soil movement, and the future of the regime, away from the worship of the golden calf of popular sovereignty. In the peroration of the Cooper Union speech, Lincoln said, "Let us have faith that Right makes Might, and in that faith, let us to the end, dare to do our duty as we understand it." Such a faith in reason, makes reasonable the faith in faith.

My demonstration of both the possibility and the necessity of natural right becoming political right, in the example provided by Lincoln, adds a practical and political dimension to Strauss's project, a dimension that cannot be achieved by any philosophic argument detached from those circumstances in which political action always takes place. At the same time, it puts the American concern with justice, in the context, not only of that "eternal present" in which the philosophic debate takes place, but in the context of that experience of justice, attested "three thousand years ago." In carrying on the struggle for the conviction that we live in the presence of such a debate, and of such an experience, do not we the living, carry on that unfinished task, so nobly advanced, each in his own way, by Abraham Lincoln and Leo Strauss?

* * *

Lincoln prefaced his peroration in the Cooper Union speech by warning his followers not to be "slandered from our duty by false accusations against us." To take up Lincoln's argument and to be slandered by false accusations, is then but a single burden. My shoulders are broad enough. But it is sad that such slanders should come from such as yourself. You tell me that "it is impossible for you to have a decent association with anyone . . . except with the student sycophants you surround yourself with." The slander of cultivating "sycophantism," as you must surely remember, is the one that was made most often against Leo Strauss. After all, you were one of the leading sycophants, and I was another. And were we not a happy band, taking the malice of our detractors as a badge of honor, like so many members of the Order of the Garter? The spring that Strauss went to Chicago (1949) I once spent an hour with Clara

Meyer, who had been one of Strauss's patronesses and friends at the New School, and who was then the Dean, listening to her complain about him in just such terms. This complaint, however, comes sometimes even from the well-meaning. But its cause is not far to seek. We live in an age of unbelief. Or, to be more precise, we live in an age in which conviction is grounded neither in reason nor in authoritative tradition. We live in an age of charlatans and so-called "charismatic" leaders. (The two are not necessarily identical.) We live in the age of Lenin, Stalin, Hitler, Jim Jones, and the apostles of permissive egalitarianism. As a critic of Modernity, Strauss criticized the falsity of un-founded belief, but in such a way as to restore belief as a rational enterprise. This restoration of rational conviction, which is certainly what turned me toward Strauss in the first place, was utterly unintelligible to most of his colleagues. Before I met Strauss, I too thought it obligatory to preface every assertation about things good and bad, right and wrong, with the disclaimer that it was a "value judgment." To maintain, for example, that the difference between just and unjust (and, in particular between tyrannical and non-tyrannical) regimes, was a matter of reason and experience, and not of liking and disliking, was taken to imply a return to the ages of superstition. And so Strauss's critics could only put down to some kind of intellectual prestidigitation, the means by which he made followers of his students. For such critics, to believe that there was any ground for belief other than unsupported preference, was to be deluded. Of course, their own beliefs were invariably the merest echoes of those "mass effects in modern society," which constituted the tyranny of the majority. Never were the cool, skeptical, "scientific" members of the academic community more credulous, than when denouncing the credulity of those who differed with them. It is unworthy of you, to ridicule or reproach, the enthusiasm of the young Claremonters for political philosophy. It is only the renewal of what you yourself once were. Look westward, Walter, the land is bright!

* * *

You would have me believe that a bad opinion of me has now "become almost universal." Yet in recent years, I have had "golden opinions, from all sorts of people." Of course, I do not conduct opinion polls to discover what I ought to be doing or thinking. Do you? Were opinions as hostile to me as you say, I do not see why that should influence my course. To prefer noble failure to vulgar success is of the essence of moral freedom and of human dignity. As a teacher of natural right, I am cleaving to a path, equally anathema to ideological liberalism and ideological conservatism. I was well taught by Leo Strauss, not to underestimate the difficulties I was likely to encounter. But I will say to you, as Socrates did to Polus in the *Gorgias*, that I care not how many witnesses you bring against me. I care only for one witness: yourself. For be assured, my old friend, that you must either refute my *logos* — in which case you will have my agreement and my thanks — or you must testify in my behalf. That you must do, either by your speech or by you silence. But only by the former can you acquit yourself with honor.

* * *

Much of your harshness towards me is founded upon the soreness you feel about "Political Philosophy and Honor," in which I set forth my objections to the Leo Strauss Dissertation Award. What matters, once again, are not the personal reflections in which you indulge, but whether the philosophical ground of the argument of that essay is sound or unsound. On that — as usual — you say nothing. When the article was in typescript, however, I sent it to you. You replied to me, that you yourself had had doubts about the Award, but that you could not have expressed them as well as I had done. By this, I thought you had conceded the points of the argument. However, you went on, you did not think that I should publish it, because it referred to something that was "past"! What in the world did you mean by this, except that you wanted me to suppress the truth, because it was inconvenient? I replied that Lincoln did not accept the repeal of the Missouri Compromise, because it was "past." And it was clear, that I called for the "repeal" of the Strauss Award as much as Lincoln had called for the restoration of the Missouri Compromise. I did so, because the very language used to justify the Strauss Award constituted a denial of the possibility of political philosophy. For it was said to constitute a recognition of political philosophy as "one of many" disciplines within political science. But political philosophy is by its nature the architectonic practical discipline. It can no more be "one of many" than happiness, which is the end of all practical activity, can be "one of many" good things. As I have argued at length herein, Reason and Revelation are the two irreducible principles of human action, which human thought has discovered. The sovereignty of Reason, as a guide to human action, itself depends upon the unity of the discipline whereby Reason becomes such a guide. The sovereignty of God depends equally upon the unity of God. "Hear, O Israel, the Lord thy God, is One!" Can you imagine the ancient chant concluding that God is "one and a half," or "One point zero zero one"? But the logic of the unity of political philosophy, to repeat, is the same. No restoration of classical political philosophy is or was possible, if the supposed adherents of it concede to their scientistic-historicist colleagues the most vital point dividing them. This was not building bridges to the profession — as I often heard it — it was burning the bridges to classical political philosophy. It was, as I said at the time, not honoring Strauss, but burying him.

George Anastaplo, in an otherwise favorable review of *How to Think About the American Revolution*, did not accept at my estimation, my critique of the Strauss Award. While being careful to say that he himself was not a sponsor of it, and had had no part in it, he noted in its favor that "hardly any of [Strauss's] thoughtful and devoted students were troubled by the enterprise." But this was merely begging the question, of whether those "thoughtful and devoted" students were thoughtful and devoted when they made the all-important concession to Modernity. Certainly these thoughtful and devoted students—or many of them—were and are—like yourself—great and famous scholars. Some of them can spin a cobweb of interpretation to cover the Super-Dome, out of the slenderest thread of esoteric text. But they forgot the One. Or, more precisely, the *one* thing they forgot was the meaning of *One*. They forgot that if there are many gods, then the gods fight among themselves (see *Euthyphro*), and man cannot be guided by divine revelation. And they forgot that if there are many separate and equal sciences of human things, then there will be many separate and equally authoritative opinions concerning the human good. These too will become "fighting gods." These will issue either in "permissive egalitarianism" or unpermissive totalitarianism. Thus the Strauss Award conceded the very premise and purpose of Strauss's life and work. It left Reason as impotent to guide human life, as is Revelation, in the presence of a Hesiod's Theogony.

The very formulation of the problem of the One and the Many, means that the One implied in the Many, cannot be One among Many. (This is the logical defect of the Kentucky Resolutions which I shall develop at some length in *A New Birth of Freedom*.) If this is denied, we do indeed live in a Multiverse and not a Universe; or, perhaps, the Universe of the Absurd, from which there is indeed "No Exit."

The foregoing theoretical argument supported my contention that the Strauss Award could only become—and indeed was intended, willy-nilly to become—an "affirmative action" program. Since you have written so well about the defects of another kind of affirmative action, how is it that you accept it in this case? It had to become a log-roll among contending factions because, by definition, there was no common (i.e. One) standard of judgment to which appeal could be made. In one of the "odd" or non-Straussian years of the Award, it was given for a dissertation on the French Marxist Louis Althusser. (Althusser has gained notoriety recently for murdering his wife.) The dissertation, which I read in part, was entirely an exercise in intrasectarian Marxist dialectics. It was praised by the committee making the award, for the excellence of its textual exegesis in the manner of Leo Strauss! Could there be a more graphic illustration of the account in my essay of how the award would be made?

You objected to the fact that I had signed my last letter to you, "As ever." That was because you professed to discover a great change, between my "earlier self and work," and the later. I considered whether I ought to subscribe myself "Your humble and obedient servant," but then I reflected upon the origins of this form of baroque politeness, in satirical infidelity. And yet it is fidelity to political philosophy, to which I herein lay claim. Churchill wisely says, that a statesman can only remain consistent amid changing circumstances, by changing with them, while preserving the same dominating purpose. I do not think anyone can find any change in the dominating purpose of my life, over the last thirty years. Certainly you have not done so. And therefore I must once again remain,

AS EVER,

HARRY

*In Shakespeare as Political Thinker, edited by John Alvis and Thomas G. West, Carolina Academic Press, 1981.

Nine

The Primacy of the Good
Leo Strauss Remembered

I n the eulogy of Leo Strauss that I delivered in November, 1973, shortly after his death, I said that I would leave to others, "more detached and more objective, the judgment of Strauss's place among the political philosophers." That warning needs to be repeated, in the light of developments in the near decade that has intervened. The interest in Strauss's work has grown apace. A bibliography of the articles about him would be a substantial one. The character of his work, no less than its merit, has become matter of ever-increasing controversy, with every passing year. But this, we must remind ourselves, has also been true of all the great figures of the great tradition that Strauss himself did so much to bring back to life. It would then be less than candid to conceal from my readers that I myself appear to be at or near the center of the disputations about Strauss. Anything I write should then be taken with all the caution with which one approaches the views of a partisan.

* * *

Readers of the January 22, 1982 *National Review* will be aware that I was roundly abused by Walter Berns for "presenting [myself] as the chosen spokesman for Leo Strauss." I was not in the least aware of having done any such thing. Certainly I did not see myself as "speaking" for Strauss by writing about him—and interpreting his work—more than I had "spoken" for Abraham Lincoln, for example, in writing about him. Nor did I think that I had written differently about Strauss than Strauss himself had done about the political philosophers before him. In an essay entitled "In Defense of Political Philosophy" published in that same issue of *National Review* I had written that

> *Leo Strauss's life and work had a motive that was not less political than philosophic. The political motive was to arrest and reverse "the decline of the West." That decline consisted in the West's loss of its sense of purpose. It no longer believed in its purpose, because it no longer understood that it had a purpose.*

In this I thought I was merely repeating thoughts encountered many times in Strauss's writings, as for example the following from the Introduction to *The City and Man* (1963).

The crisis of the West consists in the West's having become uncertain of its purpose. The West was once certain of its purpose—of a purpose in which all men could be united, and hence it had a clear vision of its future as the future of mankind. We do no longer have that certainty and that clarity. Some among us even despair of the future, and this despair explains many forms of contemporary Western degradation.

Walter Berns, after denouncing my presumption, declares unhesitatingly that

Strauss did not believe he, or political philosophy could save Western civilization (or reverse "the decline of the West"). It is precisely hopes of this kind that distort the quest for truth. Eternity, not history, is the theme of philosophy, which Strauss believed, must beware of wishing to be edifying. Jaffa, like Marx, wants to change the world, not to interpret it; he does nothing but edify.

In the revised and enlarged edition of *On Tyranny*, also published in 1963, Strauss included a forty-five page critique of his interpretation of Xenophon's *Hiero* by Alexander Kojève, whom Strauss regarded as the most competent philosophic interpreter of Hegel. Kojève (nè Kojevnikoff), originally a refugee from the Bolshevik revolution, was a French civil servant, and one who, if not strictly speaking a Stalinist, did not object to a Stalinist regime. He believed that a homogeneous world state, ruled by someone like Stalin, was inevitable on the basis of the dialectic of world history, and for that reason desirable. It was from this perspective that he criticized—and rejected—Strauss's understanding of tyranny in *On Tyranny*. Whatever the defect of Kojève's political philosophy, he made absolutely clear Strauss's disagreement with him, concerning both the necessity and the desirability of that "end of history" that Strauss had identified with the decline of the West. Strauss's thirty-seven page "Restatement," in reply to Kojève, completes what may well be the most philosophically competent intellectual confrontation of our times. It is sufficient to note here that, had Strauss resigned himself to the "decline of the West," as Walter Berns says that he did, he neither would nor could have written his "Restatement."

Berns says that I am "like Marx" in wanting to "change the world" rather than "to interpret it." He accepts Marx's dichotomy, in the "Theses on Feuerbach", between "change" and "interpretation." He pretends not to notice the difference between that kind of change which aims to prevent the destruction of decent constitutional regimes, and their replacement with the homogeneous world state, and its opposite. Yet Walter Berns himself, in the late 1950's, wrote a brilliant essay entitled "The Case Against World Government," which was precisely in the service of that philosophic understanding of politics, for which he now denounces me as being "like Marx."

In "What Is Political Philosophy?" Strauss wrote that,

All political action aims at either preservation or change. When desiring to preserve, we wish to prevent a change to the worse; when desiring to change, we wish to bring about something better.

Thought about better or worse necessarily implies thought of the good. Political philosophy clarifies the opinions of the good implicit in the political actions of men, and clarifies them in such a way as to replace these opinions with genuine knowledge. Moreover, Strauss says, "political philosophy deals with political matters in a manner that is meant to be relevant for political life; therefore its subject must be identical with its goal, the ultimate goal of political action." Political philosophy is thus meant to guide political life, in the light of its ultimate goal, "the good life," or "the good society," which is "the complete political good." In this, Strauss certainly followed Aristotle, who criticized Plato's idea of the good, as being insufficiently "relevant for political life." And he also followed the Aristotle who declared near the beginning of the *Nicomachean Ethics*, that the end of political philosophy was "not knowledge but action." Aristotle also declared (in Book II) that political philosophy "does not aim at theoretical knowledge . . . for we are inquiring not in order to know what virtue is, but in order to become good, since otherwise [our inquiry] would have been of no use." It is for this reason, Aristotle proceeds, that "we must examine the nature of actions." We must examine them, in order to know "how we ought to do them." Clearly, if Walter Berns thinks that wanting to know about actions, for the sake of knowing how to do them, as distinct from the purely theoretical exercise of knowing how to interpret them, is being "like Marx," then Aristotle, not less than Strauss and Jaffa, falls into that category.

Berns, in the context of this structure, says (as we have noted) "Strauss believed [philosophy] must beware of wishing to be edifying. Jaffa. . . does nothing but edify." Now the last two sentences of *Thoughts on Machiavelli* are as follows.

> *It would seem that the notion of the beneficence of nature or of the primacy of the Good must be restored by being rethought through a return to the fundamental experiences from which it is derived. For while "philosophy must beware of wishing to be edifying," it is of necessity edifying.*

The restoration of the idea "of the beneficence of nature," which may alternatively be called the restoration "of the primacy of the Good" by a "return to the fundamental experiences from which it is derived" is as good a summary statement of the intention of Leo Strauss's life work as I can imagine. Strauss thought that the fundamental human experiences had become almost inaccessible, because of what modern science, modern technology, and modern philosophy had done to obscure and distort those experiences. He sometimes compared modern life to a cave beneath the "natural" cave represented in

Plato's *Republic*, and he compared his own work of philosophic recovery to an ascent to the natural cave. Nevertheless, this return was not in the service of understanding the truth about those experiences in the light of "Eternity" alone. In the Introduction to *The City and Man*, he spoke of the "return to classical political philosophy"—which provided access to those "fundamental experiences"—as being "both necessary and tentative or experimental."

> *Not in spite of but because of its tentative character, it must be carried out seriously, i.e. without squinting at our present predicament. There is no danger that we can ever become oblivious of this predicament since it is the incentive to our whole concern with the classics.*

Let us repeat that, according to Leo Strauss, "our whole concern with the classics" was a hope that, according to Walter Berns, is "precisely" of the kind that distorts the quest for truth. Strauss did here warn against "squinting at our present predicament." What he meant by this, I am confident, was that—to use his oft-repeated dictum—we must understand the classical texts as their authors understood them. We must, in this, exclude everything peculiar to our situation, but alien to theirs, from the work of interpretation. But the "fundamental experiences" to which he referred at the end of *Thoughts on Machiavelli* were of course fundamental human experiences, experiences of the human condition *qua* human. At issue is the question of whether there is a human condition intrinsic to man's humanity, as distinct from an infinite number of possible human conditions, thrown up by history, necessity, or chance, from the void of an unknowable universe. Strauss never, so far as I can tell, doubted that all possible human conditions might be denominated human. That implied that the distinctively human underlay all its possible manifestations. While he called the "return" to classical political philosophy "tentative and experimental" he also called it "necessary." This implied that there was a necessity underlying the possibility of this return. Such a necessity was constituted by a nature that was "everywhere and always," a nature that determined what was intrinsically just and good.

When Strauss, at the end of *Thoughts on Machiavelli*, said that philosophy must beware of the wish to be edifying, he was quoting Hegel's *Phenomenology*. Although Strauss agreed with Hegel—as far as he went—Strauss himself went farther. He corrected Hegel's thought by adding to it. Walter Berns fails to notice Strauss's addition, which is that philosophy "is of necessity edifying." When therefore, Berns, in his role as Inquisitor, accuses me of the ultimate heresy, he says that "Jaffa . . . does nothing but edify." In so doing, however, he pays me a compliment as hyperbolic as the condemnation he intended.

The conviction that philosophy is intrinsically edifying is at the heart of that idea of natural right which is ultimately indistinguishable from the idea of political philosophy itself. Philosophy is intrinsically edifying because progress in wisdom is possible, even when wisdom itself appears to be always beyond our grasp, even when opinion about the whole seems unlikely ever to be replaced by genuine knowlege of the whole. Although "we know that we know nothing," there is a a sense in which we know something about the whole, however incomplete and inadequate. If I understood him aright, Strauss—like Socrates—always rejected Meno's rejection of the Socratic quest. When Socrates convicted Meno of ignorance of virtue, Meno wanted to abandon the quest for virtue, on the ground that his ignorance appeared to be so complete as to provide no basis upon which to recognize the truth, even if he were to discover it. In this Meno seems to have anticipated certain popular opinions associated today with Nietzsche and Heidegger. Certainly, Meno's despair would explain Meno's degradation. It was in this context that Socrates—or Plato—introduced the doctrine of learning as recollection. That doctrine is of course not a solution, but only a reformulation, of the problem, since it leaves us with the conundrum of how and when the soul which recollects first learned what it recollects. But that we can learn somehow, and even learn something about the highest things, the things upon which we can confidently ground our life and work, is a conviction— a faith perhaps, but a rational faith—upon which the natural right tradition is founded. I believe that it is upon the rock of this conviction that the work of Leo Strauss stands foursquare.

The remark about philosophy and the edifying, which appears at the end of *Thoughts on Machiavelli*, is repeated by Strauss near the end of "What Is Liberal Education?" This is the first essay in *Liberalism: Ancient and Modern*. It belongs to one of many passages of surpassing beauty that one comes upon in the writings of Leo Strauss, one of many in which, in reflecting upon an experience easily accessible to everyone, Strauss has touched, and touches us, with that kinship with the divine, which is our birthright.

Philosophy, we have learned, must be on its guard against the wish to be edifying—philosophy can only be intrinsically edifying. We cannot exert our understanding without from time to time understanding something of importance; and this act of understanding may be accompanied by the awareness of understanding, by the understanding of understanding, by noesis noeseos, and this is so high, so pure, so noble an experience that Aristotle could ascribe it to his God. This experience is entirely independent of whether what we understand primarily is pleasing or displeasing, fair or ugly. It leads us to realize that all evils are in a sense necessary if there is to be understanding. It enables us to accept all evils which befall us and which may well break our hearts in the spirit of good citizens of the city of God. By becoming aware of the dignity of the mind, we realize the true ground of the dignity of man and therewith the goodness of the world, whether we understand it as created or as uncreated, which is the home of man because it is the home of the human mind.

Ten

"In Defense Of Political Philosophy" Defended

A Rejoinder to Walter Berns

I n his "Reply to Harry Jaffa" (*National Review*, January 22, 1982), Walter Berns writes:

> *There is no substance to Harry Jaffa's criticism of me. In 1972, he wrote that the Declaration of Independence displays an "openness or vagueness" as to forms of government, so much so that "the people are not even obliged* [by the Declaration] *to set up popular governments" (*The Conditions of Freedom, *p. 158). I agree with this now and I have always agreed with it. Therefore, one must look elsewhere for the source of Jaffa's dispute with me.*

Walter Berns contributed an essay to a volume entitled *How Democratic Is the Constitution?* This volume is the first in what is intended to be a series observing the Bicentennial of the Constitution, sponsored and published by the American Enterprise Institute. Hence I associated him with the editors' assertion that, in seeking answers to the question posed in their title, they had sought out "spokesmen as authoritative, thoughtful, and instructive as could be found." I pointed to the presence in the volume of a noted academic Marxist, who gave an unequivocally—indeed brutally—Marxist answer to the question. And I pointed out that there was no representative in the volume of that contemporary of Karl Marx, whom Marx himself so greatly admired—Abraham Lincoln. Yet there was and is no more direct answer to the question, "How democratic is the Constitution?" than that given in the Gettysburg Address. There, as in countless other pronouncements, Lincoln identified this nation as dedicated to the proposition, "that all men are created equal," and by virtue of that dedication, devoted to the cause of "government of the people, by the people, for the people." It was astonishing to me that both the editors of the volume, and Walter Berns, might raise this question for consideration, in connection with the Constitution's Bicentennial, while utterly ignoring the name and argument of Abraham Lincoln. Whether Lincoln was right or wrong ought not to be taken for granted, but that his opinion should be passed over as not being among those deemed "authoritative, thoughtful and instructive," was almost beyond belief.

Whether or not Walter Berns shared responsibility for the editors' omission, his own essay, "Does the Constitution 'Secure These Rights'?" equally ignores the Lincolnian postion. It is hardly in keeping with the spirit of the Gettysburg Address that Berns writes approvingly that "for the Federalists, representation was a way of keeping the people out of government." He thinks, moreover, "that the Declaration does not contain a presumption against kings in general but only against tyrannical kings." Yet Lincoln believed that "the Declaration promised something better than the condition of British subjects...." Senator Stephen A. Douglas, and Chief Justice Taney, said Lincoln, thought that the "equality" of the Declaration applied only to British subjects in Britain, and British subjects in America. They did not see any "promise that, having kicked off the King and Lords of Great Britain, we should not at once be saddled with a King and Lords of our own."

Walter Berns thinks that there can be no dispute between us, concerning the interpretation of the Declaration of Independence, and its relationship to the Constitution, because he says he agrees with something I wrote in 1972. If then I wrote something different in 1978 (or at any other time), he implies that my other statements must be mistaken. Why? It seems that I (like any man) am as capable of being mistaken at one time as another. What counts is not who has agreed with whom, and when, but what is right. Which argument, whether mine—earlier or later—or Abraham Lincoln's, or Stephen A. Douglas's, or John C. Calhoun's, is the right one? The relevant differences can be reduced to a very sharp point: is the Declaration "neutral" towards all non-tyrannical forms of government, as Berns, following Martin Diamond, maintains; or does it contain within itself a profound preference for democratic republicanism—for government of, by, and for the people—as I and Abraham Lincoln maintain. I have given a comprehensive argument in support of the thesis I uphold, in *How to Think About the American Revolution*. This thesis and this argument Walter Berns and the editors of *How Democratic Is the Constitution?* have pretended not to see. They and Walter Berns will apparently go to any lengths, and make any excuses, rather than meet this thesis and this argument in fair and open discussion and debate. I need not repeat the argument of *How to Think About the American Revolution* here. Suffice it for the present that the Declaration, in my opinion, allows the people, in the exercise of their sovereignty to choose among a wide variety of regimes, or forms of government. Such a choice ought to be in accordance with the dictates of prudence. A prudential choice is one in which the form of government chosen is best adapted to the circumstances in which the people find themselves. But prudence relates to means, not ends. An understanding of ends is not provided by prudence. It must be provided to prudence. An understanding of the ends of government, "safety and happiness," from the perspective of the Declaration, indicates that a popular government, one of, by, and for the people, is the best form, the one that ought to be chosen, if circumstances do not in any way hinder the people's choice. It is, moreover, according to Jefferson and Lincoln, the only perfectly non-tyrannical regime.

The Declaration follows the paradigm of the relationship between prudence and political justice, embodied in the natural right teaching of the classics, as well as in Aristotelian scholasticism. There is then no question but that the people might, in deference to their circumstances, out of prudence, choose or accept nondemocratic or nonrepublican forms of government. But such choices will not themselves be prudent, unless they are informed by the understanding that some form of democratic republicanism is best. The Declaration cannot then be "neutral" towards the different forms of government. To maintain, as Berns does, that the Declaration is neutral, would mean that it is indifferent to the moral choices inherent in the differences of regimes. But the Declaration is in no sense morally indifferent, as the laws of nature and of nature's God are not morally indifferent. Lincoln believed that one could not be indifferent to the differences between, let us say, monarchy, aristocracy, and democratic republicanism, without ultimately being indifferent to the difference between slavery and freedom. Here is the crux of my difference with the school with which Berns has allied himself. No amount of indignant exclamation, or personal reproach can disguise his unwillingness to face the issue. Walter Berns is tied by interests he cannot admit, to a position he cannot defend. Like the antebellum South, he has the wolf by the ears, and is unable either to hold on or to let go. Without an argument, he is full of sound and fury. But the longer he pretends that there is nothing to debate, the plainer will become the reasons for his refusal to debate.

Concerning what I wrote in 1972, Berns has, in an abbreviated quotation, ignored the context of that quotation. That context was supplied by my critique of the Warren Court's ruling, in its reapportionment decisions, that the Constitution of the United States forbids state constitutions from apportioning upper houses of state legislatures, in a manner in which districts of unequal numbers of people would be equally represented. In short, the Warren Court held that the Constitution forbade the people of any state from doing what the people of the United States had done in representing the states in the Senate of the United States. In particular the Warren Court forbade Hawaii from giving equal representation to the smaller islands with the larger islands, in the upper house of their legislature; and it forbade Colorado from giving equal representation to the districts west of the continental divide and those east of the divide in their upper house. It forbade Hawaii and Colorado from doing these things, even though they were approved, not only by majorities of the whole people in both states, but by majorities within all parts of those states, including those that would be "discriminated" against. This limitation upon the authority of the people was, I argued, not founded upon any just reading of the Declaration of Independence. My argument was directed not only against this arbitrary limitation upon the people's sovereignty, but against the denial of any role for prudence—the proper choice of means—in the implementation of that sovereignty. The argument of that essay did not go to the question of ends, as in the question of the best regime. This latter question I did address in *How to Think About the American Revolution*. In so addressing it, I do not believe I contradicted what I had written earlier.

* * *

Walter Berns reproaches me because he says my letter, "In Defense of Political Philosophy," is "a frank imitation of Socrates's *Apology*." Jaffa, he says, has "identified his person and his fate with political philosophy and its fate." I do not see what grounds I have given Berns for this accusation, other than manifesting a serious concern with the questions of the right way of life, and of the best regime. Aristotle, in the spirit of Socrates (with whom he did not hesitate to differ), says that when all the errors have been refuted, what remains is the truth. Jefferson says that "truth is great and will prevail ... unless by human interposition disarmed of her natural weapons, free argument and debate, errors ceasing to be dangerous when it is permitted freely to contradict them." If then I have been free in contradiction, it is within the civility of the tradition of Socrates, Aristotle, and Jefferson. In the philosophic tradition, the truth may be personified in metaphor, but the truth itself is not understood to be a person. It is a *logos*, a rational explanation, or the result of such an explanation. An apology, in the Socratic sense, is neither a confession of error, nor an assertion of rectitude. It is a "giving of an account," by which one has submitted one's reason or reasons to the judgment of one's peers. To be inspired by Socrates's apology to give an account of one's own life and work is nothing for which, I am tempted to say, anyone need apologize.

It would appear, however, that if Walter Berns does not have a very good opinion of my apology, neither does he have a very good one of Socrates'. After saying that he will leave it "to the reader to judge how impressive are the similarities," viz., of Socrates's and Jaffa's apologies, he goes on to add that he "would remind them (sic) ... that it is an error of logic to conclude, as Jaffa does, that because Socrates was a pest, all pests are Socrates." But nowhere, and never, have I said or implied that Socrates was a pest. That, or something like it, was the opinion of Socrates's accusers. It is not my opinion, and it is not (as Berns alleges) the basis of any self-justification on my part. In writing as he does, Berns may have had in mind the following passage from Plato's *Apology of Socrates*:

> *For if you (men of Athens) kill me, you will not easily discover another like me, who—even if it is rather ridiculous to say—has simply been set upon the city by the god, as though upon a great and well-bred horse who is rather sluggish because of his size and needs to be awakened by a gadfly. The god seems to me to have set me upon the city as someone of this sort: I awaken and persuade and reproach everywhere upon you the whole day.*
>
> [20 E—31 A. Trans. Thomas G. West]

Socrates's comparison—which he calls "rather ridiculous"—is of himself to a gadfly, and of Athens to a horse. In this comparison, the gadfly irritates the horse, but in so doing does what is good for the horse. The word "pest" suggests pestilence, that is, disease and death. But the irritant supplied by the gadfly—Socrates—to the horse—Athens—keeps the subject from falling into a comatose condition, akin to death. The gadfly, far from being a pest, is life-giving and health-bearing. The passage in the *Apology* reminds one of another in the *Gorgias*, in which Socrates anticipates his trial by comparing it to the case of a doctor being tried before a jury of children, on charges brought by a confectionary cook. The doctor stands accused by the cook of preventing the cook from peddling his sweets among the children, and of compelling them instead to eat plain food, and sometimes to take bitter medicine. As the jurors are children, they do not understand that the doctor—like the gadfly—is their true friend and benefactor, and that the cook is their enemy. And so they will vote to convict and condemn the doctor.

In his catalogue of my crimes, Walter Berns writes that I am unlike Socrates. Socrates, he says, "was gentle and urbane," while I am "harsh and vindictive." Yet even while denying a resemblance, he affirms it. "Jaffa," he says, "adopts in earnest the heroic pose that Socrates adopted in jest." But how does Berns know that Socrates was not in earnest, or that I am not jesting? Or how does he know that there is not a jesting-in-earnest? Finally, he says that what I do is "a far cry from Socrates, who lived quietly with his fellow-Athenians while hardly letting them know that he philosophized." And, he concludes, Socrates "certainly never tried to be their king." I have taken pains to quote Socrates declaring—according to Plato—that, like a gadfly, he awakens and persuades and reproaches each of his fellow citizens, and does not stop doing this during the whole day (this being the original form of philosophic journalism). I have done so to enable the reader to judge for himself how quietly Socrates says he lived in Athens. Surely, if Socrates did what he did as quietly as Berns says he did it, it would hardly be possible to understand why his fellow-citizens executed him for doing it!

But Berns also says that I am unlike Socrates, because Socrates "never tried to be...king." Yet Socrates, in the *Gorgias*, says that he is the only genuine *politikos* or statesman in Athens. And in the most famous passage in the literature of political philosophy Plato puts in Socrates's mouth the assertion that evils will not cease from the cities until philosophers become kings, or kings become philosophers. Putting together the passages in the *Gorgias* and the *Republic*, might one not infer that Socrates believed himself to be a king, in the sense that he possessed the art of ruling, however much he may have lacked a *polis* or political community in which to rule? If Socrates was in truth the only *politikos* in Athens, then his rule, had it come about, must of necessity have been monarchical rule. It is true, that Socrates's monarchical qualifications were not the result of *trying* to be a king. Genuine kingship, from the Platonic (perhaps Socratic) point of view is a by-product of philosophy, not the other way around. Moreover, *being* a king does not imply *becoming* a king, since genuine philosophers do not wish to rule, and the idea of non-philosophers compelling them to rule is absurd.

There is even further unintended irony in Berns's accusation against me, of all people, of harboring monarchical ambitions. Certainly, if I am known at all, it is as an admirer of Abraham Lincoln. And my differences with Walter Berns, which have led to his angry accusations, arose when he ignored, or brushed aside, Lincoln's doctrine, that the Declaration of Independence indicates a preference for a regime as far from the monarchical as possible. It was, I remind the reader, Berns, not I, who wrote "that the Declaration of Independence does not contain a presumption against kings...."

* * *

In his anger, Walter Berns declares that I am "a textbook case of someone converting philosophy into ideology, of abusing theoretical teachings... for practical ends." Berns does not say how I do this, and I do not know what it is that he considers to be such an abuse. But he also says that I am "like Marx" in wanting to change the world rather than interpret it (paraphrasing the theses on Feuerbach). I have dealt at length with this comparison between myself and Marx in "The Primacy of the Good: Leo Strauss Remembered." Suffice it for the present, that I show there that if I am "like Marx," so also are Leo Strauss and Aristotle. From Berns's perspective, as it seems, *any* use of philosophical or theoretical teachings for practical ends becomes an abuse of those teachings. For Berns, political philosophy itself has become identified with "ideology." Berns's quarrel is with the very idea of that enterprise which clarifies the meaning of the good, in order that we might not only know what is good, but become good, by acting well.

Berns excuses his refusal to face the questions I have raised with him for debate, by saying that "The reason some people avoid Jaffa is not that they are afraid to debate him, but that he follows Hobbes, not Socrates in holding that to disagree with him is to insult him." But where does Hobbes — one of the ablest and most unrelenting controversialists who ever lived — say that "to disagree with him is to insult him?" And who will believe, for one moment, that Walter Berns ever refused to debate anyone, fearing lest his opponent think that he had been insulted! But Berns has a strange way of transposing facts. It was I who, in the best of tempers, invited him to share a platform with me at the annual meeting of the American Political Science Association in 1981, to debate the differences I have described concerning the Declaration of Independence. It was he who, in the worst of tempers, declined, on the ground that, in differing with him as I did, I had insulted him. Therefore, I herewith extend to him again the invitation to debate these matters, at the next meeting of the American

Political Science Association, or at any other time or place. And I assure him, and everyone, that I will never consider myself to be insulted, by any contradiction whatever.

Berns says that I am "a slayer of imaginary dragons." I leave it to the reader to decide whether the questions I have raised about the interpretation of the Declaration of Independence are imaginary or real. At stake is the question of whether "the laws of nature and of nature's God" really exist, and whether the political life of the United States—or of any other polity—ought or can be guided by them. For in the Declaration of Independence, ideas of natural law and natural right become for the first time in human history the explicit and public ground of positive law and positive right. Ideas of natural law and natural right reflect the tradition of political philosophy, whose founder was Socrates. There is a sense in which the Socratic enterprise faces its supreme test —certainly its supreme test in the post-classical world—in the fate of the American political tradition. There was a time when Walter Berns was one of the most enthusiastic advocates I knew of this view of the relationship of political philosophy to political history.

Now, however, Berns writes that Leo Strauss "did not believe he, or political philosophy, could save western civilization (or reverse the 'decline of the West')." "It is precisely hopes of this kind," Berns adds, "that distort the quest for truth. Eternity, not history, is the theme of philosophy..." Much depends upon how one understands what saving western civilization means, or how "the decline of the West" might be reversed. I believe that the enterprise of western civilization is consummated each time a soul is saved from the dark night of fanatical obscurantism. It is consummated whenever one soul is released from the pessimism that truth is unobtainable, or not worth the trouble to obtain. It is consummated whenever a single soul is disabused of the proposition that the subjective intensity of one's convictions matters more than their objective validity. Eternity is indeed the theme of philosophy, but it becomes such when the individual soul becomes aware of its power to know, and when it discovers in this power the immortal ground of its mortal existence. This, above all else, is what is meant by saving western civilization, and reversing the decline of the West. Whether there will be enough of such souls, or whether the influence of such souls will be sufficient, to inform political action on a sufficient scale, is something no one can foretell. But unless we surrender to pessimistic determinism, a pessimism born of the denial of the possibility of philosophy, unless we surrender to the nihilistic doctrine that there is no objective difference between doctrines except the subjective intensity with which they are held, we have no reason to believe that we must fail. If we do not know that we must fail, we have duty to persevere in our political efforts to reverse the decline of the West. With that duty, we have the sure knowledge that, whatever the outcome, we will, by doing our duty, have lived our lives well. For the heart of the enterprise of political philosophy lies in the distinction between vulgar success and noble failure, and in the reasoning that teaches us why we should prefer the latter to the former. The destiny of the human soul does indeed lie in eternity, not in history. But the destiny of souls in eternity is reflected in how they act in history, in their moral and political lives in this world. Western civilization is above all the historical phenomenon constituted by a concern for eternity, whether by the instruments of reason or of revelation. That our concern with eternity be reflected in our lives in this world, is so far from distorting the quest for truth, that it is the very condition of that quest.

*   *   *

Walter Berns writes that Jaffa "did not learn from his teacher, Leo Strauss, that moral indignation is the greatest enemy of philosophy." In this, Berns is most assuredly right. I did not learn from Strauss that moral indignation is the greatest enemy of philosophy, because Strauss never taught that moral indignation is the greatest enemy of philosophy. Moral indignation would be the enemy of philosophy, only if political philosophy was not part of philosophy, or if political philosophy was unphilosophical, or if political philosophy was identical with ideology (as Berns seems to think).

If Strauss had believed that moral indignation was the greatest enemy of philosophy, he would certainly have expressed that belief in his writings. But where does Strauss say anything of the kind? Socrates, in the Platonic dialogues, identifies "misology" as *the* enemy of philosophy. This means "hatred of reason," even as philosophy means "love of wisdom." If philosophy is a form of "love," its greatest antagonist would necessarily be a form of "hate." What the philosopher loves is wisdom, but wisdom understood as the perfection of reason, of dialectical reason, or of *logos*. Hence what the enemy of philosophy would hate above all, would not be wisdom, however understood, but wisdom understood as the result of *logos*. Misology, and not moral indignation, is then the greatest enemy of philosophy.

If Walter Berns had said that moral indignation may become an obstacle in the quest for truth, he would certainly have been correct. The quest for truth should be dispassionate, or at least animated by no other passion than by the passion for truth. Moral indignation arises when we become angry at threats to what we believe to be our own, and when we identify our own with the good. But moral indignation, taken by itself, is indifferent to the distinction between our own and the good. It is the task of political philosophy to teach us the difference between our own and the good, to the end that we make the good our own. But if political philosophy is possible, it is possible for us to replace opinion about the good, with knowledge of the good. And to the extent that we have knowledge of what is good, and have made good purposes our own, we ought to act well in the light of that knowledge. Acting well in the light of such knowledge, means summoning the passions to the defense of reason. It means making use of moral indignation in the defense of good against evil. Certainly, we do not, and cannot, philosophize, while we are morally indignant. Neither can we philosophize while we are acting to relieve or protect ourselves, as we must, from cold, hunger, or danger. Only God can philosophize without interruption, without having to take care. Philosophy may belong to the perfection of human life. But it is not the whole of human life. Moral indignation, under the direction of reason, also belongs to the perfection of human life, although to a lesser perfection than philosophy. According to Aristotle, there is no human situation less conducive to philosophizing, than that embracing the act of love. But he does not say that therefore sexual love is the greatest enemy of philosophy. On the contrary, he recommends it, at the right time, and in the right place, and with the right woman! And so with anger: we ought to be angry, at the right times, and in the right places, and with those things—evil, injustice, mean-spiritedness, cruelty—which offend all decent men, philosophers and non-philosophers alike. This was Aristotle's teaching; and, so far as I can gather from my nearly thirty years' association with him, and from the continual study of his writings, it was the teaching of Leo Strauss.

November 1982

The Doughface Dilemma: Or The Invisible Slave in the American Enterprise Institute's Bicentennial

Doughface: In the 1850's, a Northern Man with Southern Principles

... this Revolution was to bring our political institutions into a more perfect correspondence with an actual "American way of life" which no one even dreamed of challenging.
IRVING KRISTOL, "The American Revolution as a Successful Revolution," 1973

It is to the Constitution [of 1787] that we must ultimately turn as the completion of the American Revolution.
MARTIN DIAMOND, "The Revolution of Sober Expectations," 1973.

What a stupendous, what an incomprehensible machine is man! who can endure toil, famine, stripes, imprisonment, and death itself, in vindication of his own liberty, and, the next moment, be deaf to all those motives whose power supported him through his trial, and inflict on his fellow men a bondage, one hour of which is fraught with more misery than ages of that which he rose in rebellion to oppose.

THOMAS JEFFERSON, 1786

The April 30, 1982 issue of *National Review* carried a letter, running nearly three columns, from Robert A. Goldwin, Director of Constitutional Studies of the American Enterprise Institute, of Washington, D.C. It is a vigorous attack upon me, alleging that I had misrepresented the views of the late Martin Diamond, concerning the relationship of the Declaration of Independence to the Constitution. According to Goldwin, Diamond's position was "exactly—*exactly*—the opposite" of what I had said that it was.

The place in which this "exact" misrepresentation is alleged to have occurred, is in the remarks with which I introduced the publication of my letter to Walter Berns, "In Defense of Political Philosophy," in the January 22, 1982

National Review. In those remarks I said that I had, in *How to Think About the American Revolution* (Carolina Academic Press, 1978), examined a number of opinions, widely thought to be authoritative, concerning the Declaration of Independence, and the principles of the American Revolution. Among these were opinions of Irving Kristol and Martin Diamond, as they had been delivered in a Bicentennial program sponsored by the American Enterprise Institute. I had, I said, subjected them (together with others) to "dialectical commentary," in the course of which I had "discovered—or perhaps I should say uncovered— a core of meaning that corresponded to, if it was not identical with, opinions that had been advanced earlier by John C. Calhoun, and that were associated with the historicist and positivist defense of slavery in the ante-bellum debate."

The allegation that Kristol's and Diamond's interpretation of the central document of the American Revolution—and of the Founding it inaugurated —agreed in the most important respects with present-day defenders of the Confederacy, and with the historic interpretations by the historic defenders of American slavery, rankled deeply at the American Enterprise Institute, as it should have done. I had, by such assertions, called into question the American Enterprise Institute's credentials in regard to their highly publicized celebrations of the Bicentennials.

Kristol's and Diamond's lectures inaugurated the A.E.I.'s Bicentennial series. They were originally published individually—as were the other lectures in the series—in magnificent rag paper pamphlet editions. Later, all the lectures were collected into *America's Continuing Revolution*, published by Anchor Books in 1976. In addition, however, the Seagram Corporation published the Kristol and Diamond lectures as another, separate volume. This was lavishly illustrated, and expensively printed and bound in hardcover. It was, moreover, widely distributed, free of charge, to teachers of American history and government. It must have been one of the most heavily subsidized publications of our time. Recalling that these same lectures were also broadcast over innumerable educational radio and television channels, one might say that never in the field of American history and American political thought have such slender efforts received such stout publicity.

It is however appropriate that Robert A. Goldwin, as the officer responsible for carrying on the American Enterprise Institute's Bicentennial celebrations, should step forward in their defense. In the case of Martin Diamond, there is an office of piety and friendship to perform. Goldwin writes, "Walter Berns and Irving Kristol can defend themselves, but someone else must take up the argument on behalf of the late Martin Diamond. I do so, sadly aware of how much more instructively and humorously he could have responded to Harry Jaffa's tiresome and laborious attempt at journalistic philosophizing." Goldwin is doing no more, however, on behalf of one departed advocate of a controversial viewpoint than I, on my part, am doing on behalf of another. The other, in this case, is Abraham Lincoln, who was also known, on occasion, to be humorous and instructive. After something approaching a lifetime of study of Lincoln's writings and speeches I can, however, say that Lincoln seldom or never showed anything like levity when the questions of freedom and slavery came under discussion.

* * *

Goldwin's letter begins with two imputations of fact which are wholly erroneous. One concerns my assertion that Diamond's "no guidance" thesis was "traceable, through Willmoore Kendall, to John Calhoun." Goldwin says that this assertion was made in my "introduction" to "In Defense of Political Philosophy." It was indeed made there, but it was repeated there, as something I had given as a conclusion from the argument of *How to Think About the American Revolution*. Goldwin makes no reference to my book, and writes as if a conclusion derived from some eighty closely printed pages, had been made gratuitously, without the mass of supporting evidence and argumentation that actually accompanied it.

The other imputation is that Martin Diamond, during his lifetime, had no opportunity to respond to my critique of his "no guidance" thesis, and of the elaborate misreading of the historical record that had accompanied it. But the facts are far otherwise. Diamond's Bicentennial lecture for the American Enterprise Institute was delivered, with much ceremony, in Congress Hall, Philadelphia, October 24, 1973, and was published the following year. My critique of his and Kristol's lecture (which was given twelve days before Diamond's), was originally incorporated in a paper prepared for the 1975 annual meeting, in San Francisco, of the American Political Science Association. It was called "How to Think About the American Revolution", which later became the title of the book. The panel for which it was written was chaired by Irving Kristol. Some two hundred copies were distributed at the time, many of them being mailed out several weeks before the meeting. In the first mailing were copies addressed to Irving Kristol and Martin Diamond. I also addressed a letter to Diamond, inviting him to the panel, where I was confident Kristol would extend him every courtesy. I should mention that, had Diamond responded, and had he expressed a wish for more time than the panel offered, we could have arranged a special bicentennial panel for one of the evenings, when the regular panels were not in session. There were several of these at the San Francisco meeting. But Diamond never responded to my invitation. Although he was present in the hotel when our panel was in session, and not otherwise engaged, he did not appear. His untimely death occurred two years later. Those were perhaps the most active of his career. Although he spoke and wrote many times on the themes to which my critique was addressed—a critique which was in his posession all of this time—he gave no indication of intending to respond to it. I am glad therefore that Robert Goldwin has undertaken a defense of Diamond's Bicentennial lecture, and the position it represents. I hope he will not flag or fail in carrying on what he has undertaken. In doing so, he will be doing what Martin Diamond had every opportunity to do for himself, but which he did not do and, I am convinced, did not know how to do.

* * *

The center of what has come to be known—thanks to the American Enterprise Institute—as "the Diamond position," that center from which, one might say, all its minor thoughts radiate, is the assertion that the Declaration of Independence offered "no guidance," either to the Framing, or to the construing or interpreting of the Constitution of 1787. Collateral with this is the assertion that the Declaration is "neutral" with respect to what form or forms of government the people ought to choose, when instituting "new government," after they have acted to replace an existing government, as being destructive of their unalienable rights. These two assertions are at bottom one, since it is the alleged neutrality of the Declaration towards the many supposedly non-despotic forms of government, that is the cause or reason why it is unable to furnish the guidance in which it is alleged to be deficient. Diamond, and now his followers, has relied upon a text in John Locke's *Second Treatise of Government*, in which Locke says that the people, being sovereign, *may* institute what government they please. But what the people *may* do is an entirely different question from what it is that they *ought* to do. Diamond has confused these two separate matters, thinking that because the people are not subject to any external authority, they are not directed, by the principles intrinsic to their authority, towards any particular form of government, with a view to their safety and happiness. This position, which regards the Declaration of Independence as neutral or indifferent, towards the many possible forms of government, is in direct contradiction to the life-long position of Abraham Lincoln, the position immortalized in the Gettysburg Address. There Lincoln plainly affirms a direct relationship between dedication to the proposition that all men are created equal, and government of, by, and for the people. The argument that connects the end of the Gettysburg Address with its beginning, may be said to constitute, above all else, the theme and purpose of Lincoln's life and work. That the negation of despotism—slavery—is the affirmation of democratic or republican constitutionalism, is assuredly the core of his greatest Civil War utterances, beginning with that of July 4, 1861.

In *Crisis of the House Divided* I presented Lincoln's critique of Douglas's doctrine of popular sovereignty. According to Douglas the people might, in the plenitude of their sovereignty, unrestrained by any moral imperatives binding upon their will, vote slavery up or vote slavery down. The only "right" that Douglas acknowledged in the premises was the right of the people to decide for themselves. But Douglas drew no distinction between the people's right and the people's power. Douglas pretended to be "neutral," to be the people's servant merely awaiting the decision of their will. It was as if the gravest question was no different in principle from the question whether to adopt the right or the left as the rule of the road. Lincoln, in the Peoria speech of 1854, and ever after, called this a "*declared* indifference" but a "covert *real zeal* for the spread of slavery." (The emphasis is Lincoln's.) By what reasoning could Lincoln justify calling a proclaimed neutrality a secret zeal for slavery? In 1858, in the House Divided speech, Lincoln charged the four workmen, Franklin, Roger, Stephen, and James, with a conspiracy to extend slavery, not only to the free territories, but to the free states, making the United States "all slave." Historians have not been tender with Lincoln for making this charge. I, in *Crisis*, and Don E. Fehrenbacher, in *Prelude to Greatness*, have substantiated Lincoln's legal and political argument. Here I would only notice that Lincoln's moral argument, his ascription of pro-slavery zeal to Douglas, did not rest upon any merely subjective judgment concerning Douglas's motives. It rested rather upon the logical force of the argument that, as between the right and the wrong of slavery, there was no middle ground. As he was to say at Cooper Union, the quest for such a ground was as vain as the quest for a man who should be neither living nor dead. To pretend indifference to slavery, to deny that it is wrong, is tantamount to affirming that it is right. As Lincoln often said, if slavery is not wrong, then nothing is wrong, and "there is no right principle of action but self-interest." And Douglas did indeed testify to this interpretation of his motives, when he said at Alton during the joint debates, (and at other times elsewhere) that "We in Illinois ... tried slavery ... and finding that it was not profitable ... abolished it for that reason ...."

Aristotle says that man is the best of animals when perfected, but the worst when separated from law and justice. Lincoln saw slavery as the manifestation of the worst in man, because slavery meant the unrestrained rule of man over man, without the intervention of law or justice. Arbitrarily depriving a man of the fruits of his labor, and arbitrarily depriving him of his life, are not ultimately distinguishable by any moral principle. Under slavery, men are governed without their consent. But more than this: the slaves are bound by an entirely different set of rules than those by which the masters live. Lawful government, Lincoln believed, meant first of all a government by the consent of the governed. But it also meant a government under which those who governed lived under the very same laws that they made for others.

Diamond's argument—what I take to be now the American Enterprise Institute's Bicentennial argument—falls to the ground, in the face of the argument of Lincoln and Jefferson, by which there is, strictly speaking, only one form of non-despotic government. Let us bear in mind that law is a means of distributing the good things and the bad things, the benefits and the burdens, that are incident to our membership in the political community. Lincoln once summed up the meaning of slavery by saying that it meant, "You work: I'll eat." Slavery occurs, in its pure form when, so far as possible, all the benefits are on the one side, and all the burdens are on the other. The problem, for which constitutional government is the remedy, is that of preventing those who hold the power of government from using that power unfairly or arbitrarily to allocate more of the benefits, and fewer of the burdens to themselves; and, conversely, fewer of the benefits and more of the burdens to those who are subject to their authority. Who but cannot see, that the distribution of work and reward, as between master and slave, is determined mainly by the force at the master's disposal, and not by the right of distributive justice? But the relationship of force and right, although more subtle, is not different, when some person, e.g., a king, or some classes of persons, called, for example, noble are privileged by the law. For the distribution of benefits and burdens to have as little as possible of arbitrariness—that is, of despotism—it is necessary that all those who make the law live equally under the law that they make; and that all those who live under the law have as equal a share as possible, in making the law they live under. It is for this reason that, strictly speaking, only a democratic or republican constitutional government is non-despotic. It may be nonetheless be true, that not all despotisms are equally grievous. Jefferson, in 1786, declared that "one hour" of the bondage of American negro slavery was "fraught with more misery than ages of that" which the men of the Revolution had fought against. Nevertheless, both were to be denominated as despotisms. And resisting the first steps towards even the mildest of despotic or tyrannical regimes was the most prudent way of avoiding its ultimate evils.

Diamond's argument, and that of his coadjutors at the American Enterprise Institute, fails in the face of the logic of the Declaration of Independence, properly interpreted as it is by Jefferson and Lincoln. By this logic there is, strictly speaking, only one non-despotic form of government. In Jefferson's words in 1790, "The republican is the only form of government which is not eternally at open or secret war with the rights of mankind." And, as Lincoln said on the eve of the Civil War. "As I would not be a *slave*, so I would not be a *master*. This expresses my idea of democracy. Whatever differs from this, to the extent of the difference, is not democracy." It follows from this, moreover, that whatever differs from democracy, to the extent of the difference, is despotism. This is the argument of Lincoln and Jefferson. If we are true to our heritage, it will be the argument of the Bicentennial of our Independence and of the Constitution embodying the promise of that Independence.

*   *   *

The proposition that the Declaration of Independence supplies "no guidance" to the Constitution, and that it is "neutral" as between the different forms of allegedly non-despotic government, was not always Martin Diamond's opinion. In fact, for the greater part of his professional career, he held the opposite position. Diamond made his debut, so to speak, with a brilliant article, entitled "Democracy and *The Federalist*: A Reconsideration of the Framers' Intent," published in the March, 1959 issue of *The American Political Science Review*. This was not his first published article, but it is the one that arrested the attention of the profession, by challenging the accepted view, that the Constitution represented a conservative, or "Thermidorean," reaction against the democratic and egalitarian spirit of the Revolution, a spirit that was both symbolized by, and embodied in, the Declaration of Independence.

Diamond challenged the conventional wisdom, not by questioning the democracy of the Declaration, but by denying the charges of oligarchy made against the Constitution. His article asked, "In what way is the Constitution ordinarily thought to be less democratic than the Declaration?" That the Constitution was thought to be less than democratic, was the opinion against which he directed his argument. That the Declaration was democratic was the very premise of his question, a premise never challenged anywhere in his writing—so far as I know—before 1970. The democracy of the Declaration is not only his premise, but it is in the Declaration that he discovered the criteria by which the Constitution itself was to be judged either democratic or non-democratic.

Here is how Diamond, in 1959, met the argument that the Constitution and the Declaration embodied different regime principles.

> *The argument is usually that the former is characterized by fear of the people, by preoccupation with minority interests and rights, and by measures taken against the power of majorities. The Declaration, it is true, does not display these features, but this is no proof of a fundamental difference of principle between the two. Is it not obviously possible that the difference is due only to a difference in the tasks to which the two documents were addressed? And is it not further possible that the democratic principles of the Declaration are not only compatible with the prophylactic measures of the Constitution but actually imply them?*

In the foregoing, we see that the "democratic principles of the Declaration" appear to be taken for granted. But Diamond did not then merely take them for granted. It is not the case that he only later examined what had hitherto been an unexamined premise. Here he says why the Declaration is democratic:

> *The Declaration of Independence formulates two criteria for judging whether any government is good, or indeed legitimate. Good government must rest, procedurally, upon the consent of the governed. Good government, substantively, must do only certain things, e.g. secure certain rights. This may be stated another way, by borrowing a phrase from Locke, appropriate enough when discussing the Declaration. That "the people shall be judge" is of the essence of democracy, is its peculiar form or method of proceeding.*

In his Bicentennial writings — those which have become canonical at the American Enterprise Institute — Diamond insists that the Declaration of Independence requires for legitimacy only that governments be "instituted" with the consent of the governed, that is, that they need not be democratic. Here, however, he sees both "good" and "legitimate" government standing upon the same ground. "Legitimate" clearly refers to the "institution" of government, and "good" to its being democratic. Diamond emphasizes this by referring "good" to the "procedural," that is, operating aspect of government. He founds this, correctly, upon John Locke's famous aphorism that "the people shall be judge," which Diamond calls "the essence of democracy," "its peculiar form of method of proceeding."

Robert A. Goldwin sent me a copy of his letter to *National Review*, prior to its publication last April 30th. In a passage deleted by the editors, he made a great point of the alleged fact that Leo Strauss, in many of his classes at the University of Chicago, notably when he and Diamond were graduate students, had taught that the Declaration of Independence was "neutral" with respect to the forms of government. Why Strauss's authority should be introduced into this discussion was not clear, and the editors of *National Review* evidently thought it irrelevant. Be that as it may, it is not irrelevant to ask Goldwin why it was Diamond never learned the lesson from Strauss that he charges me with ignoring. For it was fifteen or more years *after* he left Strauss's classes that Diamond discovered the "neutrality" of the Declaration with respect to forms of government.

That Diamond continued for a long time to regard the Declaration of Independence as democratic, and as therefore supplying guidance, in principle, to the Framers of the Constitution, is proved by the introductory paragraphs of *The Democratic Republic*, published by Rand McNally in 1966. Chapter 1, written by Diamond, begins on page 3. The epigraph of the chapter is supplied by the Declaration of Independence, beginning with the words "We hold these truths to be self-evident ..." and ending "... deriving their just powers from the consent of the governed ..." Separation from Great Britain, Diamond said, "was grounded upon principles of just government held to be valid for all men at all times." In so writing, he is clearly echoing Lincoln, in his Jefferson's birthday letter of 1859, when he wrote:

> *All honor to Jefferson — to the man who, in the concrete pressure of a struggle for national independence by a single people, had the coolness, forecast, and capacity to introduce into a merely revolutionary document, an abstract truth, applicable to all men and all times....*

The American people were, we see, "a single people." But this single people had by reason of the prophetic truth embodied in the Declaration of Independence, become "an almost chosen people," the representatives of all mankind.

That was assuredly the theme of the Gettysburg Address, which declared that the Civil War was a test whether the nation constituted by that single people, or any nation conceived in and dedicated to that abstract truth, might long endure. In *The Democratic Republic* Diamond explicitly endorses this view of the origin of the regime, and of the relationship in it of the Declaration and the Constitution. He repeats substantially what he had written in his 1959 *APSR* article, with the addition of Lincoln's authority.

> *The Declaration* [Diamond wrote] *places two principles at the center of the credo. First, just government must rest upon "the consent of the governed" and, second, just government exists to secure "certain unalienable rights." Four score and seven years later at Gettysburg, Lincoln ... restated the two principles when he spoke of the "new nation, conceived in liberty, and dedicated to the proposition that all men are created equal." In Lincoln's formulation, we see the shape the two principles acquired: On the one hand, there is the equality of men from which results the democratic idea of government "by the people"; on the other hand, there is liberty from which results the idea that government may do only certain things and those only in certain ways.*

One might cavil that Diamond thinks there is a difference between "the shape the two principles acquired" in "Lincoln's formulation," and the shape they possessed in the Declaration itself. The evidence suggests the view, however, that when Diamond wrote those words he believed that Lincoln's formulation was the true formulation, and that Lincoln, at best, made more explicit than hitherto, the doctrine inherent in the Declaration itself; as he had stated in 1959.

In the very next paragraph, Diamond offered a commentary upon a text in Jefferson's inaugural address, which he quotes in part, but may be quoted here in full.

> *All, too, will bear in mind this sacred principle, that though the will of the majority is in all cases to prevail, that will to be rightful must be reasonable; that the minority possess their equal rights, which equal law must protect, and to violate would be oppression.*

Diamond argued—correctly, I think—that "The Declaration's two principles are not automatically harmonious." That is to say the rule of the majority is not of itself necessarily rightful or reasonable. From this perspective, the rule of the majority is the *necessary* but not the *sufficient* condition of just or non-oppressive government. Diamond thought, reasonably I would say, that the Declaration of Independence propounded "a problem which it does not itself solve." That problem, he thought, found many elements of a solution—although not a complete or perfect solution—in the Constitution. Certainly, the theory of the extended republic, which he was justly to celebrate and expound, is not propounded in the Declaration of Independence. What is crucial to the present discussion is this: the earlier Diamond held that the criteria of just government, the criteria that guided the Framers of the Constitution in their work, were laid down for them in the Declaration of Independence.

* * *

In the 1950's, Diamond began his *"deuteros plous,"* his second voyage of discovery, having abandoned the Marxism and socialism of his youth. He was to discover all, and even more than all, that he had once sought in the utopianism of the Left, in the sober decency of the American Founding. And he was to become one of the most eloquent spokesmen for the view that the Founding —and notably the Constitution of 1787, as expounded in the *Federalist* papers —represented sobriety and decency in its wisest political manifestation in the post-classical West. When Diamond began his studies, the prevailing scholarship, and the prevailing opinions, were still those of the Progressive Era, and of The Progressive movement in American politics. As we have already noted, the dominant view, equally supported, for opposite reasons, by both Right and Left, was that the Constitution of 1787 represented an oligarchic or "Thermidorean" reaction, in favor of the special interests of property, against the populism and democracy of the period of the Revolution, and of the period of government under the Articles of Confederation. This view of the regime character of the Constitution was associated above all with the work of Charles A. Beard, but also with that of Vernon L. Parrington and J. Allen Smith. The parroting of their opinions continued long after the research and scholarship which presumably supported those opinions had been exploded. From this, it may be inferred that the reasons for believing the conclusions fostered by Beard's *Economic Interpretation of the Constitution* were different from, and more powerful than, the shoddy research that went into that book. In fact, the thesis that the Constitution was designed to buttress and protect the interests of private property from the intrusions of the popular majorities in the state governments was also supported by the impeccable scholarship of Edward S. Corwin. In his "Development of Constitutional Theory from the Declaration of Independence to the Meeting of the Philadelphia Convention" (1925), Corwin pointed out that, although the doctrine of, for example, separation of powers, as necessary to the rule of law, was enshrined in the rhetoric of the state constitutions, it was not being implemented in practice. Private rights were, in fact, being subjected to the political, as distinct from the judicial process. Debts, and equities in mortgages, for example, were sometimes being decided by private bills in legislatures, instead of by juries in impartial trials in courts. It was precisely such things that Madison had in mind, when he wrote in the tenth *Federalist* that conflicts of interests were being decided, "not according to the rights of the minor party, but by the superior force of an interested and overbearing majority." Corwin's work, while strengthening sympathy for the Constitution, did not, however, do much to undermine the view that it was non-, if not anti-, democratic. Those who looked upon the economic interpretation of history with favor, from the Left, saw in the injustices of popular majorities—notably in such movements as Shays's Rebellion—evidence of the desperation of the debtor classes under capitalism. They saw the remedy, not in strengthening the protection for property, but in abolishing it, or at least in bringing it under the political control of "the people." Diamond was one of the first, and certainly one of the most eloquent, in the defense of the thesis that the Constitution of 1787, precisely in its safeguards of private property, was rendering an inestimable service to the cause of popular government, and to democracy.

Diamond pointed out in nearly everything he wrote in the 1950's and 1960's, that "democracy" was a bad word, in the political vocabulary of the 1780's and 1790's, because of the just reproaches under which popular governments had ever fallen, in the perennial conflict between majority rule and minority rights. Diamond's—and James Madison's—real antagonist, however, was not Beard or Parrington. It was Aristotle. For it was Aristotle who, in the third book of the *Politics*, had discussed the tendency inherent in democracy, as the regime of the poor, to use the weight of numbers in the assembly to divide up the wealth of the rich. One of the two oaths that appears in the *Politics* is when Aristotle impersonates a demagogue—in the purest sense of that term —defending the justice of expropriation, by saying, "By Zeus, it was done by the sovereign justly." Aristotle implies that, for democracy, sovereignty resides in the majority, and that democrats believe that nothing done under the forms of law, by the sovereign, can be unjust. But, Aristotle insists—and Madison and Diamond agreed—such actions destroy the political community, and nothing that destroys the political community can be just, no matter where sovereignty lies, and no matter what the forms of law are supposed to be. Aristotle saw the heart of the political problem to consist in preventing the numbers of the many, who are poor, from oppressing the few, who are rich; and, conversely, of preventing the wealth of the rich, who are few, from being used to oppress the many, who are poor. Aristotle's solution to this problem was the mixed regime, the regime in which the influences of numbers and wealth were so balanced off against each other, so blended in the mixture of institutional devices, that neither could become oppressive. But Diamond followed Publius (Madison) in declaring as he did in the 14th *Federalist* that although we owed to modern Europe "the great principle of representation," Europe had not exhibited the operation of this principle "in a government wholly popular." "America," Publius wrote, "can claim the merit of making the discovery the basis of unmixed and extensive republics." And so Diamond argued that the American form of government, under the Constitution, continued to be as "unmixedly" popular or democratic as the states of which it was composed. Paul Eidelberg, in *The Philosophy of the American Constitution* (1968), challenged Diamond's argument on this point, maintaining, on the contrary, that the Constitution established a regime decidedly mixed, in the Aristotelian sense. It is a matter of lasting regret that Diamond never saw fit to engage Eidelberg in a dialogue that might have resolved this question for the benefit of a genuinely puzzled and interested public. But Diamond was correct upon the main point, *provided* that it is understood that an unmixed government is one based unequivocally *upon the proposition that all men are created equal.* Our government is unmixedly popular because we recognize in "the people" not the poor, but *everyone.* Because all men are created equal, civil society is a voluntary association, and government arises by the *unanimous consent* of all those who agree to become fellow citizens, all those who henceforth will be governed by a species of majority rule. Democracy, as Aristotle understood it, meant the rule of the poor. For Madison, popular government was *not* rule of the poor; it was rule of a part of the whole in behalf of the whole, rich and poor alike. For Aristotle, the wealthy are not part of the *demos.* For Madison, and the Founding Fathers, they are. Eidelberg did not take sufficiently into account the transformed meaning of democracy, a meaning whose transformation was embodied in the Declaration. Diamond was correct because, but only because, his argument for the Constitution rested foursquare upon the new meaning of popular government recognized in the Declaration of Independence, and assumed by the Framers of the Constitution.

The examples upon which Publius drew, in emphasizing the reproaches under which popular government had traditionally fallen, were usually — but not exclusively — ancient. Roman history was drawn upon most frequently, but the perspective from which popular governments were condemned was that supplied, as we have seen, by Aristotle. Behind Aristotle, although alluded to only obliquely, was the condemnation of democracy by the tradition originating with the pupils of Socrates, Xenophon and Plato. And that tradition may be said to have had its origin in the circumstances that culminated in the trial and death of Socrates. The democracy that has its origin in the principles of the Declaration of Independence is the democracy that utterly separates our civil rights from our religious opinions. The Statute of Virginia for Religious Freedom came from Jefferson's pen, as did the Declaration of Independence. Both of them were inscribed upon his tombstone, as being two of the three things by which he wished most to be remembered. Religious liberty was, however, implicit in the Declaration of Independence, because, as Diamond himself commented, the Declaration limited the function of government to the security of man's natural and unalienable rights. Athenian democracy — or popular government before the Declaration of Independence — knew no such limitation. Athenian democracy, moreover, not only subsisted together with slavery, but was peculiarly dependent upon it. It was the labor of the public slaves in the silver mines that supplied the money that paid the way of the Athenian *demos* to the assembly, in the hey-day of that democracy. Slavery, and religious intolerance, were among the reproaches to popular government that had made it less eligible, especially to political philosophers, than it became in the course of the American Revolution. The peculiar justice of American democracy rested upon the proposition that, in being created equal, each man, by the laws of nature and of nature's God, owned himself. American democracy derived its justice from this doctrine. American democracy would respect the rights of property, not because of the claims of wealth as contrasted with those of freedom (as in Aristotle's *Politics*), but because each man had a natural right to the fruits of his labor, as he had a natural right to his own body and his own soul. It was to secure his equal right to his life, to his liberty, to his property, and to that happiness that he might pursue in virtue of his enjoyment of his life, liberty, and property, that he entered civil society, and was entitled therefore to an equal share in the government, in the making of the laws under which he lived. Hence it was that Diamond, in all his writings in the 1950's and 1960's, saw the criteria that the Constitution meant to satisfy, as being those set forth in the Declaration of Independence.

* * *

Diamond was well qualified to become the critic of the political thought of the Progressive Era. He came to his studies, having turned away both from Trotskyite Marxism and Norman Thomas socialism. His doctoral dissertation was an account of how "reason and experience" had turned him, and most of the other socialists in his circle, into becoming supporters of democratic capitalism. The argument of his dissertation was along these lines. Socialism had asserted that capitalism could not solve the economic problem. It declared that it could not provide that ever higher standard of living, in which everyone, or nearly everyone shared, which was its original and continuing promise. But, said Diamond, looking at our post-war prosperity, the American economy, spurred by "risk, uncertainty, and profit," had in fact provided a higher standard of living, and one more widely shared, than anything imagined by a turn-of-the-century Progressive Era socialist. Recalling even his own recent Norman Thomas brand of socialism, of the 1930's and 1940's, he saw around him greater material well-being than anything he had earlier anticipated, in the unlikely event that the Socialist Party had been elected to power. But Diamond argued that socialism's profounder claim was not economic, but moral. And this claim was characteristic of all brands of socialism, Marxist and non-Marxist alike. It was the belief that the solution to the economic problem was at the same time the solution of the human problem, the problem of human well-being. But Diamond was convinced that the very success of capitalism had given the lie to socialism: in the proof that material well-being did not bring with it that satisfaction that must be the mark of genuine happiness. Diamond's turning away from socialism prepared him to understand the crisis of capitalism, the crisis, long developing, that came to a head in the later 1960's. It was the crisis of the upper middle classes, in particular the children of these classes —the ones who predominated in his classrooms—the pampered darlings of the most economically privileged class the world has ever seen. Many of these supremely privileged beings became a "counterculture," and rejected the system that privileged them, as if in fact they had been the most oppressed class in history. In doing so, they became the most powerful empirical evidence for a proposition that should not have needed any empirical evidence: the proposition that even an infinity of means cannot become a substitute for ends. Human happiness, Diamond was convinced—as indeed were all those who had turned from "moderns" to "ancients" for guidance on *this* question—consisted in a proper relationship between means and ends. Socialism, born of radical modernity, denied that there were any ends of human life, either of God or of nature, either of faith or of reason. It had substituted in their place the project of infinite means. The classless society of the future, projected by Marx in the *German Ideology*, was one in which there was no external obstacle to the will as the now "free" human being turned aimlessly from poetry to painting to criticizing, or whatever. Marx was one of the few who had actually thought this through—although he had no sooner done so, than he denounced as "utopian" anyone else who dared to raise the question of what man in the classless society would actually do. That the success of socialism would culminate, not in felicity, but in despair, was however as implicit in the socialism of Norman Thomas and Clement Atlee as in that of Marx. Diamond saw this was also proved by the success of capitalism. He saw the children of the counterculture vainly seeking happiness by "doing their own things." What they were in fact trying to do—although few of them had any sophistication about it—was to try to live the life described in the *German Ideology*, without taking the trouble of first making the prescribed revolution. As they became ever more frustrated, they did in fact turn towards revolution, convinced, as Marx was, that destroying the "system" was a precondition of genuine enjoyment. But Diamond saw that what was wrong in their lives was not the presence or absence of any system. An aimless life was bound to become frustrated at any time and place, no matter how perfect the opportunities offered to the human beings in that time and place. Man does not make himself, and therefore he cannot invent the ends that prescribe his well-being. To do so, is to recognize the ends as spurious. The act of self-deception, whereby one treats the ends one has invented as if they were real, leads to nothing but fanaticism, and to the unspeakable tyrannies that have in fact characterized our time. Diamond saw, as did others, that only the Constitution of the United States stood between the counterculture kids and something very much like the Hitler Youth (or Mao's Red Guards).

Diamond saw then that the ultimate defect of capitalism and of socialism was one and the same. Capitalism was better than socialism, first of all because it could actually deliver on its promise of economic well-being. But the historic commitment to capitalism (although it was not called that at the time) in the American Revolution was better, in that it never saw the solution to the human problem in the plenitude of means alone. Lincoln, in 1838, had spoken of a system of government, conducing more essentially "to the ends of civil and religious liberty," than any other that history had recorded. But civil liberty was understood to be in the service of political justice, and religious liberty in the service of religious truth, or at least that version of the truth that might put each man's conscience at rest, that he was doing "right, as God gave him to see the right." Diamond was however scornful of those "free market" defenders of capitalism, who saw in the "freedom to choose" the highest purpose, not only of the economy, but of the polity. "Freedom to choose," as an ultimate end, was empty of promise for human well-being, whether preached by Karl Marx in the *German Ideology* or by the enthusiasts of the free-market who called themselves conservatives.

The discontent of the wealthy offspring of the prosperous middle classes stemmed from generations of Progressive Era propaganda, dutifully transmitted by the universities to all levels of the educational system. All personal misery tended to be blamed on "the system." "Alienation" came to be the fashionable term, to explain the misery of those who had all the means they could employ, but did not know how they ought to employ them. Freudianism, on the surface, seemed to be at the opposite pole from Marxism, since Freud found personal misery to be an indefeasibly personal phenomenon. Yet it was one that the individual could do nothing about by taking thought as to how he should live his life. Psychoanalysis only offered to restore to each individual the aimless freedom that was the starting point of his trouble. In attributing each individual's "discontent" to "civilization," Freud, no less than Marx, made "civilization" the cause of evil. It was inevitable that Freud's pessimism be absorbed by Marx's revolutionary optimism, in the popular culture (or, rather, counter culture). What neither Marx nor Freud, nor their disciples, in the endless varieties and combinations of varieties thrown up by the Progressive Era, knew, was that the ends of man which had, over the millenia, been sought in God or Nature, in Reason or in Revelation, might not be found in "Doing One's Own Thing." For the One, whose Thing was to be Done, turned out, quite literally, to be No Thing. Revolutionary socialism has in fact turned into Nihilism in our time. The burden of Nothingness has found relief, quite characteristically, in the drug culture and in terrorism. In the 1960's, the spiritual emptiness of the counterculture sought compensation in frenzy; today that same emptiness is manifest—but only for a time—in listlessness.

* * *

Diamond turned to the Constitution, in part because it was geared to modest but attainable ends. Those ends gained dignity, not merely because "comfortable self-preservation" was both modest and attainable, but because they were never thought to substitute for those larger ends of human life, such as the immortal salvation promised by Christianity, or that dwelling on "the isles of the blest," promised to the philosophers in Plato's *Republic*. A political teaching that required political institutions aimed at fulfilling what was highest in man, he thought, more often ended in tyranny than in felicity. Diamond believed that the divorce of man's highest ends from his political ends was desirable, as a means to avoiding tyranny, and the indecency that, in the name of man's highest ends, had characterized the political life of the Christian West. This, at any rate, was the perspective of the American Founding, as he saw it. His rejection of Marxism—of the attempt to guarantee perfect freedom and perfect felicity by political means—was at one and the same time a rejection of the similar attempts, made in the name of Christianity, in the Christian centuries. In principle, the attempt to make the City of God determine the form of the City of Man, was the same cause of tyranny as that he had come to see in revolutionary socialism. The theocratic politics which the American Founding sought to end, and the ideological politics of Marxist socialism, were ultimately indistinguishable. The decency of the American Founding lay in its moderation, but that moderation was in the service of a rational analysis of the human situation. It was not moderation in the service of moderation, for that would be merely another form of the infinite regress which empties life of genuine meaning.

The American Founding was better than the regimes that preceded it, and better than the regimes which, in the Progressive Era, offered to succeed it. It was better because it aimed at a moderation that was rational. This moderation was rational, because it was consistent with man's highest ends. It was open to the possibility of Creation, as the biblical religions proclaimed. But it was a universe designed to be apprehended—at least in part—by reason, for the premises by which it was apprehended were called "self-evident truths." If man's destiny transcended reason, and required faith, this faith might not contradict what was to be known by reason. Divine law might transcend natural law, but it might not negate it. This was what made possible that separation of church and state that promoted religious liberty no less than civil liberty, and with them, human decency. The American Founding limited government, and in its limitations of government, emancipated the private sphere of human life, in a way that was not recognized as meritorious in classical political philosophy, any more than in exclusively Christian (or Jewish or Muslim) doctrines concerning the right or good polity. This might be seen merely as "lowering the goals" of political life, so as to make the achievement of these goals more possible or feasible. This in truth is what the American Founding did. But it did not understand itself to be promoting a form of polity inferior in its actual dignity to any other. In connecting "the interest of the man" with the "constitutional rights of the place," one is not being cynical. One is, on the contrary, recognizing man's non-angelical nature. It is because men are not angels that government is necessary. The perfection of government is a perfection of man's non-angelic nature. The political achievement of the American Founding, Diamond thought, reflected man's capacity for perfection, by its promotion of reasonable behavior, quite as much as the necessity of government reflected man's non-angelic nature.

Diamond's work was concentrated mainly on the *Federalist*, as a commentary on the work of the Constitutional Convention. The burden of his argument was the "workability" of the regime. But the strength of that argument depended absolutely upon the understanding, characteristic of the men of the Founding, of what the ends of human life, and of political life, were, with respect to which the workable can be said to be workable. In his essay "Conservatives, Liberals, and the Constitution" (1966) Diamond shows why the Ideological Liberalism of our time, the core of the political thought that dominated Progressivism from its beginnings until now is totalitarian. He wrote as follows.

> *The liberal aim is thus clear. In order to transform the human condition, which is his deepest aim, the liberal seeks to make the political order fully dependent upon a transformed people. To achieve the transformation, he seeks the right kind of constitutional institutions to produce the right kind of party to produce the right kind of majority. At the very center of liberalism there is the theory of the truly democratic party — unified and coherent and thus capable of summoning up from the unformed mass the majority acquiescence in the liberal goals that, the liberal believes, is the natural inclination of the true majority. To such a majority, the Constitution with its "auxiliary precautions" does indeed obstruct the way.*

From this it is clear that Diamond did not see any ultimate or intrinsic difference between "liberalism" and the "democratic centralism" of Lenin. In both cases, an elitist minority defines *a priori* what it is that a majority must believe to be truly democratic. There is, of course, an element of logic to "elitism." Jefferson and Madison and Lincoln also believed that the majority must act only in certain prescribed ways, when acting as trustee for the security of the unalienable natural rights of all: that is, the majority must believe that its authority is limited to acting only in certain ways, if it is to secure the equal rights of all, including the rights of the minority. A majority that acts to institute a despotism is acting illegitimately, as well as wrongly. The American Founding was grounded upon a certain kind of unanimity ("... with respect to our rights and the acts of the British government contravening those rights, there was but one opinion this side of the water," Jefferson wrote in 1825). The concept of unanimity in the constitution or institution of civil society is implicit in the idea of the social contract or compact: men who are by nature equal act to form that voluntary association called civil society, or government under law. The doctrine of the

Declaration of Independence is spelled out in the Massachusetts Bill of Rights, thus:

> *The body politic is formed by a voluntary association of individuals; it is a social*
> *compact by which the whole people covenants with each citizen and each citizen*
> *with the whole people that all shall be governed by certain laws for the common*
> *good . . .* [to the end] *that every man may, at all times, find his security in them.*

Unanimity thus underlies diversity in the American Founding. In this it does not differ from the Liberal ideology that rejects the Founding. The unanimity of the Founding is however unanimity upon the proposition that "the body politic is a voluntary association of individuals." This proposition itself is however inferred from the more fundamental proposition which, in the Massachusetts Bill of Rights is that "All men are born free and equal," a proposition expressed more succinctly in the Declaration of Independence, "that all men are created equal." The meaning, in both cases, is identical. Being *equal*, means that one is not subject to another, and one who is not subject to another is *free*. This equality and freedom refers to *nature*, to the relationship of man to man *by nature*, and in the *state of nature*. This relationship is the one that is logically antecedent to the one that results from men voluntarily agreeing, one with another, to become fellow citizens, and thereby to place themselves in a relationship of that subordination to government and law which characterizes a free civil society. For civil society to be free, it must rest upon the unanimous consent of its members. But this unanimous consent is consent to be governed by the majority. Action by the majority follows necessarily as the only way by which unanimous consent can be turned into government. Civil society, constituted by unanimous consent, cannot act by unanimous consent. The majority is the part that acts for the whole. Its purpose in so acting is however to secure the equal rights of all, not only of those who happen at any time to constitute the majority. Indeed, the majority, in a free society, recognizes itself as a temporary trustee for the whole, and recognizes that the individual members of the majority for the time being are likely themselves to be as frequently members of the minority. Hence all have an interest in those "auxiliary precautions" that will help to insure that the action of the majority will not by intention or design or foreseeable mischance discriminate against the interests or rights of the minority. From this analysis the reader will see that, in the American Founding, the requirements, both of majority rule and of the constitutional safeguards of minority rights, flow logically and prudentially from the primordial principle of human equality.

Ideological Liberalism differs from the American Founding, not in the fact that the one requires an agreement upon principles, and the other does not. Rather is it the case that the principles are different. The agreement of the

American Founding, the central idea from which all its minor thoughts radiate, as Lincoln declared, was the proposition that all men are created equal. This proposition was a moral, a political, and a constitutional proposition, as the foregoing exegesis has, we trust, established. It implied that there is a human nature—itself part of a non-human nature that is both higher and lower than man's—and that such nature is the unchanging ground of all changing experience. Because man is and would forever be possessed of a reason that ought to govern, and of passions that would always require government, democratic republican constitutional government would always be the form of government intrinsically in accordance with nature.

Ideological Liberalism looked forward to a state or condition in which there would be no government. Henry David Thoreau, whose essay on civil disobedience was published the same year as the Communist Manifesto, declared that that government was best that governed least. But he added promptly that that government was better that did not govern at all. In this, he was merely affirming the non-Marxist Liberal equivalent of the doctrine that, in the best circumstances, the state must "wither away." The desirability and the necessity for the ultimate abolition of government is intrinsic to Ideological Liberalism. The ultimate aim of such Liberalism, as of Communism, may be described poetically as a return to the Garden of Eden. In this Second Coming of the Garden, or perhaps one should say Second Garden, there would be no forbidden fruit. There would be no forbidden fruit, because the Lord of the Garden would be man himself, now omnipotent because the power of God would have been transformed into the power of science, now in human hands. The difference of man and God would be overcome. The forbidden fruit—the knowledge which is the basis of God's power—would no longer be forbidden, because man, having eaten it, would indeed have become—as the Bible says he would—"like God." The moral virtues, symbolized by the prohibitions of the Second Table of the Decalogue, are precisely those restraints imposed upon man because he is not God. Private property is seen by Ideological Liberalism to be the source of all evil. The Marxist version of this thesis is perhaps the best known. But the Marxist version is not the first, or the most potent. It was Rousseau who first told the West that the introduction of private property was the phenomenon that turned man away from his natural goodness into a being possessed of envy, pride, the lust of the imagination (as distinct from that of the body), and the will to dominate others as a means to one's own sense of well-being. What the American Founding believed to be human nature—from which the permanence of "factions" was to be inferred, and from which the permanent necessity of "auxiliary precautions" in constitutions also followed —was not nature at all, but the consequence of private property. Hence the Ideological Liberal believes that the abolition of private property will make systems of restraint upon the majority such as are found in the Constitution of

1787 superfluous. Indeed, the Constitution of the United States, insofar as it impedes or prevents the kind of political action that can lead to the total reform of society, is pernicious. Constitutionalism is fundamentally repressive. Revolution alone is fundamentally liberating.

* * *

The most serious objections to Diamond's defense of constitutionalism arose from the misuse of the Fourteenth Amendment, by the Conservative "priests" who interpreted the Ark of the Convenant, during the Progressive era. The Liberals of that era became the enemies of the Constitution, with its salutary restraints upon uncontrolled majoritarianism, precisely because they accepted the identification of the Constitution with its reactionary interpretation. It was this identification of the Constitution with the defense of indefensible privileges that constituted the heart of the rhetoric of the Progressive movement. Between 1890 and 1937 there was a long line of Supreme Court decisions, in which the work of majorities, first in the states, and then in the federal government, were struck down as unconstitutional. The most pernicious of these were like the famous *Lochner* case of 1905. The New York legislature had passed a law providing that no bakery could employ anyone to work more than 60 hours a week, or more than 10 hours a day. The Court—by a 5 to 4 majority—held that the law was unconstitutional, because it violated the freedom of contract, which the Court said was "part of the liberty of the individual protected by the 14th Amendment of the Federal Constitution." Here and elsewhere the Court held that laws regulating the hours or conditions of labor, not only for men, but for women and children, constituted a violation of the due process clause of the fourteenth amendment. In 1918, in *Hammer v. Dagenhart*, the Court held an act of Congress unconstitutional, that prohibited the interstate or foreign shipment of commodities produced in factories employing children under 14, and in mines employing children under 16. Since state regulation of child labor drove industries across state lines, this decision effectively prevented regulation of the hours of child labor. In this decision, the Court relied on the tenth amendment, and the strict construction of the doctrine of enumerated powers. Justice Day, writing for the majority in a 5-4 decision, noted that "[i]n interpreting the Constitution it must never be forgotten that the nation is made up of states, to which are entrusted the powers of local government. And to them and to the people the powers not *expressly* delegated to the national government are reserved" (emphasis added). This was the doctrine upon which the South had relied in the secession crisis! It was now being used by Republican judges to exempt property from virtually any political control by the majority. In this case, the Marxist interpretation of the Civil War, as a war for the protection of Northern capital from the restraints of a quasi-feudal South, attained perhaps its highest degree of plausibility. The same kinds of judges also protected the alleged freedom of contract from the intrusions of labor unions. It was in this period that the labor injunction reached its height of notoriety, and gave added credibility to the growing theme of "the people versus property," in the interpretation of the Constitution. It was this experience of a conservative judiciary rather than Beard's scholarship, that made the "Economic Interpretation of the Constitution" popular.

It was in the post-Civil War era that has come to be known as Progressive, that the Liberal-Conservative dichotomy that has so largely governed political discourse in our time came into prominence. Diamond's defense of the Constitution of 1787 faced as its major obstacle the follies of the Conservatives, whose attachment to "property rights" seemed to put them into opposition to "human rights." The attachment to "human rights" was seen in the attempts of reformers to break the power of trusts and monopolies, to restrict the hours of labor, to outlaw sweat shops, and to assist workingmen to bargain with their employers on more equal terms, by means of labor unions. The Fourteenth Amendment had been passed to assure that the freedmen would be citizens, and that the states might not, by the unequal protection of the laws, create what would in effect be a second (or third) class of citizens. In turning this amendment into a sanctuary for property, and in particular for business property, it seemed to throw into question the very purpose for which the Civil War was fought. This was all the more so when, after the end of Reconstruction, the free Negroes were in fact reduced to a peonage in many respects more oppressive than slavery. The Jim Crow system, the legal "freedom" of the freedmen to the contrary notwithstanding, removed from the persons of the former slaves many of the protections they had enjoyed by reason of having been valuable possessions.

This perversion of the Fourteenth Amendment was all the more striking, when it is remembered that it had as one of its purposes the reversal of the Dred Scott decision. Chief Justice Taney, in *Dred Scott*, had declared that a Negro, whether free or slave, was incapable of becoming a citizen. Since this decision had not been reversed in 1868, the Thirteenth Amendment, by itself, was incapable of conferring citizenship upon the former slaves. But the Fourteenth Amendment could not have had the intention of reversing Taney's assertion that Negroes were incapable of becoming citizens, without intending to repudiate the reasoning by which Taney had supported that assertion. Taney had declared—not as his own opinion, but as the opinion of those who had framed and those who had ratified the Constitution—that Negroes, whether free or slave, were "regarded as beings of an inferior order; and altogether unfit to associate with the white race, either in social or political relations," and that they were "so far inferior that they had no rights which the white man was bound to respect . . . ." Taney supported this view of the Constitution, moreover, by appealing to the authority of the Declaration of Independence. That document, he said, notwithstanding its actual words, did not include Negroes in the class of human beings, when it said "that all men are created equal." As Abraham Lincoln put it, in Stephen A. Douglas's paraphrase, Taney's interpretation meant no more than that "British subjects on this continent [were] equal to British subjects born and residing in Great Britain." It was "too clear for dispute," Taney said, "that the enslaved African race were not intended to be included" in the proposition of human equality. Otherwise, he said, "the conduct of the distinguished men who framed the Declaration of Independence would have been utterly and flagrantly inconsistent with the principles they asserted."

The opinion here expressed by Taney has been one of the most persistent and mischievous in all human history. Today, it is the almost unquestioned dogma of Ideological Liberalism. It is one of the favorite "proofs" of the existence of what Marxist-Leninists call "bourgeois ideology." The Marxist interpretation of the American Revolution is that it naturally expressed the demands of the bourgeoisie in universalistic terms (e.g. "all men"), because the bourgeoisie tacitly identified itself with all humanity, but that it did so because it could not recognize the humanity of the non-bourgeois. By reducing all human relations to the "cash nexus" it saw all labor, and certainly the labor of slaves, as non-human. Taney's view of the Declaration became the Orthodoxy of Liberalism with the publication of the Report of the President's National Advisory Commission on Civil Disorder (appointed by Lyndon Johnson) on the civil disorders of the late 1960's. The major cause of the urban riots of the period was said to be "white racism." And the most profound evidence that the aforesaid racism was endemic in the American polity was said to be the "fact" that Negroes were not included in the Declaration of Independence! I recall confronting the Staff Director of the Commission at a conference on civil disobedience at Kenyon College in 1968. I pointed to the contradiction, and refutation, of Taney, contained in Justice Curtis's dissenting opinion in *Dred Scott*, as well as in Lincoln's Springfield speech of June 26, 1857. I asked the man why the Commission's Report had followed Taney, and ignored Curtis and Lincoln. All he could say was that he had followed the weight of scholarly opinion consulted by the Commission. In 1978 Don E. Fehrenbacher published his classic work, *The Dred Scott Case*, which will, I believe, be as definitive, certainly in its condemnation of Taney, as any such work can ever be. Yet Fehrenbacher could add little but detail to the judgment recorded of the central questions in *Dred Scott*, in Lincoln's speech of 1857. It is indeed true that many distinguished scholars placed their weight behind the characterization of the United States as "white racist," as evidenced by the exclusion of Negroes from the Declaration of Independence. But they did so for much the same reason that these or other scholars continued to subscribe to the the economic interpretation of the Constitution. Their reasons were at bottom ideological. But they were buttressed in the one case by the behavior of Conservatives, on the Supreme Court and elsewhere, in seeming to prefer "property rights" to "human rights," in matters of public policy dealing with the regulation of the economy. And they were buttressed in the behavior of these same Conservatives in matters dealing with civil rights, notably those of freed slaves, and their descendants. It was for this reason that Martin Diamond, in his writings in the 1950's and 1960's, criticized the Conservative defenders of the Constitution, as being foolish, by denying that the Constitution was democratic. Being democratic, for Diamond meant (then), being devoted to the equal rights of all, and refining and enlarging the public views, for the sake of all, and *not* for the sake of those who had merely vested interests in the privileges, either of wealth or of race. But this was because—and only because—Diamond (then) saw the entire Constitution as an elaborate device, or series of devices, implementing the undoubtedly democratic principles of the Declaration of Independence. When Diamond came, as he did, in 1970, to abandon the idea that the Declaration of Independence was democratic, he lent himself, not only to the heirs of John C. Calhoun, but to those of Roger B. Taney. Since the argument of the Declaration—as we have seen—is one that combines, by the ineluctable force of the purest demonstrative reasoning, the case *against* slavery, and the case *for* democratic government, it was not possible for Diamond to abandon the case *for* democracy in the Declaration, without simultaneously abandoning the case *against* slavery.

But what of the argument that, since the Founding Fathers did not abolish slavery, they could not have intended to include Negroes in the proposition of human equality? This argument is the core of Taney's position, and of that Ideological Liberalism of which he has, ironically, become the high priest. It would be tedious to refute this contention, again and again and again, were it not that it is so freighted in the public mind with the morality of the Constitution. Lincoln observed, however, that the Founding Fathers did not "at once, *or ever afterwards,* actually place all white people on an equality with one another." (Lincoln's emphasis.) Precisely what Lincoln had in mind, we cannot say. Perhaps it is sufficient to notice that the Fifteenth Amendment, guaranteeing Negro suffrage, precedes the Nineteenth Amendment, guaranteeing female suffrage. And it is also the case that in 1857, the legal position of free male Negroes was in many respects superior to that of free white women. They certainly had much more freedom to buy and sell and control property. And Lincoln, as early as 1836, had endorsed the principle of female suffrage.

More generally, however, Lincoln regarded the assertion of human equality as the assertion of a great and beneficent principle. It was little less than miraculous, that the principle which, above all others, condemned human slavery, should arise and emerge in a society characterized so largely by human slavery. That this principle would in fact have the effect of putting slavery "in course of ultimate extinction," Lincoln never doubted. That it has had the effect Lincoln expected—little as he expected to be the instrument of that effect—we all know. That it was simply impossible that the announcement of the principle would be accompanied instantly by such an effect, no reasonable man can doubt. Why then are the Founding Fathers believed to be either hypocrites, who said what they did not believe, or knaves, who did not act upon the principles they claimed for themselves? The answer is that Ideological Liberalism is in the grip of a theory of History, which declares that each age—except the Last—is one of contradictions. The Founding Fathers were not insincere—so the argument runs—nor could they have acted upon their principles, rightly understood, because they were dupes of History. They pronounced ideals which had a bearing they did not grasp, and which could not be realized except by a revolution—another revolution, beyond the one that they themselves had made. All of Martin Diamond's scholarship in the 1950's and 1960's was designed to disprove the necessity or desirability of this further revolution, in which he himself had once so passionately believed. His argument for the Constitution of 1787, excogitated (and brilliantly) from the pages of the *Federalist*, saw the Constitution as an exercise in practical or prudential reasoning. It was an exercise in such reasoning, as would illuminate the way in which principles may be wisely implemented, by being implemented only insofar as circumstances allow and permit. It was an exercise in such reasoning, in the appreciation of which, he meant to present us with a model of how we ourselves might wisely proceed in our own circumstances. Diamond thought, it is true, that our circumstances showed no good reason to abandon or greatly modify the institutions we had inherited from the Founding Fathers. But he also thought that, in seeing the continuing utility of these institutions, we would understand the meaning both of boldness and caution, in approaching those problems which were distinctive to our own time. In doing so, he meant us to understand the deadly hostility of Ideological Liberalism. But he meant us also to understand the folly of Conservatism, that Conservatism that had brought into question the genuineness of the Founding in its commitments *against* slavery and *for* democracy. Yet when Diamond came, in 1970, to deny the democracy of the Declaration, he called into question the whole enterprise in which he had himself been so eloquently and profoundly engaged.

* * *

Let us now turn to Robert Goldwin's charge that I have misrepresented the views of the late Martin Diamond. Goldwin, we recall, says that on the vital points at issue, Diamond's opinions are "exactly—*exactly*—the opposite" of what I have represented them to be. It will be recalled that I had, in *How to Think About the American Revolution*, asserted that I had discovered, or uncovered, "a core of meaning [in Diamond's "no guidance" thesis, concerning the relationship of the Declaration of Independence to the Constitution] that corresponded to, if it was not identical with, opinions advanced earlier by John C. Calhoun." I had also noted that Calhoun had characterized the principles of

the Declaration as being both "false" and "dangerous." Goldwin takes exception
to this, as follows.

*Jaffa's introduction asserts that Diamond ... somehow was heir to an argument
traceable, through Willmoore Kendall, to John Calhoun regarding the relationship of the Declaration of Independence and the Constitution. Kendall wanted to
disconnect the two as part of his "warfare against the Declaration." Calhoun was
worse: he considered the principles of the Declaration "false" and "dangerous."*

*Did Diamond agree? No. In fact anyone who reads the lecture can see
Diamond's position is exactly — exactly — the opposite: he considered the Declaration and the Constitution inseparable, and he considered the main tenets of the
Declaration as the fundamental truths of the American Republic. Diamond
made these points not just in passing, but as the emphatic and chief theme of his
lecture, from beginning to end.*

*Consider this from the beginning: "When we look back to our origins we look ...
to the Declaration and the Constitution. They are the two springs of our
existence. To understand their relationship is to understand the political core of
our being ... It is to this never-to-be severed relationship of the Declaration and
the Constitution that I address my remarks."*

*Consider this from the end of the lecture: "I have tried to turn our attention to the
two founding documents of our national being — the Declaration of Independence and the Constitution — and I have tried to make it impossible for us to
think of the one without simultaneously thinking of the other. In this I have
followed but also reversed the magisterial effort of Lincoln ... When the men of
his generation spoke of the Constitution, he wished them always to think of the
Declaration and hence of the liberty in which the nation had been conceived and
of the proposition regarding equality to which it had been dedicated.*

*Today our needs are otherwise. Our two documents must as always be seen as
indissolubly linked. But now we need to train ourselves, when hearing the
Declaration's heady rhetoric of revolution and freedom or when it is foolishly cited
as authority for populistic passions, always to see the Constitution as the
necessary forming, constraining, and sustaining system of government that
made our revolution a blessing to mankind and not a curse."*

"These quotes," Goldwin thinks, "suffice ... to establish clearly that Diamond's
argument was not at all as characterized by Jaffa, but quite the opposite."
Having said so much, Goldwin somewhat uneasily and inconsistently concedes
that he must "credit [me] with one half-truth." That half-truth is that

*Diamond did say, repeatedly, that the Declaration did not guide the writers of the
Constitution in devising institutions that would secure the rights set forth in the
Declaration: " ... the Declaration is devoid of guidance as to what those*

institutions *should be.*" "*The Declaration . . . offers no guidance for the* construction *of free governments. . . .*"

At this point one is moved to ask, what in the world was it that the Declaration
did do, other than declare independence, which Diamond sometimes noted that
the Congress had already done, by a simple resolution, on July 2, 1776? At one
point, Diamond speaks of the Declaration "richly nurturing in humanity a love of
free government," and throughout he regards it as a document of "sentiment"
while contrasting it with the Constitution, as a document of "intellect." But all
this is the merest buncombe, designed to conceal the depreciation of the
Declaration of Independence, and the hard logical idea it incorporates, which
logical idea is as far as any idea in the history of political thought can be from
mere thoughtless sentiment. It is that idea, which we have described throughout this essay, which connects the condemnation of despotism or slavery, with
that form of government—democratic constitutional republicanism—which
alone of all the possible forms of government, by its very nature, negates and
prevents despotism.

   Goldwin would have it that Diamond did not agree with Calhoun, because
Diamond praised the Declaration, and said that the Declaration and the Consti-
tution together were the inseparable documents of the Founding. But it is not
enough to say that both documents are *there.* Diamond could not make the
Declaration disappear. Once upon a time, as we have seen, he saw the
Declaration as propounding that form and essence of democracy, which the
Constitution attempted—however imperfectly—to implement. Then he said
that it provided the *criteria* by which the Constitutional Convention, and the
American people, might measure and judge any government. Now however this
"indispensable" document seems to have had no other function than to make
people into excitable revolutionaries, who would have to be calmed down in
order to become well governed. But the reader should know that Calhoun, and
all those who died for the Confederate cause, and all those who still believe in
the Confederate cause today—and they are many—believed that the South
was defending the cause of freedom. They did not see any inconsistency
between democracy for themselves, and slavery for others. No less a nineteenth century liberal than Lord Acton falsely advertised the cause of the
South as a defense against the tryanny of the majority. The whole point about
the cause of freedom, notably as developed by Lincoln's dialectic in the ante-
bellum debate, was that it was impossible to separate the defense of freedom
from the attack on slavery, and that it was impossible to demand, in the name of
freedom, the security of the rights of white men, without conceding the equal
right of black men to have their rights secured. Diamond's "no guidance" thesis
is one that divorces the Declaration from the Constitution, in the most vital
point of principle. It is no good to put the Declaration and the Constitution back
into the same bed together *after* that divorce. The issue will not be legitimate.

Diamond's assertion, endorsed by Goldwin, that the Declaration tells us nothing about separation of powers, federalism, or any of the "auxiliary precautions" which, as defended in the *Federalist*, are justly praised elements of the Constitution, is simply not true. The very idea of the rule of law—that those who make the law must live under it, and that those who live under the law must share equally in its making—is derived from the Declaration. Moreover, in the indictment of the King and Parliament, the offenses characterized as despotic constitute a very syllabus of constitutionalism. In his Bicentennial lecture, Diamond insisted that the Declaration of Independence only required the consent of the people for the "instituting" of government, but not for its "operation." As I pointed out in *How to Think About the American Revolution*, in saying this Diamond simply ignored the text of the Declaration, which makes it an act of abject despotism to raise taxes without the active consent of the people. "Taxation without representation is tyranny," was the slogan of the Revolution, and the principle in this slogan is as surely incorporated in the Declaration as that more fundamental principle, from which it is derived by logical necessity, "that all men are created equal." But if taxation without representation is tyranny, then taxation *with* representation is democracy, or democratic republicanism. The only way in which taxation with representation might have been reconciled with a non-democratic republicanism, would have been if the British argument of 1765, that the Americans had been "virtually" represented in the British Parliament, had been accepted. But it was in the categorical *rejection* of the idea of virtual representation that *popular* republicanism or democracy became the only acceptable form of non-despotic government to Americans, as the only intrinsically or truly non-despotic form of government.

While it is true that the specific form of the argument for the extended republic in the Tenth and Fifty-first *Federalist*, is not to be found in the Declaration of Independence (as it is not to be found in the Constitution), it is a fact that only the argument of the Declaration made the argument of Publius possible. I have already shown above the argument by which the Declaration upon the ground of universal human equality, transformed the foundation of legitimate civil society, and in so doing transformed the idea of democratic government. It transformed the idea of democratic government from that of the *poor*, who are a *part* of the regime, to that of the government of *all*, who agree voluntarily to be members of civil society. The very fact that the majority now includes, as a matter of principle, rich as well as poor, or those who hold as well as those who are without property, means that the rights of property must be protected as one of the original purposes of *democratic* government. The protection of "different and unequal faculties of acquiring property" becomes "the first object of government" because, but only because, of this transformation in the idea of democratic government, a transformation from classical political philosophy achieved by the logic of the Declaration. It was this transformation in the definition of democratic republicanism that set the task for the Constitutional Convention, and that laid the groundwork for the argument of Publius which the earlier Diamond was so justly to celebrate. It is also the ground of what now—and forever—must be the *conservative* defense of the Constitution, that defense which is at once truly conservative because truly liberal.

Goldwin would have us think that because Diamond praised the Declaration, he thought well of it, and that therefore "anyone . . . can see" that Diamond's position is the opposite of Calhoun's. But Diamond's praise of the Declaration is of the damning variety, since it deprives the Declaration of that function, without which it is an empty shell: the function of prescribing the form and essence of popular or democratic republicanism. Yet even as the robes of Diamond's rhetoric flow over his truncated version of the Declaration, the cloven hoof peeks through. We must always, Diamond says, and Goldwin repeats, "see the Constitution as the necessary forming, constraining, and sustaining system of government that made our revolution a blessing to mankind and not a curse." This of course was precisely Calhoun's point of view. The Revolution, insofar as it merely reflected the Declaration's "heady rhetoric of revolution and freedom" would have been "a curse." There was a time when Martin Diamond would have characterized such writing as of the darkest reactionary die, as abandoning the Constitution to its worst enemies, by separating it from the luminous principles of intelligible freedom and democracy in the Declaration of Independence. And he would have been right.

* * *

Goldwin's defense concludes with the following quotations from Diamond.

It is to the Constitution that we must ultimately turn as the completion of the American Revolution.

And:

The American Founding . . . is only begun by the Declaration. It reaches its completion with the Constitution.

These are remarkable assertions. The preamble to the Constitution, itself speaks of "a more perfect Union." To say that the Union is "more perfect" does not differ in meaning from saying that it is "less imperfect." Even the book in which Diamond's lecture was published, the book which collected the American Enterprise Institute's Bicentennial Series, was entitled *America's Continuing Revolution*, which certainly seems to imply that the America's Revolution is, and always has been motivated, by a principle never to be perfectly achieved or completed. But to speak of the Constitution of 1787 as "completing" the

Revolution begun by the Declaration of Independence is grotesque in a most specific sense: The Declaration denounces at every turn, what it considers despotism and tyranny. The Constitution of 1787 contained legal guarantees and legal advantages to the institution of chattel slavery—despotism—which were absent from the Articles of Confederation. The intention or purpose of the Constitution, concerning these guarantees and advantages, could not be inferred, in any anti-despotic sense, from the language of the Constitution itself. Only as the language of the Declaration of Independence could be brought to bear upon the Constitution, as expressing the authoritative intention of the Framers, as to the form of government intended, and the nature of the rights to be secured, could the Constitution yield a democratic and republican meaning. Let us see.

We have commented above on Lincoln's argument, rejecting Taney's opinion in *Dred Scott*, which denied that Negroes were included in the Declaration's proposition with regard to "all men." Lincoln insisted that the Declaration was a charter for the freedom and equal rights of all men, of all races, everywhere. The Constitution was, he thought, a very imperfect attempt to secure the rights enumerated in the Declaration, but it was such an attempt as wise men could prudently make, while allowing time and circumstances to improve upon that attempt. The Framers of the Constitution, Lincoln thought, had made concessions that were necessary. If they had grasped for more, they would have achieved less. Only the stronger Union, Lincoln thought, could contain slavery, and in the long run, place it "in course of ultimate extinction." It is in this light that one must interpret the concessions —above all the concessions to despotism or slavery—that are indeed made in the Constitution of 1787.

In order to make the ratification of the Constitution of 1787 possible, in order to get slaveholders to agree to a regime in which the powers of the central government would be far greater than they had been under the Articles of Confederation, it was necessary for the Convention to incorporate great and powerful measures, adding great and powerful securities, for the institution of Negro slavery in the United States. Concerning these, Martin Diamond, in his Bicentennial lecture, is completely silent. And Robert Goldwin, while denying any relationship between Diamond's views and Calhoun's, is silent about Diamond's silence.

If however we turn to the text of the Constitution, if indeed we turn first of all to the one and only provision in the Constitution to which Diamond can point as democratic—Article 1, Section 2—what do we find? We find that, in the House of Representatives, the one branch of the government in which the people are represented directly, "the electors in each state shall have the qualifications requisite for electors of the most numerous branch of the state legislature." Diamond in his Bicentennial lecture makes the preposterous claim that it was here that the American people made their commitment to democratic government. In fact, they made it in the Revolution, when they rejected the idea of virtual representation in the British Parliament. But Article 1, Section 2, does not specify what the qualifications for electors to the House shall be. It leaves that to the states, which varied widely in what they required. That the states were in fact on a democratic course, that the franchise was, and would increasingly become, democratic, is true. But that depended upon causes at work in the states, none of which was more powerful than the conviction that all men are created equal. How equivocal Article 1, Section 2 is, within the confines of the Constitution itself, is shown by other language in the section, to which Diamond makes no reference. It is that, in counting the persons to be represented in the House, "to the whole number of free persons ... [there shall be added] three fifths of all other persons." Now who are these "other persons"? Slaves. Every slaveowner cast, in addition to his own vote, three-fifths of a vote for every slave residing in his Congressional District. Or, to put it somewhat more dramatically, any man who owned a hundred slaves, in effect cast sixty-one votes. Here was something that was not only a reward for despotism—in and through the operation of the "democratic" principle—but a powerful incentive for the slave interest to expand slavery as a way of expanding its political influence within the Union.

No one will now, we presume, assert that the slaves were "virtually" represented by their masters. On the contrary, we do presume that the slaves' interest was in freedom, and whatever strengthened the political interest in slavery, was *against* the welfare of the slaves. Yet it is this provision of the Constitution, which is Diamond's *sole* evidence of the democracy of the Constitution, a democracy which he says owes nothing to the Declaration of Independence.

Article 1, Section 2, could have no parallel in the Articles of Confederation, because there was no direct representation of the people in the Congress of the Confederation. But neither is there any parallel in the Articles for Article 1, Section 9, of the Constitution which declares that "The migration or importation of such persons as any of the states now existing shall think proper to admit, shall not be prohibited by the Congress prior to the year one thousand eight hundred and eight ..." Here again we are confronted with the Constitution's magnificent circumlocutory euphemisms for the words slave or slavery. What this section of the Constitution does, however, is place it beyond the power of Congress to outlaw the foreign (or African) slave trade, for a period of twenty years. Let us remind ourselves of what this trade was, by recalling Jefferson's language, in his original draft of the Declaration, in holding the King responsible for it.

He has waged cruel war against human nature itself, violating its most sacred rights of life and liberty, in the persons of a distant people who never offended him, captivating and carrying them into slavery in another hemisphere, or to incur miserable death in their transportation thither.

It was this vile trade, piracy of the most brutal kind, a traffic the most execrable of human record, that the Constitution preserved—by, as we have said, an apparently irrepealable provision—for twenty years. But the effects of this provision did not end with twenty years. Indeed, they are with us to this very day. This trade was not slack during the period of its constitutional continuance. In *How to Think About the American Revolution* I estimated, on the basis of information given in *Time on the Cross*, that nearly as many slaves were imported in this period as during the previous one hundred and sixty years. From this one might say, with as much confidence as one can predict any "might have been" of history, that but for this provision in the Constitution, there would have been no Civil War, nor any race problem since the period of the Civil War such as we have in fact known. The slave population in 1860 would have been much smaller—perhaps by half—and so the political interests tending towards the preservation and perpetuation of slavery—including those fostered by Article 1, Section 2—would have been much smaller and weaker.

Why was such a dastardly provision included in the Constitution? Why indeed was Jefferson's condemnation of the foreign slave trade in the Declaration excised by the Congress? The answer is too well known. In both cases, the Southerners who clamored for cheap labor, and the Northerners, mostly New Englanders, who owned the ships that plied the trade, and who wanted its profits, combined. In the Declaration, however, the proposition of human equality remained, to condemn both slavery and the slave trade, in the minds of all who could understand the meaning of the words. Nothing is in the Constitution, however, to contrast this provision with any other provision of the Constitution, or to pronounce it a moral exeception to the rules laid down for a "democratic" or popular republican government.

Finally, we come to Article IV, Section 2, and to the paragraph therein which states that "No person held to service or labor in one state, under the laws thereof, escaping into another, shall, in consequence of any law or regulation therein, be discharged from such service or labor, but shall be delivered up on claim of the party to whom such service or labor may be due." This is the famous—or infamous—fugitive slave clause. Again, there is no parallel to it in the Articles of Confederation. It committed the government of the Union to the strengthening of the institution of slavery, by making it a federal responsibility to assist in the rendition of innocent fugitives from perpetual bondage. This provision, like that in Article I, Section 9, had a political effect far beyond what was immediately visible. The number of fugitive slaves never was large enough to endanger the peculiar institution, even in the border states. But the growing moral repugnance to slavery in the North, after 1832, was matched by a steadily growing moral sensitivity, by political public opinion in the South, to the condemnation of slavery on moral grounds. The fugitive slave law that was part of the Compromise of 1850 contributed mightily to the sectional strife of the last decade before war itself. In this period it was affirmed with ever increasing stridency, south of Mason and Dixon's line, that slavery was one of the moral elements of the Constitution, and that reluctance in enforcing the fugitive slave law—designed as it was to implement an undoubted Constitutional provision —was evidence of moral delinquency from the polity incorporated by the Constitution. As such, it was justification of the slave states in withdrawing from the Union which now condemned them, by condemning a constitutional obligation that they saw as vital to their life.

It was moreover because of the language of Article IV, Section 2, that Taney, in the *Dred Scott* decision, could say—however incorrectly he might have cited the actual language of the Constitution—that "the right of property in a slave is distinctly and expressly affirmed in the Constitution." Because of this, Taney held, the government of the United States "is pledged to protect it [viz., slave property] in all future time, if the slave escapes from his owner . . . ." According to Taney in 1857, "The only power conferred [by the Constitution upon the Congress, over slave property in the territories] is the power coupled with the duty of guarding and protecting the owner in his rights." This reading of the Constitution relied upon—besides Article IV, Section 2—the language of the Fifth Amendment, which says that "No person shall be . . . deprived of life, liberty, or property, without due process of law . . . " A slave was unquestionably a "person," since he is referred to as such in the euphemisms employed in all the sections in which slavery is signified. By the language of the Fifth Amendment he ought not, as a person be deprived his liberty. But neither ought his owner, as a person be deprived of the slave, who is his property! When the slave enters the federal territory, which takes precedence: the owner's right to his human property, or the human person's right to his liberty? Taney had no doubt about this question, because he believed that Negroes were not included in the humanity referred to in the Declaration. John C. Calhoun had no doubt either. Calhoun of course was dead in 1857, but he had, in many speeches in the 1840's, and in speeches dealing with the territorial question in 1850, indicated that slaveowners must be free to take their slaves with them into the federal territories. Any discrimination against the property that citizens coming from one part of the country took with them, as against the property of other citizens from other parts of the country, would be a violation of the Constitution that could—and ought—to lead to disunion. Calhoun had no doubt that the chatteldom of the slaves took precedence over their personality, in the interpretation of the Fifth Amendment, because he was convinced—as the later Martin Diamond was convinced, and as Robert Goldwin seems to be convinced—that the Declaration of Independence's proposition of human equality gave no authority, gave "no guidance" either to the framing or to the interpreting of the Constitution.

* * *

Goldwin completed his defense of Diamond, by laudatory citation of the passages wherein Diamond sees the completion of the American Revolution in the Constitution of 1787, the Constitution whose essential and virtuous moderation derived from its non-guidance by the heady, revolutionary rhetoric of the Declaration of Independence. As we have observed, this sage view of the Constitution seemed not to notice among the "necessary forming, constraining, and sustaining" provisions of this Constitution some extraordinary legal guarantees to human slavery.

Having ended his devastating ripostes on Diamond's behalf, Goldwin continues on his own account. "But Jaffa made another error," he says. This in in reference to my remark in *National Review* (January 22, 1982, p. 36) that "this series [viz., "A Decade of Study of the Constitution,"] initiated by *How Democratic Is the Constitution?*] seems destined to have as its central idea the same negative view of the principles of the regime [i.e. "no guidance by the principles of the Declaration of Independence"] as its predecessor." "I don't know when he began to lay claim to powers of divination," Goldwin writes, "in characterizing the 'central idea' of books not yet written by authors not yet chosen." Goldwin nevertheless assures his readers that the books in this series, of which he is senior editor, "will be books of controversy, designed to provide solid ground for readers to think for themselves." We will, he assures us, "try to get the best writers we can, of differing views and disciplines, to give reasoned answers to the questions."

It seems somewhat unfair of Goldwin, to call a "claim to powers of divination," my statement of what only "*seems* destined" to be the "central idea" of his series. We all judge the future by the past, and I judged Goldwin's future actions, in choosing writers on other controversial questions about the Constitution, by his actions, in choosing writers concerning the controversial question, How democratic is the Constitution?

I ventured to speak of a "central idea" in Goldwin's Bicentennial series, because of Lincoln's famous aphorism on this very topic. "Public opinion," Lincoln said in Chicago, in 1856, "on any subject, always has a 'central idea'" from which all its minor thoughts radiate. The 'central idea' in our public opinion at the beginning was, and until recently has continued to be, 'the equality of men.'" Lincoln of course repeated this thought when, at Gettysburg, he spoke of a nation dedicated to a certain proposition, and thereby to a certain form of government. The result of the central idea, Lincoln believed, was the form of government intended—however imperfectly it was achieved—in the Constitution.

When Robert Goldwin and his associates addressed themselves to the question, How democratic is the Constitution? they sought out—we are told in their Preface—"spokesmen as authoritative, thoughtful, and instructive as could be found" for the differing answers to their question. They did—quite properly—give particular place to the views of Martin Diamond, which were in direct opposition to Lincoln's. They also gave place—also quite properly—to a present-day representative of that contemporary of Abraham Lincoln, who admired Lincoln greatly: Karl Marx. But no one in the pages of *How Democratic Is the Constitution?* argued in favor of the thesis of the Gettysburg Address, or even set it forth as a serious point of view. I trust I will be forgiven for entertaining the thought that an omission of such a magnitude was deliberate. The Lincolnian point of view, after all, is not the esoteric doctrine of an esoteric cult. Is it then "divination" to think that whatever kept the Gettysburg Address, and all that it represents, out of the first volume in this series, will continue to operate to keep it out of subsequent volumes? But I will venture one further attempt at what Goldwin may choose to call divination. And that is to say that, if the American Enterprise Institute continues to celebrate the Bicentennial of the Constitution, in the Doughface tradition, noticing neither the Slave nor the Emancipator, its series will be in the purest sense a series *ad infinitum*, an exercise in futility.

Endnote

William Schambra of the American Enterprise Institute is coeditor, with Robert A. Goldwin, of *How Democratic Is the Constitution?* In the May, 1980 issue of *Interpretation: A Journal of Political Philosophy* he published "The Writings of Martin Diamond: A Bibliography." In it, he listed the *second* edition of *The Democratic Republic*, but not the *first*. It will be recalled that it was in the first edition that Diamond subscribed in the fullest degree, to the thesis that the Declaration of Independence propounded the "popular and liberal principles" of government that were incorporated into the Constitution. The second edition, however, reversed this position by 180 degrees, and said that the Declaration of Independence was "neutral" and gave "no guidance" to the Framers of the Constitution.

In the same issue of *Interpretation*, Schambra included "An Excerpt from LINCOLN'S GREATNESS." This was a speech Diamond delivered to the Los Angeles Lincoln Club, on Lincoln's birthday, 1960. It was published in a pamphlet, now very rare, entitled "With Firmness in the Right," by Claremont Men's College, in 1960. The pamphlet also included a speech on Lincoln by George C. S. Benson, President of the College. Although I remembered the speech very well, it took me nearly a year to locate a copy of the pamphlet. Schambra accompanied the reprinting of the "excerpt" with an essay about it, in the course of which he said, and said truly, that it is "a delightful lesson in the giving of lessons ... It is, perhaps, a piece more representative of his work than are his scholarly writings...." But one must wonder why, with all this praise, Schambra stopped short with this excerpt. The remainder of the speech might have extended its space from less than four, to no more than seven pages. (The part Schambra left out was no longer than Schambra's superfluous essay *about* the speech.) Could it be that the omitted part of the speech contained a powerful statement of Lincoln's "guidance" by the Declaration of Independence? And that Diamond's source for his understanding of Lincoln was *Crisis of the House Divided?* Surely this mutilation of the record is unworthy of scholarship in free society. It is, in the words of John Locke, both "foolish and dishonest."

Twelve

Willmoore Kendall: Philosopher of Consensus?

An article by Jeffrey Hart, with the foregoing title, but minus the question mark, appeared in *National Review*, September 1, 1978. In it Hart asserts that "Kendall's position ... though not widely or fully grasped ... *is* the essence of American conservatism." (Emphasis by Hart.) Quoting Henry Regnery, Hart characterizes Kendall as having a mind "which is capable of seizing upon parts of a problem." The result "was an extremely fragmentary production." Out of these fragments Kendall was never able "to pull the entire position into a coherent statement." Notwithstanding such an unpromising prelude, Hart goes on to proclaim that "Kendall's final position had a formidable coherence and consistency." And "all it needs to prevail," he continues, "is a brief and clear articulation." This, he modestly says, he "will now try to provide."

It may at first seem that Kendall was remarkably fortunate in having as a disciple Jeffrey Hart. For Hart offers, in less than 1,000 words, to distill out of the torrential flood of Kendall's writings, that brief, coherent, and clear articulation—an articulation that Kendall apparently could not provide for himself —that will now at last gain Kendall's views the influence that they deserve. One must of course wonder why Kendall, who certainly desired to be influential, could not have taken these simple steps in his own behalf. But one must also wonder why Hart has waited more than a decade after Kendall's death to perform this service for him. Central to Kendall's interpretation of the American political tradition, is the thesis that July 4, 1776, is *not* the birthday of the United States. Why did Hart allow the fake bicentennial to go unchallenged? Could it be that the recent publication of my *How to Think About the American Revolution*, with its brief, clear, and coherent account of Kendall's position, as derived from that of John C. Calhoun (the Marx of the Master Class, as the late Richard Hofstadter aptly called him), provided the occasion? I even cited the exact passages in Calhoun's 1848 speech on the Oregon question which Kendall had paraphrased in his denunciation of Abraham Lincoln for having "derailed" the American political tradition. I showed that Kendall had merely substituted Lincoln for Jefferson, as having given notoriety and authority to what Calhoun called "the most false and dangerous of all political errors." It is this identical "error" in the Declaration of Independence which is the nest of what Hart now calls "the viper theory" of equality.

My critique of Kendall was embodied in an essay called "Equality as a

Conservative Principle," and was originally presented to a panel presided over by William F. Buckley, Jr., at the 1974 meetings of the American Political Science Association in Chicago. The theme of the panel was "Conservatism's Search for Meaning." I examined in great detail Kendall's arguments in *Basic Symbols of the American Political Tradition*, a book edited and completed by George C. Carey, and published in 1970. Hart was a member of that panel. Neither he nor Carey has ever written—nor so far as I know ever uttered—a word of rebuttal to my critique. Professor M. E. Bradford, of the University of Dallas, attempted such a rebuttal in the Winter, 1976 issue of *Modern Age*. My reply to Bradford was published in the Spring, 1977 issue of that same journal, and is reprinted in *How to Think About the American Revolution*. How effective Bradford and I were, either in rebuttal or in surrebuttal, I hope every reader of *NR* will decide for himself. That Hart should think that the dull repetition of such a debatable hypothesis is sufficient to enable it "to prevail" is astonishing. Such mindless indifference to evidence and argument certainly seems to tend to confirm the worst suspicions of ideological liberals concerning the intelligence of conservatives.

* * *

According to Hart, Kendall's teaching is the teaching of the Founding Fathers. The "theory to which they subscribed" is also the theory "to which Kendall subscribed," and it "remains the central issue of our politics." But every major figure of the Founding period, and every major document expressing the thought of the Founders, subscribed to a doctrine of natural rights—of which the doctrine of human equality was the core—a doctrine largely but not exclusively derived from the teachings of John Locke. Kendall loathed this doctrine and tried to re-write the Founding as if it hardly existed. But an account of the Founding without natural rights would be like an account of the story of Moses, without any reference to the Ten Commandments, or of Jesus without any reference to the Sermon on the Mount.

Here now is how Hart goes about propounding the Kendall-Founders theory.

> *It assumes that people, living their lives, accumulate experience and knowledge. It means to prevent them from converting temporary moods and transitory judgments into public policy. Waves of popular feeling will not prevail. This novel instrument of government puts all sorts of buffers in the way of popular feeling ... Nothing really serious could happen without due reflection and the formulation of a consensus. Nevertheless, in the end, the "sense" of the people would prevail.*

Later, Hart supplements the foregoing with the following:

The people, in their deliberate sense, on the basis of their lived experience, will, in Kendall's opinion and the opinion of the Founders, affirm what is true, valuable, feasible.

* * *

Before examining this alleged theory, I would say a few words about Willmoore Kendall, partly to absolve him of the odium which must attach to such a statement of his views. To call him the "philosopher of consensus" must strike anyone who knew Kendall, or who knows his writings, as having a certain *prima facie* absurdity. Consensus means agreement, and Willmoore Kendall was gloriously and uproariously in disagreement with nearly everyone about nearly everything during most of his life. Nellie Kendall gave to that wonderful treasure house of his writings, published posthumously, the apt title of *Willmoore Kendall: Contra Mundum*. Among Kendall's writings is a defense of the people of Athens for condemning and executing Socrates. Like most things Kendall wrote, the argument will not in the end stand up. Yet Socrates would have liked it. For one thing, he would have chuckled to himself that the people of Athens would have executed Kendall a lot sooner than they did him, had they been given the chance. But Socrates would also have been sick of the ACLU-type free speech arguments by which he is usually defended today. For Socrates, no more than Kendall, defended absolute freedom of speech. What he did defend, was freedom of speech for *philosophers*. In his love of paradox, Kendall was eminently Socratic. In his ability to catch people in the toils of paradox, he was something of a genius. That is why he was a superlative teacher. But his arguments were eminently *ad hominem*, and to confuse his paradoxes with sound doctrine is both foolish and dangerous.

At the end of his life Kendall became a disciple—more I think than he had ever been anyone's disciple—of Leo Strauss. In his recognition of Strauss's greatness he showed a largeness of soul that placed him head and shoulders above any American political scientist of his generation. There was about him none of the "envy with which mediocrity views genius," because he was no mediocrity. Among Strauss's familiar sayings was that agreement—or consensus—may produce peace, but it cannot produce truth. And Kendall, whatever his failings, was a truth-seeker. He would have scorned attempts to patch up his fragments with pieces that did not fit.

* * *

Hart's summary of Kendall speaks of "people" living their lives and accumulating "experience and knowledge." Of course all people and all animals possessing sense perception and memory accumulate experience. Human beings however, unlike other animals, form opinions about their experience. Whether such opinions are ever justly denominated "knowledge" is another matter. Hart has collapsed the distinction between opinion and knowledge as if it did not exist. Yet this distinction is the ground of all philosophy, including all political philosophy, as it is of all science. Looking at the "peoples" of the world, past and present, we can say that there is no opinion so absurd or so vicious that it might not be affirmed as the ground of some consensus. Cannibal societies rest upon a cannibal consensus. Bolshevism rests upon a Bolshevik consensus. National Socialism (a species of cannibalism) rests upon a National Socialist consensus. Recent events in Guyana remind us that there can be a suicidal consensus. To say that a consensus is "deliberate" or is the result of "due reflection" tells us nothing of its quality. How much reflection is "due"? The quantity of reflection does not in any case assure us of its quality. Reasonable men may take time to reflect; but the fact that men take time to reflect does not mean that they are reasonable. The Jonestown people apparently rehearsed their suicide ritual many times. Some of us suspect that there is a suicide ritual of the West, which has been forming for over one hundred years, with much reflection. It is called — loosely — Marxism. What is crucial, and what has escaped Hart, is that there is nothing in the idea of consensus, taken by itself, which enables us to distinguish a good consensus from a bad consensus. I believe that the consensus that formed the American Founding was indeed a good consensus. But that was because, in the words of George Washington in 1783,

> *it was not laid in the gloomy ages of ignorance and superstition; but at an epocha* [sic] *when the rights of mankind were better understood and more clearly defined, than at any other period.*

To say that the people will "affirm what is true" must mean that there is a standard of truth independent of what the people affirm — otherwise one will be talking oneself in a circle. Washington's standard of truth, and of enlightenment, was supremely expressed in that document of the Founding which proclaimed self-evident truths, namely, the Declaration of Independence. Yet the doctrine of the Declaration is to be found in virtually all the documents of the Revolutionary period. I have, for example, reviewed all the state constitutions' bills of rights in *How to Think About the American Revolution* and showed that all of them, in language usually less succinct and less eloquent, express the identical convictions that we find in the Declaration. So does Jefferson's *Summary View of the Rights of British America* (1774), and so do the *Declaration and Resolves of the First Continental Congress* (1774) and the *Declaration of the Causes and Necessity of Taking Up Arms* (1775). Yet Hart ignores all this, and has the audacity to declare in this third century of American independence, that the theory of the Declaration is the "viper theory" which stands in opposition to the Founding!

In truth, however, the proposition that all men are created equal, so far from being opposed to the idea of consensus, is the very ground of consensus. All the documents aforesaid, agree that men are by nature free, equal, and independent. By this they understand that no man, by nature, has more authority over another, than the other has over him. For this reason, legitimate authority — that is, authority arising not from mere force, or from fraud — arises from *consent*. And the *consent* that gives rise to legitimate government — to the "just powers of government" — is identical with the *consensus* that gives rise to such government. "Consensus" is merely a substantive derived from the Latin verb *consentire*. Hence the consent or consensus of the American Founding is precisely that that is derived from the recognition of the natural equality of human beings, and of their rights. Equality and consent, so far from being antithetical to each other, as Hart (following Kendall) proposes, actually are reciprocals of each other. Each implies the other, as concavity does convexity, and convexity concavity. They are distinguishable but inseparable.

* * *

Kendall himself was well aware that a consensus may embody principles, but cannot itself be a ground or source of such principles. But he never successfully resolved in his own mind what the American principles were, or even what they ought to have been. Like the man who didn't know much about art, he knew what he liked, and what he didn't like. This is why his work appears fragmentary and why he never produced that "coherent statement" which Hart so blithely offers to supply for him. When Kendall attempted to read the natural rights teaching of the Declaration out of the Founding, he simply moved into an intellectual vacuum. For the teaching in regard to equality is the ground of consent: to repeat, it is *because* men are originally equal, that political obligation arises from consent. Consent apart from equality is simply a nullity.

Kendall's attempt to separate equality from consent corresponded to his attempt to separate the Declaration from the Constitution. In his mind the Declaration was — quite erroneously — a merely egalitarian document; while the Constitution was — equally erroneously — a consensual document. Hart alludes to this when he writes,

> As Kendall was fond of pointing out, the Preamble to the Constitution, in which the goals of the new government are set forth, makes no mention of rights.

But Kendall always treated the Constitution as if it were some kind of new beginning of government, without any reference to what went before it. Yet the Preamble to the Constitution begins,

We the People of the United States, in order to form a more perfect Union ...

The Preamble thus presupposes an existing people of the United States, and an existing Union, which is to become more perfect. But when did the people of the United States *become* a people, and when did they form their Union? The answer is that the people of the thirteen colonies became the people of the United States, on July 4, 1776, and their union was formed in and by the Declaration of Independence. The principles of the Declaration were and remained the principles of the people of the United States. The Declaration of Independence was and is the first of the organic laws of the United States, and is so denominated to this day by the United States Code. The Constitution does not repeat the assertion of natural rights which is in the Declaration, for the simple reason that to have done so would have been redundant. Had the union formed by the Declaration been dissolved at any time in the intervening thirteen years, a new declaration would have been necessary and proper. But as it had not, a further declaration would have been unnecessary and hence improper.

Why did Kendall ignore or deny the foregoing? In *Basic Symbols*, he flatly asserts that the Declaration of Independence was not the work of "one people" and did not create one nation, but rather what Kendall called "a baker's dozen" of new sovereignties. This was the doctrine of John C. Calhoun and was adopted by his political heirs who formed the Confederate States of America in 1861. By it, the Union, or nation, was formed by the Constitution alone. Hence the instruments by which the states had ratified the Constitution became the instruments by which the Union or nation was formed. But if the Union was formed by ratification, it could be dissolved by de-ratification. Secession—considered as de-ratification—became therefore a constitutional process. In fact, some of the ordinances of secession, adopted in 1860 and 1861, were called ordinances of de-ratification.

Kendall was a loyal son of the Confederacy. For him, as for many of his brother Confederates, this was no mere lost cause, which they might celebrate privately, like the Jacobites they so strongly resembled. It remained the ground for the true understanding of the American political tradition, for which they were willing to fight in the political arena, now and forever. This is the key to his otherwise unintelligible conception of "consensus." The consensus he revered was the one that embodied within itself the legal sanctions given to the institution of slavery. The recognition of slavery in the Constitution of 1787—a recognition accorded (however indirectly) by the three-fifths clause, the fugitive slave clause, and the twenty year guarantee of the foreign slave trade—were not prudent compromises with a necessary but transient evil. For Kendall, they were positive expressions of the moral sense of the community. From a strictly rational standpoint Kendall was unable to defend slavery. But from a deeply emotional standpoint—from the standpoint of that America that he carried "in his hips," as he said—he was sure that the community that had embraced slavery was "the people of the United States" at its best. It was *this* people whose consensus was the true American consensus. Kendall believed that this people and this consensus was still there, and might yet be revived by a genuine conservative revival. But readers of *National Review* should know, and Jeffrey Hart should know, that a "distinctive American conservatism" in this sense, would be a distinctive American fascism, or national socialism.

* * *

Kendall's Constitution was *not* that of the Founding Fathers: it was that of John C. Calhoun, Jefferson Davis, and Alexander Stephens. Madison, for example, declared that the words "slave" and "slavery" had been carefully excluded from the text of the document written in Philadelphia, in the summer of 1787, because the Framers expected that slavery would eventually disappear, and they did not want its shameful traces to remain upon their handiwork. But nothing is more striking, or more authoritative, of the understanding of the Founding, than a correspondence between Madison and Jefferson, in the year 1825, the year before Jefferson's death. The two men—the Author of the Declaration and the Father of the Constitution—had been personal and political friends for more than fifty years. Jefferson charged Madison, the younger man, to be the custodian of his reputation, after he was gone. Such things would have led anyone except the Kendallites to be suspicious of the idea of the great gulf between the Declaration and the Constitution. Both men—retired Presidents of the United States—were members of the Board of Visitors of the new University of Virginia. Jefferson, the Father of the University, was at this time also its Rector. The subject arose, as to what should be the instructional principles of the faculty. Jefferson wrote:

> In most public seminaries textbooks are prescribed to each of the several schools, as norma docendi *in that school; and this is generally done by authority of the trustees. I should not propose this generally in our University, because I believe none of us are so much at the heights of science ... as to undertake this, and therefore it will be better left to the professors* until occasion of interference shall be given.

I have emphasized these seven words, to show how utterly free Jefferson was of any latter-day ACLU or AAUP notions of academic freedom! "But," Jefferson continued,

> there is one branch in which we are the best judges, in which heresies may be taught, of so interesting a character to our own State and to the United States, as

*to make it a duty in us to lay down the principles to be taught. It is that of
government.*

Jefferson and Madison then deliberated together—in an episode I have recon-
structed with some pains in *How to Think About the American Revolution*—as
to what principles of government should be taught at the Law School of the
University of Virginia. There was as yet no separate faculty of government or of
political science. The conclusions at which they arrived were embodied in
resolutions drafted by Jefferson, and adopted by the Board on March 4, 1825.
But they followed closely recommendations made by Madison to Jefferson, and
certainly may be considered to reflect the opinions of both of them.

The resolutions provide that it is the duty of the Board to the government
under which it lives

> *to pay especial attention to the principles of government which shall be inculcated*
> [in this University], *and to provide that none shall be inculcated which are
> incompatible with those on which the Constitutions of this State, and of the
> United States were genuinely based. . . .*

The resolutions then proceed

> *to point out specially where these principles are to be found legitimately developed.*

With respect to

> *the general principles of liberty and the rights of man, in nature and in society,
> the doctrine of Locke, in his "Essay Concerning the True Original Extent and End
> of Civil Government"* [otherwise known as the *Second Treatise of Civil Govern-
> ment*] *and of Sidney in his "Discourses on government," may be considered as
> those generally approved by our fellow citizens of this, and of the United States . . .*

I sincerely trust that all readers of *National Review* will take note, and forever
remember, that according to Jefferson and Madison, Locke's *Second Treatise*,
which is the classic source of the doctrine of universal, natural, equal human
rights (Jeffrey Hart's "viper theory"), was one of the two books they considered authoritative according to the opinion of "our fellow citizens of this and of
the United States." That is to say, Locke was part of that very consensus
praised by Kendall, but from which he attempted to exclude Locke!

The resolutions continued, however, by declaring what were the "best
guides" to "the distinctive principles of the government of our State, and of that
of the United States." The first of these "best guides" is

> *The Declaration of Independence, as the fundamental act of union of these
> states.*

There are three other documents recommended for the "distinctive principles" of American government. They are: the *Federalist*; the Virginia Resolutions of 1799; and Washington's Farewell Address.

What is said about the Declaration is striking and decisive. Let us first note that according to Jefferson and Madison, the Declaration of Independence is "the fundamental act of union of these States." That is to say, it is not only the act of *separation* from Great Britain, but the act of *union* of the states. That should put an end, once and for all, to the Kendall-Calhoun hypothesis about a "baker's dozen" of separate states emerging from the Declaration. This explains why, to this day, the Declaration remains the first of the laws of the United States, and why all other acts of the United States are dated from the Declaration, and not from the Constitution.

Secondly, we observe that the Declaration is described as the first of the best guides to "the distinctive principles" of American government. Neither the Preamble to the Constitution—nor any part of the Constitution—is mentioned as a guide to any principles. The explanation for this is that there is nothing in the Constitution itself to enable us to distinguish the *principles* of the Constitution from the *compromises* of the Constitution. All the documents recommended by Jefferson and Madison assist us in interpreting the Constitution. But the Declaration is unique, in that it alone is at once a law of the United States, and a source of the principles of the government of the United States. Nor is there in these resolutions any sense of any tension between the doctrine of the *Federalist*, the second item on the list, and the Declaration. Yet Kendall pretended to regard the *Federalist*, as if it were a guide to an anti-Declaration consensus!

* * *

National Review is a journal of conservative political opinion. Certainly there is a conservative tradition much older than the tradition of the American Founding. Certainly there is much in this older tradition which might lead us to have reservations about the American Founding, as it might lead us to have reservations about any modern regime. But such reservations are theoretical, or hypothetical. In the regime of freedom, which the United States protects and preserves, we can each of us still save his soul by the light of whatever ancient wisdom seems best to him. The standards of political decency recognized in the western world, as in the world generally, have been down, not up, since the American Revolution. If the United States flags or fails in its unique mission, and in its unique destiny, the tradition of civilization, of more than five thousand years, may well be expunged from the memory of mankind.

Doubt as to the nature and worth of the American Founding is today endemic, not only among our youth, but among their teachers, and among the citizens generally. "Better red than dead" is no longer a slogan, as it was twenty-five years ago. Instead, it is a deeply ingrained conviction, so deep as hardly to need articulation or repetition. But nothing contributes more to such a conviction than the opinion that when this nation was born, we did not mean, or should not have meant, what we said, when we declared "that all men are created equal."

1978

Thirteen

The Madison Legacy: A Reconsideration of the Founders' Intent

George Will has written a homily on James Madison as the Father of this country, for the December 7, 1981 *Newsweek*. The nation, by this account, is of dubious legitimacy. Perhaps the Pearl Harbor Day appearance of this article is fortuitous. But it certainly suggests that the principles by which Americans have lived, and for which many of them have died, are of questionable dignity.

Will thinks that Washington, D. C. should have been named Madison, D. C. The pen, he says, is mightier than the sword, and Madison's pen was the ablest of the Founding Fathers. It was Madison, Will writes, who "more than any other founder, clearly understood and unsparingly articulated the nation's premises." It is these premises, however, "which contribute to today's problems." The reason he thinks the nation's capital should have been named after Madison is the same as the reason that a famous avenue in New York City is named after him. Not civil and religious liberty, but advertising, reveals the nation's "premise." "Advertising," writes Will, "tries to be a pyromaniac, igniting conflagrations of desire for instant gratification. It is fuel for our Madisonian society. It spurs economic growth, and hence specialization, diversity, and the multiplication of factions that Madison favored." Will speaks of Madison's "cheerfulness about the uninhibited self-interestedness of the multiplying factions," and describes the constitutional regime of which Madison was the leading architect as one that is supposed to work "without anyone having good motives—without public spiritedness." It is a regime which "gives people an easy conscience about pursuing private interests through public motives." That is to say, it is a regime in which you are encouraged to believe that whatever seems good (or, rather, pleasant) for yourself, must be good also for the country.

Will thinks that Madison achieved a "revolution in democratic theory." This theory was addressed, Will says, to the problem of the tyranny of the majority. Tyranny in a popular government could be avoided—according to Will's account of Madison—partly by separation of powers and federalism, but mainly "by having so many minority interests that there is no stable majority, only shifting coalitions of factions." Before Madison, one presumes, citizens of popular republics were subjected to vain moral exhortations—such as those of Washington's Farewell Address. But Madison's revolution, says Will, consisted in saying of factions, "the more the merrier." As a consequence of this teaching, Will thinks, "the churning of the government by factions [today] is more violent than anything [Madison] envisioned." And even Madison might be "chagrined at what his philosophy promoted."

Whether or not Madison would have been chagrined, there is no doubt about George Will. Will began his article by quoting Thomas Jefferson as saying that James Madison was "the greatest man in the world." This, Will says, "was a smidgen strong, considering that Edmund Burke was then in the world." Will thus implies that Edmund Burke was a greater man than any of the Founding Fathers. That Thomas Jefferson might have ranked Burke above Madison hardly takes into account the opinions of the day, however. The factional strife in American politics in the 1790's — George Will to the contrary notwithstanding — exceeded in violence anything we have known. Jefferson, in fact, detested Burke for his attack on the French Revolution. It was, he said, "evidence of the rottenness of his mind." Jefferson was solidly on the side of Paine, in his debate with Burke, and Madison was on the side of Jefferson.

There is another American, not a Founding Father, yet fondly remembered as a Father. "We are coming Father Abraham, three hundred thousand strong" was a marching song of the Civil War. George Will, in a recent column, repelling "A Shrill Assault on Mr. Lincoln," described Abraham Lincoln as "the greatest statesman in the history of democracy." If I am not mistaken, Will thereby ranks Lincoln above even Burke. Will declared of this recent attack on Lincoln (which, I might add, I had myself repelled some three years before Will seems to have noticed it), that it "provoked those, like me, who revere Lincoln, and still smolder with indignation about the Kansas-Nebraska Act of 1854." But if Lincoln is the greatest statesman in the history of democracy, are we not justified in regarding his principles, as the principles of democratic statesmanship? We can hardly think Lincoln to be as great as we say he is, without giving him credit for having an intelligent conviction as to why what he was doing was right. Socrates discovered that he was the wisest of men—as the Delphic oracle had prophesied—because, although he knew that he knew nothing, the others (especially the politicians of Athens) thought they knew, but did not know. They could not give a rational account of their actions. They had no principles which they could articulate and defend. But Lincoln was as self-conscious of the principles of his actions as ever Socrates could have wished. It was his sublime articulation of those principles that entitles him to the accolade of George Will.

Lincoln's opposition to the Kansas-Nebraska Act was due to its repeal of the Missouri Compromise restriction of slavery. His opposition to the extension of slavery, whether by a popular vote or by any other means, was founded squarely upon his conviction that it violated the principles of the Declaration of Independence. The Declaration, Lincoln thought, embodied the central truth upon which American government—or any free government—was founded. In

February 1861, on his way to Washington, Lincoln spoke in Independence Hall, Philadelphia. In that sacred precinct—where *both* the Declaraction *and* the Constitution first saw the light of day—Lincoln spoke not of the Constitution, but declared that he had "never had a feeling, politically, that did not spring from the sentiments embodied in the Declaration of Independence." When Lincoln spoke those words, it was less than two weeks before he would take an oath to preserve, protect, and defend the Constitution. On the eve of the Civil War, Lincoln told the nation that he would look to the Declaration, to learn best how to fulfill his constitutional duties. In looking to the Declaration, Lincoln thus became the greatest of all interpreters of the Constitution. Surely, George Will must agree to that.

The core of Edmund Burke's polemic against the French Revolution went beyond the circumstances of that event. It was a denunciation of an allegedly theoretical politics, which embraced the principles of the American Revolution no less than of the French. Political wisdom, Burke argued, was prudential wisdom. Prudence, he maintained in opposition to Aristotle no less than to the American and French revolutionaries—consisted in an unrelieved attention to circumstances, unguided by any abstract or universal principles. Abraham Lincoln, however, deriving his political principles immediately from the Declaration, founded his policy upon "an abstract truth, applicable to all men and all times." It was opposition to such statesmanship by Burke, that lay at the root of Jefferson's hostility to him.

Will, in repelling the assault on Mr. Lincoln, writes disparagingly of "the nostalgic Confederate remnant in the conservative movement." But this remnant *in* the conservative movement is not a remnant *of* the conservative movement. The attack on "rationalism in politics" is at the root of American conservatism, and has characteristically been directed against both Lincoln and the Declaration of Independence. American conservatives have characteristically looked to Burke, for that "better guide than reason" which they, with Burke, find in the "funded wisdom of the past." These "Nostalgic Confederates" will also denounce Jefferson's denunciation of slavery, in the *Notes on Virginia*, as their ancestors did, in the ante-bellum debate. In repelling Jefferson's account of the demoralizing effects of slavery, they turn to Edmund Burke. For in Burke's speeches on the American question, he warned Lord North that there were no more high-spirited defenders of their own liberties, than the owners of slaves. Burke thus implicitly denied any contradiction between slavery and the principles of American freedom. If there is any stultification in American conservatism, it is precisely at this point, at which it fortifies itself against the alleged evils of modernity with the romantic feudalism of Edmund Burke, against the reasoned convictions of Jefferson and Lincoln.

According to Abraham Lincoln, this nation was not conceived in a "conflagration of desire for instant gratification." It was conceived not in license, but in liberty, and dedicated to a certain proposition. It was this proposition, which, more than any other, was the nation's "premise." The man who had the honor of articulating it, was not James Madison, but Thomas Jefferson. This proposition was also, said Lincoln, the "central idea" of the Founding, the one from which all its minor thoughts "radiated." In that same Peoria speech that arouses George Will, Lincoln called it "the leading principle—the sheet anchor of American republicanism." It was, moreover, "the father of all moral principle among us." Our heritage, from the Founding, according to the "greatest states-man in the history of democracy," is the one of public spirit founded upon moral conviction. The argument for many factions is, as we shall see, altogether contingent and subordinate.

* * *

James Madison was a very great man, although not because of any revolution in democratic theory. His contributions to the cause of human freedom are incalculable—greater than Edmund Burke's, although Burke too was a great man. Aristotle said of the discourses of Socrates, that they showed brilliance, originality, and keenness of inquiry. But excellence, he added, is not to be expected in all things. Not, we may add, in Socrates, Edmund Burke, or George Will. Nor do we depreciate Madison, when we follow Abraham Lincoln in assigning a certain priority, in the Founding, to Thomas Jefferson. Lincoln said of Jefferson—in that same Peoria speech—that he "was, is, and perhaps will continue to be, the most distinguished politician of our history." And there was nothing pejorative in Lincoln's use of the word "politician." If we exclude Washington—which in any larger view, we cannot do—the three men who together did most to articulate the premises of the Founding were Jefferson, Madison, and Hamilton. It is a popular, and by no means altogether mistaken conception of the American political tradition, to see it exhibiting a sustained conflict between Jeffersonianism and Hamiltonianism. Whatever the merit of that conception, there can be no question of the bitterness of the political conflict of the 1790's. A self-evident objection to placing James Madison on a pedestal above Hamilton and Jefferson, is that his career is divided between his partnership, first with the one, and then with the other. And he seems to have argued with almost equal zeal on both sides of the issues that divided Jefferson and Hamilton in the 1790's. There is not yet a satisfactory, consistent account of the anomalies presented by the words and deeds of James Madison.

The late Martin Diamond built a brilliant career as an interpreter of the *Federalist* papers. He did so by making an assumption that no student of that book had done before him. That was to take seriously the literary conceit of the book itself, that its author was a single person, known as "Publius," the pen name affixed to the papers themselves. Before Diamond, scholarship largely turned around the matter of identifying the authors of the individual papers. It was assumed, that this would be the key for interpreting each paper. By hypothesizing a single authorship, Diamond was able to uncover an internally consistent argument that made the papers collectively into a true book. I believe that Will and I have both been persuaded by this approach. Because of it however, we have no right to impute unqualifiedly to James Madison, in his proper person, anything that came from his hand as "Publius." George Will has taken virtually all of his account of the alleged Madisonian revolution in democratic theory from the tenth *Federalist.* But there is not the slightest reason — if we accept the authority of Martin Diamond — to regard this theory as a whit more Madisonian than it is Hamiltonian. In fact, there is a good reason — although one never developed by Diamond — why we might regard it as *more* Hamiltonian than Madisonian. That is because James Madison seems to have *rejected* this theory not long after he and Hamilton together urged it in the argument for ratification. Hamilton, however, continued unwaveringly on in its implementation and its defense.

Will himself links the theory of the more factions the merrier, with the equal "protection of different and unequal faculties of acquiring property," and hence with the equal protection of "different degrees and kinds of property." These phrases had a more specific connotation in 1787 than the present-day reader might be aware of. The movement for the Constitution, in which Hamilton and Madison were leaders and partners, was pre-eminently a movement to protect creditors from debtors. There is a text in Aristotle's *Politics* which sheds a great light on the central problem to which the *Federalist* was addressed. In Book III Aristotle raises the question of where the ruling power — or, as we would say, sovereignty — ought to lie in the political community. Among the alternatives are: the many, the rich, the gentlemen, the one who is best of all, or the tyrant. Aristotle begins his consideration of the different claimants, by saying that none of them, taken separately, are satisfactory. The claim of the many — of democracy — he rejects in this way. Suppose the poor (who are the many) take advantage of their greater numbers to divide up the property of the rich. Is this not unjust? No — say the leaders of the democracy, the demagogues — because the law was passed in proper form (that is, supposing the law to be in every respect constitutional). But, asks Aristotle, is this not the extreme of injustice? Does not the political community destroy itself, when it destroys property? Justice is not self-destructive, but the people will in effect destroy themselves if they destroy the wealth without which the city cannot live.

When Hamilton and Madison began their celebrated partnership, popular government, in the United States, was being destroyed by the very excess (or defect) celebrated in Aristotle's *Politics*. The popular majorities, mainly of farmers, were bringing their voting power to bear on the state legislatures, demanding the printing of paper money, and the legalizing of moratoria on debts. Shays's Rebellion brought this trend to a crisis, of which the Annapolis and Philadelphia conventions were the principal outcome. In 1787, the United

States was overwhelmingly an agricultural nation. The tenth *Federalist* speaks of a "landed interest, a manufacturing interest, a mercantile interest, with many lesser interests. . . ." But the problem of faction at that time was very largely one of preventing the interests of farmers from unjustly dominating those of the others. The problem would have been insoluble, if the agricultural interest was homogeneous, if, that is, farmers were not divided by local attachments, as well as between those who raised grain and those who—for example—raised cotton, tobacco, rice, or pork. Any ideological consolidation of the agricultural interest could enable it to ride roughshod over all other competing interests. Nothing bespeaks Hamilton's and Madison's constitutional purposes—or their reasons for writing the *Federalist*—more than the prohibitions laid upon the states in the Constitution, to coin money, to emit bills of credit, or to impair the obligation of contracts.

The foregoing is a necessary reminder, before noticing the sharp change of course that Madison pursued, immediately after the ratification of the Constitution. He became, in effect, the floor leader in the House of Representatives in the first Congress. George Washington was now President, and Alexander Hamilton Secretary of the Treasury. Professor Marvin Meyers, in his collection of Madison's writings called *The Mind of the Founder*, writes that "Hamilton's Virginia collaborator in the nationalist movement of the 1780's might reasonably have been expected to lead a government party in the House." This reasonable expectation, Meyers says, was founded upon the fact that "Madison had consistently advanced policies closely paralleling those that Hamilton now proposed: funding the national debt without discrimination between original and current creditors; assuming state debts; expanding federal power over taxation and trade; even, with some constitutional doubts, chartering a national bank."

All of Hamilton's measures, but most notably his financial measures, were designed to protect those "faculties of acquiring property" that were vulnerable to the tyranny of an agricultural majority. Aristotle—and Hamilton—had noted that the envy of the many who are poor is easily excited against the wealth of the few, and for this reason popular government is particularly in need of policies to protect wealth from depredation under the color of law. Because of this Madison and Hamilton together, as Publius, had opted for an extended republic, and the diversification of the factional element in our politics.

This however brings us to a most painful and puzzling difficulty: to explain James Madison's articles for the Republican Party press, during the political warfare of the 1790's. In them, Madison restated Jefferson's celebrated praise of farmers, not just as one of many interests and factions, but as unique repositories of republican virtue. "Those who labor in the earth," Jefferson had written in the *Notes on Virginia*, "are the chosen people of God, if ever He had a chosen people, whose breasts He has made His peculiar deposit for substantial and genuine virtue." Here is Madison's echo, in 1792: "The class of citizens who provide their own food and raiment, may be viewed as the most truly independent and happy. They are more, they are the best basis of public liberty and the strongest bulwark of public safety. It follows, that the greater the proportion of this class to the whole society, the more free, the more independent, and the more happy must be society itself." Here is Madison saying, not the more factions, but the fewer; not the greatest diversity, but the least possible; not "shifting coalitions of factions," but a permanent majority of a single one. However, this faction will not now be called a faction, as Publius would have called it, but will instead be endowed with all the attributes of transcendent virtue.

The crisis of the 1780's, that drove Madison and Hamilton together, was one brought on by the resistance of the farming interest to the obligations they had incurred to those from whom they had borrowed money. This was reflected all the way up the ladder of authority, to the default of the states, severally and collectively (as the United States), in their debts to foreign lenders. But in 1792, Madison viciously attacked Hamilton—a man who never profited by one penny from the policies he urged—as being of the party that had been "induced by the most obvious motives, to strengthen themselves with the men of influence, particularly ... moneyed...."

By the argument of the tenth *Federalist*, nothing could be worse, for the stability and justice of popular government, than to attempt to give "to every citizen the same opinions, the same passions, and the same interests." Those are denounced as "theoretic politicians" who would suppose that "by reducing mankind to a perfect equality in their political rights they would, at the same time, be equalized and assimilated in their possessions, their opinions, and their passions." Yet what was James Madison striving for, in 1792, but an assimilation—not perhaps of possessions—but of opinions, passions and interests? For he denounced the Hamiltonians for "taking advantage of all prejudices, local, political, and occupational [to] prevent or disturb a general coalition of sentiments." This coalition was what the Republicans sought "in banishing every other distinction than that between enemies and friends to republican government, and in promoting a general harmony among the latter wherever residing or however employed." But "however employed" meant only that interests other than the agrarian might, if they wished, attach themselves to the agrarian party. The public interest was now defined, in flat opposition to the theory of the tenth *Federalist*, as the interest of that "class of citizens who provide their own food and raiment."

Neither Madison's nor Jefferson's greatness lay in their patronage of the agrarian hypothesis—the foundation of all later agrarian populist movements. Certainly they must have adopted it, in part because they saw in the promotion of commercial and financial factions, some of that vulgar "conflagration of desires" that repels George Will. Yet in his resistance to this agrarianism, in his fidelity to the doctrine of Publius, Hamilton was their superior. Hamilton saw that financial stability was one of the most important practical grounds of moral stability. Hamilton had no illusions—such as Jefferson and Madison seemed to have had concerning farmers—concerning the moral superiority of bankers or financiers. But the patronage of their interests made it possible for the nation —individually and collectively—to pay its debts. In a commercial society men must pay their debts, not with feudal dues or services, but with money. Paying one's debts is not the definition merely of commercial justice: it is the definition of justice. Using one's political power to devalue money is defrauding one's creditors. Inflation, we might add, to give the discussion its contemporary application, is a way of transferring wealth from creditors to debtors. It was to stop this process, that Madison joined with Hamilton in the 1780's, and that Hamilton carried on, in the face of Madison's opposition, in the 1790's.

George Will makes much of the fact that Publius, in the fifty-first *Federalist*, speaks of a "policy of supplying, by opposite and rival interests, the defect of better motives," and thinks that this is evidence of a belief that the American system can work "without anyone having good motives—without public spiritedness." Yet Publius also calls the means by which such a policy is implemented "inventions of prudence." A blinding light is cast upon the meaning of such inventions, in particular those by which "the private interest of each individual" is made "a sentinel over the public rights," by the Whig doctrines of Abraham Lincoln. For Lincoln belonged to the Whig Party for twenty-five years. The political question that dominated the formative years of this party was Jackson's veto of the re-chartering of the second Bank of the United States, and Van Buren's subsequent removal of the deposits of the Federal Treasury funds from the Bank to Sub-Treasuries in the several states. The Whig Party of the 1830's and the 1840's, was, in all its 'essentials, the party of Alexander Hamilton *redivivus*. On the great questions of the 1790's, dividing Jefferson and Madison, on the one side, and Hamilton, on the other, Abraham Lincoln was firmly on the side of Hamilton. I think that this shows, among other things, that Lincoln did not view these differences as anything like a struggle between monarchy and republicanism, and that he must have viewed Jefferson himself as wiser when, in his inaugural, he said "we are all federalists, we are all republicans." In any event, Lincoln became a Whig largely because he believed in the Bank of the United States, the linchpin of Hamilton's financial measures. Here is Lincoln, in 1839, arguing for the Bank, and against the Sub-Treasury system, "We ... do not say ... to maintain our proposition," Lincoln said,

> that Bank officers are more honest than Government officers, selected by the same rule. What we do say, is, that the interest of the Sub-Treasurer is against his duty—while the interest of the Bank is on the side of its duty ... And who that knows anything of human nature, doubts that, in many instances, interest will prevail over duty, and that the Sub-Treasurer will prefer opulent knavery in a foreign land, to honest poverty at home? But how different is it with a Bank. Besides the Government money deposited with it, it is doing business upon a

large capital of its own. If it proves faithful to the Government, it continues its business, if unfaithful it forfeits its charter, breaks up its business, and thereby loses more than all it can make by seizing upon the Government funds in its possession. Its interest, therefore, is on the side of its duty ... Even if robberies happen in the Bank, the losses are borne by the Bank, and the Government loses nothing. . . . [All emphasis is Lincoln's.]

This is the language of Hamilton, and of Madison as Publius. Coming from Abraham Lincoln, it shows that a precaution taken against the "defect of better motives" can be prudent, without implying in any way an abandonment of morality as an end of public policy. Another way of putting it, is that one has not abandoned the cause of virtue, when one minimizes the occasions of vice.

In the fifty-first *Federalist* Publius declares that "A dependence on the people is, no doubt, the primary control on the government; but experience has taught mankind the necessity of auxiliary precautions." Like other commentators on the *Federalist*, George Will disregards the "primary control," as if the "auxiliary precautions" were all in all. It is true that the focus of attention is on these auxiliaries, but they cannot for that be supposed to replace what is primary. In a famous passage of the fifty-fifth *Federalist*, Publius (Madison) declares that

> *As there is a degree of depravity in mankind which requires a certain degree of circumspection and distrust, so there are other qualities in human nature which justify a certain portion of esteem and confidence.* Republican government presupposes the existence of these qualities in a higher degree than any other form.

We have emphasized the last sentence to put the need for those famous auxiliary precautions in their proper perspective. The popular revolution of the Founding is not to be sought exclusively in its auxiliary precautions, although the excellence of these makes more justifiable than otherwise, the degree of "confidence" that republican government presupposes. Publius notes that it is enemies of republican government who say that

> *there is not sufficient virtue among men for self-government; and that nothing less than the chains of despotism can restrain them from destroying and devouring one another.*

Madison's "democratic revolution," as seen by George Will, has nothing in common with what Publius in the thirty-ninth *Federalist* calls "that honorable determination which animates every votary of freedom, to rest all our political experiments on the capacity of mankind for self-government."

We notice once again that the "auxiliary precautions" of the *Federalist* are called "inventions of prudence." The philosophic discoverer of prudence was

Aristotle. Books four through six of the *Politics*, the so-called practical books, have many hundreds of such devices, whereby governments can be made to function better, by supplying non-virtuous inducements to virtuous behavior. The very concept of "polity," the original classical model upon which the idea of popular republican government is founded, is that of a mixture of two defective regimes. It is addressed to precisely the same central problem which preoccupies Publius: how to moderate the conflict between the poor and the rich, so as to make possible a rule of law, a non-tyrannical way in which the citizens rule and are ruled in turn. Aristotle concentrates on the ways and means by which the defects of the two classes neutralize each other, while their just claims reinforce each other. And nothing could be more "realistic" than Aristotle's advice to tyrants on how to appear to be less tyrannical without actually being so. Aristotle's approach is not "Machiavellian," but that of a political doctor discussing a problem of political pathology. There are cases in which, if you cannot actually help the patient to get well, you can at least make him more comfortable! The hard "common sense" of Publius has much about it that is Aristotelian.

Being "practical" however does not imply, either in the case of Publius or that of Aristotle, that virtue and happiness are not the ends of the regime. In designing the regime so that it will usually be in men's interest to obey the "rules of justice," Publius is not declaring that the moral virtue of justice is useless, either to private or to public happiness. In the famous fifty-first *Federalist*, Publius declares without qualification, that "Justice is the end of government. It is the end of civil society." It is Aristotle's teaching that men become just, by becoming habituated to just actions. If they can be induced to act justly, even when they are not just, the habit of acting justly may in time make them just. Publius observes, in the seventy-second *Federalist*, "that the desire of reward is one of the strongest incentives of human conduct." For this reason, "the best security for the fidelity of mankind is to make their interest coincide with their duty." These apothegms are, however, mere truisms of classical political philosophy. The question for the legislator, is how to channel the desire for reward, and how to teach men the interest that they have in virtue. In the same number, Publius makes his famous observation that "love of fame" is "the ruling passion of the noblest minds." Noble minds are no less desirous of reward than ignoble minds. But their ruling passion is a noble one. The fame sought by these noble minds, is a noble fame: the kind, above all, aimed at by Publius himself. Publius' every line then presupposes political philosophy: the ability to discriminate between the different characters of men, not by the presence or absence of self-interest, but by the kind of interest that predominates in each self. In Plato's *Laws*, the Athenian Stranger declares, "Let us all be lovers of victory when it comes to virtue, but without envy. The man of this sort —always competing himself but never thwarting others with slander—makes cities great." A wise legislator takes care that men do their duty, if necessary for the wrong reasons. But when men take pride in doing their duty, they may come to do it for the right reasons. There is no reason to doubt that Publius, less than Plato or Aristotle, shares the hope that the prudent frustration of base motives may not become the ground upon which virtue is cultivated.

* * *

In the fortieth *Federalist*, Publius defends the Convention for having gone beyond the boundaries of its commission. The heart of the matter, he says, is "that in all great changes of established governments, forms ought to give way to substance; that a rigid adherence in such cases to the former, would render nominal and nugatory the transcendent and precious right of the people to 'abolish or alter their governments as to them shall seem most likely to effect their safety and happiness.'" There is a footnote in the text, by Publius himself, marking the quotation (which is imperfect) as coming from the Declaration of Independence. But Publius reminds us here that the entire purpose of the Convention is comprehended by the revolutionary right of the people, as set forth in the Declaration. That right of revolution becomes the right of a people, only by the incorporation of that people—who are, as human beings, created equal—under the laws of nature and of nature's God. The right of revolution is not something adventitious, it is not something that may be exercised by any chance aggregate of human beings calling themselves a people—a gang of robbers, for example. Nor is it something that may be exercised for any chance purpose—conquest, for example, or the preservation of slavery. The right of revolution comes into existence only to implement—when all other means fail—the moral purposes of "the laws of nature and of nature's God." It is because they were conscious of such purposes, and satisfied in their own consciences that they were acting in accordance with them, that the Signers of the Declaration could appeal "to the Supreme Judge of the World for the rectitude of [their] intentions." In this consciousness of righteousness, these same Signers acted "with a firm reliance on the protection of Divine Providence." Nor was it merely to emancipate their acquisitive passions—as the misreading of the *Federalist* might lead someone to suppose—that they pledged to each other their lives, their fortunes, and their sacred honor.

* * *

In 1825, Thomas Jefferson asked James Madison to recommend texts that might embody the political creed that ought to be regarded as orthodox, by the faculty and students of the Law School of the University of Virginia. Madison —now writing in his own name, and not as Publius—replied, that "on the distinctive principles of the government of our own State, and of that of the United States, the best guides are to be found in—1. The Declaration of

Independence, as the fundamental act of Union of these States. 2. The book known by the title of the "Federalist," being an authority to which appeal is habitually made by all and rarely declined or denied by any, as evidence of the general opinion of those who framed and those who accepted the Constitution of the United States on questions as to its genuine meaning." Madison then added the "Resolutions of the General Assembly of Virginia of 1799," and the "Inaugural and Farewell Address of President Washington." But the Father of the Constitution called the Declaration the "fundamental act" of the union.

The doctrine of the Declaration of Independence is presupposed by every word of the *Federalist*. To attempt to read the *Federalist*, or to understand the Constitution, as it was understood "by those who framed and those who accepted" it, except in the light of the Declaration, is utterly vain. It was the movement whose presiding genius was John C. Calhoun, that separated the Constitution—and the *Federalist*—from the principles of the Declaration. It was Calhoun's rebellion against the anti-slavery meaning of the doctrines of the Revolution, that paved the way for that so-called "conservative" movement that, both in 1861 and in 1981, would substitute a hypothetical "funded wisdom of the past" for "the laws of nature and of nature's God." No one can defend the vulgar philistinism of the pyromaniacs of Madison Avenue. But no one has a right to declare that this is what James Madison's "philosophy has promoted." That philistinism is the result of a later, radical modernity, that denies that there are any such laws of nature—or that if there were, denies that they could be moral laws. At this point, the libertarian-anarchists of the Right and of the Left are one. But the tradition of the West, the genuine as opposed to the hypothetical tradition, is a natural law tradition. The neo-Burkeans among the so-called conservatives, by their attack on rationalism, attack the very foundation of genuine tradition. George Will's simultaneous denigration of Madison, and praise of Lincoln, is that of a mind divided against itself.

1982

Postscript

The foregoing essay was written some six months before the publication of George F. Will's *Statecraft as Soulcraft* (Simon & Schuster, New York, 1983). Now that I have read it I feel justified in saying that my essay, based upon two of Will's columns, stands as a perfectly adequate critique of the central argument of his book. I had reason from the outset to believe that this would prove true, since I had what turned out to be a thoroughly reliable report of Will's Godkin lectures at Harvard, upon which *Statecraft as Soulcraft* is based.

Like Burke himself (but like Rousseau no less than Burke) Will invokes the concept of the public-spirited virtue of the great republics of antiquity as the ground of his attack upon a narrow, egotistic, bourgeois materialism. This critique Marx also inherited from Rousseau and Burke. Will finds this low, and mean-spirited materialism, to be the characteristic spirit of modernity, by which he seems to understand that form of modernity associated in particular with Hobbes and Locke. In *Statecraft as Soulcraft,* as in his earlier writing, Will declares the Founding Father, *par excellence,* to be James Madison, and it is he thinks through Madison that this low morality of modernity became the soul of the American polity.

Yet Will continues to celebrate Abraham Lincoln as the heroic embodiment of virtuous statesmanship and virtuous citizenship. One would almost think that Will had discovered Lincoln in the pages of Plutarch. Yet Will disregards everything Lincoln himself has said about the principle of human equality, as the "central idea" of the Founding, from which all its minor thoughts radiated. And Will is light years removed from entertaining the slightest consideration for what Lincoln said and meant, when he declared this same principle to be "the father of all moral principle among us." Will thus disregards that link, supplied by the Declaration of Independence, between modern men and classical virtue. He sees the American Founding as wholly and unambiguously modern, although Jefferson himself had mentioned Aristotle and Cicero, as well as Locke and Sidney, among the "books of public right" which had contributed to the formation of the American "public mind." In seeing the American Founding as he does, George Will refuses to understand it as it understood itself.

Will's celebration of Burke amounts to a categorical rejection of Lincoln's tribute to Jefferson, as the man who had "the coolness, foresight, and capacity" to introduce into the American Founding, "an abstract truth, applicable to all men and all times." Yet how does one re-found American Conservatism, as Will apparently wishes to do, by teaching disrespect for the American political tradition? *Statecraft as Soulcraft* embodies a thesis in its title: the thesis that classical political philosophy, the political philosophy originated by Socrates, is superior to any form of political teaching, embodying different, or contrary views of the human soul. The central purpose of politics is rightly held to be the formation of character. Central to the formation of character, is the ranking of the ends or purposes, by which human life may be guided. In classical political philosophy—above all, in that of Aristotle—the moral virtues, and practical wisdom, are grounded in the natural order of ends. In this order, philosophic wisdom is paramount; and it is only by philosophic wisdom that this order can come to light, and thereby guide human life. Yet the Burke to whom Will turns for "soulcraft" is the same Burke who—according to Leo Strauss in *Natural Right and History*—by his sustained attack on "metaphysics" joined Hume, Kant, and the ranks of modern positivists and historicists in denying the possibility of philosophic wisdom in the classical sense. It is Lincoln's commitment to the idea of "abstract truth" as the ground of moral and political wisdom, which is consistent with "soulcraft."

Tradition, in the legacy of Burke, is not the tradition of tradition! It becomes the substitute for philosophy and nature as the ground of virtue. Will accordingly follows in the footsteps of those modern thinkers—Rousseau, Marx, and Nietzsche—who begin by attacking bourgeois modernity, but end with a romantic elitism much farther from classical republicanism than anything merely bourgeois and egalitarian.

June 1983

Fourteen

Human Rights and the Crisis of the West

F ew political questions of recent years have been discussed at greater length, with greater heat, and with so little light, as the question of human rights. No question reveals so completely the poverty of contemporary political thinking in the Western world, and not only in the United States. But it is in the United States that the crisis has its focus, and where it may prove fatal. More particularly, there is a crisis today in the American conservative movement, a movement which is expected to provide intellectual guidance to an American conservative government.

The question of human rights is usually looked upon as a question of foreign policy. How do we admonish foreign governments that mistreat their own citizens or subjects? In particular, is there any prudent way that we can discriminate between friendly governments that misbehave and the unfriendly ones (notably the U.S.S.R., but not the People's Republic of China, at least for the time being). We cannot admonish foreign governments for not living up to American principles, merely because they are American. All Americans are human beings, but not all human beings are American. To demand that foreign governments respect the rights of human beings—as distinct from fellow-citizens, dogs, cats, proletarians, or bourgeois—implies that there is a common human nature, in virtue of which there are rights shared by all men everywhere. Because the nature which is the cause of these rights is every-where the same, the duties to respect these rights are equally universal. But it is precisely this idea of a common, or universal nature, with correspondingly universal rights and duties, a concept known for millenia as natural law, which is today held in nearly universal disesteem. Indeed, it is held in greater disesteem in the West than in Marxist-Leninist regimes.

The Marxist-Leninists denounce the idea of natural rights and natural law, in the name of history. The idea of nature, they say, has emerged from the class struggle (like all other ideas claiming universal validity). It has emerged from the class struggle as an expression of the class interest of the bourgeoisie (or its predecessors among the ruling classes). It confounds the nature of bour-geois man, with the nature of man simply. Man as such will be that kind of man that will develop in the classless society of the future. The humanity of this kind of man will reveal itself in the development of the totality of his human powers. But such will be possible only *after* the abolition of private property and the withering away of the state. When the government of man has been replaced by the administration of things, then and then only will human nature reveal itself. It will reveal itself in and through the projection of the human essence by the emancipation of the human will. The only genuine human will is one unconstrained by any necessity, moral or material. What has hitherto been called human nature, has been a blurred and partial concept, reflecting not man himself, but man as seen in the light of the class struggle. Philosophers have been as limited as anyone else, in their perception of reality, by the exigencies of this struggle. They have not been able to distinguish the myths that have served the class struggle, from the reality underlying it. Indeed, the essence of ideology is the identification of such myths with reality.

Marxism-Leninism presents itself as an objective, comprehensive, and scientific account of the past, present, and future of the human condition. Indeed, it presents itself as the first such account in the history of the world. It offers to guide human behavior in the light of this account. In short, it offers mankind the highest—as well as the final—morality. It denounces "bourgeois" morality in the name of this higher morality, and insists that the contest concerning human rights is a contest between class-bound and obsolete conceptions, and the genuine, progressive truth of Marxism-Leninism. In this, Marxism-Leninism has been enormously successful: so successful that there is a question whether most churchmen in the West do not today accept it largely on its own terms, and interpret Christianity itself as largely a prologue, whose fulfillment can come only with the proletarian revolution. Today, Marxism (if not Marxism-Leninism) is more often seen by Christian theologians in the West as the fulfillment of Christianity, than as its deadly enemy.

In the United States today—and in the Free World generally—there is no doctrine that claims authority in any comparable sense. Intellectuals of the Left, if they are not themselves some species of Marxist, are usually relativists, historicists, or positivists, or some combination of all three. Intellectuals of the Right, while usually disclaiming relativism, do so by proclaiming their belief (or faith) in "absolute values." When they describe their values as those of Christianity or Judaism (for example), they oppose religious values to non-religious (or anti-religious) values. But absolute values, *qua* values, are as subjective as relative values. What is decisive is their subjectivity, which makes them inherently relative—inherently relative to the evaluating subject. Calling a value "absolute" does not make it less subjective. It merely suggests that the value in question is being held with a peculiar intensity. As Leo Strauss liked to point out, there is no difference in the subjective assurance of the lunatic and the philosopher. Unless there is an objective difference between them, we cannot distinguish them on the basis of their "values." After all, many a lunatic has called himself a philosopher, and many a philosopher (e.g. Edgar in *King Lear*) has had to go disguised as a lunatic. (Consider also such philosophic books as *In Praise of Folly*.)

Intellectuals of the Right are however also accustomed to calling themselves "conservative," and distinguishing themselves on the basis of their commitment to "traditions" (and hence to "traditional values"). Their hero is Edmund Burke, who in his polemic against the French Revolution appealed to the "funded wisdom of the past." One presumes that this wisdom, being "funded," is therefore non-speculative. Burke also called this wisdom the wisdom of the "species," which he opposed to the meretricious wisdom of the "individual." But in this appeal to collective, as opposed to individual intelligence, the Burkeans are almost indistinguishable from the Marxists. Both denigrate the rationalism and individualism of the Enlightenment (which they seem to suppose is the only kind of rationalism and individualism), and therefore denigrate both capitalism and democracy.

Tradition, *qua* tradition, records only what men have thought and done. It cannot say what has been done wisely and what has been done foolishly. It may record successes and failures, but it does not of itself distinguish between noble failure and vulgar success. Success and failure, for Burke and Marx, seem to depend upon much the same criteria. Marx's History and Burke's Providence have a certain resemblance. Both seem to say that the winning cause is the right one. In the words of Leo Strauss, "Burke comes close to suggesting that to oppose a thoroughly evil current in human affairs is perverse if that current is sufficiently powerful; he is oblivious of the nobility of the last-ditch resistance ... he is too certain that man can know whether a cause lost now is lost forever or that man can understand sufficiently the meaning of a providential dispensation as distinct from a moral law." Strauss characterizes Burke as being "at the pole opposite to Cato, who dared to espouse a lost cause." We might add that he is equally opposite in this to Lincoln and Churchill. In a speech in 1839, Lincoln declared, "If ever I feel the soul within me elevate and expand to those dimensions not wholly unworthy of its Almighty Architect, it is when I contemplate the cause of my country, deserted by all the world beside, and I standing up boldly alone, and hurling defiance at her victorious oppressors ... Here, without contemplating consequences ... I swear eternal fidelity to the just cause ..." These are the accents, a century beforehand, of Winston Churchill, hurling defiance across the English Channel at Hitler's Nazi legions, in what, in the light of all human foresight, was as forlorn a cause as the human record knows. But Churchill says, in *The Second World War*, that one cannot guarantee success, one can only deserve it. And this applies, by Churchill's principles, as well as by Lincoln's, to the actions of peace no less than to those of war. The heart of the great tradition, the genuine tradition, is the ability to draw the distinction between deserved and undeserved failure, and between deserved and undeserved success. According to Strauss, Burke did not "consider that, in a way no man can foresee, resistance in a forlorn position to the enemies of mankind, 'going down with guns blazing and flag flying,' may contribute greatly toward keeping awake the recollection of the immense loss sustained by mankind, may inspire and strengthen the desire and hope for its recovery, and may become a beacon for those who humbly carry on the works of humanity in a seemingly endless valley of darkness and destruction." In short, only those who are willing to risk everything in resisting evil, are capable of those great actions in which human nature reveals its ultimate destiny, not in time, but in eternity.

No one articulated the principles of traditional morality better than Thomas Aquinas. Thomas defined the natural law as the rational creature's participation in the eternal law. The eternal law he defined as the law by which God governs the universe. Hence man, according to Aquinas, when he governs himself by the rules of reason, participates in the divine government of the universe. This is precisely the doctrine of the Declaration of Independence. The appeal to self-evident truths, and to the inferences and deductions from them, is an appeal to unassisted natural reason, as the ground of participation in the laws emanating from the Creator, which are also the laws of nature. However little he may have known it, Thomas Jefferson was standing on common ground with Thomas Aquinas. For both, human nature was such, and the human good was such, that man could attain felicity only by actions for which he was genuinely responsible. The axiomatic premise underlying the Declaration of Independence, the premise assumed by the idea of self-evident truths, was that "Almighty God hath created the mind free...." This great pronouncement of the Virginia Statute of Religious Liberty reminds us also of the words of Jefferson carved in his memorial in Washington: "I have sworn upon the altar of God eternal hostility against every form of tyranny over the mind of man." For Jefferson the tyranny over the mind of man was the fundamental form of tyranny. Political tyranny was derivative from it. The denial of the freedom of the mind, in the West today —not only by Marxism-Leninism, but by the many versions of determinism which dominate the teaching of philosophy, of the so-called humanities, and of the social sciences—makes the academies of the Free World and not the KGB, what Lincoln called "the van-guard, the miners, and sappers, of return-ing despotism."

According to Aquinas, there may be a natural inclination to the good within man, but there is no determination, no necessity, governing his passions or his actions, not by God, not by the Devil, and not by History. It is indeed the function of the human will to act in accordance with reason. Reason is ordered towards truth, and truth lies in an objective order of reality, an order external to the mind, as the moral law is external to the will. For the distinction between good and evil lies in the truth about reality. This truth is "metaphysical," and the Burkean attack on metaphysics is an attack on the possibility of that theoretical wisdom without which there can be no moral wisdom. To know the order of reality is the function of theoretical reason. To guide one's actions by the light of this order is the function of practical reason. To train the passions to obey practical reason is the purpose of moral education. The great tradition of the West is the one that comprehends this relationship between practical and theoretical wisdom, a relationship which comprehends the just or right way of life for man. Both Burke and Marx oppose the idea of *a* right or just way of life, that is according to reason and according to nature. Burke's praise of the British Constitution, for having no "unity of design," and being therefore consistent with, "the greatest variety of ends" (cf. *Natural Right and History*, p. 314) is virtually the same as Marx's praise of the classless society in the *German Ideology*. When we are told as well that Burke called Aristotle's natural philosophy "unworthy of him," while he praised Epicurean physics as "the most approaching to rational," (Ibid., p. 311) we are less and less astonished at the facility with which in our time Marxists have turned into Burkeans, and vice versa. (See Chapter five, "Inventing the Past.") In truth, both Burke and Marx are epigones of Rousseau—whatever the nominal antagonism between Burke and the Rousseauians of the French Revolution. For it was Rousseau who claimed to have discovered that man is by nature free, but not rational, so that human perfection (or perfectability) according to nature is constituted by an emancipation of the will, not merely from custom or convention, but from reason itself. But in the principles of the American Founding—which the Marxists hold in contempt as "bourgeois," and the Burkeans denounce as "rationalistic"—we see the same harmony between freedom, reason, and nature, that we see in Aristotle and Aquinas.

Jefferson wrote to Henry Lee, in 1825, that the object of the Declaration of Independence was "to place before mankind the common sense of the subject; in terms so plain and firm as to command their assent, and to justify ourselves in the independent stand we were compelled to take." All its authority rested, he added, "on the harmonizing sentiments of the day, whether expressed in conversations, in letters, printed essays, or in the elementary books of public right, as Aristotle, Cicero, Locke, Sidney, etc." Jefferson thus invoked a public opinion formed by the tradition of political philosophy. That tradition also informed the other great documents of the Founding, which together expressed what may be called a public philosophy. The central elements in this philosophy were never understood to be peculiarly American. Indeed, they could not be, considering the "books of public right" upon which they relied. The confidence of the Founding Fathers was grounded in their sense of this tradition of public right. This tradition of a right of nature and of reason, and not of prejudice or custom, was one that allowed for endless change in what was contingent, without abandoning what was essential. Jefferson once declared, "Nothing is unchangeable, but the inherent and inalienable rights of man." That is to say, institutions must and should change, but not their principles. George Washington, no more than Jefferson, was an admirer of the past for its own sake. "Our empire," he wrote in 1783, "was not laid in the gloomy ages of ignorance and superstition; but at an epocha when the rights of mankind were better understood and more clearly defined, than at any other period."

The public philosophy of the American Founding is the only moral and political teaching in the contemporary world, comparable to Marxism-Leninism in its scope and in its inherent claims to authority. But the crisis of the West is visible and palpable in nothing more than in the contrast between the confidence of the leaders of the Communist world in the principles of Marxism-Leninism, and the unbelief of the intellectual leaders of the Free World, in the principles of political freedom. It is characteristic of this crisis, that leaders in the West continually proclaim their conviction that the Marxist-Leninist leaders do not really believe what they profess. In this, however, they are merely projecting their own skepticism towards all principles — their own included — upon their enemies. Consider, for example, President Reagan's letter to Soviet President Brezhnev, quoted in his speech of November 18, 1981, in which he asked Brezhnev whether "we" have not "permitted ideology, political and economic philosophies, and governmental policies to keep us from considering the very real, everyday problems of our peoples?" The President's contrast between "reality" on the one hand, and "political and economic philosophies" on the other, is breathtaking in its simplicity. One can imagine the boys in the Kremlin backroom, slapping their thighs and guffawing, and asking "Who do you mean by 'we,' Paleface?" Whatever the innermost convictions of the leaders of the Marxist-Leninist regimes — and no man's innermost convictions can be known with certainty to anyone except his God — they have been unwavering in their professions of belief. The flexibility of their tactics has never been evidence of uncertainty concerning their ends. The opposite has been true. Within the West, "pragmatism" (to which President Reagan was unconsciously appealing) refers to a concentration upon "means" because of the unknowability of "ends." In such a context, dilemmas concerning means become the source of doubt and confusion concerning ends. In such a context, means then become ends-in-themselves (for example, nuclear arms reduction). But for the Marxist-Leninist, the historical and dialectical necessity (and hence knowability) of the end, permits a perfect flexibility in tactics without implying any doubt or irresolution with respect to the end itself.

The crisis of the West consists in this: that men seeking bread will not accept a stone. They certainly will not accept a stone that calls itself a stone, while its alternative calls itself bread. We have already alluded to the fact that many professors of revealed religion in the West have concluded that Marxism-Leninism is Christianity, or the form that Christianity must take in this age of science. When confronted by the materialism of Marxism-Leninism, they say that the opposition between form and matter, between body and soul, has been transcended — or superseded — by science. After all, if science can promise immortality — well, if not *actual* immortality, then indefinitely prolonged life, by a combination of immunology and organ transplants — then one need not wonder about such metaphysical curiosities as immaterial substances, or separated substances, as the ground of being. The fate of the immortal soul was interesting only so long as the soul seemed doomed to an early separation from the body. That is why nuclear war, or nuclear war plus chemical and biological war, seems so terrible. Science seems to put into the hands of mankind the alternatives of extinction and endless life. It is only in the light of an obsolete conception of morality (and mortality), that one can say to the nuclear protestors, why don't you protest in Red Square? They would reply—or at least the more intelligent among them would reply—that one-sided nuclear disarmament is all that is needed. Two-sided, or multi-lateral disarmament might be preferable, but it is not necessary. In fact, a monopoly of nuclear weapons by the Kremlin is preferable to one by the West. The proof of this is that the West once had such a monopoly and allowed it to escape. Now, only the USSR can end the possibility of nuclear war. If the Kremlin has such a monopoly, one can be confident that it will not repeat the folly of the United States. Once science cannot be employed for universal destruction, it must be employed for the universal preservation, or enhancement, of life. No one will then have any incentive to do anything else. That is the true alternative, and the only horizon within which moral decision can now take place. As things now stand, American conservatives with their Burkean predilections have no answer to such reasoning.

* * *

As a notable example of present-day thinking about human rights, we would point to a recent article by Professor Irving Kristol, in the *Wall Street Journal*, April 8, 1981, entitled "The Common Sense of 'Human Rights.'" It is certainly one of the more intelligent pronouncements on this troubled topic to come from the American Right since Mr. Reagan's election to the Presidency. It is characteristic of the Right to oppose "moralism" with "realism" in foreign policy. We should, it is thought, help our friends and injure our enemies in a non-ideological manner, keeping uppermost our "interests" and not our "ideals." Unfortunately, however, once "interests" take over from "ideals," we find the Right alternately backing regimes that simply embarrass us, and rushing pell-mell to make money by deals both with Red China *and* the Soviet Union. In the end, the depreciation of "ideals" in favor of "interests" leads directly to that kind of ideological reasoning which understands the only permanent and durable interest as that of universal peace. And this interest becomes well-nigh invincible when it is identified with Christianity.

Professor Kristol is too sophisticated to fall into this trap. Indeed, he has built his highly successful career precisely around his skill in teaching capitalists to live comfortably with their profits. Professor Kristol abandoned socialism at about the time when the last flicker of life went out of the old Calvinist doctrine of election, as the motive and justification of capitalism. It was at the time when Hayek and Friedman were perfecting their teaching, which persuaded Professor Kristol, as it persuaded me, that the free market produced and distributed goods more efficiently than any other form of economy. But Professor Kristol who understood profoundly the meaning of R. H. Tawney's dictum that the last of the Schoolmen was Karl Marx, knew that the efficiency of the market was as much a moral weakness as a material strength. The Friedman-Hayek defense of the market stressed its compatibility with freedom, but it was a freedom defined in an entirely negative way. According to Milton Friedman, the market did not care whether one "bought" leisure by not working, or "bought" ulcers by working an eighteen hour day. The market was simply a cold-blooded utilitarian mechanism for registering preferences; it had nothing to say (and the free market economists had nothing to say) as to which preferences should be preferred. It was this neutrality towards "values" that made the market economy so hateful to the Radicals, particularly those of the academy. As Winston Churchill said, "The vice of capitalism is the unequal distribution of its blessings. The virtue of socialism, is its equal distribution of misery." But for the reasons that Tocqueville has made famous, the Radicals have always preferred the equal distribution of misery. That is seen as the moral position. Irving Kristol's genius was to understand the moral vulnerability of capitalism as the free marketeers did not. He saw that socialism was appropriating to itself the legacy of Christianity, and he meant to take it back for capitalism. He saw that it was both unnecessary and unwise to attempt to reason capitalists out of their guilt feelings. Instead, he set out to teach them to live with their guilt, and eventually to enjoy it. He saw that just the right touch of guilt is what, in a Christian civilization, seasons pleasure. So he told the capitalists that they had to preserve capitalism as a duty to the poor. In the pursuit of this duty they had, like all successful ruling classes in history, to cultivate life-styles that would evoke the wonder and respect of those less fortunate than themselves. They had to give their money cleverly, generating admiration for their philanthropy. In particular they must give their money in such a way as would generate legitimacy for their life-styles in the academy, much as the medieval clergy generated respect for the medieval nobility (and as the Lockean-Calvinists had generated respect for the first generation of Captains of Industry.) Professor Kristol, in effect, taught his capitalist friends to imitate the model Shakespeare presented in *Henry V.* You will all remember the King's great speech, comparing his own sorry plight, to that of the meanest plowman in his realm. The real, substantial good was that of his subjects who worked hard, ate well, and slept soundly. But the King, bearing the responsibilities for the common good, although surrounded with all the appurtenances of comfort, had no comfort. It was he who kept the long vigil of the night, that others might sleep. And all his recompense was ceremony, vain, idle ceremony. Having thus convinced himself that the keeping of the crown his father had usurped was a supreme act of self-sacrifice, Henry clung to it conscientiously and with a grip stronger than death.

Professor Kristol's *Two Cheers For Capitalism* has carried far more of conviction than the "three cheers and a tiger" of the free market evangelists. For this, we are all in his debt.

* * *

Professor Kristol is at heart a moralist. This is another way of saying that he is a political man who understands political things. He understands, as did Abraham Lincoln, that appeals to self-interest which do not at the same time appeal to the moral sense are weak. Here is the thematic statement in his article on human rights.

> *I want to emphasize that we really must integrate a conception of human rights into our foreign policy—into our alliances, our military aid programs, our economic aid programs, our cultural exchanges, etc.: Our polity, after all, is founded on the idea of an individual's rights. Our foreign policy, to the degree that it rubs this idea the wrong way, will be guilt ridden, uncertain, lacking in self-confidence ... Elements of Realpolitik will surely have to be incorporated into our foreign policy.... but such "realism" has to be conceived and expressed in a way that allows us to live, if a bit uncomfortably now and then, with our moral selves.*

These are wise words, as far as they go. Professor Kristol and I—and Abraham Lincoln—are thoroughly agreed that we should and must identify "our moral selves" with the principles upon which "our polity ... is founded." And "our moral selves"—or, more specifically, our consciences—cannot go to sleep, merely because the matter at hand is foreign policy. Professor Kristol would never say so, but "our moral selves" found their first and greatest expression, in the Founding of our polity, in the Declaration of Independence, a document which was addressed to "a candid world."

If the central idea of our foreign policy is to be the same as that upon which our polity was founded, then we must be accurate in making this identification. Professor Kristol says it is "the idea of an individual's rights." In a general way, I agree with him. But in such a case, generalities do not suffice. They do not suffice for the reason that the Marxist-Leninists say the same thing. It is moreover characteristic of Professor Kristol that, although he constantly appeals to the ideas upon which "our polity is founded," he rarely if ever expresses these ideas in the language of the Founding. The expression, "an individual's rights," for example, occurs in no document of the Founding that I can recall. In fact, "individual," or "individuals," is comparatively rare. One place the latter occurs, however, is the Massachusetts Bill of Rights of 1780. In the Preamble of that classic repository of Revolutionary doctrine, we read that

The end, institution, and administration of government, is to secure the exis-
tence of the body-politic, to protect it, and to furnish the individuals who compose
it with the power of enjoying in safety and tranquility their natural rights....

And again:

The body-politic is formed by a voluntary association of individuals....

There is no question, as between Professor Kristol and myself, that the idea of
an individual's rights is fundamental. What is at issue—and this is an issue
between Professor Kristol and the Founding Fathers—is his refusal to see that
all the precious rights of an individual *within civil society*, according to the
Founding, depend upon the prior recognition of the individual's rights *by nature*.
Speech about "human rights" is utterly unintelligible, except in the light of the
distinction between "civil rights" and "natural rights." According to the Founding,
all our civil rights are derivative from our natural rights. Professor Kristol, by
abandoning the conception of natural rights, has nothing upon which to ground
civil rights. "Human rights" that are not seen in the light of this distinction
between "natural" and "civil" are wholly vulnerable to that interpretation that
is given them by the Marxist-Leninists.

In the Massachusetts Bill of Rights, the reason why the body-politic is said
to be formed by a voluntary association of individuals, is that (as Article I
states)

All men are born free and equal, and have certain natural, essential, and
unalienable rights.

Here the words "natural," "essential," and "unalienable" are synonymous.
More precisely, they reflect differing aspects of an underlying identity. "Free"
and "equal" are also, in this context, synonymous. By nature men are equal in
authority, one over another, and hence no man is subordinate to another. Since
no man is by nature under authority, by nature men are free. This is the
necessary premise for declaring that civil society is a voluntary association, and
hence that the just powers of government are derived from the consent of the
governed. The fact that the authority of legitimate government over the governed arises from consent, and that the meaning of consent can be understood
only in the light of natural equality, wholly determines the American Founding's
conception of "the idea of an individual's rights." Marxist-Leninist regimes, as
we have noted, are nominally no less committed to the rights of the individual.
But such rights do not arise from nature. Rather they arise from the collective
consciousness of the proletariat, as this emerges historically from the necessities of dialectical materialism. This consciousness is moreover claimed on

behalf of the proletariat by the Central Committee of the Communist Party of the USSR. But the mere phrase, "the idea of an individual's rights," is absolutely neutral as between the two competing conceptions, the one of the American Founding, the other of Marxism-Leninism.

Nature makes all men the same in certain respects. In these respects they cannot differ, so long as they remain human beings. They remain human beings so long as they live, or, by an impossible assumption, until they change into beings of a different kind. That is to say, if one imagines a man turning into a dog, one can imagine him belonging to someone else. It is the nature of a dog to belong to a man, but it is not the nature of a man to belong to another man. Slavery is "according to nature" for dogs, but it is against nature for human beings. A man may alienate his legal right to his chattels; e.g. he may sell his dog. But a man cannot alienate his right to his freedom. To sell himself into slavery, as a voluntary act, is against nature. It is something no human being possessed of his human faculties — that is, possessed of his reason — can be conceived as doing. It is therefore according to nature that men rule dogs. It is against nature that dogs rule men, *or* that men rule other men as if they were dogs.

There is nothing in the Massachusetts Bill of Rights — or in the Declaration of Independence — that implies that it is impossible for human beings to be governed as if they were cattle. But to do so is despotism. It is also possible that some men will fawn before and flatter other men, in a canine-like subservience. In extreme cases, men may have to choose between dying as free men, or living like slaves. Nevertheless, those who arrogate to themselves a species like superiority over other men, or accept a species-like inferiority, are equally mistaken, and equally deserving of moral reprobation. The former, however, should be met with indignation and anger, the latter with contempt.

The natural rights of human beings are *equally* possessed, because all are born to the *same* nature. Because civil society is a voluntary association of naturally equal individuals, the law of civil society has a certain character. It is devoted to securing, as equally as possible, their natural rights. Pursuing their happiness with equal right within the bounds of civil society, different individuals may justly achieve different kinds and degrees of recognition by others, and different kinds and degrees of rewards for their efforts. What is truly individual about an individual human being is not what he shares by nature with others: it is what makes him different, and possibly unique, for example, in his ability to play the violin, discover the theory of relativity, or make money. The individualism of the American Founding, grounded in nature, requires systematic discrimination between natural rights, and political or civil rights. And the latter require discrimination between the equal security which justice demands for the rights of everyone, and the unequal rewards to which each individual has a right, by virtue of something by which he may differ from others. Marxism-Leninism, denying nature as the ground of rights, ultimately reduces all individual differences to mere appearances, whose underlying reality is something called "undifferentiated homogeneous labor power." If Einstein discovered the theory of relativity, it was merely because the collective human scientific consciousness happened to achieve that particular form of self-consciousness in him. In Marxism-Leninism individualism and collectivism simply merge into each other. But nothing in Professor Kristol's conception of individualism prevents that merger from taking place.

* * *

Professor Kristol complains with much justification about the numerous

> *United Nations resolutions which list as "human rights" such items as vacations with pay, maternity leave, full employment and free medical care.... The American government in its moments of silliness has actually signed such declarations and resolutions. But the American people never have subscribed to such nonsense.*

I agree with Professor Kristol that these things are nonsense. But it is important to understand *why* they are nonsense. If we understand why they are, we may also understand why intelligent people are deluded by them, and how we may reason them out of their delusions. Obviously, it is not simply nonsense to say that there is a human right to food or to medical care. Human beings need food and medical care, and it is right that governments pursue policies that make it possible for them to have the food and medical care that they need. What is wrong then with saying that governments ought to consider the needs of people for food and medical care as "human rights"? The answer is that the right to food and medical care are already comprehended, in our Declaration of Independence, by the right to life. It is to "secure these rights," of which the first is the right to life, that our government, or any just government, is instituted. To secure the right to life becomes a purpose —indeed the first purpose—of such a government. Providing food and medical care are among the means by which the purpose of securing the right to life is implemented. But it is also implemented in other ways: by providing for physical security, through police and armed forces. Securing private property is another way of securing the right to life. It is by securing private property that, in general, men are secured in the right to the possession of the fruits of their own labor. By the fruits of their labor, generally speaking, men provide themselves with food and medical care, together with other necessities as well as comforts of life (e.g. vacations with pay; maternity leave, etc.). As a rule, governments provide for security services directly, and leave the provision for the other necessities, and the comforts of life, to the citizens themselves. But there is no *a priori* rule in these matters. Whether a given need is best satisfied by public or private agency is a matter of deliberation and prudence. Perhaps the best general rule is that of Abraham Lincoln: that government ought to do for the people what they cannot do at all, or do so well, for themselves. I think it is clear that a market economy can provide vastly more food, in greater variety, and at lower cost, than can any system of collective farming. I think the same is true of medical care, and most of the other goods of life. But this can be debated, just because it refers to means, which require deliberation, and hence prudence. "Human rights," properly so called, refer to ends and not means. Ends are not the subject matter of deliberation, means are. It only confuses our understanding of what government ought to do, to treat means—however vital—as if they were ends. The expression "human rights" refers then properly to the ends of government. These ends flow from man's nature, are therefore unchanging, and are of themselves not subject to deliberation or prudence. A government may not deliberate over whether it shall act to secure the lives and liberties of those who have consented to be governed by it. It may only consider how best to do these things. Human rights, to repeat, define the ends of government, those things that cannot, as Aristotle says, be otherwise. Deliberation is about things that can be otherwise: there cannot be *a priori* knowledge about how men may best secure their lives and their liberties. That men pursue happiness as their highest end, is an ineluctable necessity of their natures, according to both the *Nicomachean Ethics* and the Declaration of Independence. How best any man—or any polity—seeks to secure happiness, is subject always to the dictates of prudence.

What then is wrong about placing desirable means among those things properly regarded as ends? If, let us say, vacations with pay, or free medical care, are extremely desirable, why not call them human rights? One answer is that the number of things that human beings regard as desirable is infinite, and the resources to gratify those desires is finite. Desirable means to life, liberty, and the pursuit of happiness are not always or equally so. To make medical care a "human right" means that it is not subject to deliberation: it becomes a categorical duty of government to provide it. This then makes the provision of medical care take precedence over any other good that has not been elevated to the status of a human right. Resources may have to be diverted from, let us say, housing, or food, or education. But, it is said, let us make them all human rights. To do so would be exactly like solving the question of scarcity by printing money. Human rights, like money, are simply debased in the process. There is no way that ends and means can be confused, without destroying the practical wisdom that ought to govern human affairs.

Marxist-Leninist regimes are founded upon an analysis of the human condition that denies that scarcity is inherent in the human condition. It denies the need to rank means in relationship to ends. That is the significance of the famous passage in Marx's *German Ideology*, which envisions socialist man changing his pursuits from morning to afternoon to evening. Socialist man knows no distinction between work and play. He is not tied to the division of labor. He moves only to gratify his desires. For the same reason that there is no distinction between work and play, there is none between means and ends. This is the meaning of the "leap into freedom" that marks the end of history. This happens when all private property has been abolished, when the state has withered away, and when "the government of man has been replaced by the administration of things." It is this utopian vision of the future which Marxism-Leninism offers to mankind, with the explicit intention of replacing the Christian vision of the after-life. In both, the possible is completely absorbed into the desirable. Marxism-Leninism assumes without any argument or proof, that when human life is emancipated from the internal contradictions generated by the class struggle, there will be no obstacles to the satisfaction of human desires arising from scarcity of resources. According to Marxism-Leninism, the actualization of this utopia is not a matter of faith—as in Christianity—but something guaranteed by the laws of history, which are known without possibility of doubt by scientific reason. Of course, it is also true that, by reason of the abolition of private property, all cause of selfishness is eliminated from the human condition. Socialist man will be so constituted that he will be incapable of desiring things that his fellow-man cannot enjoy simultaneously. That is to say, no envy will enter into human satisfaction. The elimination of envy (or possessiveness) as a cause of satisfaction will eliminate scarcity as a cause of inequality. For example, no one's pleasure from a work of art, or from a woman, will be increased or intensified by the phenomenon of private possession. Such "logical" distinctions as those between ends and means, instrumental and final, natural and conventional, objective and subjective, will be cast into the dustbin of history. All of them are antinomies whose intelligibility arises from the inner contradictions of human experience within a dialectical history which no longer exists.

To place vacations with pay, maternity leave, free medical care, permanent full employment, etc., etc., among human rights is therefore to remind mankind of its proper goal: the leap into freedom, at the end of history, after the Revolution. It is to remind mankind that its proper duty—the one duty whose fulfillment marks the end of all possible duties—is Revolution. By treating the totality of all desirable things as if they were both possible and necessary, is to remind mankind of the heaven on earth that Marxism-Leninism promises. It marks those who oppose such things as reactionaries. Professor Kristol calls these promises nonsense. But it is no laughing matter. These promises may be those of a God who has failed, but there are millions upon millions around the world who do not know he has failed. As we have already noticed, this God seems to have converted great numbers—perhaps a majority—of the Christian clergy. No argument against dialectical materialism can be successful, merely by saying that it contradicts the facts of "common sense." Dialectical materialism—Marxism-Leninism— asserts that it represents the highest (or final) form of the scientific consciousness. And it is the nature of science to contradict common sense. According to common sense, the earth is flat, and the sun revolves around it. According to common sense, human nature is an essence, something permanent. But Marxism-Leninism tells us that this "essence" is in fact a "contingency," a by-product of the historical process, and that the dialectic of history itself is the only "essential" or unchanging ground of changing reality. Without refuting the concept of history, not only as we find it in Marx and Engels, but as we find it in their predecessors, including Hegel and Burke, can we make an effective response to the Marxist-Leninist understanding of human rights. Only if nature, rather than history, is understood to be the unchanging ground of changing reality, can the rights of the individual be defended in the sense intended by Professor Kristol.

* * *

Irving Kristol's instinctive understanding, that neither our economy nor our foreign policy is defensible without a moral argument, is sound. His difficulty — and it is the problem of American Conservatism as a whole — is that he does not have a moral argument. He makes a series of *ad hoc* arguments which simply do not bear the weight that he places upon them. Let us see.

Professor Kristol declares that "The right to emigrate is the most basic of all individual rights, since it tends automatically to set limits to what an authoritarian or totalitarian regime can do." But the right to emigrate does *not* automatically set such limits. Hitler offered to send Germany's Jews out of the country in the 1930's, but there was no other country, including the United States, that would take them. To call the right to emigrate "basic" is correct. But to call it "the most basic" is to deprive it of its authority, by omitting the ground of that authority. Even the Supreme Court of the United States has declared that the right to emigrate is a natural right, because it is a direct inference from the proposition that the just powers of government are derived from the consent of the governed. The just powers of government are derived from consent, because all men are created — or are by nature — free and equal. Only as an inference from a more fundamental natural right, whether one chooses the language of the Declaration of Independence, or of the Virginia or Massachusetts Bills of Rights (or other Revolutionary sources), can one say that the right to emigrate is a basic right of the individual. Without saying so much, one really says nothing at all. We do not recognize the right to emigrate as a means for evading the payment of one's lawful debts, and certainly not as a means for evading criminal prosecutions. All the Soviets have to do to justify lawfully keeping Jews — or anyone else — from emigrating is to accuse them of anti-Soviet propaganda. With what right do we say that the Soviet Union has no right to have a law forbidding anti-Soviet propaganda? Their right to have such a law is identical with their right to prevent counter-revolution, a right flowing from the very nature of Marxism-Leninism. Thus without attacking Marxism-Leninism as the ground of Soviet legality, there is no argument possible against Soviet denials of the right to emigrate.

Professor Kristol says that "The practice of torture — not 'harsh treatment' but literal torture — against political opponents is so fundamentally obnoxious as to be always and everywhere unacceptable to us. Torture is an assault on the metaphysical concept of human dignity itself, from which our belief in human rights is derived." Here Professor Kristol comes close to invoking the conception of what is right and wrong by nature, in support of his conception of human rights. Some things, he says, are "always and everywhere unacceptable to us." In classical political philosophy, what is "always and everywhere" is also "by nature." But Professor Kristol spoils his formulation, by calling what is always and everywhere *wrong* as being always and everywhere "unacceptable to us." A Marxist-Leninist would, with perfect right, ask what makes *you* competent judges of moral matters. Calling our moral judgment "bourgeois" automatically disqualifies it as *human* moral judgment. Professor Kristol shows himself to be somehow aware of this problem, by adding that torture violates "the metaphysical conception of human dignity," and adds that it is from this conception that "our belief in human rights is derived." He here concedes — what he seems not to admit anywhere else — that the conception of human rights is "derived" from something more fundamental than itself. We wish Professor Kristol had said more about it, since on his own reasoning — in this one place — it is the foundation of everything else he has to say about human rights. Let us here notice that the word "physical" is perfectly synonymous with the word "natural," the one being derived from the Greek, and the other from the Latin. And "metaphysical" is nearly synonymous with "supernatural," as when Lady Macbeth refers to the witches' prophecies as "metaphysical aid." But can we with Professor Kristol's assurance declare that the practice of torture is always and everywhere wrong? Does not this involve the fallacy of confusing means with ends? Do we not have here an example of what Aristotle meant, when he said that that part of political right which is natural right, is all changeable. Consider the following example. Professor Kristol is walking through Kennedy Airport. There is a great hubbub as the airport guards arrest a Puerto Rican terrorist, one of the FALN. The guards discover that the man has planted a bomb in an airport locker, and the terrorist admits that this is the case. The guards ask, "Where?" The terrorist replies, "That's for me to know and for you to find out." The guards then turn to Professor Kristol, as the nearest expert on human rights, and ask him what limits he would place upon their procedures, considering that a number of innocent persons, including no doubt women and children, will be blown apart unless the necessary information is promptly forthcoming.

Hard cases make bad law, no doubt, and bad morality as well. It is a general rule in moral casuistry, that the ends do not justify the means. But it was as well known to Aristotle as to Machiavelli, that good regimes cannot always deny to themselves evil means, if by so denying themselves, they doom themselves to become the victims of the evil regimes. Professor Kristol, taking his stand against evil means, apart from a stand against evil ends, is stultified once again by his own argument.

* * *

"Religious toleration," writes Professor Kristol, "is an idea so fundamental to the American way of life, so rooted in American traditions, that we simply cannot be indifferent to violations of that idea." The origin of human rights, in "the metaphysical concept of human dignity," is forgotten in the space of a single paragraph, although one would have thought that if any human rights would have reminded Professor Kristol of this metaphysical concept, it would have been the rights of the human conscience. Professor Kristol is somehow aware that an idea that is "rooted in American traditions" is not for that reason an idea which we can insist that others respect. We cannot, for example, respect untouchability, or the burning of widows, because they are rooted in Hindu tradition. He steps back, accordingly, adding "Mind you, I am talking about religious toleration—i.e., freedom from religious persecution—not religious equality and definitely not separation of church and state. These last are American ideas, not necessarily exportable." Yet he concludes that "freedom from religious persecution is a human right whose universality we must insist upon."

Clearly, Professor Kristol is playing a game, in which you lose if you say why anything is right or wrong. But what an absurd game it is! The ground of the rights of conscience is first said to be rootedness in American traditions. American traditions are then divided into the exportable and the non-exportable. The exportable are said to have "universality." But the ground of their universality is itself said to be nothing but what "we must insist on." The argument has moved in a perfect circle. And, of course, the reason *why* we must insist, is that otherwise "we shall be guilt-ridden, uncertain, [and] lacking in self-confidence." I can easily imagine the Kremlin wags recommending psychiatry to Professor Kristol and his friends, as a superior method for dealing with their guilt.

Here we must remind Professor Kristol, that according to Marxism-Leninism, religion is "the opiate of the people." While the Soviet Constitution guarantees freedom of religious and anti-religious propaganda, from the official Communist perspective, belief in God is essentially counter-revolutionary. Belief in God is intrinsically nothing but ideology, serving to justify the appropriation of surplus value by the owning classes. The victory of the proletariat in the persons of the Central Committee of the Bolshevik Party, in the October Revolution, was the first stage in the emancipation of the human race from History and the Class Struggle. There can be no human right that stands as an obstruction or impediment to this Revolution. Religion, in a bourgeois regime, is a part of the ideology by which the regime maintains itself. In a proletarian regime, such as the USSR, religious belief can be nothing more than the vestigial remains of the class consciousness which lingers from the pre-Revolutionary era. That is to say, it is either vestigial, or counter-revolutionary anti-Soviet propaganda. It can be expected to wither away—like the state itself —as the forces of the Revolution replace those of all *ancien regimes* within the souls of the Soviet citizens. Historically, working classes believed in God as recompense for the surplus value that they produced, but which was appropriated by the ruling classes. Ruling classes believed in God for the much better reason that such a belief sustained the system of privileges of which they were the beneficiaries. They enjoyed the real pleasures of the real world, while the exploited workers accepted in lieu of payment the imaginary pleasures of an imaginary world. Hence religion was indeed "the opiate of the people." How then can Professor Kristol argue that treating the purveyors of religion in the Soviet Union like drug pushers—which is what it comes down to—is persecution? How can he deny the Marxist-Leninist argument, that religious freedom (so called) in the bourgeois world is nothing but a cover for pushing the drug called religion? Encouraging religious belief has no other purpose but undermining the Revolutionary consciousness that would lead to the demand for the abolition of capitalism!

Professor Kristol draws a distinction—as we have noted—between "freedom from religious persecution" and "religious equality." The former he wants us to "insist on," but the latter he says is an American idea, "not necessarily exportable." If he had said that it was not prudent always to insist upon all the implications of religious freedom everywhere, he would have said something unobjectionable. After all, there were religious establishments in several of the states, during and after the American Revolution. The First Amendment forbade *Congress* to establish a religion in the United States. It did not forbid the people of any state to establish religion. It was not until long after the Civil War that the Supreme Court of the United States decided that, under the equal protection clause of the Fourteenth Amendment, the rights guaranteed by the First Amendment, might not be denied to any person by any state. By this, we are further reminded that slavery itself was abolished in the United States only by the Thirteenth Amendment, although the Constitution of 1787 declares that the United States shall guarantee to every state "a republican form of government." Does Professor Kristol think that slavery was not a contradiction of the principles of republicanism? The "more perfect union" of 1787 was still not a perfect union. Still, it was perfected, insofar as it moved towards an implementation of its genuine principles, the principles both of civil and religious liberty. Such an implementation ought to take place, in accordance with the dictates of prudence. But prudence has no dictates, except as they become visible by the light of the principles. The true and complete policy, with respect to religion and the rights of conscience, was embodied in George Washington's celebrated letter to the Hebrew Congregation of Newport, Rhode Island, in 1791. "The citizens of the United States," wrote Washington,

> *have a right to applaud themselves for having given to mankind examples of an enlarged and liberal policy; a policy worthy of imitation. All possess alike liberty of conscience and immunities of citizenship. It is now no more that toleration is spoken of, as if it was by the indulgence of one class of people, that another enjoyed the exercise of their inherent natural rights. For happily the government of the United States, which gives to bigotry no sanction, to persecution no assistance, requires only that those who live under its protection should demean themselves as good citizens. . . .*

Religious liberty is grounded upon the doctrine that all men have an inherent natural right to liberty of conscience, and that their immunities of citizenship are and of right ought to be perfectly independent of how they exercise such liberty. On this ground the United States might commend to other nations a policy which they *might* imitate. That they *ought* to imitate it follows from the fact that it is a policy in accordance with natural right. Without the appeal to natural right, neither the opposition to persecution nor to "religious inequality" has any power of persuasion. Marxism-Leninism must be unmasked as the bigotry it is, in its denial of the rights of human nature, if we are to defend the rights of conscience in a "candid world."

When Professor Kristol comes to discuss the human rights of racial minorities, his argument turns upon itself in a manner that is positively embarrassing. "The rights of racial minorities," he writes, "were not always thought to represent a fundamental human right, but they have unquestionably acquired that status in recent decades." "A nation which fails to recognize those rights," he continues, "inhabits a different moral universe from us and is unacceptable as friend and ally." But what has happened to "the idea of an individual's rights" upon which "our polity was founded"? Are not members of racial minorities "individuals"? If they are, why have we only come to recognize their rights "in recent decades"? If they are not, why do we recognize them now?

One thing we can assert with complete confidence: nothing can be asserted as binding upon our — or anyone else's — conscience, because it is "fundamental to the American way of life" or because it is "rooted in American traditions." The American way of life, and American traditions, are respectable because of the dignity of the principles incorporated in them, and for no other reason. We should indeed insist, so far as it is in our power to do so, that the members of racial minorities — like the members of religious minorities — enjoy the exercise of those rights to which their humanity entitles them, under the laws of nature and of nature's God. As in all cases, we should act according to the dictates of prudence, recognizing that sometimes we do more harm than good, if we insist too far. In declaring that all men are created equal, our Founding Fathers set up a principle that they were themselves powerless to implement, except in part. But Professor Kristol shows little respect for the American political tradition, when he says that it is only recently that we have discovered that the rights of racial minorities represent fundamental human rights. In saying that all men were equally endowed by their Creator with the same unalienable rights, the Fathers went as far as the nature of words and the nature of things admitted, to assert that fundamental human rights were independent of any distinctions among men. In attributing the source of the rights, both to nature and to the Creator, they invoked both reason and revelation, in support of such rights. This was certainly more authoritative than anything merely American.

Professor Kristol, in judging that the rights of racial minorities attained the status of fundamental rights only in recent decades, confuses the implementation of a right, with the recognition of a right. But if the recognition of a right did not *precede* its implementation, what reason would there have been to implement it? It was the proposition that all men are created equal, introduced into a slave society, that ultimately persuaded and compelled that society, to abolish slavery. After the abolition of slavery, that same society bestowed its civil and political rights unequally. But the man who, more than any other, had acted to abolish slavery, had declared as long ago as 1854, that the principles of the Declaration of Independence, which were the principles of self-government, required that *all* the governed have an *equal* voice in the government. And so that same society has moved ever closer to full equality of rights, civil, political, and religious. The principles have always been there, although their implementation has always been subject—as the Declaration itself also says—to the dictates of prudence.

When Professor Kristol says that any nation that fails to recognize the rights of the different races "inhabits a different universe from us," he invites a response, from a wide variety of persons and places, that "we do not, in any case, care to inhabit your moral universe." Indeed, nothing is more commonplace among professors on American campuses, than to say that in any event each person's "value judgments" accord only with his own moral universe. Human freedom, they will say, is above all manifested in the free choice of the moral universe within which we choose to live. What right, they may ask Professor Kristol, do you have to impose your moral universe upon anyone else? By making the moral universe to which he appeals merely "ours" he refers moral choice once again back to whatever it is that we decide to "insist upon." But if that is the case, why not persuade ourselves that that only is moral which is in accordance with our "interests"? Professor Kristol, in opposing our "conscience" to a foreign policy of mere "interest," arrives in fact back at the position he began by opposing.

In 1857 Abraham Lincoln spoke out against the *Dred Scott* decision. Chief

Justice Taney had concluded that under the Constitution black men had no rights which white men were bound to respect. He believed that this opinion had been authorized by the Declaration of Independence, because Negroes had not been included in the proposition, that all men are created equal. The Signers could not have included Negroes, said Taney, because if they had, they would have immediately abolished slavery. Lincoln replied as follows. Those who drafted, and those who accepted, the language of the Declaration of Independence,

> *did not mean to assert the obvious untruth, that all were then actually enjoying that equality, nor yet, that they were about to confer it immediately upon them. In fact they had no power to confer such a boon. They meant simply to declare the* right, *so that the* enforcement *of it might follow as fast as circumstances should permit. They meant to set up a standard maxim for free society, which could be familiar to all, and revered by all; constantly looked to, constantly labored for, and even though never perfectly attained, constantly approximated, and thereby constantly spreading and deepening its influence, and augmenting the happiness and value of life to all people of all colors everywhere.*

I commend Lincoln's words to you, for they are as wise as they are beautiful, and as true as they are wise. Let us abide by Lincoln's standard maxim for free society, even as Lincoln abided by it, and we may yet rise above the confusion in which our policies are now confounded, and above the difficulties in which we ourselves are entangled. Let us then go forward in the building of the "proud fabric of our freedom," here and abroad, and so build that "as truly as has been said of the only greater institution, 'the gates of hell shall not prevail against it.'"

February, 1982

Fifteen

The Declaration and the Draft

Two young men were convicted recently in federal courts for refusing to register for military service. A great deal of publicity attended the cases. The fathers of both were interviewed on network television, and denounced the government for prosecuting their sons. It was not so much prosecution as persecution, they said, since the young men had acted from conscientiously held moral beliefs. Their sons possessed the highest moral character and therefore the government had acted immorally! The assertions about their sons' characters seem to have been borne out, at least in part, by the fact that they did not run away to Canada (or elsewhere) and did not appear to evade any of the legal proceedings against themselves. In this respect, they appeared to be in the tradition of Henry David Thoreau, Mahatma Gandhi, and Martin Luther King, Jr. It was in this vein perhaps, that their families were claiming martyrdom for them.

In comparison with the high moral ground claimed by and for the young men, the government's prosecutors were singularly inarticulate. For them, the only question at issue was whether the law was being obeyed and, if not, whether those who disobeyed it were punished in accordance with the provisions of the law. Perhaps this is all that should concern a federal prosecutor. If so, the perspective of a federal prosecutor is—at least in such a case—shockingly inadequate. If there is any duty which needs to be enlightened by reason it is the duty of military service. "A frequent recurrence to fundamental principles" is enjoined upon us by the very nature of our Founding and our Constitution. Certainly a nation which took up arms to gain its freedom, and which found it necessary to justify to the entire world that taking up of arms, ought to be able to justify to its own citizens the obligation to serve in its defense. That it should appear that those who suffer punishment by defying the obligation of military service are somehow braver and better than those who accept this obligation, is shameful, as well as inconsistent with our interest in survival.

The nature of the obligation of military service in a free society has been obscured of late by the fact that President Reagan has for some years opposed a peacetime draft, on the ground that it is a violation of personal liberty. But the obligation of military service transcends the distinction between peace and war. Preparation for war must take place in time of peace. The military draft law which was in effect at the time of Pearl Harbor, December 7, 1941, had been renewed some six weeks before, by the margin of one vote, in the House of Representatives. Unprepared as we were on that day of infamy, one shudders to contemplate what our condition would have been, had that one vote not been forthcoming. Given the swiftness of the onset and progress of modern wars, the nation cannot make the duty to serve await the enemy's attack. This does not, of course, imply that a draft law is always necessary in peacetime, any more than it is never necessary. But the President should never have said, or implied, that the moral argument for compulsory military service turns on the distinction between peace and war.

What are we to say, however, of the claim that is frequently made, that there is a moral duty, higher than the law, not to engage in military service, because of the duty not to take human life? Is this not a respectable claim? At the least, one must concede that it is a claim that has often been made by respectable people. As such, it has been recognized in all our selective service laws of this century. One reason for recognizing it is the comparatively small number of those who have made it. Most of us believe that we possess a natural right of self-defense. Such a right may be exercised individually, as when we repel an attacker who invades our home in the dead of night; or it may be exercised collectively, as when we send our armed services against our country's attackers. The commandment, "Thou Shalt Not Kill," has not been understood—except by an eccentric few—to preclude killing those who would make an unprovoked attack upon ourselves, our families, our friends, or our fellow-citizens. Nevertheless, for those few who seem genuinely to believe that they have been commanded by God to abstain from all violence, even to defend themselves and those nearest to them, the law has (rightly, I think) granted an exemption. But such an exemption can only be granted by the law. It is not something anyone enjoying the protection of the law can claim apart from the law. In order lawfully to secure an exemption from military service on conscientious grounds, one must register, and follow the prescribed procedures to ascertain whether one's claim is, in fact, conscientious. To do otherwise, would be to leave this exemption open to all who did not choose to serve. This would make the law a nullity. The young men recently convicted of refusing to register had no right whatever on their side. If they were in fact conscientious objectors (as their families seemed to say) then they should nonetheless have registered. If called to service, they might then have applied for the exemption, which they would have received if their claims were valid.

In conceding the wisdom or prudence of granting religious objectors exemption from military service, we must not leave an inference in any one's mind, that those refusing service, on this or any other ground, occupy a higher moral status than those who serve. Military service in a free society is a moral no less than a legal duty. Just because someone says he is obeying God does not elevate his character. To obey the law requiring military service is to obey the dictates, not merely of a positive law, but of the natural law. It is to obey the dictates of a rational morality. The ground of the moral obiligation to military service may be found in the Declaration of Independence, and in those "laws of nature and nature's God" which the Declaration propounds. Central to the doctrine of the Declaration is the great proposition, "that all men are created equal." This proposition, to which Abraham Lincoln said the nation was dedicated at its birth, was also called by him "the father of all moral principle among us." By this proposition, no man can lawfully exercise political authority over another, except with that other's consent. In the words of the Massachusetts Bill of Rights (1780),

> *The body politic is formed by a voluntary association of individuals; it is a social compact by which the whole people covenants with each citizen and each citizen with the whole people that all shall be governed by certain laws for the common good.*

Those who do not become members of a body politic at its institution, are nonetheless voluntary members by consenting to remain in it. It is a hallmark of a free society that it does not hinder anyone who wishes to leave from emigrating, and taking his property with him. The right to emigrate is a corollary of the principle that the just powers of government are derived from the consent of the governed. A government based upon consent may therefore place no barriers to emigration, other than the payment of honest debts. However, everyone reaching the age of consent, who consents to remain, consents at the same time to obey the laws founded upon that same consent.

By the laws of nature and of nature's God, we are endowed with unalienable rights, the first of which is the right to life. Whatever else may be embraced by the term, "the common good," there can be no question but that safety is fundamental to it. For safety is the condition for the enjoyment of all the peaceful fruits of civil society. The voluntary association called the body politic is then nothing, unless it is an agreement that no one need defend himself alone, but that henceforth each shall be defended by all. But each cannot be defended by all, unless all will defend each. When someone says — as these so called conscientious objectors seem to say — that they will be good citizens in everything else except in joining in the common defense, they are removing the linchpin of citizenship, upon which everything else depends.

It is moreover a necessary conclusion from the proposition of human equality, that I cannot lay claim to an equal right with my fellow-citizens, to the protection of the laws, while rejecting the equal obligation, to share the risks without which there can be no protection by the laws. To make a demand that can be interpreted to mean that some lives are intrinsically more worthy of protection than others, is to deny fundamentally that all men are created equal.

What of the objections of those pacifists who say that if only everyone refused to serve, there would be no war? That all could live peacefully in a messianic age, "when the lion shall lie down with the lamb"? For the lion to lie down with the lamb — that is, with the lamb outside the lion, not inside — is however not in accordance with "the laws of nature." The religious vision of the messianic age, when God shall rule on earth no less than in Heaven, does not tell us what our moral duties are here and now. The principles of the Declaration of Independence are not utopian. The Declaration was made by a nation in arms and at war. The pledge made explicitly to each other by the Signers, of their lives, their fortunes, and their sacred honor, was a pledge made implicitly, by every other citizen to his fellows. The regime established by the Declaration of Independence was the most tolerant with respect to differing religious beliefs that the world had ever seen. Opinions like those of certain pacifists which presuppose a miraculous transformation of human nature (if not of non-human nature) cannot be cast into the balance against the reasoned and realistic moral arguments of the Declaration. These reasoned arguments are the foundation of religious no less than of civil liberty. The obligation to respect religious opinions cannot be understood in such a way that the government that guarantees religious freedom may not survive.

One might, however, reply that our argument hitherto has established the moral justification only of *universal* service, but not of *selective* service. Is not the latter unjust to those comparatively few actually called into service? Certainly, when all are equally obligated, it seems unjust that that obligation fall unequally on a few. And is it not also unjust that those selected should be young, while their elders do the selecting? But the laws made for the common good must be adapted to the ends they serve. Certainly the laws should seek to make the burdens of the common defense as equal as possible, but not by making the laws ineffective. There should be selective privileges for those who serve selectively. The end of military service is however the safety of the body politic. The primary object of the law is not the equality of the sacrifices it exacts—important as this is—but the fighting abilities of the services created. Service in the ranks requires men rather than women, the young rather than the old, the able bodied rather than the halt, the more intelligent rather than the less intelligent. The reasons are necessities of nature, to ignore which would be to ignore the very danger we seek to meet. Ineptitude is itself a form of injustice. The laws of nature command us to defend ourselves. The necessary means to a just end cannot be unjust, for the very reason that justice cannot be unjust.

October 27, 1982

Sixteen

Dred Scott and the American Regime

No one can speak now of the case of Dred Scott without paying homage to that magisterial masterpiece, *The Dred Scott Case: Its Significance in American Law and Politics*, by Don E. Fehrenbacher. In writing on an episode of ante-bellum American history, Professor Fehrenbacher has brought into focus nearly all the great disputed questions attendant to the coming of the Civil War. His book requires, and deserves, many readings, more than I have yet been able to bestow on it. My judgment of many of its broader arguments, as well as of its details, must therefore await better knowledge. Still, I have no doubt that, despite the many honors it has already received, it is destined for those weightier honors that time alone can bestow. Among writings on the great crisis in the American regime, I believe it will become a classic of classics.

Because Professor Fehrenbacher's book is a study of the law and politics of Dred Scott's case, as well as an attempt to locate it as an event "in the stream of history," I should like to comment on certain issues which seem to me to be outside the sphere he has marked out for himself. The Dred Scott case is indeed an important episode in the transformation of American law, culminating in the Fourteenth Amendment. The adoption of the Fourteenth Amendment was itself, as we all well know, not only an end but a beginning. But let us mark this end and this beginning. Chief Justice Taney, speaking for the Court, had declared in his opinion in the Dred Scott case, that a Negro, *whether free or slave*, might not become a citizen of the United States. The Thirteenth Amendment, ending chattel slavery in the United States, did not reverse this judgment. To do so, the Fourteenth Amendment was required. The question that the Court was called upon to decide in the case of Dred Scott, Taney said at the beginning of his opinion, was this:

> *Can a negro, whose ancestors were imported into this country and sold as slaves, become a member of the political community formed and brought into existence by the Constitution of the United States, and as such become entitled to all the rights, privileges, and immunities, guaranteed by that instrument to its citizens?*

Taney's negative answer to this question was reversed by the first sentence of Section 1 of the Fourteenth Amendment, which declared that

> *All persons born or naturalized in the United States, and subject to the jurisdiction thereof, are citizens of the United States and of the States wherein they reside.*

But Section 1 continues, extending the privileges of the Fifth Amendment to the newly defined citizen and adding as well that no state may "deny to any person within its jurisdiction the equal protection of the laws."

This prohibition of the denial to any person of the "equal protection of the laws" marks a beginning of an essentially new element in American Constitutional jurisprudence. Before this, the Supreme Court might rule under the supremacy clause that a state constitution or statute was in conflict with a valid federal law, or that a state had done something prohibited to it by the Constitution. But now it might judge that a state, merely within itself, and not by virtue of any other conflict with the Constitution, had violated the Constitution, by denying to some person within its jurisdiction "the equal protection of the laws." As we all know too well today, what constitutes the equal protection of the laws has become an increasingly complex, if not an altogether arcane question. As it does so, the questions which were at bottom at issue in Dred Scott's case, have reappeared in questions as to what it is that "all persons" are entitled to when they are entitled to equal protection. For it was Taney who first set the pattern which has, for example, reappeared in the *Weber* case. It was Taney who said that, although the Declaration said that *all* men are created equal, it nonetheless meant only that *some* men are created equal. This is precisely the mode of judicial construction popular today. It is called "result oriented," meaning that you decide first what you think the law ought to be, and then decide from this what the law is. But Taney, in deciding in this way what the Declaration and Constitution meant, did so by denying the conception of an objective order—the natural order—which the language of the Declaration invoked. He substituted in its stead a subjective order, based upon what he believed the real (or radically motivated) preferences of the Founding Fathers to be. Abandoning the objective for the subjective understanding of the meaning of equality, he laid the foundation for how the Court today decides what is meant by the "equal protections of the laws." I would sum this up, by the dictum that anyone has a recognizable claim to have been denied the "equal protection of the laws," who *feels* that he has been denied the "equal protections of the laws." And I think this brings with it the corollary, that any defendant in an equal protection suit, has upon him the burden of proof to establish that anyone feeling discriminated against, has not in fact been discriminated against.

I submit then that if the cause of Abraham Lincoln seems to have triumphed over that of Roger B. Taney, this is so merely on the surface. Taney's opinions have proved more tenacious in the realm of opinion. And Lincoln himself insisted, in a free government, he who molds opinion goes deeper than he who enacts statutes or pronounces decisions. There can then be no genuine or durable triumphs in law or politics, which have no foundation in opinion. The work of Lincoln must be done again, or it will be undone. We cannot rest on his laurels.

Judge Leon Higginbotham, Jr., is a distinguished jurist as well as a distinguished historian. As a former United States district court judge, and a present member of the United States Court of Appeals for the Third Circuit, he is a representative voice of the law. As the author of *In the Matter of Color: Race and the American Legal Process, The Colonial Period* (Oxford University Press, 1978), he represents authoritative scholarly and academic opinion. When however he declares in his book that "if the authors of the Declaration of Independence had said—'all *white* men are created equal' or even 'all white men who own property . . . ' they would have more honestly conveyed the general consensus," he is subscribing to a fundamental premise of Taney's opinion in Dred Scott's case.

According to Judge Higginbotham, the history of the United States is a "sordid history." Yet he thinks that the promise of equality in the Declaration of Independence, from which blacks were excluded, nonetheless had an impact "in the corridors of history." The idea of equality in the Declaration, he says, was merely "embryonic." Having called it such, one might think that he would have found that the gestation of the embryo resulted in that "new birth of freedom," of which Lincoln spoke at Gettysburg. However, although Judge Higginbotham thinks well of Lincoln for having construed the Declaration "as having a broader scope and impact that that suggested by Taney," he never departs from his conviction that it is Taney, and not Lincoln, who construed the Declaration in accordance with the intentions of those who made the Revolution, and who drafted and adopted the Constitution.

Yet Judge Higginbotham still finds good in the Declaration. The good he finds is particularly well expressed, he says, in the following passage from a book by Dean Louis Pollak, of the University of Pennsylvania Law School (*The Constitution and the Supreme Court: A Documentary History,* [World, 1968]):

> *The ever-widening impact of the nation's early commitment to the equality of "all men" compellingly illustrates what Benjamin N. Cardozo, one of the handful of great American judges, termed "the tendency of a principle to expand itself to the limit of its logic." In this sense, the Declaration of Independence is the apt progenitor of the Emancipation Proclamation, the Gettysburg Address, the Fourteenth Amendment's guarantee of the "equal protection of the laws," and the Supreme Court's recent decisions invalidating governmentally ordained racial segregation in public schools and elsewhere.*

I hope that Judge Higginbotham, as well as Dean Pollak, sticks to the judgment that it is the logic of the idea of the equality of all men which is responsible for the widening and deepening justice of the Constitution, including the emergent jurisprudence of the equal protection clause of the Fourteenth Amendment. But I do not think that it is possible for them to do so, if they think that that meaning is not intrinsic to the Declaration itself. But if that is what the Declaration *always* meant, it must have meant this to those who framed it and adopted it. To say that the Declaration had an intrinsic meaning different from the the conscious intention of all of its authors sounds very much like attributing to them the same feat that is attributed to the mythical monkeys with typewriters, who reduplicated Shakespeare's achievement in composing *Hamlet*.

In suggesting that the "real" meaning of the Declaration is different from the actual meaning of those who were originally responsible for it, Dean Pollak and Judge Higginbotham seem to me to be saying this: that the Declaration ought to have meant what the Judge and the Dean know that it ought to have meant. In his Epilogue, the Judge observes that "In every major respect, the colonial law was an instrument of injustice." "Even in the birth of the new nation," he adds, "the founding fathers still subjected blacks to a persistent cruelty that was far more oppressive than the deprivations over which white Americans waged the Revolution." "But," he continues, "it need not have been that way. The branding of any group as inferior or less than human on the basis of color was not inevitable. There were sufficient legal, theological, and philosophical foundations upon which a more uniformly just and humane social structure could have been built."

Judge Higginbotham here concedes what he does not elsewhere admit: that the social structure built by the Founding Fathers was "just and humane," although not uniformly so. But what was the foundation upon which the Fathers ought to have built, if it was not the foundation provided by the Declaration of Independence? He says that the branding of any group as inferior on the basis of color "was not inevitable." Of course, it was precisely the generality and universality of the concept "man" which proscribes such condemnation, and which in time in fact has tended towards its proscription. But this is not to say that it was within the power of the Founding Fathers to have acted freely upon the principle that they proclaimed. The Founding Fathers were political leaders. Is it surprising that their followers were enthusiastic about principles, insofar as they saw in them direct benefits for themselves? And is it surprising that they were less enthusiastic, when they discovered in the same principles benefits for others, which they believed however shortsightedly involved disadvantages for themselves?

Lincoln, we know, insisted that the Declaration always included Negroes in the expression "all men." He noted that Taney, in his opinion, had conceded that the language of the Declaration was broad enough to have included the Negro. Taney thought, however, that the authors of that instrument could not have meant what they seemed to say, because they did not actually and at once, place Negroes on an equality with whites. Lincoln observed that "this grave argument comes to just nothing at all, by the other fact that they did not at once, *or ever afterwards*, actually place all white people on an equality with one another." Lincoln might, had he not been a politician, have mentioned that among the white people not placed on that level of equality, were white women. As early as 1836 Lincoln, in a call for universal white male suffrage, added "by no means excluding females." Votes for women was certainly an idea whose time had not come in 1836, but Lincoln never doubted that the "logic of the idea" of equality might comprehend it.

Judge Higginbotham, like Judge Taney, assumed that Lincoln must have been wrong, because he could not conceive that the Founding Fathers would in their own minds have understood "all men" to have included Negroes, and not have acted to abolish slavery. This is Taney:

> *The conduct of the distinguished men who framed the Declaration of Indepen-*
> *dence would have been utterly and flagrantly inconsistent with the principles they*
> *asserted, and instead of the sympathy of mankind . . . they would have deserved*
> *and received universal rebuke and reprobation. . . . Yet the men who framed this*
> *Declaration were great men . . . high in their sense of honor, and incapable of*
> *asserting principles inconsistent with those on which they were acting.*

Judge Higginbotham would not agree that the Fathers were men of such high honor. Yet he concedes that there was a "general consensus" of the American political community in 1776, and that within that consensus slavery could not have been abolished. The question then remains, whether the Fathers were hypocrites, for not attempting to take action *outside that consensus*.

Let us review the logic of the Declaration and what it prescribes to its votaries. The proposition that all men are created equal is a proposition derived from "the laws of nature and of nature's God." It implies that "all men" share a common nature. This nature, while distinguishing man from beast in such a manner as to make man by nature the ruler of beast, does not distinguish man from man in such manner as to make one man the ruler of another man. As Jefferson was to put it, on the eve of his death in 1826, some men are not born with saddles on their backs, and others booted and spurred to ride them. Because the authority of one man over another does not arise from nature, it does arise—when it is lawful and just—from consent. The American Revolutionists, when they repudiated the authority of Great Britain over them, appealed to nature for their rights. Having done so, they appealed to that nature which distinguished men from brutes on the one hand, and from God on the other. The only government they would obey, was one that they had consented to obey. Would they have consented to obey a government that insisted upon abolishing slavery, and placing blacks on an equality with whites? The answer is, of course, No. Judge Higginbotham knows that as well as Taney knew it. Taney of course approved of this, and Higginbotham disapproves, but there is no dispute about the facts. But Higginbotham and Taney agree further upon this proposition, in which agreement both are wrong: namely, that a consensus against *securing* the equal natural rights of blacks was a consensus against *recognizing* that blacks had the aforesaid rights. There is however overwhelming evidence that when the colonists turned from their prescriptive rights as Englishmen, to their natural rights as men, in the struggle with the British

Crown and Parliament, they quite understood that the rights they were appealing to were rights they shared with all men everywhere. Indeed, it was the universality of these rights which alone constituted their defense against the charge of rebellion and treason. And, further, they never denied that Negroes were men. In fact, most of the Colonial laws cited by Taney as evidence of the low opinion in which Negroes were held in America, were laws against miscegenation. And miscegenation is only possible between human beings.

Lincoln believed that the Founding Fathers were right in not attempting too much in the establishment of the first government in the world based upon the equal natural rights of mankind. How to secure the rights, for whose sake the government was established, was not dictated merely by the fact of such establishment. The leaders of the Revolution were well aware that there were inconsistencies between their principles and their practices. Paradoxically, those inconsistencies were, in a certain sense, enjoined by the principles themselves. The Declaration of Independence propounded more than a doctrine, it propounded a problem as well. The doctrine of human equality condemns, not only slavery, but government that is not grounded in the consent of the governed. In fact, it condemns government in opposition to the consent of the governed, as itself slavery. Lincoln at Peoria stated flatly, that government by the principles of the Declaration could not perfectly transpire, unless *all* the governed had an *equal voice* in the government. Yet how was this possible, until all equally recognized the equal rights of all? At what point could one replace persuasion by force, without abandoning the ostensible end for which one acted? The Declaration itself indicates what it is that must mediate between its principles and their application: that is the dictates of prudence. It is the conception of *prudence*, present in the Declaration, that is ignored by both Judges Taney and Higginbotham. Taney assumes that it is inconsistent with the high character of the Founders, that they would believe slavery was wrong, and yet not act to abolish it. But, we maintain, they *both* thought slavery wrong, *and* thought it wrong to abolish it, if that could not be done with the consent of the governed. They did indeed think it their duty to work for abolition *through* consent. Yet here is Jefferson, commenting on his own failure to secure efforts in the direction of emancipation, during the Revolution itself.

> *What a stupendous, what an incomprehensible machine is man! who can endure toil, famine, stripes, imprisonment, and death itself, in vindication of his own liberty, and the next moment, be deaf to all those motives whose power supported him through his trial, and inflict on his fellow man a bondage, one hour of which is fraught with more misery than ages of that which he rose in rebellion to oppose.*

Here Jefferson reprehends his white fellow countrymen in language as powerful as any that Judge Higginbotham could wish, for failing to take action against slavery. In the *Notes on Virginia*, whose condemnation of slavery is too well known to bear repeating, Jefferson indulged in the extraordinary hyperbole of calling the oppressed slaves, "one half the citizens." By this he indicated what the slaves would have to become, were the authority over them to become one of law and not of force. The Founding Fathers, to repeat, knew that the rights upon which they based their claim to independence and liberty, were those of all mankind. They knew that those rights were equally possessed by their slaves. But they could not act against the opinion of the community as a whole, whose consent alone authorized their exercise of "the just power of government." To act against that consent—or the opinion embodied in that consent—was not possible in a free government. We should emphasize this fact: that it was not possible precisely because the government was free. To act against the opinion of those who were their constituents—before persuading them to change that opinion—would have led simply to their dismissal from office. As I observed in *Crisis of the House Divided,* it was Douglas's chief tactic, in his debates with Lincoln in 1858, to insist that Lincoln's opposition to slavery implied a commitment to full social and political equality for Negroes. He knew that prejudice against Negroes, in the minds of the voters of Illinois, was nicely balanced against their prejudice against slavery. He hoped to tip the balance in his own favor and against Lincoln, by appealing to fear of Negro equality. Lincoln, on his hand, had to deny that he intended to bring about full political or social equality for Negroes. He had to deny that he intended that Negroes should vote, serve on juries, or be permitted to marry whites. For Lincoln to have failed to make this denial in 1858, would simply have led to his retirement from political life, and, perhaps, to the extension and perpetuation of slavery in the United States. It was Lincoln's consciousness of the concessions he himself had to make to inequality, to advance the cause of equality, which informed his understanding of the compromises made by the Founding Fathers. In a society founded upon the consent of the governed, slavery might not be abolished without that consent, without abolishing the principle of freedom *and equality* within it. That despotism might be established in and through the promise to extend freedom by abolishing slavery, was a thought that preoccupied Lincoln early in his career. It is the major theme of his Lyceum Address. Lincoln thought that the process of putting slavery in the course of ultimate extinction would indeed be a long and a painful process. But there was no alternative to doing so, except by and with the consent of the governed. He did not see any despotic cure for despotism. Nor did he see that the integrity of the principles of the Declaration—or the integrity of the men who espoused the principles of the Declaration—were to be denied or gainsaid because of the imperfect world in which their application was attempted. On the contrary, it was this very imperfection in the world which the principles of the Declaration were to cure.

* * *

Appendix

The study of human nature is not ususally thought of as a discipline within modern historiography. Yet if history is the understanding of the past, as the past understood itself, then we are obliged to notice that the United States was founded upon a conception of human nature, and that the core of the sectional conflict was over the interpretation of what that conception was. It was moreover such a conflict over the interpretation of human nature, as to call into question whether there actually was such a thing. For both Taney and Higginbotham, as we have noted, the use of the word "nature" or "natural" is merely the emphatic form of a subjective preference. Abraham Lincoln, however, never doubted that there was such a thing as human nature, and his use of the term implied that it was both a formal and a final cause, in the Aristotelian sense. His commitment to the Declaration of Independence flowed from his conviction that it embodied an "abstract truth, applicable to all men and all times." The Declaration became a positive law of the United States, by virtue of its adoption by the Congress — and the making good of that adoption by the Continental army in the field, under General Washington. But its "might" flowed from its "right," which was the right of the law of nature. "Repeal the Missouri Compromise," Lincoln declared in the Peoria speech, "repeal all compromises, repeal the Declaration of Independence, you still cannot repeal human nature." "Human action can be modified," he said at Cooper Union, "but human nature cannot be changed." Human law gains strength from the natural law, when it is in accord with it, because then there is a harmony between what men are directed to do, and their innermost inclination, which they have from nature. Those inclinations can be misdirected, or opposed, but the institutions and the men who live under them can never then be as truly prosperous. To deny nature, or the possibility that political institutions can be based upon nature is to make that "second nature," custom, the sole ground of right. Taney's and Higginbotham's interpretation of the Declaration leads to the conclusion that what is called nature is in fact nothing but the custom that gives men their predilections.

Taney's interpretation of the Declaration is however consistent with the changing view of "nature" in the mid-nineteenth century. It is no accident that it should resemble in key respects the viewpoint of Karl Marx. The "Communist Manifesto" was published to the world in 1848; Taney's opinion in Dred Scott in 1857. In the first volume of *Capital*, Marx comments on Aristotle's understanding of the exchange value of commodities. He calls Aristotle a great man, whose mind comprehended all the forms of thought in the ancient world. Aristotle, he says, saw that the ratio of commodities to money, was also a ratio of the value of commodities to each other. Aristotle saw that the apparent heterogeneity of commodities was rendered homogeneous, by reference to a common standard: money. But Aristotle did not see that the true homogeneity, underlying money, was human labor power, the ultimate cause of the value in commodities, which money purportedly measured. He was prevented from seeing this, said Marx, because of the slavery endemic in the ancient world. Since slave labor produced most commodities, he could not see that human labor was the cause of value in commodities.

Clearly, Taney saw the Founding Fathers as unable to perceive the humanity of their slaves, for the same reason that Marx thought Aristotle could not perceive the humanity of slaves. For this reason, we should also observe that Marx's interpretation of the Declaration of Independence — that is to say, of the natural rights doctrine of the eighteenth century — parallels and supports what Taney, and Judge Higginbotham, says. According to Marx, both the American and French revolutionists propounded their doctrines as being the inherent natural rights of man. Yet what they called "man" was actually "bourgeois man." In this, Marx said, they were perfectly sincere, because they identified man's humanity with his ownership of property. (Judge Higginbotham says that what the Declaration probably meant was "all white men with property are created equal.") The American Revolution's human rights teaching was summed up in the slogan, no taxation without representation. Universal man was identified with the ownership of taxable property. Yet according to Marx, this understanding, although imperfect, was yet "progressive." It was progressive, because Communists too declare all men to be created equal. But the Communists know that the rights flowing from human equality cannot be recognized as long as there are social classes with contrary, if not contradictory interests. And this will endure as long as there is private property. The propertied will never see the propertyless as full human beings. A common nature, Marx taught, can never be perceived except where there is a perception of common interests. Just as man in general sees the lower order of creation — both plants and animals — as being for his use and benefit, so he sees the lower order of humanity as partaking of this same instrumental character. Man, properly so called, can never be recognized as what he is, until private property, the cause of unequal social classes, is abolished. The internal self-consciousness of ruling classes was never completely consistent with itself. Negro slaves were seen as both human and subhuman (hence they could be three-fifths of a person in Article I of the Constitution). According to Marx, so-called free laborers were also seen in the contradictory senses of being both human beings and commodities. Both slaveowner and capitalist generated guilt feelings from the internal contradiction within their consciousness. But guilt always makes a man more dangerous to his victim. Guilt, alienation, and oppression can be overcome only by one way: revolution.

In the Lincoln-Douglas debates, Lincoln confronted this dogmatic denial of the power of philosophical reason to transcend the class struggle, when Douglas made his famous equation of the Negro and the crocodile. Douglas had said that in any struggle between the Negro and the crocodile, he was on the side of the Negro. But in any struggle between the Negro and the white man, he was on the side of the white man. In this, of course, Douglas was reflecting popular evolutionism, itself a profound current of nineteenth century thought, denying the conception of nature as a permanent reality. Lincoln declared that Douglas's argument implied the following "proportion":

> *As the negro is to the white man, so is the crocodile to the negro; and as the negro may rightfully treat the crocodile as a beast or reptile, so the white man may rightfully treat the negro as a beast or reptile.*

We see here too the implicit abandonment of "nature" as a category of theoretical orientation in understanding the manner of being of the world, and as a practical orientation in understanding the rights of (and our duties with respect to) the other beings. In this, the most fundamental respect, Douglas's view of the slavery question, and Taney's were on absolutely the same level.

In commenting on events during the Civil War, Lincoln observed that the present strife was "but human nature practically applied to the facts of the case. What has occurred . . . must ever recur. . . . In any future great national trial, compared with the men of this, we shall have as weak and as strong, as silly and as wise, as bad and as good. Let us therefore study the incidents of this as philosophy to learn wisdom by. . . ."

The study of human nature, to gain philosphical wisdom, is the true end of political study. But it cannot be such a study, unless the study of human nature is understood as Lincoln understood it, as the unchanging ground of the distinction between wisdom and folly, between badness and goodness. It was the collapse of that understanding of nature, in Taney's opinion—as well as in Douglas's doctrine of popular sovereignty—which led to the collapse of the constitutional order of the Founding in the ante-bellum period. It is the collapse of this same understanding, which threatens with the same evils, the fate of the constitutional mandate of the Fourteenth Amendment to assure the equal protection of the laws.

1981

Seventeen

The American Regime and the Only Greater Institution

Prologue

Now, it happens that we meet together once every year, sometimes about the 4th of July, for some reason or other. These 4th of July gatherings, I suppose, have their uses. If you will indulge me, I will state what I suppose to be some of them. We are now a mighty nation, we are thirty—or about thirty millions of people, and we own and inhabit about one-fifteenth part of the dry land of the whole earth. We run our memory back over the pages of history for about eighty-two years, and we discover that we were then a very small people in point of numbers, vastly inferior to what we are now, with a vastly less extent of country,—with vastly less of everything we deem desirable among men,—we look upon the change as exceedingly advantageous to us and to our posterity, and we fix upon something that happened away back, as in some way or other being connected with this rise in prosperity. We find a race of men living in that day whom we claim as our fathers and grandfathers; they were iron men; they fought for the principle they were contending for; and we understand that by what they then did it has followed that the degree of prosperity that we now enjoy has come to us. We hold this annual celebration to remind ourselves of all the good done in this process of time, of how it was done and who did it, and how we are historically connected with it; and we go from these meetings in better humor with ourselves—we feel more attached the one to the other, and more firmly bound to the country we inhabit. In every way we are better men in the age, and race, and country in which we live, for these celebrations. But after we have done all this we have not yet reached the whole. There is something else connected with it. We have besides these men—descended by blood from our ancestors—among us perhaps half our people who are not descendants at all of these men, they are men who have come from Europe—Germans, Irish, French and Scandinavian—men that have come from Europe themselves, or whose ancestors have come hither and settled here, finding themselves our equals in all things. If they look back through this history to trace their connection with those days by blood, they find they have none, they cannot carry themselves back into that glorious epoch and make themselves feel that they are part of us, but when they look through that old Declaration of Independence, they find that those old men say "We hold these truths to be self-evident, that all men are created equal," and then they feel that that moral sentiment taught in that day evidences their relation to those men, that it is the father of all moral principle in them, and that they have a right to claim it as though they were blood of the blood, and flesh of the flesh, of the men who wrote that Declaration, and so they are. That is the electric cord in that Declaration that links the hearts of patriotic and liberty-loving men together, that will link those patriotic hearts as long as the love of freedom exists in the minds of men throughout the world.

Abraham Lincoln, Chicago, Illinois, July 10, 1858

L et me call your attention at first to Lincoln's speech in Chicago, July 10, 1858. It is one upon which I relied greatly in making "the case for Lincoln," in *Crisis of the House Divided*. I expect to rely upon it still further, when I attempt to complete my interpretation of the Gettysburg Address in *A New Birth of Freedom*. Here Lincoln's style is less prophetic. Even though he had already delivered the "House Divided" speech, not even Lincoln could have foreseen the drastic change that would come upon the nation, upon himself, and upon the fate of human freedom, in that short space of time in which eighty-two years would become "fourscore and seven."

Whether from the perspective of the gathering storm, or from the center of the whirlwind, or from the aftermath, for Abraham Lincoln political history is what preceded, and what came after, July 4, 1776. As President Coolidge remarked, on our 150th anniversary, we celebrate that day, not because a new nation was born, but because a nation was born upon new principles. As the Great Seal of the United States declares, that day marked a new order of the ages. Lincoln himself declared, in Independence Hall, February 22, 1861, that the Declaration of Independence "gave liberty, not alone to the people of this country, but, I hope, to the world, for all future time." It embodied a "promise that in due time the weight would be lifted from the shoulders of all men." That "weight" was inequality, the unjust distribution of the burdens and advantages of life. Remembering Christian, in Bunyan's *Pilgrim's Progress*, with the weight strapped to his back, we recognize the analogy between Inequality and Original Sin. It was to be the role and fate of the United States, to be the means for lifting the former, as it was the role and fate of Israel and the Messiah, to be the means for the lifting of the latter. The pattern of political salvation in this world, and the salvation of souls, in this world and the next, was the analogy upon which Lincoln's understanding of American patriotism was grounded.

Lincoln revered the Constitution. He once explained the meaning of the Constitution upon a figure of speech drawn from Proverbs, 25:11. "A word fitly spoken, is like apples of gold in pictures of silver." The proposition of human equality, in the Declaration, was the word fitly spoken. This word was the apple of gold, around which the Constitution and the Union were the pictures of silver. "The *picture* was made *for* the apple — *not* the apple for the picture," Lincoln wrote. (The emphasis is Lincoln's.) Constitution and Union were means towards an end. But the end itself was set forth, not in the Constitution, but in the Declaration. In the Preamble to the Constitution, "We, the people . . . " set forth our intention to form "a more perfect Union." To say that the Union shall henceforth be more perfect, implies not only that it was less than perfect before, but that it shall be less than perfect hereafter. Yet the striving for greater perfection becomes intelligible in the light of the principles of the Declaration. Lincoln dealt with this matter in consummate fashion, in his speech on the Dred Scott decision. In it he refuted the contention, by Chief Justice Taney, repeated by Senator Stephen A. Douglas, that the Declaration of Independence could not have included Negroes among those "created equal," because the Founding Fathers made no attempt immediately to place them upon a footing of equality with white men. Lincoln observed that neither did they, then or thereafter, place all white men upon an equality with each other. In fact, he said, they had no power to do so. What they meant to do, and what they did, he said, was

> to set up a standard maxim for free society, which could be familiar to all, and revered by all; constantly looked to, constantly labored for, and even though never perfectly obtained, constantly approximated, and thereby constantly spreading and deepening its influence, and augmenting the happiness and value of life to all people of all colors everywhere.

Lincoln elsewhere compared this "standard maxim of free society" to the Scriptural injunction to "be perfect, as your Father in Heaven is perfect." The Savior, he said, did not expect men to be perfect, as God is. But God's perfection was a reason and a cause for men to strive towards perfection. It gave meaning and direction to their lives, notwithstanding the great distance that must remain, between man and God.

* * *

As I have written many times, the United States was the first nation to assert its independence, not in virtue of its own particular qualities, but in virtue of rights which it shared with all men everywhere. America's uniqueness has always been derived from its peculiar mission in exemplifying a regime founded upon the doctrine of the universality of human rights. America's assertion of the unity of the human race, with respect to such rights, has often been compared to Israel's assertion of the unity of God. The unity of God, and of the human race, are of course correlative unities. From them flow the parallelism of sacred history and the secular history of the United States, the most persistent and most powerful theme of our greatest oratory. Lincoln's sounding of this theme, in the Gettysburg Address, and in his Second Inaugural address, were already anticipated in the Lyceum speech. There, he spoke of "the proud fabric of our freedom" enduring upon such a "rock," that "as truly as has been said of the only greater institution, the gates of hell shall not prevail against it."

The "only greater institution," and its "rock," are told and foretold in the

Old and New Testaments. The New Testament, as everyone knows, begins by giving the genealogy, through three times fourteen generations, from Abraham to David to Joseph the husband of Mary, of whom Jesus was born. It is the lineal connection of Joseph with the House of David, descended from Abraham, Isaac, and Jacob, which is the necessary condition for the carrying forward of the Messianic promise. Yet the Messianic promise became a promise, not only to the descendants of the patriarchs, but to all mankind, through the Gospel's interpretation of that promise. If one had faith in Jesus as the Messiah, one inherited the promise given to Abraham, as if one "were blood of the blood, and flesh of the flesh," of the patriarchs. In sacred history, the particular becomes universal, in the transformation of the Old Testament promise by the New Testament. In the political order presided over by the United States, the universal rights of man become for the first time, the ground or basis of a particular regime. As the particular becomes universal in the sacred order, the universal becomes particular in the political order. We might even say, to elide the antinomy between the two orders, that with the American Founding the *logos*, the "word fitly spoken" became incarnate in an actual regime.

* * *

The question of the relationship of ethnicity, race, and religion, within the framework of American nationality and American citizenship, involves the relationship of the patriarchs of the older nationalities, of the "races" within the human race, and of the religious denominations within the larger family of Biblical religion. Both Judaism and Christianity understand their origins in terms of a miraculous display of divine power in regard to human generation. God's covenant with Israel resulted from a promise to Sarah, when she was more than eighty years old, that she would bear a son. Sarah, as we know, laughed. The conception of Jesus, by a young woman who had not known a man, was equally out of the order of nature. These two conceptions clearly resemble each other, as images in which the relationships were reversed. Not only do they link Judaism and Christianity, on the one hand, but they link the Bible and the ancient city on the other. For all ancient cities regarded their lawgivers as either gods, or the children of gods. And the children of gods were such by virtue of having one of their parents as a god, whether male or female. The ancient city was a patriarchal regime, but it was such, partly because the line of descent was unbroken, but also because it had been broken, viz., by the divine intervention in the line of human parentage, "in the beginning."

Lincoln's account of the origin and development of the United States, from the moment of independence, suggests the fulfillment of the Biblical promise of a land flowing with milk and honey, of a land in which the injunction to be fruitful and multiply was being carried out, and carried out with general satisfaction. The cause of that prosperity, as Lincoln says elsewhere, was the hope planted in the bosoms of all, by the divine promise implicit in the proposition of equality. Never in the history of the world had there been a regime that promised that what each man's hand had earned, belonged to the man whose hand had earned it. The energy and ambition resulting from the knowledge that the purpose of the law was to see to it that every man might have his own was the greatest spur to effort and achievement which the nature of man and the nature of things made possible. This was the inner spring and cause of American prosperity, of our becoming the greatest and freest nation of earth. Our freedom and our wealth were dependent upon each other, as forming an organic unity.

The uniqueness of the United States was uniquely dependent upon the implementing of the proposition of human equality. But the obstacle to its recognition, lay above all in the sense of the separateness of mankind, arising from its sense of the discreteness of its patrimonies, and of the patriarchs whence those patrimonies arose. Both Judaism and Christianity taught that we are all the children of the same God, that we all have the same human parentage, arising from Adam and Eve. Yet this seems to have had little effect, speaking practically or politically, upon the fellow-feeling of mankind. We all know the particular affinity between John Locke's *Second Treatise* and the Declaration of Independence. And most of us know that both in the *First* and *Second* of these *Treatises*, Locke presents himself as the antagonist of Sir John Filmer, whose *Patriarcha* grounded the authority of absolute monarchy upon the claims of the eldest line of descent from Adam. Although we may take it as settled that Locke refuted Filmer, it is not the case that a polity founded upon the doctrine of human equality—and its correlative popular sovereignty—can or should dispense with patriarchalism altogether. But then we all know, that in the popular mind, our equal descent from Adam and Eve can be regarded as a levelling as well as it can be regarded as an autocratic doctrine. "When Adam delved and Eve span, who was then a gentleman?" the old verse goes. Nevertheless, the common "gentility" of the human race does not keep each of us from looking to our own ancestors as constituting an aristocracy *for us*. And it is the natural tendency of mankind to regard it as a duty to maintain the superiority of our own gods or ancestors, among the nations, if need be by fighting to prove it. The characteristic result of that conflict, in the history of mankind, is that a conquering race lives among those it has conquered, and inequality is by this fact built into its class structure. But it is not only conquest that causes inequality to arise. It is not only descent, but legitimate descent, that marks the well born from the base born. A "natural" child is a bastard. And, as we know from Edmund's fate in *King Lear*, the gods do *not* stand up for bastards. Still further, within the line of legitimacy, not all are equal. The Bible's story—as for example that of Jacob and Esau—shows that "birthrights" within the patriarchal line are not equal, nor are they transmitted equally.

In Lincoln's Chicago speech, he speaks of the race of men living at the time of the Revolution—who made the Revolution—who "we" claim as fathers and grandfathers. The Fourth of July would not mean what is does mean, were it not part of an ancestral celebration. But what of those — e.g. Germans, Irish, French, Scandinavian — who have no family connection — as for example Lincoln himself had — with those "iron men" whose deeds were the cause of our prosperity. Settling here, they find themselves "our equals in all things." Yet they cannot trace their connection with the Fourth of July "by blood." Lincoln implies that, without that connection, their equality in all things will not truly be equality. They will not share that feeling of attachment, one to another, and to the country they inhabit, unless they can share in the sense of connection "by blood." But then they see in the Declaration of that very Fourth of July "that all men are created equal," and they understand that it is that very proposition which is the "father of all moral sentiment" in the men who become "our Fathers" on that very day. Then it is that they discover that they have the highest kind of right to claim those same men as blood of their blood and flesh of their flesh. We may paraphrase this thought, in terms of the Biblical tradition, by saying that it was God's intervention, in bringing about of the conception of Isaac and of Jesus, which established the authoritative character of fatherhood within the traditions they represented. The Hebrew patriarchs, and Jesus, became authorities for a tradition of morality, and of the right way of life, because there was incorporated into their births, a principle which was "the father of all moral principle." But although God intervened in the birth-process by which He established His tradition of revealed truth, He also created all men equal, and endowed them with equal rights. This equal Creation, and endowment with equal rights in that Creation, was grounded in self-evident truth. This meant that men participated in "the laws of nature and of nature's God," by *their* nature, which was reason. Aristotle says in his *Politics* that, although the *polis* is by nature, and is prior to each individual or family in the order of nature, that it nonetheless required institution. And the man who first united the scattered families and clans and villages into the political association, was the greatest of benefactors. It is precisely in this sense, that the American Founding Fathers, who first united men into the political association in accordance with the principles of Creation and the laws of nature, are to be regarded as the greatest of all political benefactors. Their work is to be regarded in the same light, and on the same level, as the founding of that church which provides for man's eternal salvation. Hence it is that Lincoln says that there is only one "greater institution" than that of the American Founding. And it is also the case that the regime which reflects God's Creation in its laws best reflects God's intention for man's earthly welfare, and is also equally congruent with man's eternal welfare. For the American republic, as Lincoln said in the Lyceum speech, "conduces more essentially to the end of civil and religious liberty, than any of which the history of former times tells us." Jefferson, in the Virginia Statute of Religious Liberty, laid down the principles of religious freedom, as surely as he laid down those of civil freedom in the Declaration. There he called it an "impious presumption" that "fallible and uninspired men," which is what all civil rulers in the world were, should prescribe the religious opinions which their fellow citizens should profess. Bribing people to profess such opinions, either with rewards or punishments, may beget habits of hypocrisy and meanness, but can never make true men. Any establishment of religion, Jefferson held—and Lincoln certainly agreed—could only maintain "false religions," as it had done "over the greatest part of the world, and through all time." The emancipation of our civil rights from our religious opinions was necessary, *both* for civil liberty *and* religious liberty. To say that it was necessary for religious liberty, is to say that it was necessary for religious truth. For "truth is great and will prevail . . . unless by human interposition disarmed of her natural weapons, free argument and debate. . . ." This, Jefferson held, and Lincoln agreed, was the ground equally of moral and political truth, and of religious truth.

The regime of the American Founding was then the first in the history of the world fully consistent with the ground of the truth about man's nature, whether from the perspective of divine revelation, or of natural reason. It is false to say, as some do say, that American republicanism is indifferent to man's eternal salvation. As George Washington declared in his famous letter to the Hebrew congregation at Newport, "It is now no more that toleration is spoken of as if it were by the indulgence of one class of people that another enjoyed the exercise of their inherent natural rights, for, happily, the Government of the United States . . . gives to bigotry no sanction, to persecution no assistance. . . ." In his beautiful prayer, at the end of the letter, Washington invokes "the Father of all mercies" to "make us all in our several vocations useful here, and in His own due time and way, everlastingly happy." Some see the end or purpose of the regime as that "utility" which belongs to "vocations here." Of course, our civil liberty enhances to the utmost our possibility of being thus useful. But our happiness here is certainly dependent upon our opinion as to our prospects of everlasting happiness. And such opinions are, in accordance with those opinions Washington shared with Jefferson, for which Lincoln honored them both, raised to the highest point in human experience, by those principles of civil and religious liberty incorporated into the Founding.

For the Truro Synagogue in Newport, and for all the children of the stock of Abraham who have come to dwell in the land, it might surely be said, as Washington said, that by the doctrine of natural rights, no one need worship God in his own way by the sufferance of anyone else. Everyone might then sit under his own vine and fig tree, with none to make him afraid. America might indeed become a Zion for the Jews, by becoming the Zion for all mankind.

In the course of the 19th century, nationalism, which in the American Revolution meant the natural right of all peoples, and every people, to be governed by a government deriving its just powers from their consent, was transformed into something very different. By the Declaration of

Independence, the right to be governed by one's consent was an inference from the proposition that all men are created equal. Because of original natural equality, civil society is a voluntary association, arising from the contract or compact, that each makes with all, and all with each. In the later struggle for national independence in the Old World, of Poles, Czechs, Greeks, Croatians, Jews, Arabs, and many others, the right to freedom became the historic right of historic peoples in their collective existence. Of course, by the Declaration a people also has a collective right, but it is the collective right of those who have formed a voluntary association, an association that is governed by, and limited in its government by, "the laws of nature and of nature's God." This later nationalism saw peoples as the outcome, not of voluntary association, but of historic destiny and historic necessity. This destiny and necessity was different from, and transcended, what was common to them and all other peoples. It was unique in them, and was highest for them, transcending anything that arose from their common humanity. From this perspective, it became commonplace to see, for example, a particular people, making the most heroic sacrifices in behalf of their own national independence, while displaying the utmost indifference, if not intolerance, to the claims of others (e.g. the Jews in their midst). Hereditary enmities—feudalism in its purest sense, meaning feuds carried on for no other reason than that they were inherited—became features of nationalism as it developed after the eighteenth century, but in opposition to the cosmopolitanism of the American doctrines, enshrined in the American Founding. Nothing has become more commonplace in America, and yet nothing is more extraordinary in itself, than to see Teuton and Slav, Greek and Turk, Protestant and Catholic Ulstermen, Palestinian Arab and Jew, who would in their old world habitat be busily engaged in killing each other, living as the best of friends in the framework of American life. One must add, of course, that feuds are not unknown in American life—as we recall from reading *Huckleberry Finn*. But reminding ourselves of this exception only serves to underline the fundamental reality of American life, as ways flowing from the principles of the Founding, rather than as exceptions to those principles.

Appendix A

War, Peace, and the American Constitution
A Reply to Walter Berns' *Wall Street Journal* Article on the Peace Academy

In "Congress Is Saying, Give Peace a Grant," (*Wall Street Journal*, August 2, 1982) Walter Berns subjects the currently fashionable idea of an Academy of Peace and Conflict Resolution, to a becoming ridicule. At least, that is what, at first, he *seems* to be doing. His argument circles strangely back to the very propositions which at the outset are held to be absurd. He conjures up the image of the Ayatollah Khomeini, Saddam Hussein, Yasser Arafat, and Menachim Begin, as Fellows—and Grantees—of the Academy, meeting in seminar under the auspices of our scientific conflict resolutionists. The principle of such a science, as Berns rightly notices, is at least three hundred years old. It is an idea whose time has long since come—and gone.

The idea in question was expressed most forcefully—as Berns says—in the political philosophy of Thomas Hobbes, who did not doubt that the implementation of his teaching would result in "an immortal peace." Hobbes believed that all men by nature cared above all for bodily self-preservation. He thought that the passion for such preservation was the only rational passion, and that reason itself became powerful in human affairs only as it was in the service of this passion. According to Berns, "our legislators seem unaware of the fact that they hold office under a Constitution inspired by a handful of political philosophers," preeminent among them being Hobbes (who, however, received "help" from John Locke). Berns does not doubt however that Hobbism is the core of our Constitution.

The new political philosophy (of three hundred years ago) "succeeded in discovering precisely . . . how to achieve peace," Berns says. This discovery took the form of "a radical change in the acknowledged purpose or goal of political society." "No longer," writes Berns, "would the 'city' attempt to satisfy the desires of the soul, for it is the pursuit of such desires—glory or salvation, for example—that promotes conflict and war; it would confine itself to satisfying the desires of the body, or providing the conditions under which they might be satisfied." The good citizens of this dispensation, according to Berns, would "subordinate their other desires," viz., for such discredited goals as virtue, honor, glory, or the favor of Almighty God, to the desires of the body alone. How contemptible these Hobbesian or Lockeian citizens would be, Berns does not leave in any doubt. "During the 1960's," he writes, those "would unknowingly echo Hobbes and Locke," who said, "make love . . . not war." Berns, however, spares us the elucidation which would make plain that by "love" these sixties radicals did not mean "love."

Professor Berns seems however to patronize this same Hobbism, when he declares that because of it, liberal democracies have never made war upon each other. He concludes therefore that the way to world peace, is to propagate the cause of liberal democracy. This conclusion is certainly correct, but it is nonetheless stultified because it is derived from false premises. After all, if liberal democracies were peaceful because they were Hobbesian, *they would never have gone to war at all*. According to Hobbes, courage is not a virtue, and every truly rational man, like Hobbes himself, would (as Hobbes boasted), flee at the first sign of danger. Berns does not consider that the reason liberal democracies do not go to war with each other is that those who share common principles are disposed to be friendly with each other, and are not disposed to fight over mere differences of interest.

America—and other democracies, like Britain's—have gone to war, time and again, in defense of right and freedom and without regard to bodily, or personal, self-preservation. The Signers of our Declaration of Independence pledged their lives, their fortunes, and their sacred honor, to their cause. Many of them lost their lives, and many of them lost their fortunes, but none of them were dishonored. Neither George Washington, nor Abraham Lincoln, like countless of their fellow countrymen, for a moment cared more for their lives or their property, than for those goods of the soul with which they identified the cause of their country.

When the Union armies marched to the Battle Hymn of the Republic, they sang, "As He died to make men holy, let us die to make men free." American freedom has always been seen, by its best representatives, as instrumental to salvation, both in this world and the next. Material prosperity has been seen as a sign of God's blessing, at least as often as the result of licensed selfishness, although the latter has undoubtedly played its role. But it has been the willingness of Americans to die for principle which, in the end, has sealed the faith, and given the character, to "the land of the free and the home of the brave."

Hobbism, considered merely in the light that Berns has presented it, is the very negation of Americanism. It would indeed be the principle of an Academy of Peace and Conflict Resolution. But Professor Berns, in the end, seems to repudiate the idea of such an academy, not because of its baseness, but because it would be redundant.

Appendix B

A Reply to Irving Kristol's Strictures on the Insignificance of the American Civil War for the American Political Tradition*

It was said of the French emigres of the revolution that began in 1789, that they could learn nothing and could forget nothing. Of Mr. Kristol's version of American history, one can say is that he seems never to have had anything to forget. In his celebrated bicentennial lecture, he declared that the American political tradition, in the period after the Founding, became "an inarticulate tradition." There was, he says, nothing but "intellectual sloth, engendered by success." This sloth was so pervasive, that it "rendered us incompetent to explain [our] successful Revolution to the world, and even to ourselves." Yet the period after 1800 was one in which Jefferson, Madison, Monroe, and John Quincy Adams were presidents. It was followed in turn by a period in which there was a gigantic struggle over something called "Nullification." This engaged some of the most brilliant polemics and dialectics in the political history of the world, with Madison buttressing the position of Jackson and Webster, on the one side, while John C. Calhoun stood (as he seemed to himself) like Samson in the temple of the Philistines, on the other. In the struggle over slavery extension, John Quincy Adams laid down a position followed over the next generation by Abraham Lincoln, not to mention Webster, Seward, Chase, Sumner and a host of others. Yet during all of this time, according to Kristol, intellectual sloth prevailed.

What Kristol wrote in his bicentennial lecture, I subjected to some twenty-five printed pages of critical analysis in *How to Think About the American Revolution*. To this critique Kristol has never deigned to reply. Why Kristol delivers his opinions *ex cathedra*, why he will not offer reasons either to support or defend them was explained in the course of his public remarks at Wake Forest, February 3rd last. He cited William James as authority for the proposition that "philosophy is a matter of temperament." Of course, history is but a branch of "philosophy," thus conceived. If one's temperament determines one's opinions, then there is no reason to discuss the reasons for one's opinions. This leads, as any reflective person can see, to radical historicism and nihilism.

In his current rhetorical exhibition, Kristol restates his view of the American political tradition most succinctly by saying that "the American people seem never to have been torn by conflicting interpretations of the American political tradition, though scholars may be." He says that "our very bloody Civil War had surprisingly little effect on the course of American history." He thinks that any American history textbook could replace the chapter on the Civil War "by a single sentence to the effect that slavery was abolished by constitutional amendment in 1865." "The Civil War," Kristol concludes, "was and is a memorable event—but not any kind of turning point in American history." Kristol may say that the Civil War is a memorable event, but he does not seem to remember any event that occurred in it. Had he done so, he could hardly have ignored the fact that the 13th amendment was preceded by the Emancipation Proclamation. Of course, by the Civil War, we do not refer solely to the events that divided Fort Sumter from Appomatox. We think of that deep division, within the American political tradition—the division whose existence Kristol denies—that was brought to decision and action, in the course of "fourscore and seven years." It was then decided, whether this nation, conceived in liberty and dedicated to the proposition that all men are created equal, could endure. At the same time, a larger question was also decided: whether any nation, so conceived and dedicated, could endure. The American Civil War largely answered the question of whether free, popular government would "perish from the earth."

The thesis of the Gettysburg Address—Garry Wills and Irving Kristol to the contrary notwithstanding—was not something Abraham Lincoln dreamed up *ex nihilo*. In the very first paragraph of the *Federalist*, Publius patronizes the opinion that

> *it seems to have been reserved to the people of this country, by their conduct and example, to decide the important question, whether societies of men are really capable or not of establishing good government from reflection and choice, or whether they are forever destined to depend for their political constitutions on accident and force.*

In the rebellion against his election in 1861, Lincoln reduced this question to the issue between bullets and ballots.

That the fate of much more than the United States was truly at stake in the Civil War may be seen by asking ourselves some simple questions. What would the history of the 20th century, the century of world wars, have been like, had the United States been divided into two or more rival republics, allied to rival powers in Europe and Asia? Still more, what would this history have been like, had the United States entered the 20th century, a single nation, but one in which slavery was lawful in all the states old as well as new, North as well as South? Lincoln's policy not only preserved the Union, but preserved it from becoming all slave. Kristol seems to agree with those so-called revisionists, who called the Civil War "an unnecessary war," because they thought that the question of slavery was a spurious question.

Kristol says that "there never really was a distinctively Southern political tradition, nor did the war give rise to one. A textbook on American intellectual history could safely ignore the Civil War..." The kindest thing one can say about this, is that Kristol seems never to have read a speech or pamphlet or book by a Southern (or other) defender, either of slavery or of Jim Crow. He seems to think there is no "distinctive" difference between a political tradition dedicated to equal political rights for all, and one dedicated to racial subjugation and racial oppression. If that were true, it would make no difference whether in our time the United States, as a slave nation, had supported the cause of Adolph Hitler, or, as a free one, had supported the cause of Winston Churchill. And, in that case, it would have made no difference whether or not Kristol and I were here today to differ as to the meaning of the American political tradition!

1982

*Kristol's remarks form part of the text of his lecture to the Tocqueville Forum at Wake Forest University, February 3, 1982.

Sodomy and the Academy

The Assault on the Family and Morality by "Liberation" Ethics

I n a recent article ("Our Listless Universities," *National Review*, December 10, 1982), Allan Bloom has given us a brilliant Theophrastian "character" of the life and thought now dominant in the American academy. "I begin with my conclusion," he writes,

> *students in our best universities do not believe anything, and those universities are doing nothing about it, nor can they.*

"Doing nothing" is something of a play on words, since it is nihilism that the universities "do." Professor Bloom concedes that his initial "nothing" is indeed "something," when he says that

> *The heads of the young are stuffed with a jargon derived from the despair of European thinkers, gaily repackaged for American consumption, and presented as the foundation of pluralism. . . . The new soul's language consists in terms like value, ideology, self, commitment, identity—every word derived from recent German philosophy, and each carrying a heavy baggage of dubious theoretical interpretation of which its users are blissfully unaware. They take such language to be as unproblematic and immediate as night and day. It now constitutes our peculiar common sense.*

Some time ago an article was published that might very well have formed the text for Professor Bloom's critique. It appeared in *Current*, which calls itself "The Public Affairs Magazine of Claremont McKenna College," and was written by Professor Steven Smith, my colleague in the Philosophy Department. It was a description by Professor Smith of his very popular course, "Theories of the Good Life," which the editors of *Current* proudly presented as the College's cultural complement to its acknowledged excellence in business economics.

Current went out of its way to draw attention to Professor Smith's article by illustrating the magazine's cover with a Daumier-like cartoon of a character called "Mr. Goodlyfe." Mr. Goodlyfe was praised as representing what the editors said they liked to think of as "the guiding principle" of a CMC education. I wrote an essay about the cartoon and Smith's article about his course, entitled "Looking at Mr. Goodlyfe." This *Current* refused to publish, but it may be found above in the present volume. The only point that need be repeated here from my previous criticism of Professor Smith is that he himself had declared that he had no idea (that he knew nothing) of what the good life was. He had abandoned any attempt to discover anything about it by reading great books which ostensibly bore upon the question of the good life, e.g., books like the Bible, or books by such authors as Plato, Aristotle, Aquinas, Hegel, Marx, Mill, or Dewey. Studying philosophic books had, he said, only led him into a deep "personal crisis" from which he had emerged to tell his students that they must make up their own minds as to what kinds of lives they ought to lead. He was there to "facilitate" their thinking, but he could say nothing at all as to what they ought to think.

In the new *Current* (Winter/Spring 1983), Professor Smith returns to his theme in his "Reflections on Human Liberation." Although Professor Smith insisted that he did *not* know what the good life was, he is extremely confident in his declarations about human liberation. Here we have a text-book version of that nihilism, derived from recent German philosophy, "gaily repackaged for American consumption," of which Professor Bloom wrote. Here we can see exactly what it is with which the heads of the young are being "stuffed" in "our best universities." Professor Smith's article is instructive, not because it has any significance, either of originality or profundity — since it does not — but because it is so typical of what is being said in so many classrooms.

For Professor Smith, "human liberation" is something of a misnomer. The liberation of which he speaks relates to a "self" or to "selves" which are not identifiably human. Their "genders" appear not to actually belong to them: They are labels affixed by society. The reality of actual human beings, for most of us, however, begins with those we call our mothers and fathers. But "male" and "female" do not appear to be distinctions of nature, or of genuine reality, to Professor Smith. They are instead "roles" which are "stereotyped" by society, and by "social pressure." Human liberation—better called "self" or "selves" liberation—becomes above all emancipation from those stereotyped roles. Human nature, for those of us who believe what our eyes tell us, is partitioned into men and women. Moreover, the differences between men and women are the differences which instruct us in the reality of the whole of nature. For "nature" refers primarily to all those things that have their being by generation and growth. The "natural" things are distinguished from the "artificial" things, the things that are "made" but do not "grow." We human beings are "makers" of things, and we cause our world to be filled with artifacts, some of them wonderful indeed. But we ourselves are not artifacts. We—each of us—grow from fertilized seeds or eggs, whose life is not from any human maker. Man the maker is not the maker of man, because he is not the maker of nature. He has a nature, and he is part of nature. It is the *eros* acting in and through the generation of natural things by which all living things, including human things, are endowed with vitality. The forms of human life, including the forms of human art, derive their vitality from the vitality that is in nature.

In nature, the distinction between male and female is the most fundamental of all distinctions. It is more fundamental than the distinction between man and beast, more fundamental even than the distinction between man and God. This is because human nature comes to sight as part of nature. And nature comes to sight as the *eros* subsisting in the distinction or partition within the whole of nature, which is grounded in maleness and femaleness. The radical European thought alluded to by Professor Bloom is nihilistic. It denies that we have any genuine knowledge of the external world. It begins with the observation that we have access to that world—if it can be said to exist at all—only by sense perception. Sense perception, however, takes place only internally within us. What we call "sight" refers to images that are confined within the brain. And the brain has no way of "verifying" the character of those images. There is, so to speak, no "on sight inspection" possible, that will confirm or correct the judgment made by the senses of the objects ostensibly sensed. Nihilism begins in the denial of any ground for faith in the reality of sense perception. Nihilism declares that all we can do is to frame hypotheses about a world that is permanently hypothetical. And we can frame these hypotheses, not for the sake of knowledge—which is impossible—but for the sake of power. "Knowledge" becomes the ground and cause of power. It does not consist—as the older view maintained—in comparisons of assertions made about reality with reality itself. Hence traditional morality is an illusion, or delusion, since it is an opinion, or a class of opinions, predicated upon there being a particular class of beings—human beings—among all the beings, with respect to whom norms of conduct are affirmed. A theoretical or contemplative account of the world underlies, and is presupposed by, the moral prescriptions as to how we should act in the world. Nihilism, however, sees moral prescriptions and commandments merely as manifestations of the will, a will that imposes or is imposed upon. Nihilism is essentially non-erotic, because in denying nature it denies the reality that is at the heart of nature, *eros*. Nihilism is moreover non-philosophic, or anti-philosophic. Philosophy means love of wisdom, but the wisdom with which philosophy is concerned, the wisdom for which the philosopher is erotically striving, is wisdom with respect to nature. Nihilism, denying nature, must deny philosophy as well. "Selves" then are not *a priori* human and hence are not *a priori* sons, fathers, brothers, or daughters, mothers, sisters. For the very words, fathers and sons, imply beings bound to each other by duties, by moral bonds, that the nihilist (or liberationist) cannot recognize. Man as a class of beings does not correspond to any idea of man, because there are no ideas, properly so called. There are only unconfirmed impressions. Individual consciousness is only the reaction within ourselves of the domination or subjection that results from collisions that occur in a metaphysical void or abyss. This is the perspective of liberation ethics. In the traditional morality of western man, it was taught that man was made in the image of God ("male and female created he them") and that he imitated the divine goodness by obeying the divine commandments. Alternatively, it was taught that man was endowed with reason by nature and that, by the right use of reason, he might find out the rules of conduct befitting his nature. In discovering these rules, man would understand why it was good to obey them, and to internalize them. Liberation ethics, as we shall see, places great store by spontaneity. But such spontaneity has nothing in common with that habit of acting well that we call "good character."

Professor Smith is an apostle of freedom, but it is altogether "freedom from." It is altogether different from that unalienable right to liberty esteemed in our Declaration of Independence. For that was based upon a "decent respect to the opinions of mankind." These in turn were based upon "the laws of nature and of nature's God," which elicit no respect from Professor Smith. The laws of nature are in his view grounded in "gender stereotypes," the source of what he finds to be "the most insidious of all forms of tyranny." Taxation without representation is utterly remote from the question of freedom uppermost in his consciousness. Taxation concerns property, property the family, and the family, the morality of genders, which he calls "tyranny." Freedom, for Smith, means not to be held back, or averted from any desired outcome. This means that in the most fundamental respect, Smith is an anarchist. No restraint can be justified intrinsically. Any restraint that is "appropriate" is prudential rather than moral. Certain things "ought not" to be done, from Smith's point of view, only because they get you into trouble, not because they are wrong. Whether he will admit it or not, Smith's argument is an argument for despotism, because the only way in which one can maximize one's desired outcomes is to be more powerful than any of the other selves with whom—or which—one's own self might come into collision. One cannot, within the framework of liberation ethics, distinguish freedom from license, or even attribute to freedom itself anything properly called "goodness." Absence of restraint is desirable, not because it is good, but because it is desired. This tautology may be—indeed it is—absurd. But the nihilist universe is absurd, and the liberation ethicist glories in this absurdity. And so he will speak glowingly—even eloquently—about the terrors of oppression, and of the bright sunlit uplands of liberation, without regard to how base, or even disgusting, the liberated self may be.

* * *

Here is how Smith begins what he calls "a brief excursus into philosophy," for which he himself claims "no originality or novelty."

The root notion of freedom is, I believe, the spontaneous, uninhibited expression of the integrated self. Such a notion presumes that there is a self, as more than simply a conduit for external forces funneling unaltered through the organism. Such a notion implies agency: *the self is naturally active, creative, productive, seeking to engage the world rather than passively reacting.*

It is difficult to see what the word "integrated" adds to the word "self" in the first sentence quoted above. Certainly Smith's use of "integrated" is not to be understood in a sense opposed either to "disintegrated" or to "segregated." More important, it has nothing to do with the word "integrity," which refers to the goodness of moral character. A man of integrity is one who can be relied upon, something that can hardly be said of someone who is notable primarily for being "spontaneous" and "uninhibited." Someone of good moral character is not liberated from the moral law: on the contrary, he is bound by it. Being bound by morality—in particular being bound by the obligations pertaining to "gender stereotypes"—is something Smith identifies with oppression.

But what in the world is a "self"? Smith's vocabulary appears to be derived from Kant. By saying that the self is not merely a conduit for external forces, Smith is claiming for it the status of a *noumenon* as distinct from a *phenomenon:* that is to say, it has *freedom* as distinct from being a subject of *determinism.* Freedom, for Kant, meant the ability of a rational being to obey a law that it has given to itself. The categorical imperative, according to Kant, is the form of the will of a rational being. It commands us to act so that the maxim of our will may become a universal law. Liberation ethics, however, would emancipate us from the "social pressures" of "gender stereotypes." The maxim of the will endorsed by Smith with the greatest emphasis is one that would resist the social pressures which engender "homophobia," or fear of homosexuality. By the Kantian formula, one would have to ask, could the maxim of becoming homosexual become a universal law? The answer, of course, is that it could not, without the human race becoming extinct in one generation. This, it seems to me, is something that Kant would hold contradicts the idea of a good will. Smith's claim of freedom for the self is then not Kantian.

Smith does however say that "the self is naturally active, creative, productive." But he gives no substantive meaning to activity, creativity, or productivity. All he can say about what a self does is that it "engages the world," instead of "passively reacting." But what in the world does a free "self" do—or what is it like—when it is actively engaged? At the end of his article, Smith celebrates the consummation of "human liberation" by saying that it means "simply becoming who we are: free to be . . . you and me." (The hiatus between "be" and "you" is Smith's.) Smith collapses the distinction between "being" and "becoming." Because nothing genuinely "is," nothing is prevented from "becoming" anything else. Once one has abandoned the concept of gender, then nothing can be properly said to be engendered, and there is no directedness in becoming. Becoming has taken on an entirely new meaning. In nature, being and becoming are terms correlated with male and female. In a pre-nihilist universe, it would make no sense to speak of an acorn—or anything else that grows—"becoming what it is." An acorn is an acorn: but for an acorn to "become" something, is for it to become a sapling and an oak tree. Without the distinction between potentiality and actuality, correlated with male and female, freedom can mean anything—or nothing—and can mean both anything and nothing simultaneously! "What is human liberation?" Smith asks finally. "My answer," he replies, "is unformed, open, almost empty...." In fact, it *is* empty. In the context of his primary concern, "in the context of sexism," says Smith, "human liberation means the removal of impediments based simply on sex or gender...." But selves, we remind ourselves, are according to Smith beings whose consciousness has been engendered by their "engagement" with the world. And this engagement, it seems, is nothing but the engagement with impediments. Without the impediments, there would be no engagement; without engagement, no consciousness. The end of engagement is the end of life. Liberation means death.

* * *

Smith continues his "excursus into philosophy" as follows.

> *The absence of freedom means, therefore, the presence of blocks or limitations that prevent unfettered expressions of the self. In the first instance such blocks are purely external: "I tried to go through the doorway, but he stood in the way"; "I wanted some food, but there was none in the house." This form of unfreedom ... may be called objective constraint.*

We see that a man standing in a doorway preventing us from going through it is called an "objective constraint." But there is no such thing as an abstract man standing in an abstract doorway. An actual man in an actual doorway may be a fireman, keeping real people from a burning and collapsing building. Or it may be someone from the bomb squad, keeping others out until the bomb discovered within has been defused or removed to a safe place for detonation. Smith's "self," without a gender, is also without a motive. As to the food that is wanted: we may ask, why was there no food in the house? Is the cause poverty? Or is Smith on a diet, and the house was emptied of food to help him stay on his diet? Or perhaps there was a power failure, and the food in the refrigerator was removed to a place where it could be kept from spoiling? Clearly, we cannot characterize hypothetical constraints as actual—or objective—constraints without knowing the motives and circumstances of the agents.

Smith's "second form of unfreedom" arises, he says,

> *not from outright blocks or impediments, but from threat. Because we seek to avoid certain outcomes that we find aversive, the prospect of an aversive outcome*

is felt as a constraint: "I didn't want to give him the money, but he had a gun"; "I was afraid she'd scream at me if I went home, so I stayed with a friend." This form of unfreedom, in which an actual threat causes me to act differently than I would otherwise prefer to act, is more or less captured by the term intimidation.

Anything that causes me to act differently from the way I would "prefer to act" is, according to Smith, simply and categorically a form of "unfreedom," however base or foolish my preference may be. Concerning preferences, "non est disputandum," says Mr. Goodlyfe. But let us look again at Mr. Smith's examples. Here we see that one man's desired outcome is another man's "aversive outcome." Does not the man behind the gun get what he wants? And why should he not? Perhaps he is a policeman, and the money in Smith's possession has just been stolen from a bank. And who is the woman who would scream at Smith? What in the world has he done to make her want to scream at him?

Clearly, it is not possible to speak intelligently about human liberty, or human liberation, without reference or regard to the ends for the sake of which the liberty itself is desired. The mindlessness of Smith's examples is incomprehensible. No one of ordinary common sense would be deceived by them. Here we are confronted with a trained incapacity to think that is perhaps possible only as a result of a doctorate in philosophy from Harvard. Remembering William F. Buckley, Jr.'s famed aphorism, that it would be better to be governed by the first 200 names in the Boston telephone directory than by the Harvard faculty, one wonders whether it is not just as true that it would be better to be instructed in philosophy by any of these same 200. On the ambiguity of freedom or liberation, apart from the motives of those laying claim to it, we may very profitably contemplate these reflections of Abraham Lincoln, in the midst of the Civil War.

The world has never had a good definition of the word liberty, and the American people just now [April 1864] are much in want of one. We all declare for liberty; but in using the same word we do not all mean the same thing. With some the word liberty may mean for each man to do as he pleases with himself, and the product of his labor; while with others the word may mean for some men to do as they please with other men, and the product of other men's labor. Here are two, not only different, but incompatible things, called by the same name — liberty. . . . The shepherd drives the wolf from the sheep's throat, for which the sheep thanks the shepherd as a liberator, while the wolf denounces him for the same act as the destroyer of liberty, especially as the sheep was a black one. Plainly, the sheep and the wolf are not agreed upon a definition of the word liberty. . . .

Smith seems incapable of distinguishing the sheep's from the wolf's definition of liberty or liberation.

* * *

Smith refers to a third form of unfreedom as follows.

> *. . . since we have a memory for aversive outcomes and can form behavioral habits [sic], we may internalize the external threat and come to govern ourselves by it, even when the threat is not apparent: "I know it's ok, but I'm still afraid to say how I really feel"; "I could never wear that in public."*

Once again, Smith abstracts from the external threat and the outcome that the threat averts. If, every time a wolf attacks a sheep, he is beaten by a shepherd, perhaps he will stop molesting sheep. And if, instead of a vulpine sheep molester, we have a human child molester, we can hardly regret the internalization of the external threat, or regard it as a form of unfreedom. Smith says that there is something he knows is ok, but is still afraid to say. But how can anyone properly say that this constitutes unfreedom without first passing judgment upon what it is that he wishes to say? That Smith believes it is ok does not make it ok. Is it ok to falsely shout "Fire" in a crowded theater? How ok is it to speak in support of William Shockley's theories about the genetic inferiority of welfare recipients? How ok is it to speak in support of the authenticity of the Protocols of the Elders of Zion? Or to deny that the Holocaust ever took place? I am confident that Smith himself does not think these things are ok, but he must know that there are others who do think so.

Smith regards as unfreedom the internalization of customs that dictate what we wear. But is this not silly? One would not expect President Reagan to dress for his inauguration the way President Washington dressed for his. But Mr. Reagan does not think the worse of George Washington for having followed the custom of his day. To call such things "inhibitions" and declare them to be forms of unfreedom is preposterous. Are we inhibited in being obliged to observe the rules of the road? Or to refrain from drinking while driving?

* * *

We come to the fourth and final form of unfreedom described by Smith. This is

> *the experience of aversive outcomes which may condition us so thoroughly that we suppress or deny our inner life and become literally unaware of those impulses in us that have led to unpleasant results in the past: "I'm not angry!"; "I have just no interest in sex." When self-restraint and inhibition have become so complete . . . unfreedom may be called simply self-denial.*

But how does Smith know that self-denial—in these or in any other instances—is a form of unfreedom? Both Mahatma Gandhi and Martin Luther

King, Jr., believed that the theory and practice of non-violent resistance required the elimination of anger towards the oppressor. And both of them regarded non-violence as a liberating doctrine. Gandhi also believed in the suppression, or sublimation, of the sexual impulses. His belief in this respect was similar to, although not identical with, that of St. Paul who, in I *Corinthians*, praises celibacy as a higher state than matrimony. While I myself agree neither with Gandhi nor with Paul, I would never refer to them as inhibited men. Right or wrong, their powerful convictions were an expression of their freedom, not of servitude.

* * *

Smith concedes that inhibitions—or, more generally, restraints upon the spontaneity of the self—are not always to be characterized negatively or pejoratively. Nevertheless, they are all, in the precise sense, forms of unfreedom in his way of thinking.

> *It is worth noting* [he writes] *that despite their pejorative associations, these phenomena of unfreedom are not always inappropriate or wrong. The world is not wholly malleable to our wills, and may often be objectively threatening; thus in order to survive and flourish, we must develop a complete system of self-control and self-restraint. Inhibition is appropriate in the presence of a sleeping tiger—or a menacing street gang.*

Smith does not say, or admit in any way, that anything is wrong in itself. He says that some things are "inappropriate or wrong." But the "or" is only an alternative expression for what is meant as "inappropriate." Nothing would be wrong, from his perspective, were it not for the fact that "the world is not wholly malleable to our wills." In Smith's universe, there are no moral commandments that are categorical, either in the Mosaic ("Thou shalt not . . .") or in the Kantian sense ("Act so that the maxim of your will may be a universal law . . ."). For Smith, nothing is good in itself unless it is the uninhibited spontaneity of the integrated self. What is called "wrong" is merely what is inopportunistic, because it invites the retaliation of someone who may be stronger than you are.

Smith speaks of the prudence properly elicited by "a sleeping tiger" and by "a menacing street gang." But what about the tiger and the gang? Should they be denied their freedom? Smith tacitly identifies himself with the potential victims; but suppose he represented the strong, instead of the weak, in these examples. What principle would deny him his prey? Would not his "uninhibited spontaneity" properly fulfill itself in a murderous assault? If we recall Lincoln's analogy of the sheep and the wolf, we must ask why we should—if we are shepherds—prefer the freedom of the sheep to that of the wolf? Since Smith recognizes only "selves," there is no ground upon which to prefer one self to another self. Or, perhaps we should say, there is no ground for preferring any other self to one's own self. To identify freedom with the will of a self is to authorize unlimited selfishness. Which self prevails in the jungle of selves will depend then upon who is the stronger. Justice—if one can speak of such a thing, and Smith does not speak of it—is clearly the interest of the stronger. To be as free as possible, one must be as strong as possible. The freest man, clearly, is the tyrant. Smith's argument is an argument for despotism or tyranny. Although the world may not be perfectly malleable, even to a tyrant, it is far more malleable to him than it is to any non-tyrant. If, for example, we compare and contrast the freedom enjoyed by Hitler and Stalin (and the latter, to the end of his days) with that of Churchill and Roosevelt, we would, by Smith's criteria, have to pronounce Hitler and Stalin the freer men by far. Their uninhibited spontaneity was not checked or restrained by constitutions, legislatures, courts, or laws of any kind.

* * *

Smith's article culminates in an attack upon tyranny. But the oppression which concerns him is not that of the death camps or of the Gulag Archipelago. Not the police state, but "sexist" society, is the cause of what he calls "this death of the human spirit." This death, moreover, is caused, not by the Gestapo or the KGB, but "by the dead weight of social pressure." This "oppression . . . is exercised by the strait-jacket of sex role stereotyping." He turns first to the case of women, although it becomes clear that they are not his primary concern.

> Solely on the basis of their sex, women are subject to a variety of objective constraints, usually in the form of denied access to benefits and positions that are reserved for men. Also on the basis of their sex women are made vulnerable to intimidation of various kinds, most notably as potential victims of sexual assault. . . .

That women are subject to many constraints because of their sex has, at least traditionally, been true. Parents have, for some reason, tended to worry more about the whereabouts of their teen-age daughters than about their teen-age sons. Smith himself mentions "sexual assault" as the most notable kind of female vulnerability. But it never occurs to him that the basis of this vulnerability is not society, but nature. The reason that women tend to be raped by men, rather than by other women, or that men are seldom (if ever) raped by women, is not something that happens because of sexual stereotyping by social pressure. There is a physical difference between men and women (but not between "selves"), one aspect of which is that men often, if not usually, have the physical and anatomical force with which to commit this act of aggression. What Smith calls "gender stereotyping" is then grounded, not in opinion, but in nature. The traditional morality which follows from this "stereotyping" is designed to place prudent boundaries upon the freedom of women, for their own protection. But it is also designed to inculcate into the male sex a sense of duty, not only not to abuse women by physical force, but to stand ready at every moment to fight in their defense against anyone who would use force against them. The "gender stereotyping," which Smith identifies with oppression, arose in fact to prevent oppression. Nothing is more deeply engrained in the moral code of all civilized societies—and even of many primitive societies—than the idea of respect for womanhood and the abhorrence of force against women. Smith deplores the "social pressures" by which he finds boys and men to be intimidated if they display "unmasculine" or "effeminate" behavior. But reason, as well as instinct, tells us that an effeminate male cannot, or is not likely, to play the man in the most fundamental of all human duties, the duty of protecting the weak from the depredations of the spontaneous and uninhibited strong. Certainly the importance, and the bearing, of the physical differences between men and women changes with the progress of technology. The ideas of the proper division of labor between men and women ought to change as the economy and society change. But the ultimate ground of "sex role stereotyping" is not society, but nature. This may now be less obvious than it once was, but it is no less true. In protecting women from the unjust aggression of brutal and licentious males, society is protecting its most vital interest, which is in self-preservation. Concerning this last mentioned "self," there is nothing ambiguous or abstract.

Smith objects, even as I object, to the denial of many "benefits and positions" to women. That is to say, it is right for us to object insofar as the positions in question are ones for which women are qualified and are not hazardous to their health or safety. We should bear in mind that the origins of the "welfare state" lie in the factory legislation of the late nineteenth and early twentieth centuries. This was directed towards protecting the health and safety of women and children. We should not, in the name of equal opportunity, remove these protections. We should all object to those denials of equal opportunity in which "stereotypes" become a pretext for unfairness or injustice. As human "selves," we are men and women. But we are also human beings in a sense that transcends the distinction of the sexes. Transcending that distinction is not, however, the same thing as ignoring it. As citizens of a constitutional democracy we—men and women—are entitled to equal rights and equal justice under law. The recognition of the rights to which all citizens are entitled implies the equal recognition of duties by these same citizens. There cannot be a right, in the proper sense, without a corresponding duty to respect that right. The political community is a partnership in the mutual observance of rights and duties. It is therefore a partnership in justice. We cannot speak of freedom—or liberation—except within a framework of justice. Within civil society, within this partnership, no one can have a right to be spontaneous and uninhibited except in a manner consistent with the equal rights of others, except in a manner consistent with justice. The suppression of spontaneity, the inculcation of proper inhibitions, in the interest of justice cannot and must not be regarded as a form of unfreedom. Restraining ourselves out of recognition of the equal rights of others, and internalizing these restraints until they become unconscious and habitual, is education in virtue. Far from being a form of unfreedom, it is the highest manifestation of freedom in self-governing men and women.

The political community, we say, is a partnership in justice. It is, or can be, such a partnership because, at its basis and foundation, it is a partnership of families. The family is a partnership which springs from the union of man and woman. It does not spring from "selves." It is in the family that future citizens learn to become partners in the larger justice of civil society. This they do by learning to share — by learning to share, not out of weakness, but out of love and respect — and in so sharing to hold in just regard the right and dignity of others. It is in the family that children are taught that life involves work and responsibility as well as play and freedom. They learn that the former is the condition of the latter. Spontaneity and restraint are conjoined as rights are conjoined with duties. The family has its origin in *eros*. And it is bound together in all its dimensions by *eros*. *Eros* not only unites husband and wife, but parents and children, brothers and sisters, ancestors and posterity. But the very *eros* that unites the primeval Adam and Eve places erotic boundaries upon their relationship with others, and of the others with each other, according to different kinds and degrees of propinquity. The prohibitions upon incest and upon sodomy are not primitive superstitions: Reason and nature tell us that without these prohibitions the structure of the family, and of authority within the family, would collapse. Moral education within the family would not be possible, and the family itself would not survive.

The political community is grounded not in *eros* but in *nomos*, not in love but in law. Fellow citizens do not have the natural affection for each other that members of the family may have. Yet something of the *eros* of the family must pass over into the *nomos* of the polity if there is to be a passion for justice. That is why Aristotle says that legislators are even more concerned with friendship than with justice. But where friendship is not learned in the family, it will not be learned in the polity. Fellow-citizens must respect each others' rights, but such respect must be more than a dry abstraction. Men will characteristically respect each other when they are bound together by what they feel most deeply. It is when they look to each other for the defense of their families, above all for the protection of their women and children, that they discover the ground of civic friendship. It is in the bond forged in the common defense and in war that the ground of citizenship in the deepest human passions is discovered. It is then that we discover that we are children of the same "fathers," the fathers of our country, the Founding Fathers, who gave us our laws. In the phenomenon of patriotism, we see the coming together, the uniting of the *eros* of the family with that of the laws. Only where such a unity occurs can a nation remain free. Only there can the citizens be free. But a people for whom rape, incest, and sodomy are not abhorrent has no moral foundation. It cannot be a people in any proper sense. It will not fight, and it will not survive. The fate of the Cities of the Plain was not due to the vindictiveness of the God of the Bible alone: It was what the fate of all such cities must be under the law of nature.

* * *

Professor Smith's deepest passions are evoked not by what unites mankind into families, but by that "gender stereotyping" which divides male human beings from each other by not permitting them to express their affections towards each other as they would towards members of the opposite sex. Here are his own words on this subject.

> *Boys and men who display "unmasculine" or "effeminate" behaviors* [sic] *are frequently the victims of intimidation ... the social pressures of sex-role stereotyping produce in most men a massive body of inhibitions against non-masculine behavior.... As a result men typically learn to tread a narrow behavioral path, ringed by fearful prospects of humiliation and failure, and maintained by rigid self-control. One of the saddest consequences of this oppressive pattern is the stultification of affection and intimacy among men themselves. Homophobia, the fear of homosexuality, keeps men literally at arms length from one another, denies them mutual nurturance and support, and enforces a lonely fortress mentality.*

And further:

> *The poor health and mortality records of men are related to the stereotypical image of masculinity: men are trained to tune out the complaints of their bodies and their feelings, to shoulder the harness they are expected to wear, and to grind themselves into poor health and early death.*

Let us first of all dismiss the most arrant nonsense that lies upon the surface of these assertions. The conclusion of the Camp David agreements was accompanied by a positive orgy of male huggings, first at Camp David itself and later at the ceremonies on the White House lawn. It sometimes seemed that Anwar Sadat, Jimmy Carter, and Menachem Begin would never stop embracing each other and get on with the signing of the treaties. The French or Continental fashion of male kissing on two cheeks, as an alternative to the more restrained Anglo-Saxon style of hand-shaking, seems to have spread all over the international scene in recent years. I must say that I found the spectacle of Jimmy Carter kissing and being kissed by Leonid Brezhnev at the signing of

Salt II, repulsive. Throughout our society, and in most others, fathers and sons, brothers, as well as comrades in arms may without embarrassment express their emotions by embracing. Nowadays, sport teams, both male and female, celebrate victory by those overt expressions which Smith denies take place. Smith speaks of "homophobia," which he calls "fear of homosexuality." This is a vile neologism, which I cannot find in any dictionary. It is ill-formed, since the "homo" that stands opposite to "hetero" refers to "same" in distinction from "other." "Homophobia" would properly mean "fear of sameness," not "fear of homosexuality." Fear of sameness—fear of "unisex" —would I think be a salutary fear. In truth, however, men and women generally do not fear embracing those of the same sex at treaty signings, weddings, funerals, or world series victory celebrations. It is only when the signs of male affection towards male, or of female affections towards female, are understood to point towards, or involve, a sexual consummation that the disapproval results, of which Smith complains. When Smith uses words like "affection *and intimacy*," and "nurturance and support," to characterize a proper relationship among males, he assimilates the relationship of men to each other to that of men and women. This is sodomy, and what it elicits is not so much social disapproval as natural disgust.

It is then the suppression of sodomy to which Smith attributes the oppression concerning which he waxes so eloquent and indignant. One would think he was Solzhenitsyn writing about the Gulag. But to release sodomy from such social constraints as still surround it—and they seem to be fading fast—would be to adopt a neutral attitude toward the family and ultimately toward all morality. To teach that sodomy is nothing but an "alternative sexual preference" and that sodomites represent merely an "alternative life style" is to imply that all moral choice is a matter of idiosyncratic preference. Smith paints a terrible picture of the prison within which men dwell because of their "inhibitions against non-masculine behavior." But the whole idea of moral education is to teach human beings, beginning in earliest childhood, of the necessity of suppressing their anti-social impulses in the interest of friendship and justice. No impulse is conceivable which is more anti-social than that towards sodomy. As we noted in our discussion of the categorical imperative, the consummation of sodomy implies the suicide of humanity. But Smith's argument would run athwart many other forms of behavior that are condemned by the moral law. There is nothing in any of his premises which would condemn incest any more than sodomy. Indeed, if the Oedipus (and Electra) complexes represent our deepest and most repressed urges, as some psychoanalysts tell us, then incest rather than sodomy would be the most prototypical form of human freedom. As we have already noted, the argument for the perfectly spontaneous and uninhibited self, the self that is limited only by the non-malleability of the world, is an argument for tyranny. This tyranny might manifest itself not only in sodomy and incest, but in rape and murder. We know from the melancholy annals of the police blotters that there are mass murderers both of young boys and of young women who find that they have uncontrollable cravings that can be gratified only by the rapes and murders of their victims. This may even be followed by posthumous assaults. I am not suggesting or implying in any way that Smith advocates or condones any such behavior. But I do not see any ground in his premises for distinguishing as forms of unfreedom the unsated urges of sodomites from those of the incestuous, the child molesters, the rapists, the murderers, or the necrophiliacs. If the inhibition of any spontaneity of any self is a form of unfreedom, then each and every form of self-denial, each and every successful effort at the suppression of vice, becomes a form of unfreedom.

* * *

I know that an apology will be demanded of me for paying such extended attention to such a bad piece of writing as Professor Smith's "Reflections on Human Liberation." No one, it will be said, reads house organs like *Current*. However true this may be, Smith's article reveals something fundamental about the kind of liberal education that is being offered today "in our best universities." It is in the liberal arts colleges of such universities that the elite among our youth are given the education that presumably qualifies them for the positions of leadership they will soon occupy. The parents who are making such heavy sacrifices to send their children to these colleges sometimes have a very erroneous impression of what goes on in them—even when they themselves have gone to the same schools a generation ago. It is fortunate that perhaps 90% of the instructional and study time of the average undergraduate is spent in courses which are either cramming him with facts or training him in technique. There are only a small number of courses in which education properly so called takes place, in which the mind of the student can be said to undergo training in making decisions that bear upon the ends of life, upon the kind of life that one ought to lead, and upon what kind of a man or woman the student will become. Courses taught by the likes of Professor Smith may constitute 90% of that 10%. Here then is where the corruption of liberal education makes its mark upon the minds and hearts of the young.

Professor Bloom complained that today the young do not read the great books as, let us say, Marlborough or Lincoln or Churchill read Shakespeare to comprehend the actions and passions of mankind and to find guidance in that comprehension for their own actions and passions. But for Shakespeare, or for any other great author, to be important to the students, something of infinite importance to Shakespeare himself must also be important to them. That something is nature. Someone who does not know, or greatly care, what kind of a man his own father was will make light reading of *Hamlet*. Nor will he think much or deeply of "Our fathers" who "brought forth on this continent a new nation. . . ." Growing up in the United States today is far more difficult than at any time in my lifetime, or at any time since I began teaching college students in 1945. It is hard for the young to make wise decisions about their lives, because the old moral apothegms are not being updated, they are being ridiculed and scorned. And that most ancient and powerful of all guidelines, nature itself, is being called factitious and immaterial. Yet I do not despair of the future. For we can still take comfort with the ancient Roman poet that no matter how often nature is expelled with a pitchfork, it will always return. Meanwhile, however, the lives of many of our children are being ruined by false prophecy. That is a tragic loss, and one that we ought not—that we cannot—continue to abide.